View from the Top

the story of Prospect, Connecticut

Author & Editor ~ John R. Guevin

First Edition

Biographical Publishing Company
Prospect, Connecticut

View from the Top

the story of Prospect, Connecticut

Published by:

      Biographical Publishing Company
      35 Clark Hill Road
      Prospect, CT 06712-1011

Publisher's Cataloging in Publication Data
Guevin, John R., 1943 -
View from the Top: the story of Prospect, Connecticut /
          by John R. Guevin. 1st ed.
Includes photographs, drawings, index, and bibliography.
1. Prospect, Connecticut - History. I. Title.
2. Prospect, Connecticut - Anecdotes.
3. Prospect, Connecticut - Biographical sketches.
4. Connecticut Town - Early life studies.
5. Connecticut - History.
F104.P71995.G939   974.67467   CIP 95-075335
ISBN 0-9637240-3-7: $19.50 Hardcover

Table of Contents

View from the Top

. . . is dedicated to everyone who had the opportunity to call the town of Prospect their home.

ACKNOWLEDGMENTS

The author would like to thank the following for their assistance in helping to compile this work. Without their important contributions the value of *View from the Top* would be greatly diminished.

Prospect Historical Society
Connecticut Historical Society
Mattatuck Historical Society
New Haven Historical Society
Prospect and other area Public Libraries
Waterbury Republican-American Library
Mayor's Office
Benefactors and Sponsors
All who shared their information and stories

Nellie Cowdell ~ in memory of her life-long work as Prospect's historian

THE FOLLOWING INDIVIDUALS DESERVE SPECIAL RECOGNITION
FOR THEIR TIRELESS CONTRIBUTIONS OF INFORMATION AND EDITING
IN THE PRODUCTION OF THIS WORK:

Dick Caouette ■ Boardman W. Kathan ■ Elizabeth Guevin

CREDITS

Sources for photographs, graphics, quotations, and stories are noted as they occur in the text. The bibliography contains the major sources for historical facts and data used to compile each chapter. The reader is invited to consult these resources for further study on a given topic.

ERRORS AND OMISSIONS

Every effort has been made to provide information that is accurate and complete. Whenever possible, original documents have been used rather than secondary material for factual entries. The records and the retrieval of the information they contain is subject to human error. Much of the data about the history of Prospect was not included for lack of space, time, or availability at the time of publication. The recording of a town's history is a never ending activity. At best, one can hope to capture a snap-shot view, a cross-section of events and people. Future works by other authors will expand upon the findings reported here and will correct any shortcomings.

BENEFACTORS

The Big Dipper Ice Cream and Yogurt Factory
Foam Plastics of New England
Oliver's Supermarket
Prospect Dental Associates
Prospect Pizza

SPONSORS

Chris Barrere Trucking
Buckmiller Brothers Funeral Home, Inc.
Cipriano Agency – The Prudential
ESI Electronic Products Corp.
Equipment Maintenance Co.
William M. Lanese Associates
New England Visa Services, Inc.
Noble H.V.A/C Systems, Inc.
Packard Specialties, Inc.
Prospect Dairy Bar & Restaurant
Prospect Machine Products, Inc.
Prospect Service Center & Towing
Prospect-Wolcott Veterinary Hospital
Sheldon Precision Co., Inc.
Site-Tech, Inc.
Smedes Realty
South Central Connecticut Regional Water Authority

Prospect Barn — Center Street

Drawing of the Petrauskas barn by Jane Fowler

Chapter One

Rocks and Hills —
the Geography of Prospect

From any direction there are hills. From the east, west, north, or south, one must climb them — a formidable obstacle today in winter's icy grip. How much more of a barrier they would have been to the early settlers who lacked the advantages of modern roads and vehicles. Imagine hauling your products to market in Waterbury or carrying back your supplies in an old wagon over rivers of mud and rock. Such was often the case for the people of Prospect a century ago.

Rocks! Everywhere one digs, they appear with at least one good-sized stone in every shovelful. And they seem to multiply. A plot of land cleared one year yields a new crop of rocks the next. Then, there are those boulders that defy movement. Why would anyone choose to farm here?

In the course of this book we will explore the development of the town of Prospect. We shall see how its history and its very personality was shaped by the geography of the place. To fully understand this process, we must journey back to the beginnings of this tract of land that is now Prospect, before man set foot here, before there were plants or animals, to a time when this region was under water.

Excerpts from . . .

THE PROSPECT PROPERTY, PROSPECT, CONNECTICUT

by Melissa Paly

BEDROCK GEOLOGY

Prospect occupies a unique geological spot that tells a revealing story about the history of Connecticut and southern New England. The bedrock that underlies the land's varied vegetation, stony soil, and glacial deposits represents an enormous time span in the history of the earth.

The three processes by which rocks are formed (sedimentation, igneous activity, and metamorphism) have all acted at Prospect. The rocks here are a result of forces within the earth — those that create and destroy mountains and that open and close ocean basins. Evidence of this dynamic history includes four types of rocks, a buried fault line, and a few topographic clues.

The youngest rocks are the arkose and diabase. Arkose is a type of sedimentary sandstone, composed of sand and feldspar grains that have been deposited by running water and cemented together to form rock. Igneous diabase is a dark gray rock, composed of plagioclase feldspar and pyroxene minerals. The oldest rocks are schist and gneiss. Both are metamorphic, the original rocks having been altered by heat and pressure within the earth. The schist was once a sedimentary rock that contained layers of quartz sand and weathered feldspars called clay. The gneiss was once the igneous rock called granite.

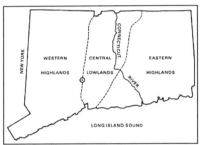

Fig 1 Geological provinces of Connecticut.   Prospect is shown at crossed circle.   Melissa Paly

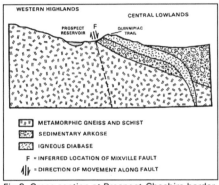

Fig 2 Cross-section at Prospect-Cheshire border.
                                          Melissa Paly

The land at the Regional Water Authority around the Cheshire Reservoir in eastern Prospect straddles two of the three major geological provinces that make up Connecticut [Fig 1]. Southington Mountain Schist and Prospect Gneiss, which underlie the western section of the property, are part of the ancient Western Highlands. The New Haven Arkose and West Rock Diabase that form the property's eastern flank and ridge are part of the Central Lowlands [Fig 2].

EARLY STAGES IN THE FORMATION OF PROSPECT'S LANDSCAPE (Fig 3)

The story behind the rocks at Prospect begins some 500 million years ago during the Cambrian period, when geologists believe the edge of the North American continent lay considerably west of its present position. The shallow ocean above the continental shelf was located in New York State. To the east, in what is now western Connecticut, lay the deep ocean. Fast-moving currents deposited great quantities of the sand and clay that compose schist on the continental slope and beyond. Soon after these sediments were deposited, forces within the earth began to rumble under the ocean. The sediments that once lay deep in the ocean were pushed up during this period of mountain building, called the Taconic Orogeny.

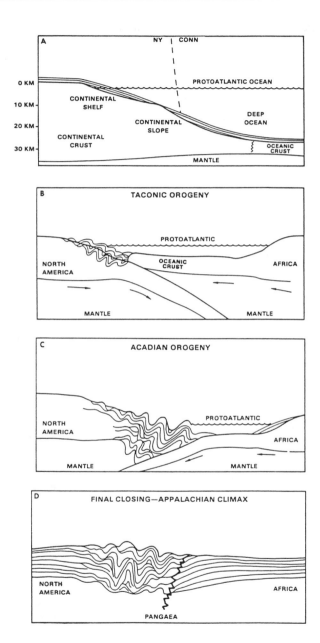

Fig 3 Early stages in the formation of Prospect's landscape.   Melissa Paly

About 360 million years ago the mountain building continued in the Acadian Orogeny period. As the ocean basin continued to close, compression forces caused the accumulation of sediments to be folded together, much like a thin rug on a slippery hardwood floor. The great pressures during this period caused metamorphosis of sedimentary and igneous rocks to form schist and gneiss.

With the complete closing of the ProtoAtlantic, the North American and African continents joined together. By the end of the Paleozoic era (the earth's "ancient" history), there was a great mountain range running north and south through the middle of an enormous fusion of continents called Pangaea. By this period the rocks of Connecticut's Western Highlands were not significantly changed.

GEOLOGIC EVENTS THAT SHAPED

PROSPECT'S MAJOR LANDFORMS (Fig 4)

The story behind the other two rock units at Prospect, those of the Central Lowlands, begins about 30 million years later in the Triassic Period. By this time the great mountains had eroded to a nearly level surface, and the unwieldy continents began to pull apart. Under tension, the stiff crust cracked open like a loaf of overheated bread, forming a series of parallel troughs called grabens. One of these eventually opened east of where the continents joined and became the new Atlantic Ocean. A much smaller one occurred parallel to the coast, all the way from Nova Scotia to Florida, and created a rift valley in Southern New England.

Millions of years of earthquakes along border faults of the graben caused the valley floor to drop downward relative to the raised walls, creating a mountain and valley landscape in what is now central and western Connecticut. Fast-moving torrents of river water carried rock fragments and sand which accumulated on the valley floors. These sedimentary accumulations were compacted and cemented together to form arkose sandstone.

During the Triassic and Jurassic Periods, volcanic activity in the mantle caused molten rock, or magna, to rise through the underlying bedrock and sediment-filled graben. Those that cooled more slowly below ground formed large crystals of intrusive rock called diabase, also known as traprock. By the end of the Jurassic, the New Haven Arkose and West Rock Diabase had been formed, though they were not yet exposed on the earth's surface as they are today.

During the Mesozoic ("Middle Ages") that ended some 65 million years ago, forces below the basin caused it to arch and bend. The domed center of the graben was now subject to climate and weathering which eroded away the entire cap of the dome.   Eventually, only two wedges of Triassic sediment remained. The eastern wedge is now the Central Lowlands of Connecticut. The ancient metamorphic bedrock is now exposed as the Western Highlands of the state. The igneous rocks that were flows of lava 200 million years ago have been more resistant to erosion than the sandstones they intruded. They

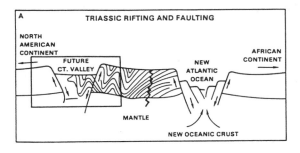

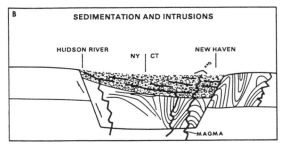

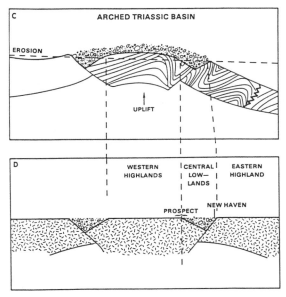

Fig 4 Geologic events that shaped Prospect's major landforms.

Melissa Paly

remain today as ridges. West Rock, East Rock, and the ridge that separates Prospect and Cheshire were all such intrusions.

A beautiful example of the relation between diabase and arkose of the Central Lowlands is visible at Roaring Brook Falls. At the base of the falls, the layers of bedded and sorted arkose form a wall that has been exposed by the running water of the brook.

A GEOLOGICAL CHRONOLOGY OF MAJOR EVENTS
THAT SHAPED PROSPECT AND THE REGION

MILLIONS OF YEARS AGO	PERIOD	EVENTS IMPORTANT TO PROSPECT	OTHER LANDMARKS
0			
2×10^{-4}		First Prospect white settlers.	
1×10^{-2}		Wisconsin glaciation ends.	
1.2×10^{-1}		Last CT glaciation begins.	Evolution of Homo Sapiens.
2	Quaternary		
			Primitive horses.
65	Teritiary	Land forms remain relatively unchanged from this point.	Dinosaurs extinct.
145	Cretaceous	Erosion of arched dome.	Climax of dinosaurs.
		Uplift of Triassic Basin.	
195	Jurassic	Deposition of arkose and diabase.	
230	Triassic	Rifting of Pangaea.	New Atlantic Ocean Basin begins to open.
280	Permian	Climax of Appalachian Mountain formation.	Most severe extinction in the history of life occurs.
345	Carboniferous	Pangaea forms.	Abundant forests become source of coal.
395	Devonian	Metamorphism & formation of gneiss and schist.	First land plants.
435	Silurian		First fish.
500	Ordovician	Appalachian Mountains begin.	Major radiation of marine invertebrates.
570	Cambrian	Taconic Orogeny.	
3800		Oldest rocks on earth.	Blue-green algae, bacteria.
4650		Birth of planet earth.	Melissa Paly

SURFICIAL GEOLOGY

The surficial geology of Prospect is closely allied to the great masses of glacial ice that lumbered southward over New England in very recent geological times. In the last two million years alone, Connecticut has been overridden at least four times, and maybe as many as ten times, by glaciers. Sometime less than 120,000 years ago, the earth's climate cooled rapidly and the last major period of glaciation began.   This last ice age, called the Wisconsin glaciation, lasted until about 10,000 years ago.

Before glaciers had advanced as far south as Prospect, the erosion that had been going on for many millions of years produced a thick soil layer on ridgetops and valleys that undoubtedly supported a diverse vegetation.   As the glacier moved, it flowed to areas of lower elevations, scraping soil from the ridges and scouring sediments from the valleys.   These particles and rock fragments accumulated in front of and below the mass of ice, which was more than 100 feet thick in southern New England.   Like an overloaded plow in winter, the glacier continuously dropped bits of its load and plastered them to the ground by its great weight.   The result is a nearly continuous mantle of glacial till, a very compact, unsorted mass of rock fragments, sand, silt, and clay.   Till is known locally as "hardpan" because it interferes with the vertical movement of water and forces it to flow laterally.   This is characteristic of much of the land in Prospect.

Other parts of Prospect are blanketed by material deposited by water that flowed from the glacier as it melted (Fig 5).   Rock fragments, sand, and silt were picked up by running meltwater and deposited when the slow current would no longer carry them.   The heavier load was dropped first while smaller particles were suspended longer in the current and transported further downstream.   The result is a deposit of size-sorted particles that is called stratified drift.   Such beds are often mined — indeed, sand and gravel beds are one of Prospect's economic resources.

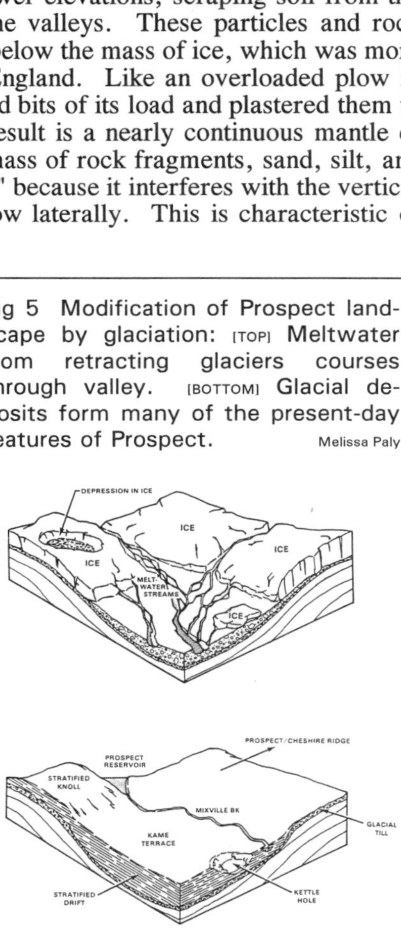

Prospect has a number of glacial kettles, including one just east of the junction of Cook and Roaring Brook Roads.   This kettle is extremely well preserved and has noteworthy soil and vegetation characteristics.   A kettle is an egg-shaped basin with steep sides

Fig 5   Modification of Prospect landscape by glaciation: [TOP] Meltwater from retracting glaciers courses through valley.   [BOTTOM] Glacial deposits form many of the present-day features of Prospect.   Melissa Paly

and is formed when a chunk of ice becomes logged in a spot and remains after the glacier advances.   Glaciers also left signs of its weighty presence in the form of erratic boulders.   Enormous blocks of igneous diabase from the traprock ridge were carried by the glacier along its path and then dropped at random.   Such boulders can be found throughout Prospect.

Since the early 1800s, man has done his own modification of surface features in Prospect.   With the creation of dams, reservoirs were formed and new paths for water flow were created.   These alterations to the natural drainage system have initiated new cycles of sedimentation which are continually changing the shape of the land.

SOILS

There are ten soil orders, but only three are common in Connecticut. All three are represented in Prospect. Entisols are mineral soils that are so recently formed that they have developed no distinct layers of organic or mineral components. These soils are commonly found in floodplains along brooks and streams. Histosols are soils with a thick layer of decomposing organic matter. These are mostly formed in aquatic environments, such as swamps and wetlands. Inceptisols are soils that have had time for the mineral and organic elements to become organized into layers. This order includes most of the soil found in Prospect.

In Prospect, as in the East in general, soils tend to be moderately acidic. This is a result of the crystalline arkose and basaltic bedrock, as well as the frequent rainfall, which leaches out many of the calcium compounds that make a soil more alkaline. Soils in this area need to be limed or "sweetened" to make a more neutral medium for crops.

VEGETATION

The blend of geologic, topographic, climatic, and hydrologic conditions at Prospect sustains an interesting mosaic of vegetation which can be divided roughly into forest and non-forest communities. The forests of much of Prospect were once cleared and used as pasture and farmland. The farmer's signature remains in the winding miles of stone walls that once delineated pastures and fields, built as the first settlers cleared the very rocky soil so that it could be tilled. The forests that have reclaimed these farms are mature and uniform in age, even though not very old. Most trees in the mixed hardwood communities are about half a century old — the few larger "wolf trees" that appear are a sure sign of an intentionally nurtured shade tree or property boundary.

Prospect lies on the northern part of a great region of mixed hardwood forest that includes much of the eastern United States. As one travels north into upper New England, conifers rather than hardwoods become the dominant species of the forest. In this region, oaks are the most abundant and characteristic tree species, though in many forests, oak may be virtually absent, replaced by a number of other hardwood species that reflect the local environmental conditions. One such determinant is the amount of moisture available in the soil. On ridgetops where soil is thin and excessively drained, nearly all large trees are oaks. As one descends the slope, oaks are replaced by other hardwoods. The dominant species in the swamps is red maple, a tree that can tolerate long periods of standing water around its roots. Prospect's forests contain a wide array of understory species and herbaceous plants, among them many wildflowers, ferns, and flowering shrubs.

An especially interesting vegetative area in Prospect occurs in the large dry glacial kettle above the headwaters of Mixville Brook (Fig 6). Here the zonation of the mixed hardwood forest exists in microcosm. The egg-shaped hole descends steeply about 60 feet, and its vegetation ranges from oak forest to a mixed forest of white ash, tulip poplar, and red maple with a thick and diverse understory. This effect of environmental gradations in the vegetative community, apparent in this kettle, is a valuable educational tool to the community.

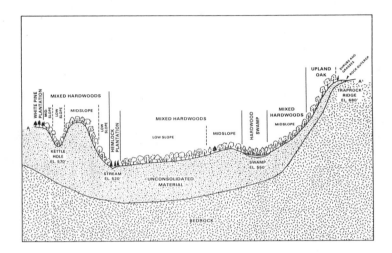

Fig 6   Vegetation cross-section from Roaring Brook Road to Traprock Ridge.

Melissa Paly

WILDLIFE

Prospect runs the gamut of vegetative communities, so it supports a wide variety of wildlife habitats. Most of the animals that can be expected in southern New England forests are found in Prospect. This terrain provides a combination of food-bearing shrubs and relatively open space for white-tailed deer, grey fox, squirrels, and chipmunks. A wide variety of birds are found in low-slope and mid-slope forest communities; some of the more notable are northern oriole, rose-breasted grosbeak, and several woodpeckers. Flocks of ruffed grouse reside in the understory throughout the hardwood forest.

Along softwood plantations around reservoirs, deer and raccoon tracks and scats are often seen. Many birds such as field sparrow, grackle, and mourning dove nest in softwood forests.

In non-forested meadows there is a colorful array of songbirds and butterflies. Mockingbird, red-winged blackbird, goldfinch, and robin as well as black swallowtail and monarch butterflies, are a few of the species that frequent these open fields. Meadow voles and mice that burrow in the fields and thickets are preyed on by hawk, owl, and red fox.

In swampy areas live beavers and muskrats. The reservoirs and ponds are populated by warm water fish such as largemouth bass and yellow perch. Waterfowl such as mallard ducks and Canada geese occasionally migrate through and feed on the fish in Prospect's water basins.

Fig 7 Autumnal scene at a pond on Clark Hill Road   John Guevin

The unspoiled property surrounding Prospect's reservoirs fulfills the requirements for highly productive wildlife populations; upland, wetland, and aquatic habitats; a variety of food and cover plants; interspersed vegetation types; and protection from urban encroachment. This fortunate combination of factors make wildlife one of Prospect's special assets, and one that should be preserved.

~

The preceding information on the geography of Prospect was largely obtained from two studies by the Regional Water Authority. While these studies focus on the portion of Prospect owned by the Regional Water Authority surrounding the Cheshire Reservoir, much of the information applies to Prospect as a whole. The reader is invited to consult these resources for more details on these topics.

Chapter Two

The Indians

Long before the first white settlers discovered what is now Prospect, the Indians roamed across our hilltop patch of land. Just when they first came, no one knows with certainty. The best estimates range from 20,000 to 40,000 years ago when America was first settled by these travelers from Asia. This long span of history dwarfs the brief stay of the white settlers. And yet, so little is known about the Indians' life and times in this area. Their imprint on the land was as transient as their moccasin prints on the muddy landscape. They treated nature with great respect — leaving precious few traces of their civilization. Most artifacts are limited to arrow points and a few simple tools and utensils. The methods the Indians used to construct buildings and their lifestyle left the land much as they found it. Compare this to the many stone walls, foundations, dams, and buildings that already define the short span of the European presence.

One lasting contribution we owe to the Indians is their influence on our language. The name Connecticut comes from the Algonquian word *Quinnetukut* for "on the long tidal-river." Other Indian words include Naugatuck from *Naukotunk*, meaning "one large tree." This was an a favorite Indian fishing point along the Naugatuck river, complete with a convenient large shade tree. Waterbury was first called Mattatuck from the Indian word *Matecoke* for the same tract of land.

By the 1630s the first English colonists found one of the densest concentrations of North American Indians in Connecticut. Yet, they were still widely scattered with only 6,000 to 7,000 throughout the state. Connecticut Indians lived largely by hunting and fishing. Using bow and arrow, they found their abundant prey of deer, moose, bear, raccoon, rabbits, and squirrels in the large forests. They also lived off partridge, turkey, quail, and water fowl. For clothing they trapped beaver, otter, and wolves. Indians of the seventeenth century found fish everywhere in vast quantities.

Indians displayed little interest in agriculture, although small clearings were made for the growing of maize (corn), pumpkin, squash, beans, sweet potatoes, and tobacco. Fields of hemp were also cultivated for fashioning nets, baskets, mats, and clothing. Maize was held in reverence as a gift from the Creator. Great effort was made to insure the corn would not become feed for the crows.   Older children would be dispersed before dawn to stand guard in scaffold-mounted watch houses near the ripening ears.   Tame hawks were also kept by the Indians to prey on the corn-loving birds.

Indian life was family oriented.   The men were the hunters, fishers, and tool makers; they had lives of relative ease.   Women were responsible for the care of the household and tended to all the agriculture (with the exception of tobacco, which was the duty of men).   The typical home for Connecticut Indians was the *ptuk-wi-en* or "round house," which would accommodate one or two families.   Built of tree saplings about ten to sixteen feet in diameter and covered with bark, the structure had two doors about three feet high. Leather curtains sealed the entrance.   Mats and paintings decorated the inside. A central hearth was used for heat and cooking.

The Indians were clustered mostly along the coast.   There were a number of tribes in the area, all belonging to the loose Algonquian confederation. These tribes had little unity and often quarreled with one another.   This proved helpful to the white settlers who used this division to their advantage. The European colonists arriving in Connecticut were, more often than not, welcomed by the local Indians who saw these settlements as protective havens against hostile tribes.   There were two main tribes that claimed the lands surrounding the region of Prospect — the Quinnipiacs and the Tunxis (Fig 1).

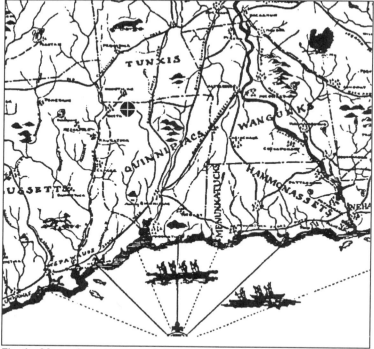

Fig 1   Map of south-central Connecticut Indian tribes circa 1625.
Approximate location of Prospect center is shown by crossed circle.

THE QUINNIPIACS

The Quinnipiacs, also known as the Quiripi, held the choice coastal land from present-day Madison to Milford. The principal village was located at the site of what is now New Haven, along the shore trail from Shawmut (Boston) to Manhattan. The path turned in its direction between Guilford and North Haven. Hence, the tribal name derives from the Indian word *quinnuppin-uk*, which means "turning about" or "changing its course." This village was quite a metropolis with three trails (besides the shore path) leading northward to the modern towns of Middletown, Wethersfield, and Farmington. These trails continued into Massachusetts and as far as Canada.

The Quinnipiac territory was bounded on the north by the lands of the Tunxis, on the south by Long Island Sound, on the east by the Wangunk and Menunketuck counties, and on the west by the Paugussett tribe. This land included the southeastern part of the bounds of Prospect. Their tribal government was divided with Momauguin sachem (a sort of chief whose duties were limited to affairs of peace) of the southern region and Montowese ruling the north. The Quinnipiacs stated their number at 47, but this only counted full-grown men. In 1638 the population of the entire tribe was about 200-250.

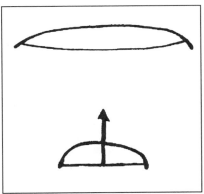

Fig 2 The marks of Momaugin (top) and Montowese (bottom).

Vision in the Sky

The whole Quinnipiac territory was purchased by the New Haven Colony from Montowese and Momauguin on the last day of November 1638. The meeting on that day was represented by the Englishmen Davenport and Eaton. A document was drawn up to confirm the purchase and contained the marks of many Indians (Fig 2), including one squaw. All the Puritan signers were men. It would appear that the Indians held their women in higher regard than the English at this period of time. The land was exchanged for one dozen each of coats, spoons, hoes, hatchets, and porengers (bowls) plus two dozen knives and four cases of French knives and scissors.

The Indians also agreed to the following terms:

1. *They must not set traps where cattle might be caught or hurt.*

2. *They must not frighten away or steal fish from the English nets.*

3. *They must not come into town on Sundays to trade or hang around the house while the English were at church.*

4. *They were not to take any boat or canoe belonging to the English without the consent of the owner.*

5. *Not more than six Indians at a time were to come into town with bows and arrows or other weapons.*

6. *They must never harm in any way an English man, woman, or child.*

7. *They must pay for cattle they killed or injured and return those that strayed.*

8. *They must not allow other Indians to come and live with them without the consent of the English.*

9. *They must promise to tell the English of any wicked plots against them.*

10. *They must agree to have all wrong-doers punished by the English.*

11. *The Indians would be paid for any damage done to them.*

12. *All those who wronged the Indians in any way would be punished by the colonists.*

Vision in the Sky

The settlers made such demands because they felt the Indians would cause trouble. In truth, the Indians were not used to the ways of the Englishmen. It never occurred to the Indians that they had to ask permission to use or take from nature what they needed. They did not have a sense of possession. The land and its bounty was for everyone. The Puritans clung to their principles of rights to privacy and property. In return, the Indians asked for only three things: a place (now called East Haven) where they could live and plant their corn; the right to hunt and fish in Quinnipiac; and protection from the Mohawks and their other enemies. While the terms of this first agreement may seem rather unfair to the Indians, they freely accepted them. The Indians put their trust in the settlers, and all parties faithfully observed the agreements.

TUNXIS

The Tunxis tribe was centered in the Farmington-New Britain-Berlin area. In 1640 the Tunxis made their land settlement with the European settlers of Farmington. Like the Quinnipiacs, the Tunxis were peace-loving but feared the more hostile Indian tribes. As part of their agreement with the English, the Indians were provided with two reservations. Relations must have been friendly as there are no reports of hostilities.

In Farmington great effort was directed toward educating the Indians. Schools were set up for them, and records indicate a Mr. Newton and perhaps a Mr. Hooker were teachers in the 1730s. Some Indian students were even admitted as freemen, and a few became members of the church.

An aged citizen in Farmington, who died some years ago, and who was born about 1730, used to say that, within his recollection, the Indian children in the district school were not very much fewer than those of the whites. In their snow-balling parties, the former used to take one side and the latter another, when they would be so equally balanced in numbers and prowess, as to render the battle a very tough one and the result doubtful. This of course, must have been at least as early as 1750.

History of the Indians of Connecticut

In 1761 the tribe was estimated at something less than twenty-five families. Some of the Tunxis moved to Mohawk county. The Tunxis and the Quinnipiacs continued dispersing to other tribes and areas; their numbers diminished until both were officially extinct by the year 1849.

THE INDIANS OF PROSPECT

Prospect was a shared hunting and fishing ground for the Quinnipiacs and the Tunxis. There is no evidence of permanent Indian villages within the bounds of Prospect prior to the arrival of white settlers. Encampments that did exist were no doubt of a temporary nature for the convenience of the hunters and fishermen. The discovery of numerous arrowheads, spear points, and stone tools in many areas of Prospect supports this theory.

Fig 3 Arrowheads, spear points, and coins unearthed at the Plumb Farm on Cheshire Road.

John Guevin

As far to the east of the Naugatuck as Malmanack is to the west, rises the height known as East Mountain, near the bounds of Prospect. This is represented in this writer's collection by a handsome black spear-head. At Prospect Centre, on ground high enough to command a view of Long Island Sound, the writer secured an interesting stone "mortar," probably of aboriginal manufacture, which now rests under a tree near his cottage at Woodmont. The material is a compact, yellowish brown sandstone. It is without definite form, but approximates to an oval. It is twenty-three inches in length, eighteen in breadth, and six in thickness. The excavation is three inches at its greatest depth and slopes gradually to the top. The longer diameter of the excavation lies across the stone and measures seventeen inches. Its width is fourteen inches, so that there is a flat margin on one side of it, measuring several inches across. This may have been a mortar in which to grind corn. If so, the "pestle" must have been used horizontally, that is, rolled. But the excavation does not afford much evidence of use.

The writer recalls with no little amusement the prolonged effort put forth to secure this "relic" from its purative owner. It lay at the time in a barn yard, filled with ice, having been set apart as a watering trough for fowls. But the farmer's son, as soon as he was asked to sell, conceived a strong attachment for it. "My grandfather," he said, "found it and *brought it home a hundred years ago, and people have come miles to see it." When finally persuaded to name his price, he said, with much deliberation, "I shall have to ask twenty-five cents for it." "Well, I am willing to give you twenty-five cents for*

it," the collector quietly replied; and then and there began to appreciate for the first time the high estimate which the hill-top farmer puts on a quarter of a dollar.

History of Waterbury

The Indians did have a frequently traveled route though Prospect — the Quinnipiac Trail along the Cheshire border. This north-south path was most likely the route of choice during the rainy times when the valley routes would be muddy. Prospect was also an excellent look-out for the movement of unfriendly tribes.

Little has been recorded about specific Indian families in this area, but here is one story that has been obtained from a family diary:

> *Frank Brooks told me this story about what may have been the last Indian family living in Prospect. This family was living in what is known as the Indian cave off of Plank Road. The Indians wanted to move away but had a young child who was too sick to travel. They left the child behind. Frank Brooks' father, Alfred Brooks, took the waif in and the Brooks family nursed the child back to health. For the next two years they cared for and raised the Indian as their own. Later the Indian parents returned and reclaimed their child. The fate of the child from then on is not known.*   Lillian Walters (1994)

THE PROSPECT RESERVATION

The Quinnipiac tribe was provided two reservations by the Puritans of New Haven Colony. One was near the Cove and the other on the river near the former home of Sachem Montowese. Over a period of time, conflicts between the Indians and the white settlers increased. Frequent drinking of alcoholic beverages (obligingly provided by area merchants) and unwelcomed visits to town led to the formation of a committee in 1706 to purchase all Indian lands and disperse the natives. The Indians were slow and reluctant to leave. After seventeen years they were still there claiming "squatter sovereignty" upon the Indian territory. About this time the last sachem of the Quinnipiacs, Charles, froze to death while in a drunken stupor.

> *But faith in missionary work was still strong enough to flicker. And so another committee was chosen "To consider whether the land belongs to the Town or the Proprietors, and whether it may be advisable to secure by Bill the land to the Indians to encourage them in the Christian faith." In 1725, a committee was authorized to sell the Indian land to four planters, and six years later, a vote was recorded that fifty acres in Waterbury [Prospect] should be purchased for the Indians in behalf of the proprietors. It seems, therefore, that the company of proprietors had taken the Indians under its protection, and probably removed them, or the majority of them, to Waterbury.*   New Haven a Connecticut Town

It may have been for noble reasons that the New Haven Colony chose to provide still another reservation for the Indians. It is curious that they should select a location outside of their boundaries.

It may be a surprise to our readers that Waterbury [now Prospect] had an Indian reservation. It was on the southeast portion of East Mountain and consisted of fifty acres, and was bought by the proprietors of the undivided lands of New Haven . . . This Indian reservation was undoubtedly occupied for we find it called "the Indian farm" down to the time of the Revolution. History of Waterbury

According to Prospect historian Nellie Cowdell, the reservation in Prospect was located on Bronson Road. A census indicated only four Indian residents there in 1774. The population at other times is not known, but most likely the use of the reservation was limited.

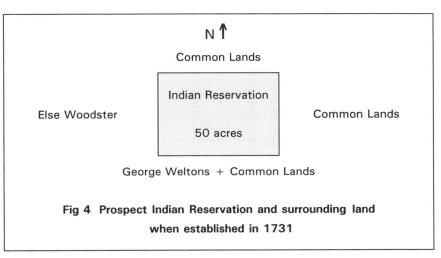

N ↑

Common Lands

Indian Reservation

Else Woodster   Common Lands

50 acres

George Weltons + Common Lands

Fig 4 Prospect Indian Reservation and surrounding land when established in 1731

1731 . . . Know all men by these presents, that I John Morris of New Haven, in the county of New Haven, for consideration of a certain quitclaim to me given by the proprietors and town of New Haven . . . give unto Samuel Bishop of New Haven . . . fifty acres of land [Fig 4] . . . in the town of Waterbury . . . bounded West on Else Woodster land, South in part on land that was George Weltons and part on Common land, and East and North on Common land; the Southeast, Northeast, and Southwest corner are rocks with stones on them and the North west corner is a heap of stones, sd land is in the south east quater of sd town of Waterbury about three miles from the Town Platt. . . . for the use, Benefit and Behoof of the Indians that now do or hereafter shall properly belonging to or descending from that tribe of Indians called or known by the name of New Haven or Quinnepiag Indians, so long as any of that tribe or family shall remain and no longer. . .

A true Record of the Original Deed Attest John Southmayd Recorder, May 7th Anno Domini 1731.

Forty-seven years later, on January 2, 1778, the Indian reservation was divided and sold (Fig 5). The need for it no longer existed as the occupants had died, moved out of the area, or assimilated into white society. Of the fifty acres, Samuel Adams of Farmington sold 14½ acres to Amos Hotchkiss, 11 acres to Isaac Tirrell, and the balance to Stephen Ives. Thus closed the chapter on the Indian reservation of Prospect.

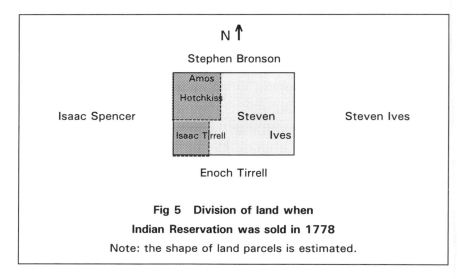

Fig 5   Division of land when

Indian Reservation was sold in 1778

Note: the shape of land parcels is estimated.

~

Chapter Three

The Evolution of a Town — the Waterbury and Cheshire Connections

---

A town is created in one of three ways. Parent towns, as I may refer to them, are the first settlements in a given area. They are formed by pioneering individuals who left the relative comfort of their birthplace to establish a new community. The reasons for such moves include freedom from oppression, overcrowding, attraction to stories of promising new lands, and the spirit of adventure from within. The settlers in a parent town must endure many hardships during the start-up of their community. The living conditions are primitive and the work is hard and long, but there is satisfaction and freedom which comes with forming a town in one's own image.

The second type is the offspring town. This town tends to be created about twenty to thirty years (or one generation) after the parent town. Often several such towns are formed in areas adjacent to or near the parent town. The founders of these communities are mostly the children of the original parent town residents. They are likely to be searching for their own identity as well as parcels of virgin land. The common belief that the grass is always greener applies here.

The marriage town is the third variety. Prospect falls into this category. Waterbury and Cheshire evolved as offspring towns. In 1827 a portion of each was combined to form the present town of Prospect.

There are some fundamental differences between a marriage town and the other two types. In parent or offspring towns, occupants of the new communities make physical moves from one location to another. The citizens share common ideals and beliefs that cause them to migrate. From the onset there is a sense of harmony and a spirit of cooperation. A marriage town is quite different. The people are already there and no pioneering spirit need be present. The residents of the newly formed town may come from different parent or offspring towns. They could have diverse beliefs and opinions as to how this new town should be run. The potential for conflict is there but so is an environment that is the cornerstone of the American way — the classic melting pot. People have the opportunity to learn to live with and accept others of different origins, beliefs, and customs. In the course of this book we will try to determine if this was a marriage made in heaven!

Fig 1   Chronology of Prospect's evolution.

THE CHESHIRE
CONNECTION

THE WATERBURY
CONNECTION

"Quinnipiac" - 1638
New Haven Colony - 1640
PARENT TOWN

"New Haven Village"
"East River"
Wallingford - 1670
OFFSPRING TOWN

"Ye Fresh Meadows" - 1694
"West Society"
"New Cheshire" - 1724
Cheshire - 1780
OFFSPRING TOWN

↓

"West Rocks" - 1694
"Columbia Society" - 1797
SECTION OF CHESHIRE

Dutch trading post - 1633
"Suckiaug" -1635
Hartford - 1637
PARENT TOWN

"Plantation of Tunxis" - 1640
Farmington - 1645
OFFSPRING TOWN

"Mattatuck" - 1673
Waterbury - 1686
OFFSPRING TOWN

"Cheshire Mountain"
"South Farms"
SECTION OF WATERBURY

Prospect - 1827
MARRIAGE TOWN

THE CHESHIRE CONNECTION

■ NEW HAVEN COLONY

The story of the founding of New Haven began in Boston in 1637. Arriving from England were John Davenport, Theophilus Eaton, and Edward Hopkins. These three men and their supporters shared the common interest of establishing a new independent settlement. The Bay Colony area did not offer the kind of harbor the merchants Eaton and Hopkins sought in order to pursue their commercial interests. The men were also concerned with the growing heretical ideas and discontent in that region. They longed to establish their own "Bible State" with their puritanical views of religion.

As a result of the Pequot War, glowing reports arrived in Boston about a new site called Quinnipiac (New Haven) which offered fertile land and a fine harbor. In early September of the same year, Eaton and a company of men visited the area. Eaton was much impressed. He built a temporary hut and left seven men to hold claim to this land until he could come back. He then returned to Boston. With much enthusiasm, he convinced the others that this was, indeed, their promised land. Together, they recruited other volunteers, and in March of 1638, they set sail from Boston in two ships. High head winds made for a rough two-week voyage to Quinnipiac. The company arrived on March 30, 1638, and on the next day, a sabbath, John Davenport convened the first religious service under a large oak tree, preaching:

> *Then when Jesus led up of the spirit into the*
> *wilderness to be tempted of the devil. . . The*
> *voice of one crying in the wilderness, Prepare ye*
> *the way of the Lord, make his path straight.*

The settlers were fortunate to find the local Quinnipiac Indians friendly and eager to sign treaties offering land in exchange for the Indians' protection (see chapter 2). The land included what is now the greater New Haven area, Cheshire, Wallingford, and parts of Orange, Bethany, Woodbridge, Meriden, and Prospect. The northern border was a line roughly twenty miles inland from Long Island Sound. This twenty mile limit also represented the southern boundary of the Hartford-Farmington settlement. The line cut through what would become Prospect, placing a portion in each colony (Fig 2).

The Colony at New Haven took form with the laying out of lots that radiated from the present New Haven Green by surveyor John Brockett. Buildings rose and the colony prospered. A wave of new settlers continued to arrive, increasing pressure to add more blocks for housing or "suburbs" and later to push the settlement further north.

An oligarchy form of government was established, based mainly on "the Word of God." A covenant was entered by all members of the colony, which simply stated that the Scriptures would decide right and wrong in all matters involving church and civil affairs. For several years there were no laws except the Mosaic laws. Trial by jury was abolished because there was no reference in the Bible. In contrast, the Hartford colony was guided by the principles of the Bible. New Haven sought a literal application of the <u>rules</u> of the Bible. Even though the settlers fled England to escape oppression by the King of England, they were content to follow the rule of their self-appointed leaders.

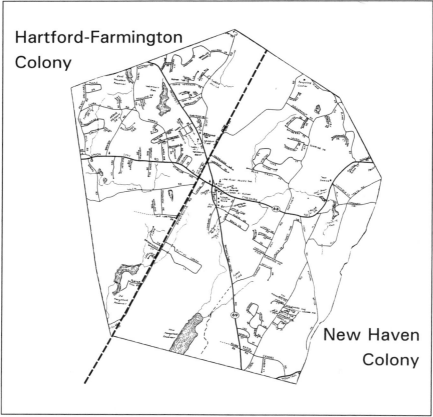

Fig 2 Dividing line of New Haven and Hartford-Farmington Colonies as shown on modern Prospect map.

■ WALLINGFORD

By the 1660s New Haven was no longer a colony, but a bustling town with a large and still growing population. Permission was granted at Hartford to establish a new village.

> *Upon the motion of the deputies of New Haven this courte grants the towne of New Haven libertie to make a village on ye East River, if they see it capable for such a thing, provided they setle a village there within fower years from May next.*   by consent of the Generall Courte at Hartford Oct. 10th, 1667

New Haven appointed a committee that selected thirty-nine people who would be the first to establish this new community. Four from this group were nominated as supervisors to oversee the orderly laying out of lots and other affairs. One member of this foursome was John Moss. Later, his son would be among the first Prospect land holders. Our ancestors did not take the surveying task lightly. Everything was planned out in minute detail. The establishment of such a village was considered a "very great undertaking."

> *The town of New Haven had been established for thirty years. The country northward was still an almost unbroken forest, infested with Indians, howling wolves, fierce bears, catamounts, and all other wild animals who made both day and night fearsome to all except the most courageous of the settlers . . . To this end arrangements were made for the enrollment of a guard, the fortification of houses, and so placing of their village that all of its inhabitants could be speedily gathered together at the call of danger.* History of Cheshire

In spite of these obstacles, the village of Wallingford not only survived, but grew to the point where some of its citizens looked with longing at the vast acres of untouched land that surrounded them. It was time to begin new settlements.

■ CHESHIRE

By 1694 Wallingford residents settled in two areas beyond its boundaries. One group formed along the Quinnipiac River to the northeast. The other group, known as the "west farmers," took up lands in "Ye Fresh Meadows" in the southern part of town. The families of Ives, Doolittle, and Hitchcock were prominent members of this group.

In 1694 John Moss, Jr. owned property on *"ye Tenn Mile river alongside an irremovable hill."* This was a 90-100 acre tract of land against the "Blew Hills" to the northwest in West Rocks, now Prospect, and represented the first royal grant of land in town. It is also the earliest record of land secured within the present bounds of Prospect. We do not know when his land was actually settled.

On June 16, 1714, the proprietors of Wallingford agreed that they should have their western land sited or surveyed. At the same meeting they voted to distribute land to men by their status in the community as follows:

Ye Loer Rank sixty acres

Ye Middell Rank ninety acres

Ye Upper Rank six score [120] acres

The land to be divided was that portion located in eastern Prospect and western Cheshire. A system of tiers running nearly north-south was chosen. The first tier began at the western edge of their territory, which was just west of the center of Prospect. It followed the present route of Straitsville Road, Old Schoolhouse Road, Summit Road, and Peter Gilkey Road. These four roads formed a nearly straight line when connected (Fig 3).

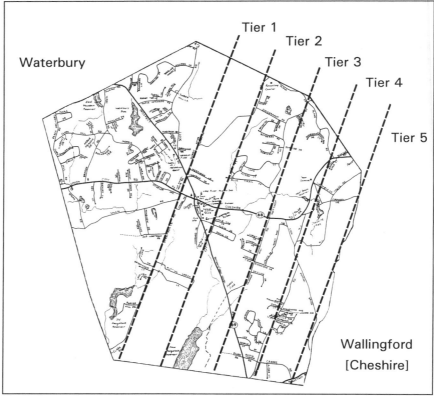

Fig 3 Approximate location of lot tiers created by the proprietors of Wallingford in 1714 as shown on modern map of Prospect.

The first tier began at the chestnut trees, known as the Three Brothers (or Three Sisters), where Prospect, Bethany, and Naugatuck intersect. This location has been a historical marker for hundreds of years and is explained in detail in the chapter on boundaries, markers, and monuments. The first lot on the first tier was designated the College Farm Lot for use by Yale. It was the custom for each new settlement in Connecticut to provide such a lot. The tiers were spaced at one-half mile intervals, with subsequent tiers getting closer to Cheshire. In between the lots, provision was made for roads six rods wide or about one hundred feet.

From the map (Fig 3) we can see that Tier 1 is bounded by Coer Road, Tier 2 by Talmadge Road, Tier 3 by Cook Road, and Tier 4 by Roaring Brook Road. There was a grid of crossroads to connect the tiers. The proprietors were practical men and made allowances for the sort of rocky and sometimes swampy terrain found on the hillsides of Prospect. They were wise to provide land for what would become the Prospect Green.

> . . . all *Dificultye about rocks or swamps or other impedy-*
> *ments that may happen in ye high ways the suvaiers & sizers*
> *shall have power to regulate by turning the highway a little*

out of a streight corse as it may be convenient, Agreed also that there shall be a hundred acres of land reserved for such use as ye proprietors see cause to put itt to near ye middel of ye second teer.   History of Cheshire

The west farmers worked their land during the week but returned to Wallingford for church services on Sundays. In 1719 a separate school was established in Ye Fresh Meadows. The residents petitioned Wallingford in 1723 that they should have a church of their own. One of the reasons for this need was the distance traveled by the West Rocks settlers.

> . . . *which hath greatly increased the burden of Travel in coming to town on all Neadfull occasions & more Especially as our Settlements are Increasing Greatly over the West Rocks where we expect a Parish will be made hereafter. Whose travel many of you gentlemen Know to be very Bad as well as a Distance of about twelve miles, those are at Extream Parts . . . all which Increasing Burthens said Inhabitants have endured for the space of Forty-six years at Least since made a society: and some Long before that Time.*
> *History of Cheshire*

In 1724 approval was given so they could form their own church. One year earlier Wallingford granted them separate village status, and the name was changed to New Cheshire. This new status did not free the west farmers from their obligations to Wallingford, who would remain the supreme authority for the next fifty-six years. The laws of Wallingford would prevail, and taxes were still levied on New Cheshire, which included the present town limits of Cheshire plus the eastern two-thirds of Prospect.

On May 19, 1780 the state legislature established Cheshire as a separate town. This day was called the Dark Day and was one of great drama. At midday candles were lit in homes. Birds began to roost. Some of the legislators meeting in Hartford to consider Cheshire's petition for township declared that the "Day of Judgement" was at hand and wanted to adjourn, but Colonel Abraham Davenport of Stamford, who was at the session, saved the day.

> *I am against adjournment. The day of Judgement is either approaching, or it is not. If it is not, there is no cause for adjournment: If it is, I choose to be found doing my duty. I wish therefore that candles may be brought.*   *History of Cheshire*

Cheshire, like many towns in Connecticut, can draw on a number of dates to point to its beginnings. When celebrating their 300th anniversary in 1994, the reference point was the first white settlers to the area in 1694. One could also use the official start of the village or its final recognition as a town to begin counting the years of existence.

Cheshire grew quickly during its early days. The availability of water power from Ten Mile River, originating in Prospect, allowed the development of grist mills, saw mills, and other industries in the northwest corner of town. The soil proved to be ideal for fruit trees and vegetables, prompting a flourishing business. By 1810, 52% of the land in Cheshire had been cleared, more than any other town in Connecticut according to *Landmarks of Old Cheshire*. The population was a little over 2,000 at the time of the Revolution but did not increase again until around the Civil War. Migration to other states and the independence of Prospect in 1827 were factors that retarded continued growth of the town.

THE WATERBURY CONNECTION

■ HARTFORD

The westward movement of the English colonists in the New World began with settlement of the Connecticut Valley. A Dutch navigator, Adrian Block, was most likely the first to see the possibilities of the fertile valley along the Connecticut River, which he called the Varsche River, when he sailed along it in 1614. Nearly twenty years passed before a Dutch trading post was established at the future site of Hartford in 1633.

Moving by land in October of 1635, the first large migration, under the direction of John Steel, left Cambridge Massachusetts and settled in Suckiaug (Hartford) next to the Dutch trading post. The following spring Rev. Thomas Hooker and his congregation followed. Hooker and others, like John Cotton, were leaving because of their destain for the autocratic nature of the government in the Bay Colony.

The English at Hartford combined the resources of settlements at Wethersfield and Windsor and soon outnumbered the Dutch who abandoned their trading post in 1654. The Fundamental Orders, inspired by one of Hooker's sermons, was drafted in 1638 and adopted by the three towns. This document is often considered the first state constitution. The court, established under John Steel and Roger Ludlow, became the supreme authority.

■ FARMINGTON

In 1639, four years after the settlement of Hartford, some of its inhabitants, along with others from Windsor and Wethersfield, petitioned the general court to establish a new community. The following year a report was made by a committee chosen to select a site. They described the beautiful valley of the Tunxis they saw when they went through the pass in the mountains west of Hartford. This territory was occupied by the Tunxis Indians, a small tribe whose chief was Sunckquasson. In two agreements (1650 and 1673) a peaceful land purchase was made with the Indians. Friendship was maintained between the Tunxis and the valley settlers who treated the Indians with compassion. Unlike other tribes, the Tunxis remained together in the community for over a century. They received schooling provided by the English and were allowed to attend town meetings and church services.

The valley community was incorporated as a town in 1645 and given the name Farmington. The boundaries extended from Massaco (Simsbury) on the north to what is now Wallingford on the south, from Hartford and Wethersfield on the east to the present Harwinton and Waterbury on the west.

The chief community interest was in the church. It was through the seating in church that one's status in the society was registered. This rank was determined by the seating committee made up of leading citizens. Everyone went to church. To fail to attend would mark one as an outcast in the community. The records of Farmington contain many examples of squabbling and quarrels over the church seating issue. This and other subjects of discontent led to dissensions from the church. In 1673 twenty-six citizens of Farmington petitioned the general court for the establishment of a plantation at Mattatuck (now Waterbury). And thus the time had come for the first division in the town of Farmington.

▓ WATERBURY

Interest in the area that would become Waterbury came in 1657 when two men from Farmington acquired mining rights from the Indians for a hill thought to contain black lead. The tract of land which included this hill was called *Matetacoke* or *Mattatuck*. The lead deposits proved to be non-existent, but the reports of fertile lands along the Naugatuck River inspired some from Farmington to settle in this region. All that lay between them were twenty miles of pathless forest.

One year after the petition of 1673, thirty-nine men of Farmington agreed to share the financial burden for establishing a settlement at Mattatuck dependent on each man's means. The amounts ranged from fifty to one hundred pounds. The land was purchased from the Tunxis for a sum of thirty-eight pounds. Each proprietor was to receive eight acres as a home lot. Additional meadow lands would be distributed in proportion to their investment. A key part of the agreement was that each person accepting an allotment must build a substantial house at Mattatuck within four years and must live there at least four years.

In the summer of 1674 some of the newly allotted proprietors began the task of building the settlement. The following was said of the first settlers of Waterbury:

> *They were tough men, and had come into tough country; a country, which for easy tillage, was in striking contrast with the plains of Farmington. With rich soil in abundance in Farmington, and most of the first settlers of Waterbury enjoying proprietor status in their former home, there must have been other causes which prompted their removal.*

Farmington in Connecticut

One cause for their determination in setting up such a community may have been the narrow political leadership in Farmington; another was the church conflicts mentioned earlier. They selected a site on the west side of the Naugatuck River, known as Town Platt. The timing would prove to be unfortunate. Hostilities erupted with the strong Narragansett Indian Confederation. The outbreak of the bloody King Philip's War put remote settlements in great danger. In October the General Court ordered these plantations to withdraw to a defendable location. Most of the men, therefore, returned to Farmington. A few men stayed on to harvest the crops in the summer of 1675 and to transport them to Wallingford for safe-keeping.

When it was safe to return to Mattatuck in 1677, some of the proprietors were so disheartened that they abandoned the project. And so, new signers were called to complete the task. By November of 1679 many households were established in the new community. The site was relocated on the east side of the river, which they thought would allow for safer retreat from the Indians if the need arose. Residents were held accountable for the time limits and building requirements. If the houses were not large enough or were without a chimney, builders were penalized or lost their proprietary rights entirely.

Although most of the first settlers of Waterbury had been trained in the religious beliefs of those days and were members of the church in Farmington, a number of circumstances prevented them from being from the beginning a religious community in the same sense as the other towns of the country. The plantation of Mattatuck was "remote in one corner of the wilderness," which made the task of building homes and protecting them against savage inroads so burdensome that they had "much charge, pains, and hardships," which prevented them from having the full enjoyment of privileges which were so dear to other colonists. Nearly a dozen years elapsed before they had a minister settle among them. History of New Haven County

In 1680 boundaries with Derby and Woodbury were decided. Beacon Hill Brook, on the east side of the Naugatuck River, marked the southern limit of Mattatuck. A stake on Twelve Mill hill was the west boundary with Derby while the western limit with Woodbury was a line eighty rods east of Quassapaug pond.

Additional land agreements were made with the Tunxis and Derby Indians in 1674 and 1686. In some cases the same land was bought two or more times. One reason for this was that the Indian culture did not comprehend the Englishmen's notion of land ownership. The Indians believed that land was sacred and eternal and belonged to everyone, so that it was not possible for someone to buy or sell it.

The streets of the new town plat were laid out around Center square, or the green, very much like they are now [1892], and on these, for the purpose of mutual defense, the first houses were built. The material was logs for the walls and split logs for the roof and the floors. The need for saw and grist mills was much felt by the early settlers, and their only recourse was to carry their corn to ground to Farmington, twenty miles through a wilderness. What lumber they used was brought from the same place. The colony committee early sought to relieve them in this matter by recommending, in November, 1697, that a mill be built, and offered a grant of 30 acres to whoever would built it and keep it up. This offer was accepted in 1680 by Stephen Hopkins, of Hartford, who built a mill on Mad river "for grinding corn." It stood on the site used since that time, and which is now occupied by the rolling mill of Scovill Manufacturing Company. History of New Haven County

The growth of Waterbury after 1686, when that name was officially adopted, was steady but not rapid. New house lots were reduced from eight to two acres. Great floods in 1692 and 1709 destroyed many good acres of fertile land. Some settlers were forced to leave. And yet, the community went forward. In 1697 "bachelor" privileges were instituted. Eligible young men were given thirty acres of (less than choice) land if they would build a house sixteen feet square or more within four years.

More troubles kept Waterbury in a perpetual state of alarm from 1702-1713. It was still a frontier town with nothing but wilderness to the north. Two sentinels were kept on duty looking out from high points (perhaps Prospect) at all times. A loss of power was suffered when parts of Waterbury began to incorporate: Watertown in 1780 and Plymouth in 1795. There was also unrest with the desire of southern residents, including some from the area that is now Prospect, to form their own ecclesiastical (church) society. This would become known as the Society of Salem.

■ SOCIETY OF SALEM

In 1765 the people living near the intersecting boundaries of Waterbury, Oxford, and Bethany grew tired of the long Sunday travel to their respective churches. They began to agitate for a nearby place to worship in the winter.

> *April 22, 1765. Forty-six petitioners in Waterbury and Oxford live from four to seven miles from places of public worship, and pray for liberty to have four months' winter-preaching.*
> Ecclesiastical Records

After some delays the petition was approved that year except for Oxford. This was the beginning of the community also called "Waterbury South Farms" or just "The Farms." Another petition in 1767 was denied for that winter, but the future residents of Prospect had other ideas.

> *Oct. 21, 1771. Thirty-nine remonstrants in Cheshire, West of the mountain, wish not to be included. They cannot get to Waterbury South Farms in winter, and hope hereafter to be constituted a separate Society.*
> Ecclesiastical Records

This break-off was the first suggestion of what afterward became the Columbia Society and the town of Prospect. The new Waterbury society was given full ecclesiastical privileges in May of 1773 and was named Salem. Seventy-one years later, in 1844, this same basic area would be incorporated as Naugatuck.

~

Chapter Four

The Evolution of a Town — the Marriage

T he marriage of a portion of Cheshire and a portion of Waterbury in 1827 to form Prospect was preceded by a very long courtship. For fifty-six years or more prior to the incorporation, the residents of this region fought to achieve their own independence. In 1771 a petition was made to the proprietors from "Waterbury South Farms" (Prospect); they requested to be made a parish. The formation of an ecclesiastical (church) society was the normal first step in the creation of a new town. Colonel Benjamin Hall and Captain Cornelius were appointed to a committee to review the matter. They "agreed" to deny the petition, and the people of "West Rocks" continued to attend church in "New Cheshire."

In 1778 the first house of worship was built on the land of John Lewis, Jr. The Columbia Parish, including a governing body called Columbia Company, was formed in October of 1797. Besides being the business arm of the church, the leaders of the company performed civil roles. Their work included laying taxes, assuring support for church and schools, electing constables, and forming a local militia. They also appointed school officials, road surveyors, grave diggers, and a tavern keeper.

The formation of the Columbia Society did not free the people of West Rocks from their obligations to Cheshire and Waterbury. They still paid taxes and were subject to the laws and ultimate authority of their parent towns. The citizens on the Waterbury side of Prospect were given the opportunity to be a part of the Society of Salem in what is now Naugatuck, but in 1771 they made it clear that they preferred to form their own society (Chapter 3). Thus they became part of the Columbia Society when it formed.

The continued unrest and longing of the Columbia Society to be a free and independent town led to a petition (the latest of several) that was presented to the General Assembly of the State of Connecticut convened at Hartford in 1827. The residents wanted Columbia Society to be made a town unto itself, incorporating the same basic territory, which was situated approximately one-third in Waterbury and two-thirds in Cheshire (Fig 1).

At a general Assembly of the State of Connecticut holden at Hartford in said State, on the first Wednesday of May in the year of our Lord One Thousand, eight hundred and twenty seven.

Upon the petition of the Society of Columbia in the County of New Haven showing to this Assembly that the Society is composed part of the town of Cheshire and part of the town of Waterbury, by means of which and of its peculiar situation great inconveniences are sustained and praying that the inhabitants may be incorporated into a town as by petition on file date the 21 day of April, A.D. 1827; Resolved by this Assembly that the inhabitants being in that part of the town of Cheshire and in that part of the town of Waterbury lying within the limits of said Society of Columbia, and their successors forever, be and they are hereby incorporated into a town by the name of Prospect, with the privilege of sending one representative to the General Assembly of this State.

And it is further resolved that the said town of Prospect shall take and maintain such portion of the present poor of said town of Waterbury as the amount of polls and rateable estate of the inhabitants of that part of Waterbury lying within the limits of the said town of Prospect bears to the whole of the list of said town of Waterbury for the year 1826 and the like proportion of the present inhabitants of said Waterbury now absent and not residing within its limits who may hereafter become chargeable and of such of their descendants who shall be chargeable to said Waterbury by virtue of the present settlement of said absentees therein.

And the present said poor of said town of Cheshire shall be apportioned and divided between the said town of Cheshire and the said town of Prospect according to the ration on the list of 1826 by the selectmen of said towns and if they shall not agree by the committee herein after named, and said committee shall have power in regard to the division of the present poor of said town of Waterbury and Prospect if the selectmen of Waterbury and Prospect shall not agree upon the same, and said town of Prospect shall be entitled to and shall hold and enjoy the same proportion of the house and land purchased for a poorhouse in said Water-

bury as is herein after prescribed in regards to the debts due to and from the town of Cheshire and the debts due to and from the said town of Waterbury. And it is further resolved that the debts due to and from the town of Cheshire and the debts due to and from the said town of Waterbury shall be apportioned to the list of the year 1826.

The said town of Prospect shall pay such proportion of the debts due from the said town of Cheshire on the 14th day of May 1827, AD: and be entitled to such a portion of the debts due to said town of Cheshire on that day on the list of inhabitants of that part of the said town of Cheshire included in said town of Prospect bears to the whole, of the said list of said town of Cheshire and shall pay a portion of the debts due from the town of Waterbury on the said day of the said list of the inhabitants of that said part of Prospect.

And it is further resolved that the Hon. Noyes Darling, Jared Basset, and Nathaniel Richardson Esqs. be and they are hereby appointed a committee to enquire and decide whether the said town of Prospect ought to pay or contribute anything hereafter towards the building or maintenance of Bridges in the said town of Waterbury and if they shall decide that anything shall be paid or contributed it shall be their duty to enquire and decide what sum or proportion shall be paid or contributed and their decision thereon shall be forever conclusive upon the parties until relieved against or altered by the General Assembly.

The first town meeting in said town shall be held on the second Monday of June 1827 at the Congregational Meeting House in said town and Samuel Peck, Esq. shall be Moderator thereof and shall warn the meeting by setting a notification thereof on the sign post in said town and where else he may think proper at least six days before said second Monday of June.

A true copy of record examined and certified under the seal of the State, Thomas Day Sect. of State of Conn. And then September 25, Edward Chittenden of Prospect entered it in the town records, certified as a true copy.

Fig 1   The Charter of Prospect as approved, April 21, 1827.

The name of Columbia for the new town was rejected because there already was another Columbia in Connecticut.   The name Prospect was chosen because of the extended view experienced from the town's summit.   While in recent years, the growth of trees has caused some limitations, the panorama from the Prospect Green has always earned wide acclaim.   Visible are the hills from Meriden to beyond the Connecticut River, the waters of the Sound, and on a clear day, Long Island itself.   Prospect is, indeed, known for its view from the top.

PROSPECT TOWN OFFICIALS ELECTED JUNE 11, 1827	
Town clerk	Edward Chittenden
Selectmen	Jared Burr, David Scott, Albert Hoppin
Constables	Orrin Hotchkiss, Franklin D. Benham, Robert H. Bronson, Andrew Smith
Grand jurors	Gideon M. Hotchkiss, Lauren Preston, Eldad Hotchkiss, Jr.
Pound keepers	Joseph Payne, David Scott, Guy Perkins
Town agents	Samuel Peck, Joseph I. Doolittle
Treasurer	David Scott
Sealer of weights	Isaac Bradley
Sealer of measures	Ephraim Nettleton
Fence viewers	Joseph Beecher, Lyman Hitchcock
Assessors	Joseph I. Doolittle, Benjamin Bronson, Benjamin Platt
Surveyors of highways	Stephen Bradley, Samuel Williams, Jr., Gideon M. Hotchkiss, Samuel Peck, Ransom R. Russell, Olcott H. Payne, Garret Gillette, Joel Brooks
Agent	Jared Burr, Esq.

Fig 2   Besides the positions shown above, school officials, school visitors, and grave diggers were selected.

The first meeting of the newly formed town was held at the Congregational meeting house on June 11, 1827.   Samuel Peck was the moderator when elections were held for town offices (Fig 2).   Thomas Wilmot moderated at many of the early town meetings which were held at Castle Tavern.   Samuel Castle and later, "widow" Hannah Castle were the tavern keepers.   This was an official position appointed by the town.   Each municipality was required to have a tavern to accommodate visiting officials from outside the community. These were not only places where one could obtain meals, lodging, and of course, libations, but they also served as the meeting place for town functions.   Castle Tavern was located on Cheshire Road opposite the present Meeting Place (old library).   The road then was on the same level as the Green.   Later, Col. George Payne and then a man named Gunn kept the tavern at the same location. The Kimball family had another tavern at the site of the Congregational Church parsonage. After the new Congregational Church building was constructed in 1841, town meetings were held in its basement.

In the text of the Charter of Prospect (Fig 1), it is clear that the leaders of the day were concerned very much about matters such as taxes, bridges, roads, and the poor. Things that we might consider more important today, such as education and public buildings, were of little concern then. The welfare of the poor, though they were small in number, represented a large portion of a town's budget. There was constant bickering and attempts to trade off the poor of one town onto another. Prospect, being low in seniority compared to its parent towns, no doubt, took more than its share of burden.

The care and associated problems related to animals of all sorts was another concern for the elected officials. On June 27, 1846, a new Prospect by-law appeared in the Waterbury American (Fig 3).

In the early years the construction and improvement of roads engaged the attention of the town more than any other matter. The appropriations for roads were very liberal, considering the limited means of the town. Nothing affected the lives of everyone in town more than the condition of the roads — especially in a hilly place like Prospect. The leading citizens were chosen to supervise the road projects. Those selected in 1890 were Alfred Brooks, George D. Fenn, Lourie Richardson, Lewis Wooding, H.N. Clark, James Bottomly, Frank Allen, A.S. Plumb, Edgar Wallace, Levi Sanford, John Cook, and Reuben Perkins.

Prospect By-Law

At a special town meeting legally warned and holden at Prospect on the 6th day of June, 1846, for the purpose of taking into consideration the subject of restraining cattle, horses, hogs and sheep, from running at large on the commons and public highways in said town:

Voted, That if any owner of any horse or horses, neat creature or creatures, hogs or sheep, shall suffer the same to run at large out of his, her or their enclosure, on the commons or public highways in said town of Prospect, from the 6th day of July to the 6th day of November next, it shall be the duty of the haywards or either hayward of said town, and shall be lawful for any other person or persons who reside in and belong to said town, to take up and impound the same; and when any person or persons shall have so impounded such a beast as aforesaid, he, she or they, shall give notice to the owner or owners thereof, if he, she or they be known, in the same manner as in that case be liable to be proceeded with and sold, except that it shall not be necessary to have regard to fences. The owner shall pay before receiving said cattle from the pound-keeper, for horses fifty cents, for neat cattle twenty-five cents, for sheep 12½ cents per head, and for swine 20 cents, and all lawful expenses paid to the owner for food and water for said beasts while in pound. One-third of the above penalty to be paid to the pound-keeper, and the other two-thirds to the impounder.

Voted, That the Town Clerk be directed to cause said law to be published in a newspaper printed in New Haven county four weeks successively, before the 6th day of July next.

A true copy of record.

Attest JAMES STREET, *Town Clerk*

Prospect, June 6th, 1846.

Fig 3 Waterbury American, June 27, 1846.

Prospect Property Owners from the First Grand List — 1828

Andrews, Miles, 1
Andrews, Samuel, 1
Asel, F.,1
Austin, Alde, 1
Balden, Daniel, 2
Balden, Isaac
Barnes, Dimon, 1
Beecher, Hezekiah, 1
Beecher, Joseph, 1
Benham, Franklin, 1
Benham, Fredus M.
Berns, Elizabeth
Blakeslee, Manning, 1
Bradley, Isaac, 1
Bradley, Stephen, 1
Bronson, Benjamin, 1
Bronson, Cornelus, 1
Bronson, Joseph
Bronson, Robert H.
Bronson, Samuel
Brooks, Amasa, 1
Brooks, Hiram
Brooks, Joel, 1
Brown, Alford
Brown, Isaac, 1
Burr, Jared, 2
Burr, Orlando
Castle, Hannah, 1
Chatfield, Joseph
Chittenden, Edward
Chittenden, Leva
Chittenden, Richard
Chittenden, Platt
Clark, Amos, 1
Clark, Merritt, 1
Clark, Selah, 1
Doolittle, Joseph, 1
Farrel, Benjamin, 1
Farrel, Lebe, 1
Giles, Ransom
Gillette, Garret, 1
Hall, Miles, 1
Hill, Stanley
Hine, Ambrose, 1
Hine, Charles, 1
Hitchcock, Daniel, 1
Hitchcock, Esther children, 1

Hitchcock, Joab, 1
Hitchcock, Lyman, 1
Hitchcock, Oliver
Hitchcock, Samuel, 1
Hoppin, Albert, 1
Hotchkiss, Abigail, 1
Hotchkiss, Abigail, Amos-w, 1
Hotchkiss, Amos H., 1
Hotchkiss, Amzi
Hotchkiss, Avery, 1
Hotchkiss, Benj. Rusel, 1
Hotchkiss, Charles, 1
Hotchkiss, David M., 1
Hotchkiss, Eldad, 1
Hotchkiss, Elden, 1
Hotchkiss, Frederick, 2
Hotchkiss, Gideon M., 1
Hotchkiss, Isaac, 1
Hotchkiss, John
Hotchkiss, Lauren, 1
Hotchkiss, Lauren, 1
Hotchkiss, Marvin, 1
Hotchkiss, Orrin, 1
Hotchkiss, Ransom, 1
Hotchkiss, Rusel Ramon, 1
Hotchkiss, Sherman, 1
Hotchkiss, Woodward, 1
Ives, William, 1
Judd, Isaac, 1
Matthew, Edmon, 1
Matthew, Feber
Matthew, Joseph
Merriams, Lucius
Merriams, Sarah, 1
Mix, William, 1
Morse, Lent Jun.
Morse, Lent, 1
Nettleton, Eli, 1
Nettleton, Ephraim, 1
Norton, Harvey
Payne, David M., 1
Payne, Joseph, 1
Payne, Olcott, 1
Payne, Silas, 1
Payne, Stephen, 1
Peck, Samuel, 1
Perkins, Guy, 1

Platt, Benjamin, 1
Platt, Benjamin II
Platt, Elisha, 2
Platt, Joseph, 1
Platt, Joseph II
Porter, Arba, 1
Porter, Luca, 1
Preston, Eliseph, 1
Preston, Lauren, 1
Roberts, Ephraim, 1
Samuel, Martin, 1
Sanford, Archibald, 1
Sanford, David, 1
Sanford, Fremon
Sanford, John, 1
Sanford, Libeus, 1
Scott, David, 1
Smith, Andrew, 1
Smith, Ira, 1
Smith, Joseph, 1
Smith, Leverit, 1
Smith, Luther
Smith, Lyman, 1
Smith, Roswell
Smith, Samuel, 1
Street, James, 1
Talmage, Josiah, 1
Talmage, William
Tuttle, Lauren
Tuttle, Moses, 1
Tuttle, Obed, 1
Tuttle, Obed, 1
Tuttle, Wooster, 1
Tyler, Fores
Tyler, Ichabod, 1
Tyler, Lymon, 1
Tyler, Richard, 1
Walles, James, 1
Weeks, R. M., 1
Williams, Abigal, 1
Williams, Albert
Williams, Samuel, 1
Williams, Samuel Jr., 1
Wilmot, Amos, 1
Wilmot, Asa
Wilmot, Silas
Wilmot, Thomas, 1

Fig 4 Complete list of property owners and number of houses they owned in 1828. Others listed had either land, livestock, clocks, or other taxable items.

The care of the poor was another priority item. Starting in 1832 the town appointed overseers to look after those who were suffering tough times or were in need. The goal was to prevent the unfortunate ones from becoming town charges. These efforts were sometimes effective, but occasionally the poor people resented the care forced on them and refused to submit to the authority of the overseers. The outlay for the poor in 1889 was $225 out of a total Prospect budget of about $2,000. Prospect was not a rich town. It did not have any truly wealthy citizens. Most residents were considered hard-working, lower to middle class people for that time. In 1890 the Grand List for Prospect was $154,641. This was the lowest of any town in New Haven County which had a total Grand List of $10,368,393.

Other concerns of the new government were the registering of voters, holding of elections, regulation of liquor sales, and perambulating (walking around) the boundaries to settle disputes with neighboring towns.

The census of 1830 was the first to show Prospect separated from its parent towns. The population was 651. Being primarily agricultural, there were about as many cattle (555) and sheep (661) as people in Prospect during the early years of the town's existence.

The first Grand List of 1828 reveals a bit of the character of Prospect. There were six mills in town, of which William Mix owned two. The only store in town was owned by Edward Chittenden. The items listed below (Fig 5) were possessions taxed in Prospect. House assessments were based on size and quality of construction, and there was quite a range. The smallest houses had assessed values of $25 each while the largest, David Scott's place, was valued at $1150 or forty-six times as much! David Scott was the wealthiest man in town with the largest house, 179 acres, 1 distillery, 1 horse, 9 cattle, 21 sheep, 1 carriage, and 1 clock. He was probably a popular man having the only registered fancy carriage in Prospect and one of the two distilleries. Joseph Doolittle had the largest piece of land at 250 acres. Clocks and in later years, watches and pianos were considered luxury items and were taxed accordingly.

Property owners	135	Horses	54
Houses	110	Cattle	555
Mills	6	Sheep	661
Isaac Hotchkiss		Carriages	1
Sherman Hotchkiss		David Scott	
William Mix (2)		Clocks	59
Ely Nettleton			
Andrew Smith		Paid Poll Tax	64
Stores	1	Distilleries	2
Edward Chittenden		Lent Morse	
		David Scott	
Land (in acres)	4638		

Fig 5   Line item quantities in the Grand List of Prospect of 1828.

In 1830 another business category was added: the manufactory. The owners and appraised values were: Levi Baldwin ($100), Lockwood Smith ($50), and Edwin Hopkins ($50). These were distinct from the mills listed that year by Gideon M. Hotchkiss ($25), Sherman Hotchkiss ($150), Isaac Hotchkiss ($50), William Mix ($500 + fishery $15), and Andrew Smith ($100).

Pocket watches were on the Grand List of 1830. Watches valued at $4 were carried by Libeus Sanford and Titus Sanford. Those sporting $5 watches were Samuel Martin, Lauren Preston, and Albert Williams. David M. Payne and Leonard Tuttle had $6 timepieces, while those of Daniel Baldwin and Wooster Tuttle were worth $10. The finest watch in Prospect was owned by Joseph Doolittle with an appraised value of $35.

The $20 poll tax was paid by sixty-four of the one hundred thirty-five property owners. If you consider that the average wage for a man at this time was about $1 a day or even less, paying for the "right" to vote was costly in those days. One must wonder what these founders would think if they saw the meager turn out at some elections today where the privilege to vote is free?

~

Chapter Five

Early Settlers and Their Houses

T he very first houses built in Prospect, long before the town was incorporated, were small and crude. Little is known about these structures or the people who lived in them. Only the foundations remain to tell us their size and location. No one knows for certain who the first homesteader was in that wilderness we now call Prospect.

John Moss, Jr. drew lots on the first tract of land here in 1694, but we do not know when he built on the site. Former town historian Nellie Cowdell thought that John Cook had the first house on Cook Road, although this has not been confirmed.

The first dwellings in Prospect date back to the early to middle 1700s. Because Prospect was primarily a farming community, most of the homes of this period were simple farmhouses scattered throughout the town. Many of these houses burned down and were replaced with others on the same site. Therefore, it is often difficult to determine the exact age of the structures.

However, the oldest public building still standing is known — the Pavlik Real Estate office on Union City Road. This building, not far from the center of town, was first owned by Asahel Chittenden and served as a store in 1803. There were once several stores, taverns, and inns located near the Green, but they no longer exist.

A GUIDE TO HISTORIC BUILDINGS IN
PROSPECT, CONNECTICUT
by Mark Guevin

In 1977, when Prospect observed its 150th anniversary, twelve homes were designated Sesquicentennial Houses. All these homes were built before the town was incorporated in 1827. Ten of the twelve homes are still standing as of 1995. One house that no longer remains is that of Ephraim Nettleton on Center Street, just south of the Green (see drawing by Jane Fowler on Page 2). This home was last owned by the Petrauskas family before the property was sold to the town of Prospect. The new Prospect Library was built on the site. The other house that was torn down is the Maria Hotchkiss house on Maria Hotchkiss Road. In the future, as more research on Prospect's history is done, additional homes will be designated Sesquicentennial Houses. This article not only focuses on the sesquicentennial houses, but also on other historic buildings built in later periods. The sesquicentennial houses are marked with an asterisk (*).

The Old Glebe House — 21 Center Street

This home is the oldest building still standing on the Prospect Green (Fig 1). It was built in 1844 as the second parsonage of the Congregational Church. A gift of $1000 by Elizabeth Beecher, a former member, helped pay for the new building. It replaced the first parsonage, which was built on the same site and purchased by the church in 1801. The new building was 24 by 28 feet and two stories high. There was also a kitchen 14-15 feet by 22 feet on the south end of the home. In 1883 the building was enlarged, and large chimneys with fireplaces were removed.

Fig 1   The Old Glebe House - 21 Center Street   Mark Guevin

Reverend Reuben Torrey was the first minister to use the new parsonage. He lived there with his wife Anne and daughters Susan and Martha. Twenty-one other ministers lived in the parsonage until it was sold in 1927, and another building was bought adjacent to the church. Today, the home is the residence of Walter Misavage.

Center School — 19 Center Street

This one-room schoolhouse was used until 1936 when Community School was opened. At that time, all of the other schoolhouses were closed. Center School was then used as a justice court and for other town functions. It was also used for civil defense during World War II. Today, the building is maintained by the Prospect Historical Society for exhibits. It is open to the public during the town picnic in June and the Grange Fair in August. Occasionally, classes from Community School visit for a short lesson on Prospect history.

Hotchkiss House — 61 Waterbury Road *

The Hotchkiss house (Fig 2) was built by Frederick Hotchkiss for his son, David Miles Hotchkiss. Work began in 1815, when timbers were cut from the family property. A well was dug in 1818, and the main house with a one-story el was built in 1819 at a cost of $660.99.

David Miles Hotchkiss, who gave Prospect its name, was the first generation of the family to live in the house. His first wife was Zeruah Stevens of Naugatuck, and his second wife was Hannah Doolittle Bristol, a widow from Roaring Brook Road in Prospect. He had a total of ten children. He operated a private school, called the Select Academy, in his house. He used several second-story rooms for classrooms and for boarding students.

After the private school closed, rooms were rented to Irish immigrants who worked on the telegraph lines in Prospect. They signed their names on a wall upstairs. The wallpaper has been peeled away in one of the rooms to reveal their signatures.

Fig 2 Hotchkiss House - 61 Waterbury Road*   Mark Guevin

Although this house was owned by the Hotchkiss family for 161 years, from 1819 until 1980, only three generations of the family lived in the house. Ruth Hotchkiss, who was David Miles Hotchkiss' granddaughter, lived in the house until her death in 1980 at the age of 91. She, like her grandfather, was a schoolteacher. She taught at Webster School while her sister Mabel was a teacher at Crosby High School.

In 1980 the Hotchkiss House was purchased by the town of Prospect and leased to the Prospect Historical Society. The Historical Society holds its meetings at the house and also holds several open house days each year to which the public is invited. The house can be toured by appointment.

Clark Homestead — 89* and 95 Clark Hill Road

Amos Hotchkiss owned 320 acres on Clark Hill in the late 1700s. He was born in 1751, fought in the Revolutionary War, married Abigail Scott, and died in 1820. His father was Gideon Hotchkiss, who represented Waterbury in the General Assembly and was an officer in the militia. Gideon fathered 19 children and owned over 1000 acres of land bounded by Salem, Straitsville, and Porter Hill Roads.

Amos built the old Clark house (Fig 3) around the 1770s, which was the first plastered house in Prospect. Sand was carried from the seashore by oxen to make the plaster. Merritt and Catherine (elsewhere Keturah) Clark bought the farm in the early 1800s when they moved from Milford. They were the parents of Merritt Clark, Jr., who was born in 1823 and died in 1898.

Fig 3 Old Clark Homestead - 89 Clark Hill Road*   Mark Guevin

Fig 4 New Clark Homestead - 95 Clark Hill Road   Mark Guevin

Merritt Clark, Jr.'s son, Halsey Steele Clark, moved into the new Clark house after marrying Fannie Phipps on May 25, 1881. The new house (Fig 4) was built in either 1881 or 1882 by John Skilton. John Skilton lived with the Clarks for nine months while building the house. He was an excellent builder and made only one little mistake on a brace upstairs. William Morris plastered the entire house (10 rooms) in only one day. He worked so quickly that four assistants could not keep up with him.

Harris Platt House — 3 Union City Road *

Asahel Chittenden was born in 1763. In March 1780 he enlisted in Col. Beecher's Regiment of Infantry. After returning to Prospect, he married Anna Lewis in 1783. He bought 15 acres from John Lewis, his father-in-law, in 1793. John Lewis was a minister in Prospect before the Congregational Church was established in 1798. He also gave five acres to his daughter.

Asahel built a house (Fig 5) and barn on the property. He also opened a store in 1803 and sold all sorts of goods. This building is the oldest public building still standing in Prospect. Asahel died in 1813 and the property was left to his wife. She married Robert Hotchkiss in 1816 and the property was given to her children.

By 1831, Asahel's son, Edward, owned the property. He became postmaster in January 1830, shortly after the town was incorporated. One old lady wrote almost 100 years ago that she remembered Mrs. Edward Chittenden selling gingerbread on "Muster Day" when the militia met to train. There was also a ballroom upstairs where people danced. In 1833 Edward sold the building and 22 acres to Woodward Hotchkiss. In 1852 Woodward Hotchkiss sold the property to Harris and Lucinda Platt.   The building is presently owned by George Pavlik and is the Pavlik Real Estate building.

Fig 5 Harris Platt House — 3 Union City Road *   Mark Guevin

Fig 6 Plumb Farm - 61 Cheshire Road*   Mark Guevin

Plumb Farm — 61 Cheshire Road *

In 1713 or 1714 a division of 90 acres was deeded to Capt. John Merriman as a proprietor of Wallingford. The property extended along Cheshire Road from the intersection of Coer Road to the intersection of Matthew Street. The land stretched north for 90 rods (.28 miles). The lot passed through several owners until it was sold to Jonathan Smith of New Haven for £ 210 in 1737. In 1755 he deeded the property to his son Ephraim.

In 1757 Ira Smith, son of Ephraim, was born at the homestead. In the spring of 1777 Ephraim was drafted into the military, but Ira went instead. He served as a private in Capt. Kimball's company under Col. John Chandler. He was at Peekskill, Germantown, Fort Mifflin, and Valley Forge. In 1779 Ira Smith married Elizabeth Judson. Ephraim gave Ira about 35 acres of the farm in 1791. In 1798 Ephraim and Ira were among the 16 original members of the Congregational Church.

Ira Smith built the current Plumb house (Fig 6) sometime between 1779, when he was married, and 1791, when his father deeded him the acreage. Ira's son, Andrew, owned and lived in the house until his death in 1878 when the Plumb family purchased the home.

Joel Matthews House — 4 Matthew Street *

Fig 7 Joel Matthews House - 4 Matthew Street*   Mark Guevin

In 1806 Ephraim Smith, who owned the Plumb farm, died and left a five-acre plot of land on the corner of Cheshire Road and Matthew Street to his son, Ephraim Smith, Jr. In 1811 Ephraim Jr. moved to New York State and sold the land to his brother Ira. However, a small ¼ acre piece was not included in the land given to Ephraim Jr. This land was sold to Hezekiah Hine in 1791 for £ 1. This property was sold several times until 1812, when the land with a house on it (Fig 7) was sold to Uriah Carrington of Waterbury for $100. In 1813 Ira Smith sold 3/4 of an acre to Uriah for $30 to round out the piece to one acre. The property was sold several times until 1833, when a two-acre lot with home was sold to Joel Matthews for $300. It is now the residence of Peter Thiel and is a fine example of early 19th century architecture.

Ambrose Hine House — 118 Cook Road

The history of the Captain Ambrose Hine house can be traced to 1716, when 120 acres were laid out for Thomas Yale. The land changed hands many times until Ambrose Hine purchased it in 1757. The exact date when a dwelling house was built on the site is not known, although records suggest the family was living on this property in 1759. The first description of the dwelling does not appear in the land records until 1794 (Fig 8).

Besides engaging in farming, records show that Ambrose Hine was a soldier who served in Col. Wadsworth's Brigade. According to a pay extract in Waterbury history, "Captain Ambrose Hine had in his company 26 able men" in August 1777.

Fig 8 Ambrose Hine House - 118 Cook Road   Mark Guevin

The Ambrose house is currently owned by George and Shirley Sabo. It is a home typical of early buildings in the area — a story and a half, two-room, wood frame structure with center fireplace. Originally, it consisted of a hall and parlor on the ground floor. Above, there was either one general area or a division of hall chamber and parlor chamber. Another room (or rooms) were located to the back of the house (north side). The measurements of the cellar appear to coincide with the original house: 30 feet by 21 feet. The main carrying beams, 10 inches by 10 inches, are virtually tree trunks. The mortise and tenon method was used to join beams and joists, and the entire house is pegged. When nails were used, they were rose-head, hand-forged, and door hinges were double H-L.

> Information on the Ambrose Hine house has been provided from a study by Shirley M. Sabo, *The Captain Ambrose Hine House c. 1759 As Compared to Other Dwellings in Prospect, CT*, August 20, 1984.

Lucius Talmadge House — 21 Talmadge Hill Road *

In 1742 Peter Curtis sold a 90-acre property with house, barn, and fences to Joseph Matthews. Eleven years later Joseph gave part of his property to his son, Samuel Matthews. Samuel sold 10 acres to Isaac Tyler, Jr. in 1768. The property was sold again in 1803 to Joseph Beecher. Joseph and Abigail Beecher joined the Congregational Church in 1818, later transferring to Cheshire in 1845. They gave the property to their daughter Olive and her husband, Joseph Williams, in 1839. The Williams also transferred to Cheshire, but in 1840. The property changed hands several more times until 1847, when Lucius Talmadge purchased the property. Talmadge Hill Road was named after the Talmadge family, who occupied the house (Fig 9) for many years.

Fig 9 Lucius Talmadge House - 21 Talmadge Hill Road   Mark Guevin

Col. Jesse Ford House - 43 Cheshire Road *

In 1768 Ephriam Smith, who owned the Plumb property, sold 5 acres from the western part of his farm to Isaac Tyler. The lot was bounded west by highway, south, east, and north by the remainder of Ephriam Smith's property. The "highway" was one of the original north-south roads laid out in 1713. It still exists today as the long driveway leading to the house.

Fig 10   Col. Jesse Ford House - 43 Cheshire Road*   Mark Guevin

The property was located 19 rods (313.5 feet) north of present-day Route 68. It was 40 rods long in the north-south direction and 20 rods wide in the east-west direction. The northern 3 acres of the 5-acre lot were deeded to Isaac Tyler's son, Amos, in 1791. Two other pieces were also transferred, 16 acres to Amos, increasing his property to 22 acres. It is assumed that a house (Fig 10) was built on the property about 1789, the year Amos married Chloe Hine, although the date of the marriage was not recorded.

In 1796 Amos sold the house and 22 acres to John Bryan. In 1800 he sold it to Jared Burr and Jesse Ford. Jared Burr was Jesse's father-in-law. Jesse Ford served as a Major in the 10th regiment, which was comprised of men from the Cheshire area. He was appointed a Lt. Colonel and Commandant in October 1810. He resigned in 1813, having served more than 22 years. He had been a Major for five years and a Lt. Colonel for 2 years. He died in Prospect in 1824 at age 49. Jared Burr died in 1829 and left the house and 33 acres to his daughter, Rebecca Ford. Rebecca died in 1862 at age 81.

Houses in this article and other historic homes are identified on the Driving Tour of Prospect map on the following page (Fig 11).

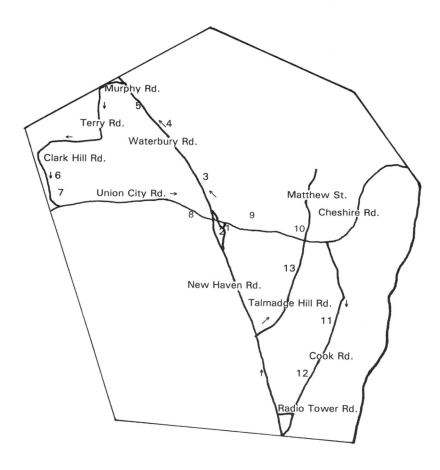

Fig 11 Driving Tour of Prospect

1 - The Old Glebe House
   21 Center St.
2 - Center School
   19 Center St.
3 - Hotchkiss House
   61 Waterbury Rd. *
4 -   110 Waterbury Rd. *
5 - Eldad Hotchkiss House
   138 Waterbury Rd. *
6 - Clark Homestead
   89 Clark Hill Road *
7 - Clark Homestead
   95 Clark Hill Road

8 - Harris Platt House
   3 Union City Rd. *
9 - Plumb Farm
   61 Cheshire Rd. *
10- Joel Matthews House
   4 Matthew St. *
11- Ambrose Hine House
   118 Cook Rd. *
12- Asaph French House
   194 Cook Rd. *
13- Lucius Talmadge House
   21 Talmadge Hill Rd. *

* - Sesquicentennial Houses

SOME OF THE HOUSES IN PROSPECT, CONNECTICUT
by Jennie Beardsley Clapp to Mrs. Fred Sanford (Julia Hotchkiss)
written about 1920

My great-great-grandfather moved to Prospect from Wallingford and settled there.   His name—Gideon Hotchkiss. Amos his son was born in this town.   It was called Columbia and belonged to Waterbury in the early days of the settlement.   Amos was my great-grandfather; his wife was Abigail Scott of Watertown. My grandfather was also born here and my mother and my sister and myself.

THE HOUSES I LIVED IN
The first house my parents lived in here that I know of was the part of Mrs. Roe's house near Warren Wilson.   I was not born then but in Feb. 6, 1852.   I was born in an old house near Prospect Hill, afterwards the site of Edwin Tyler's square house.   This new house later in 1870 was occupied by Woodward Hotchkiss' widow and her daughter Mrs. Norton.   Their home used to be near Mrs. Hitchcock's before Mr. Hotchkiss died. Mrs. Hotchkiss was Polly Castle and she lived to be 100 years, shy by less than one month.

After we came back to Prospect from Bridgeport we lived in an old-fashioned house about ½ mile west of A. Harlow Hotchkiss.   It was owned by an old lady they called Aunt Daniels who lived with Harriet Ford.   My sister was born at this house in 1855.   We moved from here to a place next south of Lorain Hotchkiss' house.   A family by the name of John McDonald lived in the south part of the house at the time.   My father died of consumption there June 20, 1857.   He was almost 40 years.   We then moved to my mother's father's place in the west of Prospect.   His name was Amos but his father having the same name most people called him Uncle Harlow.   Harlow Hotchkiss was very deaf.   In Oct. 1858 we moved to the gate house in Rag Hollow and lived there until the fall of 1875

(or my mother did) when she broke up the home.   I was living in Yalesville at this time and my sister went to Bristol and married there on July 24, 1878.   My mother had a place in West Cheshire but it was rented for several years before she lived there.   She took care of the sick and was with me some of the time.

One other house we lived in after 1852 (probably in 1853) was an old house standing where Frank Wallace afterward built.   He sold later to Moses Chandler whose wife was a Winchell. They had two sons, George and Wallie. I have forgotten his real name, they called him Wallie.   I do not know others that lived in or owned the old house we lived in.

My great-grandfather Amos, son of Gideon, owned a place he sold to a Merritt Clark before 1820.   Then he owned a house that stood in the east part of Lyman Smith's lot.   He died in 1820.

Joseph Bronson and wife Polly owned a house near the school house in the western part of Prospect.   She lived there summers until part of the house was unsafe.   Her son Harry used to care for the farm.   In 1870 I went to see her.   She was very old.   She was Grandfather's sister.   Only a part of the house was safe at that time.   She was with her children in Waterbury winters.   She was a very determined and independent old lady who would be at her own home just as long as she could and be safe.   She died in Waterbury.   I think she was 90 or more. Judge Geo. H. Cowell was her grandson.

Thus far I have written to tell of the different houses I lived in Prospect. Aunt Daniel's place has been gone for years.   The one on the road from the Summit station was burned down.   The house that stood at Edwin Tyler's site, was gone many years ago.   The Harlow Hotchkiss place was torn down 4 or 5 years ago and the old house where now stands Moses Chandler's, is long gone.

I used to find the first flowers in the spring. The blue hepaticas, anemones, yellow violets and the swamp pinks in June. I loved the wild beauties and knew where to find them too. I have never lost my love of flowers. I knew the different trees by their leaves. How I loved the tulips on the tulip trees (white wood). With but few play things I made play of the outdoors world and enjoyed it well.

THE HOMES & OCCUPANTS OF RAG HOLLOW BEGINNING AT THE TOWN LINE OF CHESHIRE AND PROSPECT

In the lot next to the one that the Cheshire line runs through was an old-fashioned house, brown with age, where a Scott family lived. Mrs. David Scott, who was a Frost, was there in 1858 and 1859. In the time of the war, Jehial Benham bought the place. He with his three brothers, Robert, Bennett, and Lewis, enlisted in Company A. 20th Regt. Conn. Vol's. He lived there until his death a few years ago.

Across the road on a hill stood a square roofed house; different persons lived in it for a little time. I do not remember their names. During the war or a little after, Richard Dorr Johns bought the place and lived there the rest of his life. It was sold by his widow but I was away from the town and do not know who bought it. They had one son Frank and three daughters: Carrie, Mamie, and Hattie. Mr. Johns was a three-months man; afterwards he enlisted again. He peddled tin for a while, then he was a dipper of matches at the match shop. Mrs. Johns was Elizabeth Wilkinson. Her father Lenard Wilkinson owned the place where the Tuckers live now. I think it's over the line in Cheshire. Mr. Wilkinson bought it of John Ives, then sold it to Mr. Smith. Mrs. Tucker was a daughter of Mr. Smith.

Early across the road from the John's place was the Titus Mix place. He had a grist mill near the gate house. I was told the mill used to be a spoon shop. In 1858 Mr. Mix had owned his house a long time. He was a brother of Ervin Mix and his wife was Flora Tuttle. They had two sons Edwin and Frederick. Across the road was the house now owned by Mr. Lomiss. Mr. S.E. Jeralds owned it when he moved there in 1858. I think he built it. When he moved to Cheshire in about 1871 he took the house of Geo. Tyler's and Mrs. Elias Mix. He left the town for Yalesville in '74. About 1864 or 1865 Professor Elton, just married, lived upstairs at the Titus Mix house.

Mr. S.E. Jeralds had the hoe, ferrule, and sewing machine needle shop. His first wife was Marintha Griswold from Bantam. They had four living children, Edgar, Welley, Roderick, and Minnie. Their oldest, a girl, died. His second wife was a sister of his first wife. Her name was Julia Ann Chandler. Her first husband was a brother of Moses and Edward Chandler. She had one son of the same name as his father, Marcus Chandler. Her three children by Mr. Jeralds were Harry, Daisy, and George Jeralds.

THE GATE HOUSE

The next house and the mill by it, around the bend towards the west, was the gate house where we lived. [Editor's note: See chapter 11 for more description of the gate house.]

In the lot joining was the Enos Gaylord place. After I left town, the Gaylords, being old, sold the place to Elmer and Ida (Mix) Brooks. Mrs. Ida Brooks owns it now. Mr. and Mrs. Gaylord had two sons named Delos and Brainord who settled in the west. They went with Delos. He used to live in West Haven or Westerville. I forget which. I think he married a sister of Leslie Russell of western Prospect. It might have been Leslie's aunt.

THE OLD ROAD

Above this house there used to be a hilly road called the old road, running west that went up the hill a mile or so. It was crossed by a road that ran past the Ed Chandler, Harry Moss and Mrs. Lent Moss and the Wm. Beecher places. The Beecher place nearly across from the end of the old road. Mrs. Lent Moss was

Mrs. Titus Mix's mother. Her first husband was a Tuttle. She lived with her son Gus and daughter Amy Moss. I remember three daughters of Tuttle, two besides Mrs. Mix. Amy Moss was a dwarf.

To return to Enos Gaylord place, the first house on the old road, was Ransom Benham's place. The road is now closed as the railroad crosses it. He lived there with his daughter Almeda Hull. Her husband was killed in the war. She had two girls and three boys. She afterwards bought a little house on a stony road nearly across from Deacon Street's near Prospect Hill. Lucien Talmadge lived I think on a street towards the south above Matthew Street. I believe a Kimball lived on that street.

The second house on the old road was Ervin Mix's house and farm. He married Margaret Atwater of Bethany. She died leaving two children. Ervin Mix who is unmarried lives in California and Ida Mix who married Elmer Brooks, son of Harry Brooks of Mixville. Ervin Mix's house and farm are sold but I do not know to whom. After his wife died her sister Lucy Atwater took care of his home and brought up the two children.

THE ROAD TO PROSPECT HILL

Next to the Elmer Brooks (Gaylord) house towards Prospect is the Bennet Royce place, now occupied by Mrs. Jane Gibbud and son Duncan. Mrs. Gibbud was Avery Hotchkiss' daughter, a brother of Woodward and Amos Harlow Hotchkiss. When the 6th Conn. Reg. of Vol. was formed Mr. Wm. Berkeley enlisted in it. They then lived in the upper part of the Bennet Royce house. Bennet Royce had two daughters and five sons. Mrs. Royce was Julia Benham of Cheshire. Her four brothers and three sons went to war. One of her brothers was killed and her son Charles was killed by a shell. Ed Royce married Jeannette Hotchkiss the night before he left for the war. After he came home he lived in the upper part of the Royce house and taught school in Mixville the winter term. Philander Royce married a distant cousin from New York State and went to Nebraska. Emily was a teacher and married

Elford Smith, brother of Mrs. Tucker and lived at that place a while, then went to Nebraska. George lives in California. Rodney was killed by Indians in the west and I do not know where Lissie is now. When old, Mr. and Mrs. Royce went to live with or near their children in the west and died there.

THE HAUNTED HOUSE

Across the bridge above the old shop was a road running by a small shop belonging to the company and went through a grove to a large house called the Wilcox House; when I was little girl it stood empty most of the time and was called haunted. Many scareful stories were told and children shunned it. There was a Mr. Wilcox built it for some reason was not able to keep it. For a number of years it was in some building company and the story was that Frederick Mix (brother of Mrs. George Tyler) was hired to care for it and keep away those who would damage an empty house—thence the ghosts and their fearful doings.

THE SHOPS & FACTORIES

Next on the road to Prospect comes the old building near the road where the sulphur matches and parlor matches were made. (I believe the building is gone now). Edwin Tyler had the business first I remember. Then Henry Judd of Prospect and Howard Ives of West Cheshire took the match making business. When I was married it was run by them.

Edwin Tyler bought the place and carried on the match business. Many a time I've enjoyed myself playing with Nellie Tyler and her numerous family of dolls. Although an only child she was a lovely and unselfish playmate. After Mr. Tyler left Prospect different families lived there. Mr. Frank Matthews lived there a long time. Also there was Mr. Delano Judd and Henry Elliott Russell's widow, Sarah Tyler Russell with her son who died there, her niece Eleanor Beecher, and a friend Lydia Thorpe. The three kept house together and worked in the match shop.

A little above the old match shop was a small shop east of the road. Before the war and until Feb. 6, 1867, Henry Judd made tin buttons or suspender buttons. Some of them were made black; some left the tin color. There was a blacking or japan shop too. A family lived in this shop for a time. Nearly across the road was the blacksmith shop of Elias Mix, father of Emily Tyler and Frederick Mix. I believe his wife was Maria Judd, sister of Henry Judd.

The next house on the west side of the road was owned by Mr. and Mrs. Elias Mix. Mr. and Mrs. George Tyler lived there, and perhaps owned part of it. They had one child, Emma Tyler who was Edgar Jeralds' first wife. Emerson Jeralds is their son. Mr. Jeralds later owned the house and now Edgar Jeralds and his second wife, Jennie Hotchkiss live there; I do not know if they own it or not. One of Edgar and Jennie's girls died. Her name was Edna and the other, named Cassie, is now living. Jennie's father Evans died at their home. Her mother was a Wallace. I think her name was Nancy. Evans and his wife were parted. Jennie lived with her mother. Harry was brought up by Bela Hotchkiss, an uncle, of Cheshire. Jennie's mother took care of her mother, "Old Lady Wallace" as she was called, in a little house above the Edgar Wallace place. I think the house was off the road a little to south or in a lane.

Above Edgar Jeralds on the opposite side of the road was his father's shops. Next house above (probably gone now) was a house for two families as far back as the war. Mr. and Mrs. Wm. Berkley lived there and a Mr. and Mrs. Hough. I know of a Mrs. Hine that lived there later and later a Mr. and Mrs. Northrup. I think families lived there who were employed by the Jeralds' shops. I think the house was owned by Mr. S.E. Jeralds.

This house was on the west side of the road as was also the next large house and grist mill owned by Capt. William Mix. In the 1850s he used to make clay buttons and I've been told that spoons were made there. Just before we reached the mill, which was close to the road, a road wound around through a large chestnut grove to the house. A dam was above the house and the two Mix ponds were divided by the road to Prospect Hill ex-

tended above the dam. Wm. Mix was called well to do. He had a large room dedicated for the meetings that were held there. He was an Advent and entertained the ministers who came. I suppose the house is gone now.

Another house above his in the same lot was where Miles Williams and his mother lived. When I first lived in the Hollow, there above the mill on a bank across the road from the pond, was a very old house where Miles William's mother lived with her grand daughter Libbie Lewis. Before the war, in 1859, Henry Mix lived in this old house.

THE ROAD TO EDGAR WALLACE

Above the mill a road went around by the widow Wallace's place bearing to the east. Edgar Wallace lived there later. [One of] Mrs. Wallace's children was Frances who married Otis Paine. They said her mother was 15 years older than her girl. They said Mrs. Wallace was married at 13 years. Also there was Josephine who married Horace Nettleton, Edward, Edgar, and Eldredge. Nearer the bend in the road there used to be a house where a Mr. Spencer lived. They had a son Garden.

Above Edgar Wallace's bearing to the north east was the Henry Judd home and near it his mother's place. Farther was a house where Robinson Williams' brother and his wife lived. I think his name was Albert. The Conklins built in that vicinity. I cannot remember just how the houses are located above the Judd place. I never was on that road above there much.

Return to Prospect road above this branch road. The road wound around from south to west between the two divisions of the Capt. Wm. Mix ponds. Just above the bridge dividing the ponds was Mr. Wilson Potter's house on the right of the road. He had one daughter who married Edwin Benham, son of Lewis on Matthew Street. Mr. Potter and daughter both stuttered.

THE BETHANY ROAD

Above this house on the left of road stood the house Frank Wallace built on the corner of the Bethany Road. In 1858 and until after the Civil War, Frank Wallace lived there. His children were Lucy, who married E. Lawton of the firm of Jeralds, Nettleton & Lawton, Kate who married J. Walter Mix who later was Comptroller of Conn., and Frank Jr. who married Tessnie (?) Munson, the daughter of Levi Munson of Cheshire.

Frank Wallace and Geo. Tyler went to war but came home before their time was out. Moses Chandler who owned the place next enlisted. I think in the same 20th reg. Conn. Vol's as also Ed Chandler, Moses brother. Their father went to war later.

About 1853 or 1854 my parents lived in an old house that stood on or near the site of Frank Wallace's house. At that time Stiles Perkins, who married Capt. Wm. Mix's daughter Marriette, lived near, I think at the Wilson Potter's place. Henry Mix, her brother lived in an old house on the east of road across from the Mix pond and above the mill. Henry Mix's wife was Charlotte Tyler, daughter of Spencer Tyler.

While we lived at the gate, on the Bethany road the first house was where Mr. and Mrs. Williams lived with their two children: son Lambert, and daughter Lavinia. Mr. Williams died soon after we came to the gate. He had a hair lip as had also his daughter. The next house was owned by Lafayette Anthony long after he moved away and Mr. Wm. Berkley lived there for a while. They were there in 1878. Soon after the war they lived in the Capt. Wm. Mix place. They also lived in a rather small house below on this Bethany road, in 1870.

Elim Sanford also lived down that way and Merritt Young's father and a Mr. Peck but I hardly ever went in that locality and cannot locate their places. The Umberfields, the place of Warren Wilson and an old lady Mrs. Roe where my father lived before I was born were there too. I cannot tell just where the places are situated but perhaps having the names you may find others that can locate them.

During the war Mrs. Wm. Berkley worked in the match shop and had several rooms in the house with Mrs. Jehiel

Benham and my mother boarded the two girls, Eva and (Birdie or) Fannie Berkley. Prof. Elton and bride Ellen Hotchkiss lived in Titus Mix place up stairs during the time.

I remember some of the houses above Moses Chandler's but do not remember clearly enough to place them in the right order but will name them as best as I can. As I remember near the Red School house, I believe before you reach it, was B.B. Brown's house. Above was a small house where in the winter of 1870 Nelson Welton lived. It was on the north side of road. Then came the Joel Matthews place on the corner of Matthew Street, the Plumb place, the Sanford place, the Andrew Smith place, the Blakeslee place, and the Deacon Street place. That is all I can remember as I have not been through that locality but twice in toward forty years. It is very hazy in my mind. I think you will be able to untangle it.

There used to be a small red house where years and years ago Stanly Hill lived. His son Wm. married my Aunt Olive. Wm. worked at one time with Mr. Kimball in the match shop. My father worked there at the same time. The shop burned down and all the accounts were burned up. Wm. Hill was a brother or a nephew of Mrs. Loran Hotchkiss, I do not know which. Wm. and Olive Hotchkiss had four girls: Stella, Bertha, Cora, and Ione Althea. Stella is in New Brunswick, Cora in Tennessee, Bertha in Brooklyn, and Ione in Havana, Cuba. I think Delos Hotchkiss' parents lived in this Stanley Hill house as late as 1867.

THE SUMMIT & PLANK ROADS

From the Summit you would probably be more able than I am to locate. There used to be the Gillet house, John, Rufus, Bennet, and Garry Gillet; Mrs. Merriman and daughter Mrs. Talmadge, Robertson Williams, and Elisha Platt houses but in 1905 when I was there so much was changed I could not tell much about it. I have been there once in about 50 years.

About a mile above the gate on the plank road lived a Mr. Hine. He married a widow Brooks. She had one son

Alfred who married Gussie Platt and built a house above Mr. Hines house. I do not know whether those houses were in Cheshire or in Prospect.

There used to be a Louisa Tuttle that lived above the Hollow. I do not know where; she was not quite normal. She used to call on Mrs. Titus Mix and stop at our houses. They said that she was disappointed in love.

THE WATERBURY ROADS

I have heard my mother tell of different families on the Waterbury roads. On the west one I have heard of the Dudleys, the Clarks, Aunt Lev. Smith, Ed. Allen, Gilbert Hotchkiss.

You probably know those on the road your father lived on. When we lived near that road in 1857, Mr. Berkley Hotchkiss lived a little above the corner. At that time there was a little house above Mrs. Laran Hotchkiss where Evans Hotchkiss and wife lived.

I have heard my mother tell of Aunt Lev. Smith (mother of Mrs. Ed Allen) having sick spells, and sending for the neighbors time and again saying she was going to die, but would recover. I suppose finally she died.

West of Prospect Hill a road went to the south where John Platt's parents lived. I never knew who lived on that road. I think Frank Wallace was an old Prospect family as his mother lived there and his father. There was a story that when they made spoons in the Hollow that they used so many rag wheels to polish with that they gave the name of Rag Hollow to the place.

THE CIVIL WAR

In the time of the war I've seen the top [of the stage coach] full of soldiers in their blue clothes. I was 13 when the war ended; 9 when it commenced. I remember when Ed. Moss was brought home for burial and when Fred Williams was killed. He was to have married Virginia Van Housan. And how a Mr. Clark and Patrick Dailey were among the missing. I believe they did not know for certain about them. I remember the mourning

when Lincoln was shot. It was too blue for me. I ran away from the mournful talk. The outdoors was all before me. I preferred it. I remember what a solemn waiting after a large battle to hear the news. It was an exciting time. I read the New York Tribune all through the war as the older people did. The older people used to say, "It will never be the same again. That they will not have the same care of men's lives and we shall have more murders." It used to be enough to scare a child.

In those days the real old people used to tell ghost stories. Warnings and presentments enough to scare the children. They used to claim they were true too.

THE ROAD FROM PROSPECT HILL WEST

There used to be a small house on the south side of road where Reuben Hitchcock and wife lived. There was a daughter, I think her name was Karietta. On the opposite side of road was Richard Tyler's house. Near the cemetery was Elias Platt's (I am not sure of the 1st name). Their children were, Frank who died young, Agusta and Lelia. I think Luther Moss' place was beyond and the Spencer Tyler place, the Harmon Paine place, Geo Paine and there used to be two houses beyond; in one a Bronson family lived, Belle and Wheaton. I do not remember all the names. Then came my grandfather's place. My grandfather (his first wife was Almira Wheeler) married for his second wife Sally Judd. Her son, Wm. Judd and wife Rebecca, lived in Prospect. He was a drinking man. They had two girls, Julia and Janey. I think that they lived at different places. Above the Harlow Hotchkiss place across the road and joining his land, was a lot with an orchard of nice apples and an old cellar place on it and an old well. My father bought this Bettie Tyler land meaning to build on it, but died shortly. My mother kept it for many years, then Richard Tyler bought it for Elmer Smith, son of the man that bought grandfather's place.

When my mother was a girl (she would be 95 yrs. old if she were alive) I have heard her tell of families that lived in the western part of Prospect. They were the Ellis family, Thadeus Hitchcock, and his son James and daughter Grace. The Fairclough's children Mary, Joseph, Charles, Thomas, and the Bracketts are all I can think of.

EARLY LIFE STORIES

I have heard my mother tell how they covered the fire in the fireplaces with ashes and how when it should happen to go out they were sent after fire perhaps ½ mile to neighbors and would run so until they reached home. How when she could not reach the wheel she had a block to stand on to do her stint, and how they used to pick geese on the barn floor.

How in the winter they had a shoemaker come to the house and stay a week to mend and make boots and shoes. How thanksgiving week the old brick oven was in use to cook the many good things for their numerous children that would come home at that time. I have a tea kettle that was my grandfather's great-grandmother's; it must have been brought over from England. Also I have the Bible that my great-grandfather Amos gave to grandfather when he married in 1809.

In 1870 a Mr. Guernsey owned the Harriet Ford place. I was teaching in Naugatuck that summer and Mr. and Mrs. Guernsey came to Naugatuck to church with their daughter Lottie. Their other children were Lynman, John and Sherman, Rebecca, Truman, and Almira.

When we lived in Aunt Daniel's place, Henry Elliott (Russell) as they called him, used to be haying at the barn and field across the road. One day Henry Eliot had evidently drank some, when a man rode by and told him Zebe Farrell was dead. He hollered back, "Is Zebe Farrell dead again?" Mr. Farrell was a

relative of his wife Sarah Tyler Russell, daughter of Spencer Tyler. Henry Elliott used to get on his horse and ride bareback through the lots to his mother's home where he lived, jumping the bars as he went. His mother was Harriet Ford. Probably Jared Ford, shoemaker was her 2nd husband. They did not live together. Jared lived somewhere below Prospect Hill; he did shoe mending etc.

MATTHEW STREET

I know but little about Matthew Street. Ester Daily lived there, as did Lewis Benham. A McDonald family lived there a short time, and Robert Matthews lived somewhere on the street. A Terrell family lived in the Wm. Beecher house.

Mrs. Joel Matthews lived on the south corner of Matthew Street and the road to Prospect Hill. I think Moses Chandler's father lived on the road at one time. He married a widow McDonald for his 2nd wife. I think Harry Moss who lived on the road towards the north from the Beecher place was a son of Lent Moss. Harry was father to Geo. and Hattie. Hattie married Friend Sanford and they built near the Gillet's. Willie Gillet married a Clark girl and lived in the Gillet neighborhood.

I think Edw. Chandler's wife was Martha Moss, a sister of Harry. She had a sister Lucy who married John Isbel, and lived at one time in part of the house where Edgar Jeralds lives. A Mr. Cherry and his wife, a Purdy girl, lived one time in the same place. I think that Mrs. Elias Mix lived with her mother above Henry Judd's for a time after her husband died but am not certain. I think that Josephine Wallace Nettleton lived once in the house where Edgar Jeralds lives. I think that Leonard Wilkinson bought or rented a house near Edgar Wallace's after he sold his house where the Tuckers live and lived on the road to Bethany at one time.

~

Chapter Six

The Churches

I t is difficult to underestimate the importance church life played in the history and development of Prospect. Like many Connecticut towns, Prospect was an ecclesiastical society (Columbia Society) before it was incorporated. Churches in the early years were the centers of society. Not only were they sources for religious training and inspiration, they were the primary social activity for the town. The daily life from Monday to Saturday was intense and demanding; there was little time to meet or converse with others except within the immediate household. Sunday services offered a chance for interaction with other members of the town. It was a much anticipated event that gave purpose to their lives.

Prospect was a hot bed of religious fervor and controversy. Radical movements, such as Perfectionism, had no stronger voice than in this town. Prospect fostered a number of churches (Fig 1). Being a marriage town (Chapter 3 and Chapter 4) may have contributed to the emergence of different houses of worship. When parts of Cheshire and Waterbury were united to become Prospect in 1827, a number of denominations were already represented. The exodus from the cities into the suburbs in the middle of the 20th century led to further diversity of religious beliefs. In this chapter we will trace the emergence and growth of these faiths.

THE PURITANS OF CONNECTICUT

The Puritan settlers to Connecticut were recognized for their zeal in maintaining theological and ecclesiastical purity. Those who colonized New Haven, Hartford, Farmington, and the other towns which preceded Prospect abandoned the Bay Colony in Massachusetts because it did not live up to their high moral standards. These pioneers sought to establish new settlements in the wilderness of Connecticut which would not be tainted by the evils (in their opinion) that had inflicted other colonial states.

The early settlers were quite intolerant of those who did not adhere to their strict codes of faith. Ironically, these same Puritans left England for the lack of religious freedom there. They sought freedom of religion for themselves but were not proponents of such liberty for others who were not within their Puritan fold. The church of the Puritans faced a continual barrage of attack from other emerging denominations. When the Quakers tried to take a foothold in the New Haven Colony, the Puritans responded:

If after they have suffered the law . . . and shall presume to come into this jurisdiction again, every such male Quaker shall for that second offense be branded on the hand with the letter H [for Heretic], be committed to prison and kept to work till he can be sent away at his own charge, and every Quaker woman that hath suffered the law here and shall presume to come into this jurisdiction again, shall be severely whipt . . . and for every Quaker, he or she, that shall a forth time again offend, they shall have their tongues bored through with a hot iron.

New Haven Colonial Records, 1653-1665

It is worth noting that these zealous Puritans were far more tolerant of the native Indians than of white settlers of different faiths. They seemed to view the Indians as religiously naive savages who only lacked the proper education in the principles of the Puritan faith to become good citizens. This was particularly true in Farmington where Indians were given many of the privileges afforded the English colonists.

The famous "Blue Laws" came into being during this era. Sundays were days of fasting and thanksgiving. Church attendance was mandatory or the fine was five shillings. Swearing in public resulted in a ten-shilling fine for the first offense and twenty for the second.

Church Law - 1676 . . . any person either on Saturday night or on the Lord's Day night, though it should be after the sun had set, who was found sporting in the streets or fields, or drinking in houses of public entertainment, or elsewhere unless for necessity, To pay ten shillings for every such transgression or suffer corporal punishment for default of due punishment. Servile work, defined as "work, not of piety, charity or necessity," was forbidden on the same date.

Connecticut - A Bicentennial History

In the meeting houses no fires were permitted, even in the coldest weather. Women would take to church small foot stoves containing hot coals which had to last through the long morning services. A church might have a "Sabba day" house nearby where a fireplace was provided to replenish the hot coals at noonday. The sermon alone might last one hour and a half during which the tythingmen moved about the church. Their function was to keep the children quiet and the adults awake. Men found nodding off during the pastor's dissertation were given a sharp rap to the head with the hard end of a long stick. The women were treated with more compassion. They were awakened by the tickling of feathers on the other end of the stick. It was expected that infants would be taken to church for baptism the first or second Sunday after birth. During the middle of winter the child was often bathed in nearly frozen water.

This atmosphere of Puritan idealism was still present when the first churches of Prospect were formed. As noted earlier (Chapter 3), the people within the present bounds of Prospect in the 1770s wanted to have their own church society. Those of the west side petitioned Waterbury, while those toward the east asked Cheshire. Their early requests were denied.

Fig 1   CHRONOLOGY OF MAJOR PROSPECT CHURCHES

Separatist Meeting House	1778
Columbia/Prospect Congregational Church	1798
Methodist Church	1805
Advent Church	~1850-60
St. Mary's Mission Church	1936
St. Anthony Church	1943
Bethel Baptist Church	1981

THE SEPARATISTS

In 1778 a church was built on the Cheshire mountains and was called Columbia Church or Society of Columbia. The members liked to be called *strict* Congregationalists but were often known as the Separatists. They permitted no "frivolities" in their life. This meant, for example, no "card-playing, frolicking, or horse-racing."

The Separatists built a meetinghouse located on the north end of Columbia (Prospect) Green (near the sign post) which faced north. The building was as "rude" as a barn. The floor boards were not nailed down and the seats were but slab benches. There was no pulpit, steeple, or bell. The only heat in winter was supplied by transported foot stoves. The structure was never finished because of little money and few members. A sixteen rod plot of land "improved" for a burial ground was located at the present site of the Grange hall. The first minister of this church was Rev. John Lewis, who was followed by Benjamin Beach and a man named Chatterton.

On March 26, 1795, land on Prospect Hill was purchased from Abraham Hotchkiss — one acre for a meetinghouse and a lesser amount (the same sixteen rods plot as above) for a graveyard. It was deeded for nine hundred and ninety-nine years in the presence of Ira Smith and Enos Tyler.

Abraham Hotchkiss of Waterbury quitclaims for the consideration of six pounds . . . to the strict Congregational church and the people on Cheshire mountain . . . To have and to hold . . . unto the said Church & people to be improved by them in their present Order and if the major part of the people should see cause to have Society lines & set up on the Congregational or Calvinistic Order it is understanding of me the Releasor that they are stil to hold the same privileges of the house & Land . . . to be undisturbed by me or my heirs & Assigns for the above said term.

acknowledged before John Lewis, Just Peace

N B   *It is the understanding of the above Grantor and Grantee that whenever the people shall think best and do get Established with Society Lines the above named Abraham Hotchkiss is to Receive from the people the sum of seventeen pounds Lawful Money.*   History of Cheshire

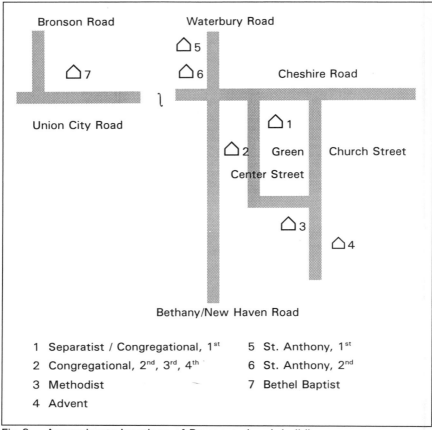

Fig 2   Approximate locations of Prospect church buildings.

The majority of members at this time were not Calvinists. They voted on March 3, 1795, to follow the strict Congregationalist line, a movement started in eastern Connecticut about 1740. The central belief of this faith was that existing churches were not "true" churches, rather they were anti-Christ. They shunned non-believers as hypocrites and sought to remain pure. Without the benefit of notes, ministers delivered sermons from the spirit "within."

In 1797 the land which very nearly includes the present bounds of Prospect was surveyed so that all who lived within it might be taxed for the support of the "Congregational Ecclesiastical Society." This organization not only supported the church (as Columbia Society) but had charge of the schools and all other matters of public concern within its territory (as Columbia Company). The first society meeting was held Nov. 2, 1797. The following positions were appointed: Jared Burr (constable), Jesse Ford (grand juror), Robert Hotchkiss (tithingman), John Ford (lister), and Asahel Chittenden and Asa Wilmot (highway surveyors). Four persons were appointed "choristers on the Lord's day in public worship," and a petition was sent to the honorable Assembly for a military company in this society.

THE PROSPECT CONGREGATIONAL CHURCH

There was a gradual shift toward regular Congregationalism, and on May 14, 1798, the Congregational Church of Columbia (later Prospect) was organized. The ministers assembled on this occasion were: Revs. John Foote (Cheshire), Abraham Fowler (Salem), Benjamin Beach, and Oliver Hitchcock. Ira Smith was chosen to be clerk.

The original sixteen founding members were:

Ephraim Smith	Thankful Smith	Damaris Tuttle
Joseph Matthews	Lois Matthews	Olly Byington
Abraham Hotchkiss	Hannah Hotchkiss	Hannah Doolittle
Ira Smith	Phebe Hotchkiss	Jerusha Hotchkiss
Eben Hotchkiss	Esther Ford	
Asahel Hotchkiss	Mehitable Byington	

The members continued to worship in the old building for three years, then made a number of improvements. Pews were installed and seating was according to status on the Grand List. A steeple and bell were installed, and a hexagonal pulpit that was supported on a pillar was added. The first pastor was Rev. Oliver Hitchcock. He received $200 in money and a supply of wood annually. The first deacon was Gideon Hotchkiss, who served from 1799 until his death in 1807 at the age of 91. Gideon had been a key organizer of the Salem (Naugatuck) church. He served as deacon there until Columbia Society formed, when he transferred his membership.

In 1800 the Columbia Congregational Church adopted the Saybrook platform. This required a rigid code of personal and moral conduct with no frivolities of any kind allowed. Reverend Oliver Hitchcock was pastor during this period. He supplemented his modest salary by laying up stone walls — a skill with which he is said to have been most proficient.

From Monday to Saturday the Rev. Hitchcock went about his parish supervising the laying of stone walls. Each Sunday found him in his pulpit ready to preach to his handful of followers. It was a rugged country and rugged people lived there. New Haven Register, Oct. 29, 1933

Under the pastorship of Rev. James D. Chapman in 1833, the doctrines of the Perfectionists began to be adopted by many of the influential members of the church. This theology originated with some students at Yale. The basic concept was that mankind was divided into three classes: the unconverted, the converted, and those who experienced new birth. The latter were considered to be the only true children of God. This movement caused a great disturbance in the otherwise tranquil town of Prospect.

They believe that none are Christians, who are not entirely freed from sin, and who do not possess the faith, righteousness, liberty, and glory of the risen Son of God. They believe that they are infallible, being under the peculiar guidance of the Spirit, and give themselves up to be guided by Him in the way of all truth, having as they say, the will of the Lord made known to them by an immediate revelation. They set aside all ordinances and holy days, such as baptism, the sacrament, with the Lord's prayer, and the observance of the sabbath, &c; saying that they are but the mere traditions of men, being no better than the forms and ceremonies of the Popish church. Connecticut Historical Collections

Anathema, the excommunication of non-believers, was preached from the pulpit. Frightened townspeople believed their neighbors were bewitched. Those convinced they were among the Perfectionist elite (or later called the Oneida Community) disregarded all orthodox ordinances. They felt no need to keep the sabbath because, to them, all days were holy, and they were already secure in their eternal rewards. The Prospect church grew to its largest membership at this time in history. Believers were attracted from the surrounding towns and joined the flock, but that began to change when Rev. Chapman's license to preach was revoked by the Congregational Church Consociation.   He continued to preach at a nearby schoolhouse which drew many key members from the church. Other ministers were called in to preach to the Congregationalists. The furor gradually ended, and most of those who strayed from the original course realized they were not angels and returned to their former beliefs. This was not before twenty-seven were cut from the fold in 1835.   Many of these carried their doctrine and worship to Wallingford.

The Congregational Church built four different meeting houses in its nearly two hundred years of existence.   There are no drawings to depict the first "rude" building. By 1840 that structure was allowed to deteriorate and a new house of worship was planned. With the growing affluence of some members, including pastor Edward Bull, who was a man of some means, the new church was dedicated in 1841 (Fig 3). It was placed southwest of the old one, approximately where the present church stands. The town excavated and built the basement which it used for town meetings. The church paid for and completed the upper portion. In comparison to the first church, this building was well-appointed.   It eventually included a furnace, cushioned chairs, and carpeting.

The period during the Civil War was one of great activity.   The church was painted inside and out. The parsonage was repaired, horse sheds were built, a melodian was purchased, two mission schools were organized, and liquor selling ceased in the town, according to an article in the *Waterbury Republican,* June 27, 1948, based on information from Nellie Cowdell. The church declined in membership and available funds in the late 19th century. In 1891 pastor Rev. Phipps spoke about the Prospect church at the celebration of Waterbury's bicentennial.

Fig 3   Congregational Church, built in 1841, and ministers who served it.

Top: (L to R): Rev. Frederick W. Chapman, Rev. Reuben Torrey.

Bottom: Rev. William W. Atwater, Rev. Franklin Countryman, Rev. William H. Phipps.

This daughter is somewhat enfeebled, and has for many years been walking with the aid of crutches furnished by the sister churches of the state . . . Columbia was for a period of time a flourishing place, supporting manufactures of some importance. But it has gradually diminished, and now there are more old cellars marking the places where houses formerly stood than there are homes in town . . . The number of members at the present time is ninety-eight. The Prospect church has no reason to regret that she was ever born, for her life has been fruitful of good.   Rev. Phipps, History of Waterbury

In July 1906 Rev. Phipps preached his farewell sermon.   In September Rev. Homer Hildreth was called to replace him.   Before taking the pulpit, the church was destroyed by fire on November 6.   Rev. Hildreth was forced to conduct his first worship service at the Grange hall.   The third church was dedicated in 1908 (Fig 4).   It was built of native field stone and trimmed with white marble.   The windows were stained glass.   The building served the town for many functions, including school graduations and the Prospect Centennial.   In 1927 ten of the horse sheds behind the church were sold when automobiles came into wide use.   Electricity also reached the center of town.

On Saturday morning, Nov. 29, 1941, Clifford Clark discovered that the stone church was on fire.   He hoisted young Leo Gonneville of Straitsville Road, a member of St. Anthony Church, through a window, and the boy succeeded in saving the church Bible.   Enough headway had been gained by the blaze that fire departments called from neighboring towns were able to save just the new parsonage.   By nightfall, only the smoldering stone walls remained, with the bell still hanging in the tower.   Ironically, a sign in front of the church read "Watch Our Smoke," in reference to a parish drive to raise funds for the new parsonage. The following Sunday was Pearl Harbor.

Fig 4 The stone church — the third Congregational Church building.
Waterbury Republican-American

For two years after the fire, services were held at the Grange hall. The basement of the fourth building was completed for Palm Sunday services in 1945. The lower section was equipped sufficiently to allow programs, such as suppers and entertainment, besides the regular worship services. The 150th anniversary in 1948 was observed there. The sanctuary on the first floor was finally dedicated on July 15, 1951 (Fig 5). A steeple and lighted tower were added before a rededication in 1956.

In 1957 Rev. Doris Belcher was called as the church's first permanent female preacher. This was at a time when women in the clergy were uncommon. She preferred being called Miss Belcher, believing *Reverend* was an implication of personal worship.

Fig 5 The fourth and present Congregational Church building.   John Guevin

She joked about her pastoral duties, *"I have married 13 men, but have never had a husband. "* During her term of service, a major addition for classrooms and other activities was dedicated to Carl Spellman in 1959. He was chairman of the building committee before his sudden death in 1958.

Pastors of the Prospect Congregational Church

1798-1812	Rev. Oliver Hitchcock
1813-1814	Rev. David Bacon
1815-1816	Abraham Fowler
1816-1816	Gideon Burt
1817-1818	John Marsh
1817-1824	Rev. Samuel Rich
1824-1825	Mr. Charles Nichols
1825-1832	Mr. John Bray
1832-1833	Rev. Peter Sampson
1833-1837	Rev. James Chapman, Rev. Albert Camp, Rev.Sylvester Selden, Rev. Zephaniah Swift*
1837-1839	Rev. Ammi Linsley
1840-1843	Mr. Edward Bull
1843-1848	Rev. Reuben Torrey
1848-1849	Mr. Ira Smith
1849-1850	Rev. John Ambler
1851-1851	Rev. William Whittemore
1851-1854	Rev. James Kilbourn
1854-1855	Mr. Asa Train
1855-1858	Mr. Joseph Payne
1858-1860	Mr. Asa Train
1861-1865	Rev. William Atwater
1866-1871	Rev. Frederick Chapman

1871-1874	Rev. Charles Pyke
1874-1877	Rev. Frank Countryman
1878-1906	Rev. William Phipps
1906-1909	Rev. Homer Hildreth
1909-1910	Rev. Charles Gaffney
1911-1912	Rev. Jacob Spoolman
1912-1916	Rev. Charles Strong
1916-1917	Rev. Howard Blanning
1918-1921	Rev. George Culbertson
1921-1921	Rev. George Farnum
1922-1926	Rev. Oscar L. Locke
1926-1926	Rev. Arthur Golder
1926-1929	Rev. Leonard Ruttan
1929-1941	Rev. Thomas Cochard
1941-1947	Rev. Daryl Williams
1947-1956	Rev. Robert Senior
1957-1966	Miss (Rev.) Doris Belcher
1966-1976	Rev. John G. Beck
1976-1987	Rev. Gregory Errgong-Weider
1988-	Rev. Howard L. Hinman

* During the Perfectionist era other ministers were called to preach in Rev. Chapman's absence.

The first parsonage during the Columbia Society era was on the east side of the Green. It was purchased with 5½ acres of land, dwelling house, and blacksmith shop from Eliphalet Hotchkiss for $366.67. The parsonage gradually fell into disrepair, and a new glebe house, still standing today, was constructed on the same site in 1844. In 1927 the Stephen Talmadge property next to the church was obtained for use by the pastor. This building had been an inn as well as a store, library, and post office. Being old and in poor condition, it was torn down in 1941, and the new and present parsonage was built on the same site.

The history of the Prospect Congregational Church and the town of Prospect are forever intertwined. For so many years the church *was* the primary center of the community. Throughout the years the church has faced many challenges — both internal and external. Somehow it has always survived these conflicts. From within, there was the struggle of the Perfectionists vs. the Congregationalists struggle. Then there were attacks from outside, such as the rise of Methodism and the arrival of the Advent Church. New challenges will continue to arise, but the Congregational Church has adjusted to its new role in Prospect. It is no longer the principal player in terms of membership or influence in the town. Prospect is now a town of diverse religious faiths, each contributing its share to the future history of this place.

METHODISM

When the Separatist Society dissolved, not all the members joined the ranks of the Congregationalists. Some became Methodists. The church was divided into "Old Lights" and "New Lights." The latter were viewed as boisterous and disorderly by the more conservative "Old Lights." Organized Methodism began in Baltimore with a conference in 1784. Francis Asbury, an itinerant preacher from England, was elected Bishop of the Methodist Episcopal Church in America. He was a man of commanding physical presence who preached and sang in a powerful and convincing style.

Bishop Asbury in his journal, under the date of September 23, 1796, speaks of passing through Waterbury, Salem and Oxford and preaching at Waterbury "in the Separate meeting-house." This meeting-house was located in that part of Waterbury called Columbia, which in 1827 became part of the town of Prospect. Some of the "New Lights" had withdrawn from the Congregational churches and formed societies of "Separates." . . . But some had already become Methodists, among them Amos Hotchkiss. He had been the chief contributor in the erection of the Separate meeting-house, and lived in a commodious farm-house near by (now the residence of Merritt Clark). His house was a stopping-place for the itinerant preachers and the gathering place on "quarterly meetings" occasions for Methodists from all the region about.

Grandchildren of this old-time Methodist speak of having heard their grandmother Hotchkiss and their mother, who was Molly Hotchkiss, tell of the visit of Bishop Asbury on the occasion referred to, and of the large company that assembled to see and hear the noted man. The Bishop and perhaps a hundred visiting Methodists were entertained at the Hotchkiss mansion, where they remained all night, the house, barn, cider-mill and other available accommodations being utilized to lodge the company.

Mother Hotchkiss and her daughters, among whom was Molly, then a girl of thirteen, provided a feast suited to so great an occasion. When the time came to surround the fragrant board, the Bishop said, "Sister Hotchkiss, have you not a spare tea-pot? I carry and make my own tea. And let me have the top crust from the loaf of rye bread; that is all I want."

It may be added that, although Mother Hotchkiss willingly provided for the Methodist guests, she remained a Congregationalist. Sometimes in after days, when the quarterly meetings were to be held in

Columbia, she would arrange for the expected visitors, then mount her horse and away to visit friends in Watertown, leaving the girls to entertain the company.
History of Waterbury

The Methodists continued to hold their meetings in private homes. Besides the house of Amos Hotchkiss, Thomas Benham offered his place, which was located one-half mile north of the Green. Daniel Hitchcock also provided a room for prayer services in his house. When Amos Hotchkiss died in 1820, three of his sons, Woodward, Avera, and Amos H., carried on the Methodist faith. Other prominent Methodists were: Milly Sanford and her son Hershel, who was a preacher, Mrs. Eunice Rowe, Abel Austin and wife, Warren Wilson and wife, Dimon Hitchcock and wife, and Elisha Preston. Lauren Preston was one of the last prominent supporters in Prospect.

When no longer used by the Congregationalists, the old Separatist meeting-house was moved to a new location at the south end of the Green at the site of the present Grange. The Methodists maintained a society and services in Prospect until 1858, by which time they had become weakened and reduced in numbers. Those who remained true to the faith transferred to Bethany and Cheshire.

ADVENT CHURCH

Fig 6   The Advent Chapel, now the Prospect Senior Center.   John Guevin

Little is known about the Advent Church in Prospect, as the records of that society have not been uncovered. The Advent movement started here about 1850, when it is believed that William Mix kept a large room in his home in "Rag Hollow" for Advent meetings. Moses Chandler was one of the most active in this movement, and meetings were held at his house as well. Other prominent members belonged to the Tuttle, Tyler, Hotchkiss, and Beecher families. In 1890 there were about a score of members and Seth Woodruff was the minister. The chapel on the east side of the Green, which later became the Chapel schoolhouse and now is the Senior Center (Fig 6), was built by the Adventists around 1886, according to J.L. Rockey in *History of New Haven County*. About 1900 the Prospect congregation merged with the Advent church in Waterbury.

ST. ANTHONY CHURCH

The history of the Catholic Church in Prospect began with the first inhabitants of that faith. The 1850 U.S. census counted twenty-nine residents who were born in Ireland. Some of these were hired to work on the telegraph lines in the area. Their signatures are preserved on one wall in an upstairs bedroom of the Hotchkiss house. The McDermotts were the first Catholic family to settle in Prospect in the 1850s. By the 1880s there were five families professing the Catholic faith. About that time, Mr. and Mrs. John Murphy arranged for the first Mass to be celebrated in Prospect, which took place at their home. Father J. O'R Sheriden, a curate from the Immaculate Conception Church in Waterbury, celebrated the Mass in their parlor. In attendance were Mr. and Mrs. McDermott, Mr. and Mrs. McDonald, Mr. and Mrs. Jeremiah Delaney, and the Meighan and Murphy families. This group constituted the entire Catholic population of Prospect.

"It was just a small farming community where everyone worked hard to make the land pay. Journeys were made to the center of the town three times a week to get mail, go to church on Sunday and do shopping. However, because Prospect is such a delightful country section within short distance from Waterbury, the farmhouses were generally alive with company especially on Sunday."

Mrs. Murphy had a big dining room table which could be pulled out to the length of the room and there were few Sundays that it wasn't filled with guests. She baked all her own bread, pie and cake and used up a barrel of flour a month getting ready for company.

"It was about half an hour's journey with a horse and buggy and most of us lived on farms so we had horses. We went to Mass rain or shine. Nothing kept us away. During the winter we went by sleigh. Sometimes in the early spring the mud was pretty thick. The roads were not what they are now. But it never occurred to us to stay away from Mass."

Bridget Murphy, Waterbury Republican-American, July 26, 1936

Similar home services were held at other houses but only on rare occasions. Every Sunday the Catholics would make the trip to Immaculate Conception Church in Waterbury. As roads improved and automobiles became popular, travel was easier. In later years the churches of Cheshire and Naugatuck were attended by some living closer to those areas.

The Catholic population grew slowly but surely. The need for celebrating Mass in Prospect was discussed when twenty-eight people gathered at the home of Mr. and Mrs. Fred Canales on Salem Road on June 10, 1936. This turned out to be, not only the first organizational meeting, but a fund-raiser as well. Leftovers from an overabundance of cupcakes baked by Mrs.

Canales for the occasion were sold to raise money for the church. The group sought advice from Rev. Richard Morrissey, pastor of St. Mary's Church in Union City. He suggested a census be taken to determine the Catholic population of the town. A total of one hundred ten Catholic families were tallied by the nine people who took the census. This information was presented to the Bishop of Hartford with a request to establish a place of worship in Prospect. Permission was granted, and a mission church was established with St. Mary's Church of Union City serving as the host.

Father Morrissey celebrated the first Mass that was held in the Prospect Grange hall on July 19, 1936. Three hundred people attended the nine o'clock service. The upstairs room was filled with more standing on the steps leading to the upper floor. This was a remarkable occasion for two reasons. It was the first public Mass celebrated in Prospect, and it was held at the Grange hall, whose members were all Protestants. Some members of the Congregational Church were very supportive in establishing the parish of St. Anthony.

The little handful of Catholics found itself a rather small and lonesome group in Prospect. Not that there was any particular enmity toward them in town, but fifty years ago [1886] small New England towns founded on firm foundations of Congregationalism did not especially welcome newcomers of other denominations. But the fact that last Sunday's Mass was celebrated in the Grange hall and that some non-Catholics are lending their support to the establishment of the church shows that times have changed.   Waterbury Republican-American, July 26, 1936

In attendance at the opening service were the members of the Guild Committee responsible for the organization of the church:

Fr. Richard P. Morrissey	Sen. Joseph Lawlor	Mrs. Richard Murphy
Patrick M. Goode	Patrick Spellman	Mrs. Emil Toscano
Emil Toscano	Joseph R. Gomez	Harry Coughlin
Mrs. Arthur Driver	Mrs. Edwin Canales	Mrs. Louise Gomez
John J. Kelly	Mrs. Harry Coughlin	Alfred E. Fournier
Daniel B. Connor	Mrs. A.F. Carrington	Thomas Scadden

As the Catholic population grew, services were moved to the auditorium of the new Community School in May 1937, using the stage as the Sanctuary. Priests continued to be provided by St. Mary's Church. With no booths, confessions were heard face to face on the school stage before Mass.

Efforts were made to construct a church building in Prospect. Land from Patrick Spellman was rejected because Bishop McAuliffe believed a site closer to the center of town would be more appropriate. Although Mr. Spellman's proposal was unsuccessful, he did help name the new church. According to tradition, he made the original offer on June 13, 1936 — the feast of St. Anthony.

Two acres of land were purchased from Harry M. Stieler at the junction of Routes 68 and 69 (known then simply as the state highways) on July 2, 1938. The bishop said that construction could begin when the small parish raised $5,000. With much determination and little regard for the Depression that overshadowed the country, the members went to work to raise the needed funds. Through bake sales, lawn parties, card parties, raffles, bingo, and donations, they quickly met the goal, and construction began in the fall of 1938. Father Morrissey chose the design for the new church based on a similar building in his home town of Knock, Ireland. When the basement was finished, services were held there for several months while the upper half was completed. The altar, pews, and statues came from a church in New Britain that was being refurbished. The church bell came from a railroad station.

On Sept. 16, 1939, Bishop McAuliffe dedicated the new church (Fig 7), which was still considered a mission church of St. Mary's. Rev. John F. Mc-Teague, a curate at St. Mary's, was appointed to oversee St. Anthony Church in 1942. One year later, in June 1943, the Parish of St. Anthony was established as an independent church. The official name is The Roman Catholic Church of St. Anthony but it often is shortened to St. Anthony Church or simply, St. Anthony's.

Fig 7 The first St. Anthony Church building under construction.
Waterbury Republican-American 1-18-39

Father McTeague was named pastor and served for five and a half years. He moved into the house of Alice McDermott Steeves on Route 69 and was the first resident priest in Prospect. He made his home there until a new rectory was created from a house owned by the Main family. This building was moved from the intersection of Center Street and Route 68 to a site next to the church. Women from the first Altar Society assumed the duties of cleaning the church and taking care of the linens and flowers for Sunday Mass.

I remember cleaning the church whenever a dignitary was to visit. We were a small group of mothers who would trudge up the road (no highway then) with our small children. We carried our own mops, pails, brooms, and cleaners (no Murphy's Oil Soap, but 99% pure Ivory Soap), and we would clean and polish the House of St. Anthony for arrival of a bishop or archbishop.

Melba Membrino, 50th Anniversary, St. Anthony Church

In 1943 a Mission Church of St. Anthony was formed in Bethany for forty Catholic families there. Father McTeague served this parish as well. Under pastors Rev. Thomas J. O'Connell and Rev. Edward J. Donnelly, the parish in Prospect grew steadily until there were about seven hundred families by 1957. The need for a larger church was apparent. Ground was broken for the new church and rectory on May 20, 1961, (Fig 8) at a cost of $430,000. Even though Archbishop O'Brien had concerns about the financial burden, the parishioners held suppers, shows, raffles, and dances to raise the needed funds. Their persistent efforts paid off when Father James F. O'Dea made the final payment of the church mortgage in 1971.

During his thirty years as pastor, Father O'Dea saw many changes in the Catholic Church. The Mass was changed from Latin to English, the altar now faced the people, and lay people took a more active role in the church as Lectors and Eucharistic Ministers. The first deacons were appointed: Nicholas Diorio and George Dinkle in 1978 and Paul Iadarola in 1982. Other positions filled included secretary, Director of Religious Education, and Minister of Health Care and Bereavement. Father O'Dea had a number of priests who assisted him over the years, including: Fathers Joseph Puzzo, Thomas Donnelly, William Baldyga, Philip J. Cascia, Richard Taberski, David Lonergan, and J. Thomas Walsh.

Fig 8   The second St. Anthony Church built in 1961.   John Guevin

In August 1989 Father O'Dea retired as pastor after fifty-one years of priestly service. He was replaced in October 1989 by Father Cascia, a former assistant. Under his direction the church has undergone many renovations and improvements, including a complete refinishing of the inside. The project was completed at minimal cost to the church after seemingly endless hours of work by many parishioners, including "Michelangelo" Cascia.

The church now has an active Mission Society which sponsors an orphanage in St. Petersburg. This complements the long term support provided to the St. Vincent DePaul Society of Waterbury and the Prospect Food Bank. Recently, a church council which provides greater input from the parishioners in the organization and operation of the church was formed. In

1993 St. Anthony Church celebrated its 50th anniversary.   Additional information about the church may be obtained from its anniversary book prepared for this occasion.

Pastors of St. Anthony Church

Rev. John F. McTeague	1943-1949
Rev. Thomas J. O'Connell	1949-1954
Rev. Edward J. Donnelly	1954-1959
Rev. James F. O'Dea	1959-1989
Rev. Philip J. Cascia	1989-

BETHEL BAPTIST CHURCH

The Bethel Baptist Church is one of the newest houses of worship in Prospect, but it has grown to have a large congregation in a short period of time.   This church had its beginnings in April 1976, when twenty-eight people gathered in a home in Waterbury for the first prayer service.   Arrangements were soon made to use the church building and small school at 101 Prospect Street in Union City across from the Prospect Street School.   This facility was rented from the Pinebrook Assembly of God.

Fig 9 Ground breaking for the Bethel Baptist Church.   Waterbury Republican-American, 4-28-81

Rev. Floyd Allen Pascall was the founder of the Bethel Baptist Church. He continued to minister to his flock in Union City until 1981, when the building there could no longer accommodate the 230 attending services each

Sunday. Ten acres of land were purchased on Union City Road in Prospect near Bronson Road. Plans were made for the 8000 sq. ft. frame building to be constructed by William Dunn of Prospect. The ground breaking was held in April 1981 (Fig 9). Prayers and a short scripture reading were followed with music provided by the Men's College Choir from the Baptist Bible College East in Shub, NY. Brother Pascall is credited with starting about 30 other churches in New England, but the Bethel Baptist Church in Prospect became his permanent home. Before he died in 1984, Rev. Pascall saw the congregation grow to over 500 worshipers each Sunday. More space was needed and the building was expanded twice (Fig 10). New wings were built to accommodate offices and classrooms. These replaced facilities were lost when the main auditorium was expanded from a seating capacity of about 300 to 450. An additional nine acres of land adjacent to the church was also purchased for future use.

The membership of the Bethel Baptist Church is mainly from Waterbury, Naugatuck, and Prospect, although some members travel from towns farther away. The church is independent and self governing. The members have recently chosen to form two mission churches rather than expand at their Prospect location. They have a satellite church in Watertown, called the Victory Independent Baptist Church, and another in Waterbury, known as the Amazing Grace Baptist Church. These churches will remain under the direction of the Bethel Baptist Church for a period of time, and then they will be on their own. A third mission church is planned in the Cheshire area in the near future.

Fig 10 The Bethel Baptist Church with two expansions.   John Guevin

The second pastor was Rev. George Dubish, who served as an assistant under Brother Pascall. He was replaced recently by Rev. Bryan Kelley who had also been an assistant pastor. Thus, all leadership has come from within.

With the expansion of the mission churches, the weekly attendance has dropped to about 300. But Brother Kelley is not concerned. He indicates that the purpose of their church is to serve as many people as possible. By placing new churches in neighboring towns, the satellite churches reach more people who will not have to travel as far. Members never worry about how to get to church. There is an active bus ministry which picks up anyone in need of transportation to services. Currently, three buses bring about 120 people to Sunday services. When membership was at its peak, there were seven buses transporting 300 members.

Interesting guest ministers have participated in the services at the Bethel Baptist Church. One was "Gorgeous George" Grant who spoke during services on July 2-6, 1984. Grant was a popular professional wrestler in the 1950s who has since become an evangelist. His dress and mannerisms made him one of the most famous wrestlers of his time. All that changed in 1965 when he was "saved" and became a preacher for the Lord. Peter Ashade was born in Nigeria and was deaf. In 1987 he came to America for an education. The Bethel Baptist Church supported him through studies at the American School for the Deaf and toward a bachelor's degree at Northwestern Connecticut Community College. In 1989 he was ordained at Bethel Baptist Church where he founded a Ministry for the Deaf.

Besides Sunday services there are Wednesday night prayer meetings, an audio cassette tape program, home Bible studies, a food bank, clothes room, visitation programs, and "Sonshine Street" programs for children. The Bethel Baptist Church is very active in world missions. Currently, they provide financial support to 80 mission projects around the world and some in the United States. This represents a major portion of their budget but is an activity to which they contribute freely. As the church nears its 19th anniversary, the membership is thankful for its success and looks forward to the future of the church in Prospect and their Mission Churches.

Pastors of Bethel Baptist Church	
Rev. Floyd Allen Pascall	1976-1984
Rev. George Dubish	1984-1994
Rev. Bryan Kelley	1994-

OTHER CHURCHES

Over the years people from Prospect who practiced a faith not represented here traveled to a neighboring town to find a place of worship. Sometimes small groups organized to conduct these services in town. These were often simple prayer services held in homes. In 1978 Gould Clark had a vision of forming an Orthodox Presbyterian church and offered prayer meetings at his Clark Hill Road home with assistance from Rev. Jenkins of Hamden. Other groups have secured public places of worship, such as the Grange hall or the Senior Center. In 1980 the Christ Messiah Church met at the Senior Center under the leadership of pastor Sandra L. Torres.

~

Chapter Seven

Education in the Town of Prospect

by Nellie Cowdell and Boardman Kathan

A ny history written today about the schools of Prospect is dependent on other town histories since the eastern ⅔ of the community lay in Wallingford originally and the western ⅓ in Waterbury. By 1718 the people in what is now Cheshire complained to the Connecticut Assembly that "by reason of the distance from town, their great disadvantage to appear at public worship and to 'eddicate' their children, they desired a distinct society." Five years later the New Cheshire Society was separated from Wallingford, and a meetinghouse and a schoolhouse followed. In later years, when the Cheshire parish petitioned to be made a separate town, they stated: "There is considerable many over by West Rocks where we expect there will be a parish shortly." In 1794 Cheshire established the boundary lines for fourteen separate school districts, and three of them were in the Prospect area.

Waterbury histories furnish little information about school districts that would have been in the western part of Prospect, what the Waterbury folk called "South Farms" or "Cheshire Mountain." One history, *The Early Schools of Naugatuck*, by William Ward, published in 1906, gives more information. There was at least one school in the southern part of Waterbury before the organization of Salem Parish, and this was located east of the Naugatuck River in what was called Judd's Meadow. Some children may have attended this school from the Straightsville, Porter Hill, Logtown, Salem, and Clark Hill areas. It would have been a long walk, and soon local schools for at least a few weeks must have been needed. After Salem Parish was created in 1773, six school districts were formed, and it is possible that two of these served the part that is now Prospect. One of the members of the school committee, Amos Hotchkiss, lived in Prospect.

Editor's note: Much of the material for this chapter was first gathered together by Nellie Cowdell and typed in preliminary form with the intent of printing it as one of the booklets published by the Prospect Bicentennial-Sesquicentennial Commission in 1976-77. The text has been revised, re-organized, and expanded by Boardman Kathan, who served as secretary of the Bicentennial Commission and chairman of the 50th Anniversary Committee of the Prospect Community School in 1986.

There are other sources of information as well. One small book with school records and some cemetery notes, beginning in 1802 and continuing to about 1855, is in existence. Another book from 1875 to 1920 has been found. Many loose pages from the earliest days give an indication of the school districts. One confusing habit of early clerks seems to have been that of using some pages, then skipping to the middle of the book for other interests of the same group. If the back of the book filled up, the subject would continue on vacant pages in the middle. Thus we have clerk and treasurer records of school committee, Columbia Society, Town, and Union School District out of any chronological order. Sometimes the clerk thought better not to write too much, and we find in the minutes: "met, transacted business and after a five hour discussion, adjourned."!!!

Putting together various papers and records is like a jigsaw puzzle. Many were found in an old chest that Albert Allen left to the Prospect Historical Society. They represent an accumulation of the many years before there was a Town Hall with a vault. Many of these items are of no value except to the historian. There are school teachers' accounts which give the lists of the names of parents with the tax for the total days of the attendance of their children. The wood tax account lists the parents and the kinds of wood which were brought for the wood fireplaces and stoves in the one-room schoolhouses. Then there are lists of the names of people where the teachers boarded and for how many days. The records of births, deaths, marriages, public offices, tax lists, census, school attendance, deeds, and law suits were all probably written at the time of the events and are reasonably correct, but handwriting, fading ink, and tattered papers make them hard to read. Another problem is that the old deeds and school district boundaries mention farms or homes or roads or even "a pile of stones" or "a hickory tree" that may not exist today. The task of writing a history of the schools of Prospect is a difficult and challenging one!

Other sources are the recollections and reminiscences of people who grew up in the town, like those of Jennie Beardsley Clapp (1852-1925), who wrote in 1920 about the different schools she attended:

> *The first one: at about 5 years I went to the school on the hill, the winter term taught by Mr. Lines, the summer term by Miss Upson. Then in the west part of Prospect I went two terms to the little schoolhouse on the bank which had a cute little brook running along across the road. Miss Mary Jane Smith taught; she was my first cousin. Cousin Jane always had a pillow so that the little ones could have a nap on the wooden benches. When I was 6 ½ years old we moved to the gate house and after that I attended the school at Mix-ville, Cheshire, as we were in that district. Deacon Benja-min B. Brown taught in the Mixville School two winters.*

In order to understand the history of the schools of Prospect, it is essential first to look at the changes in school management and control through the years. These historical periods can be organized as follows:

1)   Church Parish or Ecclesiastical Society (Wallingford and Cheshire, Waterbury and Salem, now Naugatuck), 1712-1797.

2) Columbia Parish and School Society (Town of Prospect from 1827 on), 1797-1870s.

3) Prospect Union School District, 1870s-1936.

4) Prospect Community School (from 1936) and Algonquin School (from 1957).

5) Region 16 School District, 1969 to the present.

Each of these historical periods will be reviewed in turn, followed by a section on the high school situation.

1. CHURCH PARISH OR ECCLESIASTICAL SOCIETY

In the 18th century in the American colonies there were three kinds of schools: the English common or petty schools, open to the public; the grammar schools, which were more academic, classical in studies and selective (Hopkins Grammar School in New Haven is a good example); and a growing number of private schools or academies (Cheshire Academy, for example). In Connecticut, control of the common schools had been given over to the churches, which meant the established Congregational churches in existence in nearly every community of the state. Long before the "separation of church and state," the churches were charged with the responsibility, not only of the worship of God, but the education of the children, the collection of taxes, and the recruiting and training of the militia. (Hence, the importance of town greens where the militia could drill!) In the year 1766 the churches and their ecclesiastical societies were authorized to divide the towns into small school districts, and this meant a gradual narrowing down to little schoolhouses, with all ages and levels of proficiency in one room.

The area that is now Prospect was served by two parishes. In the eastern ⅔ of the community there was the New Cheshire Society of Wallingford, which formed a separate church by 1724 and became an incorporated town by 1780. In 1769 that part of Prospect in the Cheshire Parish was given "winter privileges" which meant that people did not have to travel to the center of Cheshire for worship in the cold winter weather. Also, $^5/_{12}$ of the residents' church and school taxes could be used locally. By 1772 the Cheshire Parish agreed to divide the district for schooling, and a schoolhouse was built for the first time on Prospect Hill.

The western ⅓ of the town was served by the ecclesiastical society of the First Congregational Church of Waterbury, and a school district was organized in Judd's Meadow, with the first schoolhouse on the eastern side of the Naugatuck River in what is now Union City. A separate Salem Parish was established in this area in 1773, and the six school districts were set up prior to 1802. Two of these school districts served the western part of Prospect. One was the Pond Hill District, which built its first school building in the area of Pond Hill Road (now May Street), which was just down Salem Road from Prospect. The second was the Middle District, which erected a schoolhouse south of Straits Turnpike (New Haven Road, Route 63), just west of the Beacon Hill Brook.

It was customary for each parish to appoint or elect a school committee, and each district in the parish would have a representative on that parish-wide committee. Usually this person was treasurer for the district, receiving the town appropriation, the state grant, as well as the per pupil, per school day assessment from the parents. He also arranged for hiring and paying the teachers, and finding homes for the teachers to board in during the school term. He was also responsible for the wood tax, keeping track of the amount of wood for the fireplace in the schoolhouse. School terms were generally held in summer and winter, and it was common for men to teach in the winter term and women in the summer term. These arrangements continued at least through the first half of the 19th century. Money records usually name the committee member, and the teacher's name may be only on receipts. Cheshire history lists some school committee members in 1782 whom we know lived in what is now Prospect: Amos Atwater, Enos Tyler, Nicholas Russell, and David Hotchkiss.

At the annual meeting of the Cheshire Society on December 9, 1794, it was voted to establish fourteen school districts in the parish, and the boundaries are described in the minutes. Three of these districts were in the eastern ⅔ of Prospect, Districts 11, 12, and 13. District 11 was in the northeastern part of town and included the northeastern part of Summit Road and Matthew Street, Old Scott Road, and the area north of Roaring Brook Road. District 12 was in the center of town, and District 13 included the southern part of town. A school house was built in each of these districts.

2. COLUMBIA PARISH AND SCHOOL SOCIETY

Before the Columbia Parish or Congregational Church was organized in 1798, there was a "Columbia Company" or Ecclesiastical Society which consisted only of men with financial responsibility. A large ledger which contains some of this company's records, along with most of the early treasurer records of the Congregational Church, is deposited in the state library in Hartford for safety. This Columbia Company organized the church, but it also included men who belonged to other churches, such as Ezra Pierpont, a member of the Episcopal Church of Waterbury. The administration of the schools was the responsibility of this company, along with the care and maintenance of a cemetery. One of the first decisions was to establish a cemetery at the Prospect Green, just east of where the Grange Hall stands.

At the time of the organization of the Columbia Society, some important changes were going on in the state of Connecticut. In 1795 the proceeds of the sale of lands in the Western Reserve in Ohio were put in a permanent fund, the Connecticut Common School Fund, and money was distributed to the local parishes or ecclesiastical societies in their capacity as school societies. Before the end of the decade, the management of schools was transferred entirely from the towns to these school societies. The boundaries of these societies followed the parish lines, since they were ready-made and convenient for school purposes. The parishes of the Congregational order were selected as the most convenient of existing organizations for the establishment and supervision of schools. At the same time the Office of School Visitors was established. By 1798 the Conn. General Assembly had vested the school societies with all the powers and duties previously exercised by towns and ecclesiastical societies. Each society was entitled to receive interest from the School Fund, to appoint visitors to the schools not exceeding nine persons, and empowered to tax itself for school purposes. Ebenezer Hale, tax collector of Cheshire, turned over a proportionate amount of taxes beginning in 1797.

Fig 1 Prospect as shown on Beer's 1868 New Haven County Atlas. Boardman Kathan

Minutes of the annual School Societies meetings are contained in a record book, beginning in 1802 and ending by 1890. The term, "Societies," is instructive because this annual meeting was a joint meeting of the several, separate societies in the Columbia Parish, each society administering one of the school districts. When the meetings began there were four such districts, but by 1808 there was a petition to create a South West District in the area of

Straightsville Road and Porter Hill Road. An East District was created by 1810, but there is no report of the building of a schoolhouse until the time when a deed in 1834 conveyed land to the treasurer of the East District for the construction of one.

On Jan. 7, 1846, the boundary lines of the six districts were established, and the earliest maps of 1855 and 1868 (Fig 1) showed these district lines. We find reference to these districts, sometimes by name and sometimes by number, but there is no consistent list of districts by number, as some towns like Cheshire have. Each of these six districts had a one-room schoolhouse by the 1830s. In addition, some pupils near the Cheshire line in "Rag Hollow" attended the Mixville School in Cheshire, and some on the Waterbury Road and Turkey Hill section went to East Mountain School in Waterbury. When this happened, the home school district paid a proportionate amount of money. It was cheaper to pay another town than to maintain a schoolhouse for three or four children or furnish transportation. However, there seems to have been many times when one or more schools were closed for a year or more and the pupils transferred to another district. While state and town money was used to a certain extent, each district was responsible for its own school.

At each annual meeting reports were given of the different districts, and decisions were made to make changes in the district lines. Also, members of the School Committee and the Inspecting Committee (School Visitors) were elected. At the first meeting the members elected to the School Committee were Frederick Hotchkiss, Stiles Hotchkiss, and John Ford. Visitors elected were: Rev. Oliver Hitchcock, Jesse Ford, Ichabod Terril, Isaac Terril, John Ford, Abraham Hotchkiss, Amos Hotchkiss, Ira Smith, and Asahel Chittenden. Members of the school committee administered the financial affairs of each district while the visitors actually visited the schoolhouses and supervised the classes. It was customary to select the pastor of the Congregational Church as one of the visitors; indeed, the 1855 minutes stated: "If we have a clergyman with us in the Congregational society, he is appointed a visitor." The visitors were paid a stipend for their work, although the minutes of the 1850 annual meeting indicate that they voted "not to pay the visiting committee"!

One of the more faithful of the school visitors may have been the Rev. Frank Countryman. Among the records is a statement submitted to the Town of Prospect in 1875 for eleven visits to schoolhouses at $1.50 per visit for a total of $16.50. At the annual meeting on Oct. 1, 1877, not only did they vote to accept the report of Mr. Countryman, but they tended to him a vote of thanks for the faithful performance of his duty as a school visitor.

Even after the Town of Prospect was incorporated in 1827, the school society continued its existence and held annual meetings. In 1856 the Conn. General Assembly voted to abolish school societies and transfer all their power to the towns. It was not until the following year that the Annual Town Meeting began to hear reports of the school committee and to vote on members of that committee and the visiting committee. A special town meeting was called on Jan. 11, 1869, to authorize the selectmen to use as much of the town money as will make the schools free for six months of the year. In 1870 it was voted to make the school free for 30 weeks of that present year. In the meantime the General Assembly had voted to authorize towns to consolidate school districts into one.

On Nov. 11, 1871, it was voted that the Town of Prospect form a union district under the control of a Board of Education to care for and manage all the schools and school districts and district lines in said town. It was voted to appoint six persons to the new Board of Education: David M. Hotchkiss (Centre); John Gillett (North); Merritt Clark (West); Algernon S. Plumb (East); Smith S. Clark (South West); and Benjamin B. Brown who also lived in the East District. The South East District is not included. Most of the annual meetings in the 1870s seemed to include the matter of a consolidated district on the agenda. In 1878, for example, they voted "to go back to the old school system." Finally, in 1887 the annual meeting voted to give the town control and possession of all the schoolhouses and school property that belonged to the old school districts.

During these years of School Society and town control, the districts did not feel that they had to levy very much in taxes. Not only was money from the State School Fund available, but also in 1836 Connecticut received a windfall when the Federal government divided a large budget surplus among the states. Connecticut distributed its share to the towns, provided that one half of the income from the fund (known as the Town Deposit Fund) should be used for education.

There were some people in town who found the town schools inadequate, and at least two private schools were organized: in the 1820s at the David M. Hotchkiss house where the second floor room is still preserved just as it was when classes met there: and at the Castle public house just north of the green, organized by Seabury Scott. The 1890 History of New Haven County reported "both were well patronized."

3. PROSPECT UNION SCHOOL DISTRICT

The on-again, off-again nature of the unified school district is illustrated by the annual reports to the State of Connecticut and published in the State Register. In the 1874 annual report there is one school district in place of six, and this continues until 1880 when five school districts are reported. It is not until the 1886 report that the unified district took hold on a permanent basis. It was also during the decade of the 1870s that two of the one-room schoolhouses were abandoned; first, the Southeast and later, the Southwest. At the 1879 adjourned meeting, it was voted that the school in each district shall be open to all the children from other districts of the town where there is no school open in their own district. This was a change from the previous policy where students and their families had to make a petition to relocate. Inequities continued among the districts. In 1881 it was voted to give the West District 24 weeks of school, but the Center, Northeast, and East schools were allotted 36 weeks of school. The following year the sum of $152 was appropriated to the West and Northeast school districts while the East and Center school districts each received $190.

The minutes of the Union School District are missing for the years 1890 to 1920 although the financial records are in existence. We know that 1890 was the year that school visitors or Board of Education members were elected at the town annual meeting. It became customary for the annual meeting of the Union School District to be held before the annual town meeting. We also know that in the years between 1890 and 1920, the district built a new East schoolhouse and a new West schoolhouse, and that it purchased the old Advent Chapel near the Green as a second schoolhouse in the center of town.

In 1903 with state aid, the town voted to employ a school supervisor to be appointed by the state — his salary not to exceed $150 per year. His work would be to visit the schools and take the place of the local school visitors and instruct and advise on the ability of the teachers. The position was filled in 1910 by L.S. Miller of Waterbury who also served the towns of Avon, Beacon Falls, Bethlehem, and Middlebury. His place was taken by G.C. Swift, also of Waterbury, who covered the towns of Bethany, Beacon Falls, Goshen, and Oxford. Other state supervisors included W.H. Holmes, W.H. Bliss, Raymond N. Brown, and F. Burton Dunfield.

The primary management of the school district remained in the hands of elected Board of Education members who served three-year terms but could be re-elected indefinitely. The longest tenured school board member in Prospect was David M. Plumb, 42 years, from 1892 to 1933. Second in longevity was Halsey S. Clark, 36 years, from 1893 to 1929. Benjamin B. Brown served 28 years altogether, beginning before the Union School District was created. Others with many years of service were: Edgar G. Wallace, 27 years; Rev. William E. Phipps, 26 years; and George H. Cowdell, Charles S. Fenn, David B. Hotchkiss, William E. Clark, 22 years. In the years 1907-1909 there were three members of the same family on the six-member board: William E. Clark, Lavergne G. Clark, and Halsey S. Clark. The first woman to serve on the board was Nettie H. (Mrs. William E.) Clark, from 1895 to 1897.

4. PROSPECT COMMUNITY SCHOOL AND ALGONQUIN SCHOOL

The building of the Prospect Community School in 1936 marked an important new chapter in the history of the schools of the town. Not only was there a single consolidated school building for all the elementary grades, but there was a centralized management in the form of a Principal. The idea of a single schoolhouse for the community was not a new idea. As early as 1870, it was recommended that the districts be unified and the pupils be brought to a common center, but it was rejected because the "scholars were too remote." In June 1919 the Rev. George Culbertson spoke at a meeting for five minutes about the need for a consolidated school. Horatio Clark offered to give $500 toward a new central school building, remembering the problems he had securing an education for his children, but his offer was not accepted. Travel over muddy or icy roads took hours, and parents preferred to keep their children near home if they could.

On the occasion of the 50th anniversary of the Prospect Community School, research was done on the beginnings of the school by a group of students in the Talented and Gifted program led by their teacher, Blanche Ranaudo. They reported that on March 13, 1935, a town meeting was called to deal with the future of education in the town. A committee was appointed to investigate the conditions of the one-room schoolhouses and, in consultation with the Board of Education, to make a report. On April 15, the following month, a vote was taken to build a central school and hall to be used by the community. The vote was: "Yes" 61 and "No" 38. Plans were made by the building committee to hire Fred A. Webster of Waterbury as the architect and the Tremaglio Brothers, also of Waterbury, as the contractors. The building committee consisted of: Spencer Henn, chairman; Eugene Lewis, Sr.; John Keiper; William Mortison; Christina Staneslow; and John Gayer. Opposition arose to the plans because the building was considered too big for what was needed and too expensive.

On April 22, a vote was taken as to whether to continue the project. The vote this time was: "Yes" 43 and "No" 45. It was voted that the town could borrow not more than $25,000 for the new building and apply for a grant to the federal government through the Federal Emergency Administration of Public Works to fund the rest. A grant was given by the W.P.A. for 45% of the total cost of the building, $18,918. Adding the town's appropriation, the central school and community hall cost $43,918. On Oct. 15, 1935, a vote was taken to accept this plan and the vote was: "Yes" 196 and "No" 31, as recorded in the minutes by the Town Clerk, Mildred Talmadge.

Fig 2 Community after second addition in 1952.   Waterbury Republican-American

On Nov. 2, 1936, the new central school building was opened to the pupils of the town. The following March, the Board of Education officially named it the Prospect Community School. The members of the Board of Education in that critical 1935-36 year were: Charles S. Fenn, Chairman; Mae C. Miller, Secretary; Josephine S. Stieler; Thomas Murphy; Bessie Moshier; James L. Ives; Harold M. Bunnell; Merritt Walters; and John Keiper. In the 1936-37 year Anna Driver took the place of Murphy, and Clifford Wallace replaced Merritt Walters.

The Prospect Community School has had three additions: 1947-48, three rooms in the basement; 1951-52, classrooms, gym-auditorium, and kitchen (Fig 2); 1953-54, additional classrooms. In 1953 a Fact-Finding Committee, chaired by Carleton Benson, recommended that a new building be constructed on ten acres of land behind the volunteer fire department because the property was already owned by the town and abutted a recreation field (now Canfield Park). Both pieces of land had been deeded to the town by the New Haven Water Co. for school or other public purposes. The Coer Road Jr. High School (now Algonquin Annex) (Fig 3) was opened for 7th and 8th grades in 1957-58. Algonquin School was built in two stages, the first or eastern part in 1959-60 and the second and western part in 1961-62.

Fig 3   Coer Road Jr. High School, Sept. 6, 1957.   7th and 8th Grades started classes before the landscaping was done.   Waterbury Republican-American

When the Prospect Community School was opened in 1936, there were four classrooms with the following teachers: Catherine Cooke, Principal and 7th and 8th grades; Helen Hartnett, 5th and 6th grades; Mary Roach, 3rd and 4th grades; and Helen Sokolowski, 1st and 2nd grades. There was a health room, with Susan Cocchiola as school nurse and Dr. John Staneslow as school physician. Albert Allen was the custodian. There was a library room in the new school but no librarian, so classes made weekly trips across the Green to the fieldstone library where Nellie Cowdell was the librarian.

In 1936 Edwin Floyd was the Rural Supervisor, and he was assisted by Miss O'Neill, and was succeeded by E. Arthur and G.E. Rast. Dr. John Thorpe of Cheshire became Superintendent of Schools in 1945, followed by Charles Ritch, Eric Hirst, William Nolan, and Robert Winslow. William Welton was first hired as Principal in 1955-56 and became Superintendent in 1963. He in turn was followed by Francis Ciarfella.

The Board of Education member with the longest tenure in this era was Joseph Membrino, 18 years (1941-59), followed by Mae Miller (1933-44) and Ruth Chandler (1939-50), both 12 years.

5. REGION 16 SCHOOL DISTRICT

One of the last major decisions of the Prospect Board of Education was to build a new school building behind Town Hall. Originally, it was to be a combined Jr. High-Sr. High. However, by July 1968 the Board had ratified a 10-year contract with the City of Waterbury to continue sending high school students there, and a middle school was planned to serve a new regional district consisting of Prospect and Beacon Falls. Under the direction of the State Department of Education, a study was done by the University of Connecticut and presented to the Board on June 15, 1968. Entitled "Education for Prospect," the report found the educational program in Prospect wanting in many areas as a result of overcrowding, inadequate planning, and a lack of financial support and community involvement. It recommended that Prospect enter into a regional school district with one or more other towns on a kindergarten through 12th grade basis, build a regional middle school, and begin immediately to plan for a high school. The towns of Prospect, Beacon Falls, and Oxford entered into discussions, but Oxford had withdrawn by March 1969.

At a town meeting in Prospect on Sept. 26, 1968 (and in Beacon Falls three days earlier), it was voted to set up a Temporary Regional School Study Committee. Prospect members included: Frederic Shattuck, Eileen Mullany, Alex Rozum, Denis Broderick, and Frank Doyle. A year later the committee issued its final report, recommending that the two towns form a regional school district. Also, that kindergarten through 5th grades be housed in elementary buildings in the separate towns, that grades 6 through 8 be housed in the new middle school to be built in Prospect, and that grades 9 through 12 be housed in a new high school facility to be built on a site located in the center of one of the two towns. The new regional Board of Education would have eight members, four from each town.

The final report was accepted and Region 16 School District came into existence. The members of the new board were: from Prospect, Denis Broderick, Chairman, Gerard McCarthy, Eileen Mullany, and Richard Platt; from Beacon Falls, Walter Haas, Mabel DelVecchio, Steven Csuka, and Frank Semplenski. The following year Paul Lange took Platt's place. Mary Nolan was elected to the Board in 1971. Francis Ciarfella, who served as Prospect's Superintendent of Schools, was hired as the Superintendent of the new district.

Fig 4 Long River Middle School under construction, 1970.   Waterbury Republican-American

The Long River Middle School (Fig 4) was built in 1970-71 and dedicated on June 13, 1971. Stanley J. Lucas was chairman of the building committee,

Walter Crabtree was the architect, and Edward L. Miller was the first Principal. John Proctor succeeded Ciarfella as Superintendent of Schools in 1979, and Dr. John Buck was welcomed to the position in 1986. His place was taken by the current Superintendent, Dr. Helene Skrzyniarz, in 1994. Several attempts to build a regional high school since 1969 have failed. However, the district did build a substantial addition to the Laurel Ledge Elementary School in Beacon Falls and is in the process of doing the same with the Long River Middle School in 1995.

There have been four attempts to dissolve the region, initiated primarily by the voters of Beacon Falls because of their dissatisfaction with the "Equalization of Assets" plan, the "one-man—one vote" weighted voting, and the rejection of a suitable high school site in their town.   In 1973-74 the committee voted in favor of dissolution, but it was rejected by the State Board of Education. The same thing happened in 1976-77. The third committee in 1978-79 failed to come up with a report in the allotted time. The fourth committee in 1979-80 submitted a report, but some of the financial issues were not resolved and it was rejected by the state. The assets issue between the towns was finally resolved in 1986 under the administration of John Proctor, after going through a maze of legal proceedings.

One of the most difficult periods in the history of the new regional school district was in the years 1975-76. After many months of negotiations between the Board of Education and the teachers and the defeat of several salary agreements, the Region 16 Education Association called a strike on Nov. 3, 1975. Although it was over in another day and the teachers returned to the classrooms, bitterness continued and teacher morale was at a low point. The Conn. Education Association was asked by the local teachers to conduct an inquiry into the actions of the Superintendent of Schools and the Board. The letter of request specified that although the Board is "anticipating anywhere from a $45,000 to $80,000 surplus, teachers are being told not to order supplies essential to their everyday activities, such as duplicating paper, construction paper, etc." and the Board is not offering the $37,000 needed to pay teachers their annual increments. Also in 1975, petitions signed by 1,300 persons urged an evaluation of the Superintendent.

The Conn. Education Association carried out an extensive review in 1976, including meetings with staff and town leaders, and a public hearing. A final report was issued on Oct. 13, 1976, and it included a number of conclusions and recommendations. One area had to do with what was perceived as an inadequate level of funding. Another dealt with a lack of community support, viz: "The Region 16 School District has had, with the exception of Citizens for Quality Education, Parent Teacher Association groups, and scattered pockets of educational groups, very little community activism, interest, or support prior to the past school year."

Other subjects touched on were: the need for curriculum committees with the participation of teachers; better relations between teachers and the towns; better conflict management and policy making by the Board of Education; and improved public relations and community involvement. A number of changes took place in the region in the succeeding years, especially after new members were elected to the Board from both towns in 1977.

The Prospect member on the Region 16 Board of Education with the longest tenure was Boardman Kathan, 12 years, 1977-89.

THE HIGH SCHOOL SITUATION

Public high schools developed in Connecticut in the latter part of the 19th century. The neighboring towns of Waterbury (1852) and Naugatuck (1851) built high schools, and students from Prospect started to attend them. Transportation was difficult, but the construction of the trolley line made it possible for more students to go into Waterbury for school. Cheshire also had a small high school at the turn of the century which was attended by a few Prospect students, including Merritt Walters who was First Selectman for a number of years. At least one student requested permission to attend Southington High School. Of course the town paid tuition for these students, which in 1922-23 totalled $2,600. In 1934 a discussion was held by the Board of Education as to the future closing of the trolley line. By July of that year, a contract was negotiated with the Connecticut Co. to furnish a bus to Waterbury over state highways 68 and 69.

Because of a rapidly growing number of high school students, Prospect entered into conversation with several neighboring towns about the possibility of a regional school. On Oct. 2, 1941, representatives from the town met with their counterparts from Cheshire and Wolcott at the Waverly Inn in Cheshire. Two years later a committee was appointed to investigate the possibility of joining Cheshire and Bethany in building a regional high school. It was called Regional High School District No. 2, and in 1945 a contest was held to name the new school. Clifford Wallace of Prospect was one of the judges. The winning name was "Mt. Sanford Regional High School" and it would be built in the Town of Cheshire. By the end of the decade the district was dissolved, and Prospect voted to pay its remaining bills for participation in the planning process.

In the 1950s there were several attempts to collaborate in building a high school. On Feb. 4, 1953, Cheshire was approached about the possibility of Prospect sending its students to the new high school building, and the answer was "NO." On Jan. 2, 1957, the town discussed with Wolcott the possibility of a regional high school, but was informed two months later that Wolcott was too far along in its plans.

Rebuffed by two neighboring towns, Prospect looked at some land within its own boundaries upon which to build a high school. In 1958-59 properties under consideration included: Hotchkiss, Coer, Plumb, Wooster, Petrauskas, and Lombard (the town could have purchased 100 acres for $115,000 including the former Weyand home; this property was later developed into the Prospect Country Club and golf course, and is now a private estate). By 1960 the town had bought for $70,000 the Clifford Wallace farm on which to build a town hall and high school. By the middle of the decade, construction of a combined Jr. High-Sr. High was being urged with a capacity of 800-1,000 students. A citizens advisory committee reported that the building would be ready by 1970. What happened instead was the building of a middle school to serve Region 16, and Prospect students continued to be transported into Waterbury for high school.

A 10-year contract was approved in July 1968 with the City of Waterbury, but with the stipulation that when a new high school was built in the east end, Prospect students would be moved there. The contract was not honored, and Prospect students were sent to the new Wilby High School until 1983 when a new agreement was worked out to house them at Wolcott High School. In each decade of the life of Region 16, there has been an effort to develop a high school.

In the early 1970s a committee looked at sites in both Prospect and Beacon Falls, and the Smith family farm in Beacon Falls was one of the preferred sites. Soil tests and studies were done on the property, and the cost for about 30 acres was $425,000. However, the Region 16 Board deadlocked over a final site; the four Beacon Falls members voted against any place in Prospect, and the four Prospect members voted against any place in Beacon Falls. The board even looked at a neutral site in Bethany, but this was dropped.

In the mid-1980s another effort was made to develop a high school, but this time it went as far as a district-wide referendum. Three committees were appointed: the High School Building Committee, an Educational Program-Curriculum Committee, and a Physical Plant-Location Committee. Again, many sites were looked at in both towns, and a professional site analysis was done on three properties, two in Prospect and one in Beacon Falls. The final site chosen was the Smith family farm, but this time the cost for 26 acres was almost 2½ million dollars, in great part because the Smith family had already developed plans for a subdivision and it was ready for approval by the town's planning and zoning agency. An architect was hired for the high school, and a set of preliminary plans was presented to the public. The estimated cost was 26 million with nearly 81% reimbursement by the State. In the referendum on June 8, 1988, the plan was soundly defeated by the voters of the region by a 2 to 1 majority. The residents of Beacon Falls approved the plan by a vote of 452 to 277, but it was rejected overwhelmingly in Prospect by a vote of 522 for it and 1,649 against it.

By the mid-1990s there was another attempt to develop a regional high school; a building committee has been hard at work, several sites are under consideration, and an architect has been hired. Only time will tell whether this effort will succeed where others have failed.

~

Chapter Eight

One-Room Schoolhouses

by Nellie Cowdell and Boardman Kathan

W hen the Columbia Society was established in 1797 and given control of the schools, there were three one-room schoolhouses in the community. One was on the Green just east of where the old fieldstone library (now the Meeting House) is located. Sometime between 1772 and 1779 a schoolhouse was built on this hill by Cheshire's 12th district. The first meeting of the Columbia Parish ecclesiastical society was held "in the schoolhouse on the green." A second schoolhouse was located in the northeast part of the town on the west side of Summit Road north of the intersection with Juggernaut Road. This one was in Cheshire's 11th district. A third schoolhouse in the 13th district was built in the southeastern part of town and was located on Cook Road just south of the intersection with Radio Tower Road. A deed granting the land to build the Radio Tower Road in 1784 mentioned the schoolhouse.

It had been thought that there was a fourth schoolhouse within the bounds of the Columbia Parish, located in the western part of the town at the corner of Clark Hill Road and Union City Road. When the bounds of the Parish were established in 1794, one of the westerly boundaries was a "schoolhouse corner," but historians cannot agree on whether this was the Pond Hill District of Salem Parish or the West School of Columbia Parish. However, the reference may have been to the site of the original East Mountain School on the Waterbury-Prospect line.

Colmbia Society built two more schoolhouses soon after it was organized and a third one later. We will look at each district in turn. Unless the records were preserved, we know little about the building of each one.

1. CENTER SCHOOLHOUSES

There is more information about the schoolhouses in the center of town. The original one on the Green was apparently used until a new one was built on Old Schoolhouse Road about 1808 near where the barber shop is today. One old booklet, made of sheets of paper folded to 3 by 5 inches, describes "a tax laid on the inhabitants of the Center School district for the purpose of building

Editor's note: the same note at the beginning of Chapter 7 applies to Chapter 8.

a new school house in said district to raise the sum of $190 collectable on list of 1807. Laid at a meeting holden 16th of January 1808. To Frederick Hotchkiss, collector." The booklet continues with the list of persons living in the Center District and their property values and tax. It is hard to understand what the values are based on, perhaps a 30% valuation, and the tax was about 4½ mills on that value. Some men appeared with several pieces of property or as guardian for another. Only a few women's names appear, such as Sally Curtis and Esther Hotchkiss. The total collected for the school is $197.12. Expenses included: Isaac Hotchkiss, $12 for chimney and plastering, 700 brick for 50¢, $6 for 12 bushels of stone line; Amos Tinker, $3.50 for seven days work at the schoolhouse; Rev. Oliver Hitchcock, $1.50 for laying the underpinning; and other men, so much for the stone for the hearth, for lumber, shingles, joists and studs, clapboards. The complete list of taxpayers and workers would take two pages. This was the schoolhouse that burned about 1863. One pupil, David Hotchkiss, reported that he went to school one morning and found only hot ashes where the building had stood. There were no houses nearby and no one saw the fire.

Some educational activities also took place in a two-story building which stood just south of the green. There is no record of it in the minutes of the School Society annual meetings, but in the minutes of the Congregational Church, a meeting was called on Nov. 3, 1829, "to lease a piece of land from the ecclesiastical society, 50 foot by 20 foot . . . for to set the center school." The lower story was to be occupied by the proprietors for school and other purposes. The society's committee was authorized at this meeting to lease the above described piece of land for the consideration of 50¢ annually to be paid to the treasurer of the Congregational Society of the town. It is not clear when this two-story building became the "store with a meeting hall upstairs" that is referred to in many old papers. In 1831 the church voted to pay from the treasury $4 annually for the use of their schoolhouse on the green for society conference and singing school. In March 1843 the church voted to confer with the center school district to buy the two-story building to make an addition to the parsonage, but the following month it was reported that the building could not be bought. Some years later this building was moved down to Union City Road and became the wing of a house opposite the cemetery gates.

As to where classes were held in the center of town after the old schoolhouse burned in 1863, it is possible that a room was rented in a home. However, the records show that in April 1865 Dr. and Mrs. Henry Ducachet, through Ichabod Hitchcock, by power of attorney, sold to the Center School District "a certain piece of land situated near the center of Prospect containing two acres more or less, with dwelling house and other buildings thereon standing." The price was $450 but then the Center District committee sold the same property to Eunice Hotchkiss for $500, reserving to said district the right and privilege of using the schoolroom during the winter of 1865 and summer of 1866. School may have been kept in this house until the new Center School was built.

We know more about the Center Schoolhouse (Fig 1) which still stands west of the Green and is leased by the Prospect Historical Society. It was built in 1867 to take the place of the schoolhouse that burned. A deed is recorded on Oct. 22, 1866, whereby Henry Nettleton "for $20 sells to the

Center School District 840 square feet for the purpose of placing a school thereon." This was built for a cost of $900 and is reported in the state records in 1868. It was customary in the minutes of this time to record that the meeting was held in "the usual place" without specifying where. However, it was written that the Annual Town Meeting in 1869 was held in "the Centre School house." This center schoolhouse was shingled and the plaster repaired in 1889. In 1906 at the time the present green was built, it was voted to thank Whittemore and Tuttle for painting the center schoolhouse.

Fig 1 Center Schoolhouse, built in 1867, has served many uses including town hall and WW II telephone center. It is now used for exhibits by the Prospect Historical Society.   Prospect Historical Society

In 1919 another schoolhouse was acquired. On Aug. 14, 1919, a deed was recorded whereby Theodore Allen conveyed the Advent Chapel property to the Prospect Union School District. It had been built originally as the Advent Church in the 1880s but had been empty for a number of years before being bought by the Allens. For several years the Advent chapel building had been rented for $5 a month. After it was purchased, the upper grades of the Center and East Districts were educated at the Chapel School while grades 1 through 4 were taught at Center School on the Green. Even after the new Community School was built, this facility was used as a classroom for a number of years because of overcrowding. Today, this building is the Chapel Senior Center.

2. SOUTHEAST SCHOOLHOUSE

Not much is known about the schoolhouse that was built in the Southeast District on the west side of Cook Road just south of Radio Tower Road.

There were a number of houses in the Cook Road area before 1750, and the Cheshire Parish may have built a schoolhouse in that area by the 1770s. We know that the building existed prior to 1784, because the deed establishing what we now call Radio Tower Road was recorded on May 4, 1784, and the schoolhouse is mentioned in the deed. This was the school built by Cheshire's 13th district before the Columbia Parish and Society were organized. It is not clear when the schoolhouse was finally abandoned. In 1892 the building may have been still standing in ruins, but there is no record of it being sold. The minutes of the 1871 annual school society meeting indicate that none of those appointed to the Board of Education represented the Southeast District. The last year that a school visitor was elected from the Southeast was 1875; his name was Warren Wilson. In addition, the Rev. Frank Countryman reported on his visits in 1875 to only one "South" school and it was probably the Southwest one. The Southeast School was probably abandoned by the beginning of the 1870s.

3. NORTHEAST OR SUMMIT SCHOOLHOUSE

Fig 2 Summit Schoolhouse.   Prospect Historical Society

The schoolhouse (Fig 2) in Cheshire's 11th district stood on the west side of Summit Road, north of the intersection with Juggernaut Road, before the creation of the Columbia Society. Indeed, it may be the one-room schoolhouse with the longest continuous history in the town. There is a paucity of records regarding repairs and maintenance except for a vote in 1889 to pay not more than $75 for repairs to the schoolhouse for shingling and repairing of plaster. We know that there were some years when the schoolhouse was closed for a term and combined with another school. Summit School enjoyed one distinction: it was the site of a religious Sunday School during the early

1930s conducted by Charles Hodges and George Hill. The building survives today as a completely remodeled private home at 143 Summit Road.

4. WEST SCHOOLHOUSE

The West Schoolhouse (Fig 3) was built originally by the Columbia Society soon after 1797. It was situated at the foot of Clark Hill Road, facing Union City Road. Old-timers who attended school there remembered a pleasant brook on the east side of the school. Apparently this original schoolhouse was badly in need of repair in 1916-17. Students in that district were transported to the Center for several terms. Finally, the old building was sold to the Clarks and moved up the hill to the Clark farm, where it served as a milk house and shed for many years and is still standing today. When an article was published in the newspaper in 1933 about the old schoolhouses with a picture of the old West one, it was stated that the building was 150 years old. This would take it back to the end of the Revolutionary War which is somewhat questionable. Merritt Clark, who was born in 1823, and his sons Lavergne and Halsey and their children all attended school in that old building.

Fig 3   Teacher Catherine Brown with students at the first West Schoolhouse c. 1912-1915.   Prospect Historical Society

Julia Beers had offered to buy and give to the town a site for a new West School, and the construction was approved at a cost not exceeding $2,000. Land for a new West School was purchased in 1919. The deed recorded on July 11 indicates that Albert Simon and Alex Parvasarus sold to the Prospect Union School District ⁴/₅ of an acre of land for a new West School. The land was bounded north by Salem Road and south on an abandoned highway called Logtown Road on a site known as "Foster's Corner". When Community

School was built, this schoolhouse was sold and remodeled as a private home and is located at 139 Salem Road today.

5. SOUTHWEST SCHOOLHOUSE

The Southwest Schoolhouse stood on the west side of Straightsville Road, south of Porter Hill Road, but was not built until after 1808. It as at the annual School Societies meeting on Oct. 3, 1808, that a petition was presented to create a new school district in that part of town. The petition was signed by Asahel Hotchkiss, Elmer Hotchkiss, Chauney Judd, David Payne, John Stevens, David Sanford, Philemon Payne, Wooster Tuttle, Woodward Hotchkiss, and Amos Hotchkiss. There were times during its existence when it was closed for some terms and the students housed elsewhere, especially at the West School. It was finally abandoned by 1880 and sold at auction in 1892 to Smith Clark for $5.

6. EAST SCHOOLHOUSE

Fig 4 The graduation class of 1936 from the second East Schoolhouse.
L to R: Mary Salvatore, Elma Hintz, Elinor Chatfield, Mary C. Roach (teacher), Helen Voss, and Richard Varis.   Prospect Historical Society

The East Schoolhouse was originally built after 1834 on the southwest corner of the intersection of Cook Road and Cheshire Road. The deed for the sale of land was recorded on October 9, 1834, and reads as follows: "Hezekiah Beecher . . . for $7.00 to Isaac Judd, Treasurer of the East School District, in said district a certain piece of land situated in the certain part of Prospect containing 8 rods of ground, which is to be for the use of the said district for a building lot." Further: "The schoolhouse is to stand on the west line and the District shall have the perfect right to pass and repass on the land west of the house for the building or repairing the house, and other necessary business." "Furthermore I the grantor am to build and keep in repair all fences on the south and west boundary lines." This is the "old red school" which is referred to in some papers. This building was abandoned in 1891 and sold at auction in 1892 for $6.00 to John Cook.

The East Schoolhouse was replaced by a new building on the north side of Cheshire Road (Fig 4). Land for this new school was sold to the Union School District by Benjamin Brown in a deed recorded on August 18, 1891. The size of the building lot was 90 feet by 121 feet, and a fence marking the schoolyard was to be maintained by the school district. The building was sheathed inside with Georgia pine and finished outside with clapboards with a hall 4 feet wide on the front and the classroom 8 feet high. In 1914 the school board met in the East schoolhouse and voted to build an addition on the west side not to exceed $300. They also bought 52 new desk seats, some for the East School and some for the West. After the Community School was built, this schoolhouse was also sold and remodeled into a private home. The building was torn down in the late 1980s to make room for a new home located at 135 Cheshire Road.

DESCRIPTION OF SCHOOLHOUSES

From descriptions of other schoolhouses and from some old letters, we know something about what the early Prospect schoolhouses were like. A description of the old West school by a woman who attended it in 1860 was typical of the period. There was a shelf for writing that ran around three sides of the room and was marked by the knives of many boys. Facing the shelf was a backless bench. When it was time to recite, the children could turn around on the bench and face the teacher and rest their backs against the shelf. The teacher sat at one end or in the middle, with backless small benches for the youngest children around her. A fireplace or stove at one end furnished heat. The schoolhouses were of different dimensions according to the anticipated enrollment. Some were 16 by 20 feet, some 18 by 30 feet. The smaller buildings had two windows on the side and perhaps one or two on the end between doors. At the opposite end from the entrance was a chimney and for many years a fireplace until it was replaced by a wood stove. If large enough, there may have been a window on each side of the chimney. The teacher at the Center School (built in 1867) sat on a little platform so she could oversee the work of all the children. Boards that were painted black behind the teacher served as blackboards since they were much cheaper than slate. Sometimes one of the older boys was paid 25¢ a week to start the fire in the wood stove, and sometimes the teacher had to do it herself.

The outside of the buildings was clapboard and, if painted at all, was white. In 1864 it was reported that the five schoolhouses were "without outbuildings." When the new East School was built in 1891, the outhouse was moved across the street from the old schoolhouse.

When electricity came to town in the 1920s, those schoolhouses on the power line were wired for lights. Earlier, when it was too dark to see, school had to be dismissed, or the teacher read to the pupils using one oil lamp on her desk. In 1930 an effort was made to bring electricity to the East school, the only one without it. Electric power came from a distance in either direction on Cheshire Road, but a number of new poles would have to be set. Wells had been drilled around the year 1924 for all the schools except the Center one. There was a well outside the Grange Hall nearby, and that was the source of water except when the pump handle was broken.

There was a town meeting in early 1935 to consider the condition of the schoolhouses. Roads were better (State Routes 68 and 69 had been built) and school buses could travel around town without too much problem. William Mortison was chairman of a special committee to investigate the situation, and he reported that it would cost at least $2,500 to repair and bring the schoolhouses to decent condition. Plumbing and heating was not even considered a possibility. A new building was considered, one that would be reasonably fireproof. This led to plans for a new central school building to take the place of the one-room schoolhouses.

TEACHING

The story of the schools in Prospect needs to be set in the larger context of American educational history. When the Constitution of the United States was adopted, education was one of the important matters left to the several states, and the states left it in the hands of local communities. People in the towns resisted additional taxes and kept the decentralized district schools, which resulted in a lack of supervision, accountability, financial support, and a great deal of public apathy and indifference. Before the common school reform movement began in the 1830s and 1840s under Horace Mann and Henry Barnard, schools were deplorable and lacked equipment; classes were ungraded and crowded; teachers were untrained, ill paid, and transient; libraries were unknown; and textbooks, nonexistent. Those who could afford it sent their children to an increasing number of private schools and academies. One outstanding exception in the State of Connecticut was the school in Cheshire taught by Bronson Alcott in 1825-27. The forerunner of the state Board of Education was not established until 1838, and the first normal school for the training of teachers was not opened until 1850 in New Britain.

Not much is known about the teachers or "schoolmasters or dames" in 19th century Prospect. Some of the old fragile record fill in some details that are not in the books or minutes. Sometimes the district is named and the parents in it. It was customary for the teachers to board in different homes for a term. For example, one teacher boarded with A. Chittenden for 10 days, with Ichabod Tyler 7 days, Benjamin Bronson 3½ days, Rev. Oliver Hitchcock 4 days, David Byington 3¼ days, widow Esther Hotchkiss 7 days, Frederick Hotchkiss 10 days, Amos Tinker 19 days, Curtis Hotchkiss 3 days, Obed Tuttle 3 days, Lydia Tyler 8 weeks, 3 days; total 18 weeks. This was the record of Concurrance Garnsey for teaching in 1802.

Ansel Spencer taught for several terms. His lists of parents with per pupil days of attendance for each are in very small neat writing. He and his father Isaac, and his brothers, Selden and Elihu, all saw service in the Revolutionary

War. Ansel was still drawing a pension in Waterbury in 1840. Hannah Hotchkiss presented her bill for teaching in 1806. She listed where she boarded and included $4.00 for boarding herself the previous summer, and included $2.50 to be reimbursed for prizes, mostly books that were given to the best scholars at the end of the term. We know of a few old books that were saved because they had been received as school prizes, but this is the only entry of a district being billed for some.

In the early 1800s there were few qualifications to be a teacher; some had been hired for the position because no one else would take it. Albert Allen told about the old Southeast Schoolhouse when Fred Brown was the teacher there. Brown had lived in the East District and attended school there (he was born in 1848). When he was 15 years old he taught school, and three girls aged 16 were among his pupils: Ella Kimball, Julia Talmadge (Cook), and Hannah Munson.

The next year Ella Kimball was herself the teacher. The bell she used to summon her class to the schoolhouse was given to Albert Allen and now belongs to the Historical Society. She married Henry Hotchkiss and moved to Waterbury. Another teacher was Josephine Nettleton who lived just over the town line in Bethany and attended the "Gate School" in that town. One day a member of the Bethany school board came to the school and asked her teacher, "Who is your smartest scholar?" and Josephine was transferred at age 15 to another Bethany school to teach.

There were some teachers of good ability and also some mediocre, even poor ones. In the 1864 report to the state it was noted: "Examined nine teachers, two unqualified. Not regular attendance; parents indifferent." By 1905 it was noted that all four teachers were graduates of Normal School. Through the years, more and more of the teachers were graduates although some took only a six week course after high school graduation. The qualifications of the teachers increased when the pay increased.

The length of the school term varied in the different districts. Usually there was a summer term and a winter term. Sometimes there was no winter term in the Northeast or Summit School because of the weather or the poor roads. In 1875 there was a summer term of 17 weeks in the Northeast School, but the Center, West, Southwest, and East Schools had only 13 weeks each; they had a Fall-Winter-Spring term varying from 4 to 16 weeks. The attendance also varied. Some classes were down to 8 pupils while another district could have over 50. If the class was too small, the children would be transported to another district and the schoolhouse closed.

Total school enrollment in the mid 1800s went over 150, then declined to a low of 75 in 1883. It did not reach the number of 140 again until the 1920s and that included high school students. In 1935 there were 19 graduates from 8th grade in the four one-room schoolhouses. Commencement exercises were held as usual in the fieldstone Congregational Church building.

Most students in earlier times had walked to school but transportation had to be provided for longer distances, especially to bring students from the southern or eastern parts of town to the center. A driver with a team of horses was employed for this job. In the 1920s drivers included: Samuel Hlooshko, Anton Cocchiola, A. Harrington, and A. Haquist. By 1929-30 a bus was put into service for the first time, driven by Harry Stieler. In 1936-37 the bus contract went to Lionel LeClair.

Salaries for teachers varied a great deal. Early in the 1800s all teachers received 75¢ per week plus room and board and $12 a year for fuel except where no winter term was held. The pay for teachers and the mill tax went up and down. Votes regarding school terms, opening and closing, were taken and then rescinded until the records seem to mean nothing! Generally, male teachers seemed to receive twice as much salary as females. By 1920-21, the range of teachers' salaries had reached $1,050-$1,200 per year, but this changed to $950-$1,250 in 1931-32, followed by a 10% cut in salaries in 1933-34.

Another example of discrimination besides salaries was the unwritten rule that female teachers could not get married. This policy was enforced as late as 1939-40 when Helen Harnett, teacher and principal at the Community School, got married and left the school system. It was not until 1940s that a state law was passed prohibiting discrimination on the basis of sex or marital status in the employment of teachers and their compensation. At the same time an old law regarding homes and transportation for teachers was repealed. Also a whole new set of laws began to be passed regarding contracts, collective bargaining, termination, and other personnel matters.

There is some information regarding teaching material and activities. In the first year of reports to the State, 1846, it was noted that the schoolhouses have blackboards but no globes or maps. Gradually maps were added so that they were all equipped with them by 1858. No doubt, even if geography was not a common subject, those who had relatives moving to the Midwest traced their path on a map of the U.S.

For many years children supplied their own books and because some would inherit books from an older brother or sister, the text for a class would vary. In that same report to the State by the school visitors, the books used in the schools were listed as follows: Spelling — Webster's; Reading — National Preceptor, Worcester's Third Book; Grammar — Smith's; Geography — Smith's, Mitchell's; Arithmetic — Smith's. School libraries were nonexistent at first, but the Southwest District established one by 1857 and this slowly spread to the other districts. The usual subjects for study were: the three R's (reading, writing, arithmetic) plus spelling and geography. According to one record in the year 1868, no one studied bookkeeping, composition, drawing, history, declamation, or algebra. Some specimens of penmanship for the early 1800s still exist and are beautiful. The teacher was expected to own a "pen knife" and be able to fashion pens from the quills that the children brought to school. Usually, a bundle of switches was also a part of the teacher's equipment and hung conveniently behind her desk.

The educational program in the schools had changed dramatically by the 1900s because the teachers were trained in Normal School and they were overseen by a supervisor appointed by the State. In addition, more and more standards regarding curriculum were promulgated by the State Board of Education. By the time the new Prospect Community School was built, it embodied the best facilities and equipment in "progressive" education. It became a "model" school and was visited by teachers and students from the New Britain Normal School.

Another important factor in the progress of education in Prospect was the creation of the first Parents Teachers Association around 1930 through the initiative of Myrtle Chatfield who served as the first president. She was a grandmother of Mayor Robert Chatfield.

This section on teaching would not be complete without recognizing those who taught in the last years of the one-room schoolhouses since 1924. There are some people still living in town or elsewhere who will remember them and recollect their names.

Chapel: Clara DeReizno, Helen O'Meara, Mary Joyce, Violet Raytwich, and Catherine Cooke.

Center: Erma Geddes, Rosalind Stoddard, Jeanette Frechette, and Helen Cochard.

Northeast: Emeline Cassiday, Anna Alishansky, Gertrude Stokes, and Helen Hartnett.

East: Winiford Dauck, Mildred Hetherington, L. Norton, and Mary Roach.

West: Ann Smyth Parsons and Helen Sokoloski.

On May 21, 1995, a reunion was held of all those who had attended one-room schoolhouses in Prospect, and many more stories were shared of a period of history that has long since gone.

Fig 5   Ruth Tibbetts, Mrs. Normand, and Mrs. Galvin serve hot lunch to students at Community School in 1949.   Prospect Historical Society

Some memories had been compiled by the TAG students in 1986 when Community School celebrated its 50th anniversary. Included were: memories of the teacher stepping out of the door and ringing a school bell, signaling that class was about to be in session; memories of boys learning woodcraft in the basement while girls worked at a sewing machine in the classroom; memories of Pet Day each year when the children brought their pets to school; memories of the warm wood stove to gather around after a walk to school; memories of eating lunch outdoors on a rock under a tree or sharing the warm soup heated by the wood stove; memories of completing your own work and then observing the older pupils do theirs, being puzzled by the advanced math problems on the blackboard; memories of "teachers who were like mothers to us;" memories of close friendships in the little schoolhouse.

Memories . . . Memories . . .

~

Chapter Nine

Early Agriculture and Industry

Agriculture was the primary source of income for the residents of Prospect from the very first settlers until the middle of the twentieth century. There were times when manufacturing was of great importance, but never did it replace the dependence on farming. As shown in (Fig 1), the manufacturing production value in 1845 was about equal to that of agriculture. This chart gives a capsule summary of the crops and products that were the mainstay of Prospect's economy. Only since the suburban spread from Waterbury and other towns in the 1950s, did the complexion of Prospect change forever from its agricultural heritage. Today, the working farm has all but vanished as a way of life on these hills.

AGRICULTURE

The Indians did little farming in general in Connecticut and probably none in the Prospect area, which was a food gathering area for fish and wildlife. The first white settlers knew little except farming. Agriculture was their trade and they practiced it wherever they went. Of course, there were those among them who had other skills, but almost everyone, even the clergymen, had a plot of land to grow food or graze animals.

To the city dweller the work of a farmer may have seemed rather simplistic — the sort of thing anyone could do. In reality, the life of a farmer was complex because they needed to perform so many functions. Each farm was a micro-community with the farmer, his family, and perhaps a few hired hands. The farmer had to mend a cart like a mechanic, repair shoes like a cobbler, doctor a sick cow like a veterinarian, and build a barn like a carpenter. It has been said that a farm is a poor place for a lazy man to exercise his gifts. Life on the farm was hard and days were long. The farmer learned to be thrifty and conserved his valuable resources whenever possible. In the summer, boys and even men went barefoot to save on shoe leather. On Sunday they might carry their shoes and stockings to church, putting them on only as they approached the sanctuary. A farmer's wife needed energy, an ingenious mind, and swift hands to complete the endless list of chores to be done each day.

Money was seldom used. Taxes and church offerings were among the few debts that required cash. Most other goods and services were obtained by barter. One farmer would exchange surplus produce or meat with another who had different items. When the services of a blacksmith or mill operator were needed, payment would often be in products from the farm. According to the census reports, the farms in Prospect produced wood, charcoal, hay, ice, apples, cider, milk, butter, cheese, eggs, wool, flax, corn, rye, barley, and oats. The common farm animals were sheep, horses, swine, and cattle. The rocky soil was ideal for the grazing of sheep and fruit orchards — both of which were prolific here. In the first half of the 20th century, dairy farming and egg production were major industries in Prospect.

PRODUCTION OF GOODS IN PROSPECT
OCTOBER 1, 1844 — SEPTEMBER 30, 1845

AGRICULTURE

	QUANTITY	VALUE
Lumber	15,000 feet	$ 150.00
Firewood	685 cords	1,723.00
Charcoal	40,000 bu.	3,000.00
Sheep	233	236.00
Wool	718 lbs.	212.40
Horses	71	2,154.00
Neat cattle	456	6,076.00
Swine	171	1,848.00
Indian corn	1918 bu.	1,342.60
Rye	1124 bu.	899.20
Barley	16 bu.	9.60
Oats	1560 bu.	780.00
Potatoes	5805 bu.	2,322.00
Other esculents	2450 bu.	392.00
Hay	566 tons	8,107.00
Butter	19,525 lbs.	2,929.00
Cheese	3,060 lbs.	270.00
		$ 32,450.80

MANUFACTURING	QUANTITY	VALUE	CAPITAL INVESTED	PERSONS EMPLOYED MALE	FEMALE
Shovel, fork & hoe factory	1	$7,000	$5,000	10	
Britannia-ware factory	2	$9,000	$6,000	17	
Coach, wagon, sleigh factory	1	$ 500	$ 100	1	
Tannery (20 hides tanned)	1	$ 100	$ 50	1	
Shoe manufacturer (1600 pr.)	-	$1,389	-	3	4
Umbrella trimming mfg.	1	$4,500	$3,000	7	8
Japanned & bone button mfg.	1	$2,500	$ 900	5	7
Friction match mfg.	-	$5,500	$1,000	8	22
Pocketbook mfg.	1	$2,400	$ 800	2	9
		$32,889		54	50

Fig 1   Branches of Industry in Connecticut Report, 1846

A HISTORY OF THE CLARK HILL FARM

by Clifford Clark, August 28, 1956

Across the road from the old Clark homestead is a three acre meadow. It is called cider mill lot. There once stood a big cider mill 35 feet square with a turndown in the middle and an arm on it to hitch an ox to mash the apples as it went round and round. I remember seeing that turndown before it was destroyed in 1892. It was a bright yellow color from the apples. Amos Hotchkiss ran that cider mill when he came back from the Revolutionary War in the 18th century.

Over the fence to the west is a narrow strip of land called the neck. My father and grandfather were plowing in the neck lot one day. They looked up, and across the cider mill lot, my father's two little sisters were coming towards them dragging a leather boot. They were so small they could not carry it. Their father asked them what they wanted. They said a lady called at their house the year before and gave them some peaches. These were the first peaches the little girls had ever seen. She told them to save the stones, put them in a leather boot, bury the boot, and dig it up the next year. Then they should put the stones where they would like to have peach trees grow. They put the stones on the side of the neck lot. My father said that some of these trees gave the most beautiful peaches he had ever seen. The names of the little girls were Marion Clark and Kate Clark.

At the funeral of Kate Clark, the procession of horses and wagons was more than one mile long before the church bell began to toll the years of her short span of life. My father told me that a great many people went to the funeral that no relative had ever heard of. People that knew Kate Clark considered her personality magnetic. Her husband, Harry L. Payne, who owns the Johns farm, put a monument in Prospect cemetery that has not been surpassed in 80 years.

East of the house is a meadow called Granny Winkle lot. I do not know how it got its name, but it has been called the Granny Winkle lot for more than 150 years. Over the fence is a well about 8 feet deep. One Good Friday morning, my grandfather was looking toward the well and saw black snakes coming out. He killed as many as he could. When he placed the dead snakes end to end, they reached 110 feet.

To the north is a clump of rosebushes. I never saw roses like them. I believe that very few people have ever seen such beautiful roses. I have heard that some people think that those bushes once belonged to Amos Hotchkiss in the 18th century.

To the east is a lot called rock lot. The first Merritt Clark drilled great slabs from an enormous boulder. Some of those slabs are 14 feet long. Four of them are the underpinning to the first hog house built in Prospect. It is on the town records. Leveritt Smith sharpened the drills. Also on the records, Amos Hotchkiss built the first plastered house in Prospect. The sand was carried in from the seashore by oxen. Today the plaster will discolor wallpaper just as badly as ever.

Under the south porch is a rock 10 feet by 4 feet by 15 inches, which probably weighs about six tons. There is a well hole drilled in one end. It was carried from Cheshire by oxen. East of that rock is a flat topped rock about 4 feet square with a rivulet around the edge. It is known as the lye rock. My great grandmother used to heat the lye and run it off into a brass kettle. That lye rock is one of the rarest antiques in the state of Connecticut.

South of the house stood a tower about 15 feet high with a bell on the top. There was a little roof over the bell and a string attached to the bell leading down toward the ground. It was known as the call bell. The first

Mrs. Clark used to call the help on her 325 acre farm with the bell. The tower was eventually taken down and the bell was placed on the top shelf in the old pantry.

In 1892, my father and Lavergne were working on the road one mile from the home in front of the house were Charles Hodges now lives.

A very small thundercloud came up. As they looked toward the cloud a bolt of lightning came down. My father said that it looks as if it came down at Clark Hill. Lavergne said:

Hark, I hear the call bell. The call bell is ringing. We have got to make a break for it. Lightning has struck at Clark Hill.

When they came down the road, the rafters on my father's big barn were burning. They told me it had been burning for 18 minutes. The pitch from the knots in the boards nearest the barn ran down nine inches. That was a close call. Marion Clark was ringing the call bell. That call bell was rung for a purpose 150 years ago. It has been rung for a purpose but once in the last 150 years.

THE PLUMB FARM HISTORY

by Tom Wheeler, 1995

The story goes, that back in 1880, when D.M. Plumb wanted to move to Wolcott, his father offered him the "Smith Place" if he would stay in Prospect. And so, Plumb Farm began.

All through the late 1800s and early 1900s, D.M. Plumb made a good living from the farm and a lucrative wood business, selling cord wood to Waterbury's brass mills and lumber to the area's expanding population. He raised a family of seven with two sons, Thomas and Frank, staying at home to work the farm. Over the years, they operated a fruit farm and roadside stand selling apples, pears, peaches, strawberries, corn, and garden vegetables and a dairy supplying milk and cream. They also delivered turnips and potatoes to Waterbury's east end by the truckload.

In 1959 both barns were burned by an arsonist. A diary entry from Anne Bird Plumb (Frank's wife) reads:

The barn burned, 3 cows saved. 6 A.M. Pouring water on the barn yet. 6 Animals burned to death.

That was the end of the dairy business. As the years went on, the orchards got old and the people got old. When Frank fell off a ladder picking apples and broke some ribs, that was the end of the fruit business.

They kept the stand and through the 1960s and 1970s the family was selling corn, berries, and a few apples and garden vegetables along a busier and busier Route 68. In the late 1970s David Plumb (D.M.'s great-grandson) briefly ran an herb farm on the property. Then, in the early 1980s, Frank's daughter Florine Plumb Wheeler put up a greenhouse and started selling geraniums and annuals as well as cut flowers and a more diverse collection of garden vegetables. In time she expanded to sell hanging baskets, Easter flowers, pumpkins, ornamental corn and the like.

In the spring of 1993, Thomas E. Wheeler (4th generation) and his business partner, David B. Rubino, came to Connecticut with very little money and a lot of energy, to take over the family business. They changed the name to Plumb Farms, built another greenhouse, created a sales area in the garage and offered lots of new products for sale.

Plumb farms is now a full service nursery and flower business selling annuals, perennial, fresh flowers, silk and dried flower arrangements and seasonal items like mums, pumpkins, Christmas trees and wreaths. There are display gardens, a quarterly newsletter

and plans for teaching. With lots of
ideas for the future, Tom and Dave plan

to bring Plumb Farms and its new focus
into the 21st century.

THE YANKEE PEDDLER

The Yankee peddler was an integral part of society in farm towns like Prospect. Without him, obtaining needed goods would have been most difficult. A trip to the shops of Waterbury, Cheshire, or Naugatuck would consume the better part of a day. But the peddler gave door-to-door service. His arrival was a much anticipated event. Children would run to greet his wagon as the banging of his pots, pans, and other wares signaled his approach as he bounced down the rocky roads.

Peddlers were a rather unkempt lot. Unshaven, dirty fast-talking, and often mistrusted, they were still welcomed for the goods they offered and the gossip they passed on from neighbors and other communities. The farmer or manufacturer would barter with the peddler to buy up their goods which the peddler could sell to others down the road. Before the Sears Roebuck catalog, this was the way people shopped in rural areas. Yankee peddlers carried an astounding array of small articles like clocks, chairs, books, scissors, fabric, hats, shoes, tools, and saddlery. They might offer matches, buttons, needles, or harness and carriage hardware which the peddlers could purchase from factories in Prospect.

Besides the traveling departments stores of the Yankee peddlers, there were many other products brought door-to-door in Prospect up until the 1960s. In early years a cobbler traveled about and boarded at a farm house for a few days or a week or more. In exchange for food and lodging and a small wage, he would make or repair shoes and other leather items for the household. When his work was done, he would move on to another house in need of his service. Other products delivered door-to-door were bread, milk, and eggs. As recently as the 1950s, haircuts were given in homes by traveling barbers.

MERCHANTS

One could not always wait for an itinerant peddler to pass by. Stores and shops were the source of many staple items not produced by the family. Some shopping was done in neighboring towns. In 1827 when Prospect was founded, it had only one general store. Asahel Chittenden ran that store with partners, starting in 1802. Ozro Collins kept the general store from 1829-1834, opening it before he was of age. In 1834 Julius Hotchkiss and Fredus Benham each owned half of a store. In 1838 Luther Morse was a store owner in addition to running a manufactory.

From the records of a general store run by George Payne in 1848, we know he sold *molasses, kalerco* [calico], *hayrakes*, a *pale* [pail], and *candlewicking*. This same store was later owned by Tyler and Bronson. Other book entries from Prospect general stores list *yards of tobacco, pints of gin, barrels of kerosene, vinegar*, and *skeins of thread*. On the credit side of the ledger there would be things such as butter, eggs, or other goods traded by the housewife for the store merchandise. These items would be put up for sale in the general store or sometimes taken to other stores in Waterbury or nearby towns.

MANUFACTURING

The development of factories and shops is a fascinating era in Prospect's history. With the dawn of the industrial revolution, many farmers in town saw the possibilities of setting up a factory to manufacture goods. Since farming in the rocky soil of Prospect was a marginal occupation at best, the idea of cashing in on the industrial craze was very tempting. Years of temperance and conservatism did not allow many to abandon their agricultural roots. Most manufacturing businesses were done as supplements to the farm

1 - Allen wire factory	9 - Kimball match factory
2 - Russell's mill	10 - Benjamin Beecher factory
3 - Obed Tuttle place	11 - Bone button factory
4 - Morris Road button factory	12 - Andrew Smith umbrella factory
5 - Luke Tyler match factory	13 - Match stick saw mill
6 - Brooks Hotchkiss match factory	14 - Lime kiln
7 - Luther Morse pocketbook factory	15 - Ezra Kimball match factory
8 - Richard Tyler / Samuel	16 - John Wallace match factory
Bronson match factory	17 - Rag Hollow (Fig 5 for details)

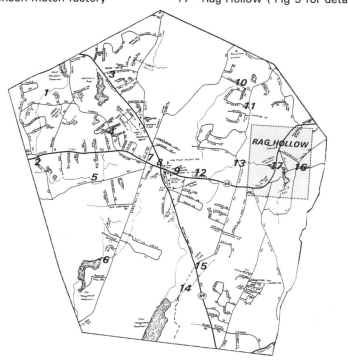

Fig 2   Location of manufacturing operations in Prospect.

work, often in the same location.

The term Yankee ingenuity has no greater meaning than in Connecticut. From the time the U.S. patent system began in 1790 until the 1930s, this state was a leader in patents granted. Connecticut averaged more than three times the number of patents per 1,000 residents than any other industrial area of the world. The peak of this activity occurred around the 1850s, a time when industry in Prospect was booming.

Prospect manufacturing can be divided into two categories. Those factories requiring water power were situated near streams or rivers. Most of the good water power was near the town borders where the slope of the land gave enough head to the water to turn the water wheels. The largest concentration of such industries was in a section known as Rag Hollow toward the Cheshire border. Industries not dependent on water power were scattered about town and often moved from one location to another (Fig 2).

MATCH FACTORIES

The manufacture of matches was a major industry for Prospect. The first parlor matches made in this country were from the Prospect factory of Ives & Judd. These gentlemen went to England and brought back a man named Gardner who knew how to make matches. They built a factory which created quite a sensation in town and attracted people from surrounding areas who were lured by the high wages. The pay was good because the work was very hazardous.

The matches were cut and then dipped by hand, first into brimstone and then into phosphorous. Fumes from the latter caused phosphorus necrosis or "phossy jaw" as it was known among the workers. It led to gangrene of the jaw and certain death. This condition was most common among men who would accumulate phosphorous on their beards. The fumes made their first inroads through the teeth, so many workers tried to protect themselves by having their molars examined frequently. Those who were careless were often stricken with the disease and died painful deaths. Even with the dangers well known, there was no shortage of workers willing to take the risk for the money. Heavy drinking was common among the match workers who had resigned themselves to an early grave. Besides the health hazards there was a high risk of fire at these factories. At least two of Prospect's biggest match factories burned to the

Fig 3   John Holley Jr. stands where match saw mill water wheel would have been positioned.   Peter Thiel watches from above.   Michael J. Holley

ground. No doubt residents found new meaning to the expression of *fire and brimstone* heard from the pulpit.

Prior to 1860 there were fifty to seventy people employed in making matches. It was a business that created a demand for other services. The boxes in which the matches were placed for sale were made in homes around town by women and children. Stephen Talmadge delivered raw materials to the homes and picked up the finished boxes. On Matthew Street a saw mill, opposite John Holley's land, was designed especially to make the wooden sticks for matches (Fig 3). Shortly after the Civil War, the Diamond Match Company took over the entire operation, and any remaining buildings were used for other purposes.

By 1845 there were five match factories scattered all about town. There was one factory in back of the store owned by Kimball, opposite the current Meeting Place on Cheshire Road. Ezra Kimball had one or two factories on the New Haven Road. Another was on Straitsville Road and was owned by G. Mills Hotchkiss and operated by his son Brooks. Luke Tyler owned one on Salem Road near the place where his grandfather had a gristmill. Another match factory was owned by Richard Tyler and Samuel Bronson. It was located across from the cemetery gates. These buildings were cheaply made since the danger of fire was high. John Wallace made matches at a location west of his house. In 1850 the factory burned down, so he built another to the east. This one also burned and he built a third.

RAG HOLLOW

The section of Prospect along the Ten Mile River near the Cheshire border contained the highest concentration of industry in town. It had as many as fifteen factories and was a small but thriving, nearly self-sufficient village (Fig 5). There were shops and at least a dozen private homes. A fine school-house and a chapel were located nearby in the Mixville section of Cheshire. The area was called Rag Hollow or Ragville because Capt. William Mix invented the rag buffing wheel there. This simple device revolutionized the manufacture of britannia and pewter ware. Previously, each piece had to be painstakingly rubbed by hand to create the desired luster. With the rag wheel, the operation was fast and efficient. William Mix was too busy with his many enterprises in Prospect to patent his invention for which he could have reaped great rewards.

Rag Hollow had factories that made

Fig 4 Mill stones used by Capt. Mix, now at the Prospect Historical Society.   John Guevin

sewing needles, britannia and pewter ware, cutlery, buttons, button hooks, hardware, and wagon wheels. Factories right on the river received their power directly from the water flowing downstream. Those set back from the river were fed water through hollow logs (see photograph on back jacket cover).

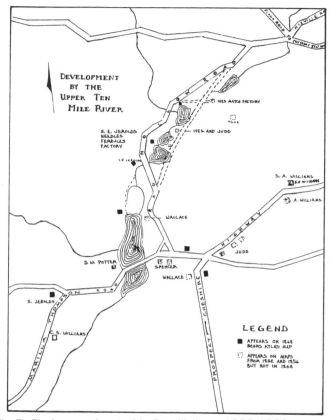

Fig 5   Businesses located in Rag Hollow, 1852-1868.

Melissa Paly

Capt. William Mix arrived in Prospect about 1820-1830. He established the first water privileges along the Ten Mile River, starting with a grist mill (Fig 4). He built a dam and later raised it to where the Cheshire Reservoir now stands. At that site he had a water wheel built by Andrew Smith, who lived up the road about a mile to the west, now called Plumb Farms. Burr Chatfield of Waterbury may have helped him build the wheel that was twenty feet in diameter. It had five buckets and furnished power for a number of the Captain's enterprises.

Mix had a pottery where he fashioned and glazed clay buttons and drawer pulls. Both were made in molds from clay and colored with saltpetre solution. This resulted in some fancy decorations for the Sunday coats of our

Prospect ancestors. Working with Robert Wallace and later by himself, he produced pewter spoons, tea pots, and coffee pots. The spoons were made with the handle and bowl separate then later joined together. It was here that Capt. Mix got the idea for the rag wheel. Edgar Wallace, who was a child at the time, recalled in 1928:

> *The pewter spoon factory which Mr. Mix operated stood about a stone's throw from the house where I was born and now live. It was Mix's manufacturing of the spoons which resulted in the invention of the wheel. Up to that time, he hired women to polish each bowl and handle by hand. To his thrifty New England mind, this process seemed not only too slow but too expensive. So he set his mind working and finally evolved the wheel. It consisted of several thicknesses of cotton cloth held between iron clamps. Revolving quickly by means of foot pressure, polishing the spoons became much faster and more effective than by the old process. While Capt. Mix worked only in pewter, Robert and John Wallace (my father and uncle) began making spoons out of German silver in Prospect. They later moved this operation to Quinnipiac.*

Waterbury Republican, August 19, 1928

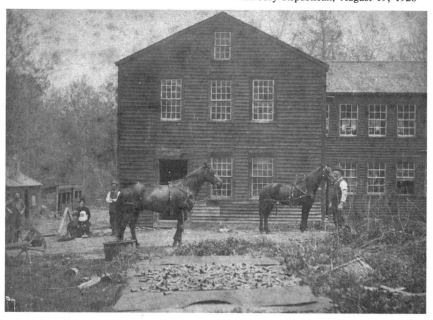

Fig 6   Jeralds and Lawton factory made hoe ferrules on the Cheshire Road. Steel handles for buttonhooks and tableware were also made here until about 1900. S.E. Jeralds is at the right holding his horse, and Lawton is at the left at the corner of the building. Ferrules spread to dry after brazing and pickling are in the foreground.   Waterbury Republican-American, 1947

In 1836 Andrew Smith was in partnership with Hervey Dwight Hotchkiss and Robert Wallace in the making of spoons at the next mill below Capt. Mix. They had a patent for strengthening cast britannia spoons by inserting a wire in the handle. After a while they sold their patent, and the plant was moved to Yalesville. According to Rockey (*History of New Haven County*), Sherman Blakeslee and Harris Smith took over the operation in the fall of 1839 from Smith and Wallace. They improved the power and continued to make spoons, coffee pots, and tea pots of britannia ware. Smith withdrew, and Blakeslee continued alone until selling out to David Hotchkiss and Robinson Williams. From 1849-1854 Bennett Jeralds and Eli Ives had that line of manufacture before selling the business to Charles Parker, which he later moved to Wallingford.

According to the 1850 industry census, three other hardware manufacturers were located downstream from Mix. David R. Williams employed about twenty people in the manufacture of suspender buckles and other small steel and brass items. William Wilcox had six employees producing tin spoons and other hardware. Fourteen workers manufactured the same products at the firm of Ives and Jeralds.

A town map in 1868 shows the Wm. Mix grist mill and spoon shop next the factories of Jeralds and E. Mix, then just before the intersection of Plank Rd., a match shop and cutlery factory. Andrew Smith and his brother started the first factory in the country entirely devoted to the production of sewing machine needles. It was located about midway between the dam and the Cheshire town line. John Isbell and J.E. Jeralds, then Nettleton and Lawton, expanded the line to include hoe ferrules, steel handles for buttonhooks, and tableware along with the sewing machine needles (Fig 6). About 1890 they made patented knife handles for the Meriden Cutlery Company. Toward the end they produced bicycle wrenches. At one time forty people were employed in a busy plant that was one of the few companies surviving until 1900. When Edgar Wallace was a boy, he worked in the sewing machine needle shop.

> *Even though I was only a boy, I earned $100 a month. The same salary is not even earned by many boys today [1928]. The needles were all made by hand too, by that I mean that they were molded and the holes punched by crude machines worked by hand. It was very close work but the pay was so good that there were always plenty to be found to do it. At that time they were sold at wholesale for $60 a thousand. Today they are worth probably $9 a thousand.*

Edgar Wallace, Waterbury Republican, August 19, 1928

The water power below Jeralds was used in the manufacture of matches by Wilcox, Tyler & Bronson, Ives & Bagley, and last by E.P. Dunham. Not far below the match factory was the buckle shop of David R. Williams described at the top of this page. The Williams property passed to Titus Mix who had three small mills and shops.

OTHER MANUFACTURING

Northwest of Rag Hollow, on Juggernaut Road, was the factory of Benjamin Dutton Beecher. Beecher was an eccentric, but brilliant individual. He invented and patented the first fanning mill. This device winnowed or separated the chaff from grain by means of a current of air from a fan. Later he invented the first screw propeller for use in a steamboat. Andrew Smith is credited with making the parts for the screw. It was assembled in Beecher's factory and first tested on Juggernaut Pond. They dismantled and took it to Beachport in Cheshire where one test run was conducted on the Farmington Canal with somewhat dismal results. Most history accounts do not give Prospect or Beecher credit for this major invention which others would improve and perfect.

On Matthew Street there were two enterprises. Near Cheshire Road was the match stick saw mill described earlier. Farther north, near the Walter Morse house, was the bone button factory owned by Obed Tuttle. This factory employed eight women and five men. Obed also operated a business on Waterbury Road opposite Maria Hotchkiss Road. He made scythes and axes that were renowned for their superior quality. Another of his enterprises made iron ferrules for hoes, forks, and rakes. In 1845 his shovel, fork, and hoe factory produced $7,000 of goods and employed ten men. Tuttle's operations grew so much, that he moved to Naugatuck where more water power was available. Eben Tuttle, the son of Obed, invented the goose-neck hoe. This tool utilized a curved piece of spring steel between the blade and the handle, relieving the user of shoulder-shock when using the tool. Beginning in 1822 and continuing for nearly twenty-five years, Eben forged hoes in Straitsville and finished them in his shop just over the line in Prospect. Like his father, he eventually moved to the more lucrative market of Naugatuck in 1846.

Fig 7 Pocketbook factory of Luther Morse on Union City Road.

Prospect Historical Society

On Cheshire Road, near the center of town, Harris Smith manufactured umbrella trimmings at the site of the present Plumb Farms. He employed seven men and eight women in 1845, turning out $4,500 worth of merchandise until interest declined. Also on Cheshire Road, there was a blacksmith shop as early as 1812. It was succeeded by one owned by Elias Mix. His brother-in-law, Henry Judd, owned a shop nearly across the street where metal buttons were made. These were enameled and japanned, then taken to Beachport for shipment to New York by canal.

A factory on Morris Road, opposite the old Morris house, made buttons of vegetable ivory. This business later merged with one in Naugatuck. Not far west on the north side of Clark Hill Road was a factory owned by Edward Allen in 1856. A map of 1860 identified it as Allen's Wire Factory. Just west of the center of town, where Harry Stieler later made his home, Luther Morse owned and operated a leather pocketbook factory in an el of the house (Fig 7). In 1845 two men and nine women were employed and produced $2,000 worth of merchandise.

On the corner of New Haven Road and Talmadge Road, Kimball had a factory making brass thimbles at one time. Across the road, in the present water company property, was a lime kiln which was abandoned when the limestone was exhausted. On Spring Road near the Naugatuck line, the H. D. Russell factory had the first power on the Fulling Mill Brook. This factory made bone buttons in 1850 and by 1856, manufactured harness and carriage trimmings. There was a saw mill toward the Waterbury line on one of the upper tributaries of the Turkey Hill Brook.

By the dawn of the twentieth century nearly all manufacturing in Prospect had ground to a halt. Many of the leaders in Prospect's industrial boom had left to make their fortunes in Waterbury, Naugatuck, Cheshire, or New York. The cities became the centers of industry. With their abundant supply of immigrant labor and better transportation systems, they offered what factories needed. Water power was replaced by steam and electric engines. The rivers cascading down from Prospect to the east, west, north, and south were no longer needed to turn the wheels of industry. Except for a few merchants, Prospect retreated to what it knew best — its agricultural roots.

~

Chapter Ten

Roads

Before the first European settlers came to Prospect, the Indians cut trails across the landscape and kept them open by burning brush along the walkways a few times a year. These routes avoided major boulders, swamps, and steep hills. It is only logical that some of these trails were widened and improved into the early roads of the 1700s. The Indians followed these paths to reach their Prospect hunting grounds and probably found them useful alternatives to the muddy trails at lower elevations during rainy periods. The Quinnipiac trail was the first to be designated in the Connecticut Blue Trail System in 1928. It stretches from Mt. Carmel to Wolcott, running along the Cheshire-Prospect border ridge. The path was continuous through Prospect until development of streets and houses truncated it at the junction of Chatfield Road and Route 68.

The first roads were laid out by the parent towns of Waterbury and Wallingford over a century before Prospect was incorporated. Each town chose two surveyors. These officials had the authority to summon all men between 16-60 years of age for one day per year to mend the highways. One early project was the laying out of the Backbone Road across Prospect connecting the New Haven road to Waterbury. Only the largest boulders and tree stumps were removed from the path.

The next day [Dec. 16, 1717], and it was December weather, two surveyors, Thomas Hikcox and John Bronson, laid out a 4 rod highway to Thomas Andrew's land at Turkey Hill. This was, in part, the same Prospect road that now passes in sight of the Turkey Hill reservoir. It is described as beginning at East Main street [Waterbury] (they called it the Country Road) . . . eastwardly up the East Mountain where the road now is [Hamilton Avenue], across one corner of Samuel Porter's farm, south by the east side of it, and along the west end of Thomas Andrew's land.

The same day they laid out a 4 rod highway from the New Haven road across the south end of the "Abrigado" to the above East Mountain road. History of Waterbury

A whole network of roads was created on the Wallingford side, which constituted two-thirds of what would become Prospect (see Chapter 3, Fig 3).

In 1803 a petition and citation from Columbia society respecting the laying out of a new highway came before the town, and Andrew Hull, Esq., was appointed agent for the town with "discretionary powers"; and at another meeting Burrage Beach was appointed to act with Mr. Hull in the matter . . . In 1805 Ebenezer Hough, Jared Bishop and John Peck were appointed "to view the Ground from the Turnpike road, near the meeting house to the highway which runs by the dwelling house of Joseph I. Doolittle for the purpose of locating a highway between said Roads and to obtain proposals from the proprietors of Lands: and make report to the next annual Town meeting." The determination to keep these highways in proper shape is shown by the purchase soon after of twelve scrapers for work on highways "to be used for that purpose and for no other."

"Floods of Water & Ice" caused much trouble in 1807, for at a special town meeting in February a tax of "one cent five mills on the dollar" was voted to be levied upon the "List of the Polls and Rateable Estate of the Inhabitants & non-resident proprietors of sd Town" for "repairing the Bridges, & other charges."

Joseph Platt was the collector of the tax in Columbia Society. . . The town in 1814 voted to lay out a road "from the notch of the mountain near Mr. Jesse Humiston's to intersect the Waterbury road near Enos Moss's" but Henry Brooks and others petitioned for a special town meeting, which was called when a motion was offered to reconsider the "vote passed at the Annual Town Meeting" to lay out this new road. Gen. Andrew Hull, Jr. and Amos Baldwin Esq. opposed the motion and after "considerable debate the question of order of the motion was withdrawn." However, a second motion on the assessment of damages, and directing the selectmen to "open said road in due time" was voted in the negative.

During the following years the road from the "Notch of the Mountain" to the Waterbury old road was widened and improved, a road from Joshua Ives' to Prospect Line laid out, and the highway from the notch of the mountain to Waterbury authorized, and from time to time other highways were opened, or the old ones repaired and improved as seemed most for the interest of town, without very much discussion.

History of Cheshire

After Prospect was incorporated, the construction and maintenance of roads continued to be a subject of great interest and constituted a sizable portion of the town's budget. The figures in the 1898 Prospect town report are typical (Fig 1). One can only wonder if the repairs to the houses were the result of

Fig 1 PROSPECT TOWN REPORT ROAD EXPENSES 1898	
Grading	$ 1,246.40
Dynamite caps & fuses	22.65
Wire & exp.	14.89
Repair to houses	5.25
Leveling for survey	1.62
Advertising	12.75
Total	$ 1,303.56

the dynamite use. Roads were constantly being repaired. New roads were created and some old roads were abandoned. In 1901 it was voted to "discontinue that portion of an old highway leading from the Prospect Railroad station to where it meets the highway near Elmer Brooks." In 1906 Prospect closed "the road called the Erwin Mix road from the Prospect Station on the Meriden and Waterbury Rail Road to the road known as Matthew Street."

The road surfaces in Prospect went through an evolution of improvements.

Some of the major dirt roads were upgraded to gravel roads, beginning in the 1920s (Fig 2). Later, the use of a mixture of oil and sand on the surface was common practice. It was better than gravel but had to be renewed almost every year. It was not until 1968 that Prospect began to use asphalt on its own roads. First Selectman George A. Sabo, Jr. followed a sugges-

Fig 2 from the CT State Register. . . Miles of Prospect roads in 1932:	
Gravel	1.51
Trunk & State Aid	6.53
Unimproved	28.21

Total	36.25

tion from the contractor who was doing the road work. About 28 miles could be done in asphalt for about the same cost as 36 miles of oil-sand coating. The asphalt would also be guaranteed for 8 years. Some of these original asphalt roads are still in use today.

The state roads (now called Routes 68 and 69) underwent major changes. They were widened and the sharper turns were removed. In some sections the roadbed was shifted to new locations. All of this was the subject of much debate in town. No stronger opinions were expressed than in 1931 when the debate raged over the placement of the Bethany-Waterbury Turnpike (now Route 69) through Prospect center. Poetry was used to influence public opinion for and against a by-pass around the Prospect Green.

FOR

Friends, Fellow Citizens.
Stand! the Green is your own, to hold
For the children of Prospect fold,
For the grass so green on the mold,
For library, worth more than gold
To Prospect — now a century old.
Spoil not these treasures of today.
Build the new road a safer way.
Fannie Clark, March 10, 1931

AGAINST

Make a road right through the Green
So our natural beauty may be seen.
Build a road with modern skill
Let travelers by, see our hill.
To our library standing high
Keep it in sight for passers-by.
For the children going to school
Make a road that's free of pools.
To the monument of our honored dead
Place it where it may be seen and read.
Time will come when we may add
A green much larger than we ever had.
H.W. Talmadge, 1931

In the end, those who advocated the preservation of the Green won. The state road from Bethany to Waterbury by-passed the center to the west (Fig 3). But there would be other battles with more victories and some losses. When the state roads were widened, many residents were upset that the old trees along the roadside were cut down.

> *Route 68 to Cheshire was bordered with cherry trees. The kids would feast on them in season as they walked to and from the center of town. Route 69 going toward Waterbury was lined on both sides with large maple trees that formed an arch over the road [see photograph on back jacket cover]. We should have organized to stop the cutting and preserve the beauty.*   Gloria Stieler, 1994

The citizens of Prospect did speak out and forced the state to alter its plans for widening Route 69. The original design would have put the road within a few feet of the front door to the historic Hotchkiss house. Earlier in 1934 the new Prospect-Waterbury Road was built. This road took out many of the curves from the original route which went via Murphy Road, along the reservoir, then snaked back and forth along Hamilton Avenue in Waterbury.

Fig 3 Looking south on the state road in 1939. The original highway was via Center Street to the left, while the by-pass is the present Route 69 to the right.

Waterbury Republican-American

The course of both state roads has been altered over the years. The southern part of Route 69 (formerly State Road № 348) passed near the New Naugatuck Reservoir and connected with the Cheshire-Naugatuck Road (current Route 42) in Bethany. Route 68 was known as State Road № 325. The early road to Cheshire went right across the Cheshire Reservoir before that area was closed-off within the New Haven Water Company property. Driving was difficult along the Union City Road when construction was begun in 1939 to make the road wider and straighter. The original road jogged along via Hydelor Avenue. The rewards for all of these road changes were great improvements in travel through Prospect. Prior to this time, most travelers avoided the hills of Prospect and went around the town, either through Naugatuck or Cheshire.

NEW PROSPECT ROAD HOLDS ALLURE FOR RIDER AND HIKER

People living today in the New Haven metropolitan area or in the built-up towns adjacent find it hard to realize that there remains close to virgin country, wooded hills and valleys, uncultivated, with dwellings far apart, country like that through which the Aborigines roamed three hundred years ago.

Today one can leave his home by automobile and fairly fly across the Connecticut countryside, at no time being far from the sight of a gasoline station or hot-dog stand. And yet within ten miles of the New Haven Green and closer even than that to Waterbury and heavily populated towns of the Nauga-

tuck Valley, there has just been opened a rural area that is as rugged, as wild and wooly, as any region in New England. This territory, truly a wilderness such as not only surprises the people of modern New Haven, but would have been a wilderness in grandfather's day, has been made available by motor cars through the completion the past week of a new direct state highway to Waterbury by way of Prospect.

. . . The scenery surpasses description . . . the wide vistas from the high Prospect Hills, that would do justice to the upper Berkshires . . . You traversed a country during the twenty-minute drive that up to now has echoed only to the heavy rumbling of ox-carts.

Folks who remember that road as it has been will recall that for auto travel at least it was impossible. After a half-mile of that kind of travel, the driver usually turned back towards Bethany and if he chose to approach Prospect, did so either by way of Waterbury, Cheshire or Union City.

The New Haven Register, October 29, 1933

Fig 4   Aerial view of Prospect center (looking west along present Route 68) showing proposed traffic rotary in 1941. The stone Congregational Church and old parsonage (lower left) would both be destroyed before the year was over. The area around the present town hall (lower right) was the Wallace farm.

Waterbury Republican-American

The improvements in Prospect's roads brought a vast increase in traffic through town. The state highways now provided a quick and easy connection between surrounding towns. The crossing of the state highways at the center proved to be a dangerous intersection (Fig 4). The combination of speed, steep hills, and frequent fog led to numerous accidents — some of them fatal.

Stop signs were often disregarded; a traffic rotary was proposed. The rotary was never constructed and it was May 19, 1956, before an automatic traffic signal was put into service. Another thirty-eight years passed before Prospect had additional traffic lights. In 1994 signals were installed at the intersection of Scott Road and Route 69 as well as at Old Schoolhouse Road and Route 68. Many new Prospect roads were laid out, starting in the 1950s as new housing subdivisions were constructed.

The Prospect Development Co. started one [subdivision] off Scott Rd. and Saunders La. It is called Williams Drive and Sherwood Dr. Williams Dr., known as Section 1, is made up of half-acre lots and Sherwood Dr., known as Section 2, is made up of one acre lots.

Knapp Dr. has been practically completed with only a few lots left on Barry La. This project consists of about 54 homes. Sunrise Dr. and Laura La. are part of the Sunset Heights project. This project is located off of Matthew St. The builder intends to put up another 15 homes next spring. Corinne Dr., off Union City Rd., and Dupreay Rd. and Anthony Rd,. off Morris Rd., another project, will commence this spring. A new project, called Cedar Hill Park, is located off Union City Rd., formerly the Johns property.

The owner intends to extend a road from Union City Rd. to connect with Salem Rd. a distance of about 2000 feet. Split level and ranch type homes will be featured in this project with a prospect of the building of about 40 homes on this site.

Dogwood and Spruce Drs., off Talmadge Hill Rd., is already building up. The builder has completed and sold about 10 homes this year and plans about 12 for next year.

A new project still in the rough is that of the Raggozini property on Union City Rd. This road will extend from Union City Rd. to Straitsville Rd. About 27 homes are planned for this project which will start next spring.

Waterbury Republican-American, 1958

At one time bus service was provided to Prospect. Beginning in 1934 CR&L buses came to the center of Prospect. When the trolley stopped running about 1935, the use of buses increased. A loyalty developed between the passengers and bus drivers. Mr. McElligot was the driver for many years on the Prospect run. He would chide commuters if he saw them accepting a ride from a passing car rather than take his bus. When someone returned from Waterbury by bus but had not taken the outbound trip that day, Mr. McElligot would jokingly ask the passenger where their bike was. The drivers were very considerate and would patiently wait while a forgotten lunch or package was retrieved. When automobiles became more prevalent, the bus ridership declined until service to Prospect was discontinued.

Nearly half of the 51.1 miles of public roads in Prospect are named for families or individuals. The most recent example is Hughes Court which was renamed from Williams Drive Extension. This road has been populated by members of the Hughes family since it was built in 1990. Selecting the name for the court was obvious.

Early roads in town were often named for their destination. Examples are Waterbury Road, Cheshire Road, "Road to old Gunn Place," and "Road or Drive around the Green." Matthew Street was the only "street" in town when Prospect began, although there are more today. The names have changed over time and multiple names often exist for the same road. Route 69 was first the Backbone Road. It was also State Road Nº 348. Another designation was the Bethany-Waterbury Turnpike. The northern end has been called the Waterbury Road throughout its history, but the southern part has been called the New Haven Road or the Bethany Road or a combination of both.

There is a document entitled *Prospect Roads* at the Historical Society, the date and author of which are not known.   It suggests new names for some of the existing roads. A few of these were adopted such as Porter Hill Road for the "Road by Horatio Clarke's." Other suggestions were not carried through

Fig 5   Delia Fields behind the wheel of one of the first automobiles in Prospect, purchased by Albert D. Field in 1916.
Rev. Alida B. Wolfe

like calling Waterbury Road "Columbia Highway" or renaming Straitsville Road to "Boundlyne Road." With the latter, it is interesting to note that Straitsville road was part of the ancient Waterbury-Wallingford boundary which extends in a nearly straight line through Wolcott where the name of Boundline Road was retained. This Historical Society document contained the names of only thirty-one Prospect roads which existed at that time compared to over one hundred forty in town today.

~

Chapter Eleven

A Turnpike, A Railroad,
and A Trolley Line
by Boardman W. Kathan

A turnpike, a railroad, and a trolley line ran through the northeastern corner of Prospect in the latter part of the 19th century or early in the 20th century. The motivation for each form of transportation was to find a more direct and easily negotiable route between the growing industrial center of Waterbury and the population centers in central and southern Connecticut and beyond. Because the Naugatuck River was not navigable, several generations of entrepreneurs sought a way to move raw materials, finished products, and people between the western highlands and the Quinnipiac and Connecticut River valleys. In so doing, they hoped to reduce the cost of freight and lessen the amount of time for travel. The completion of the Naugatuck River valley railroad in 1849 from Derby provided one possible route, but other alternatives were sought, especially after the building of the Northampton line through Cheshire to New Haven in 1848.

Early roads up the Prospect and Southington mountains were very difficult for oxen and horse drawn vehicles because of the steep grades, rocks, and swamps on the mountain. An article in the 1922 *New Haven Register* about the old Plank Road toll house expressed it this way:

> *Almost a full century ago travel between Waterbury, Cheshire, and Meriden was very poor and much more of a hazard than a pleasure trip. Not only was the road narrow and winding, but it was in a very poor condition as well. Heavy boulders were strewn along the thoroughfare and deep ruts and huge puddles resembling miniature lakes, were quite common.*

The Plank Road turnpike, laid out by the Waterbury and Cheshire Plank Road Company in 1853, was the first road built to traverse these formidable obstacles through a corner of Prospect, and it was followed by the Meriden, Waterbury, and Conn. River Railroad in 1888 and the Cheshire Street Railway Co. in 1904. Each paralleled the other because each had a common destination in the City of Waterbury and each took advantage of "The Notch" in the mountains as the most convenient gateway to the western highlands.

To quote the book, *Landmarks of Old Cheshire*:

> *The Notch, one of Cheshire's singular landmarks, is the easiest access through the long trap-rock ridge all the way from New Haven. Few people in town today remember when not only a road but also trolley tracks and a railroad trestle ran through the Notch.*

THE WATERBURY AND CHESHIRE PLANK ROAD COMPANY

Lou Mortison, the syndicated columnist and cartoonist who lived in Prospect, wrote under the name of "Lester Green," and his Nov. 16, 1947 piece about the Plank Road, began with this rhyme:

> *In the days of old*
> *The knights were bold*
> *All 'ruds' were dirt*
> *An' dusty —*
> *'You're wrong,' says Hank*
> *Some roads were plank*
> *But surrey wheels were rusty.*

Mortison was familiar with the stories of the old Plank Road which ran through his part of the town of Prospect.

In fact, the Plank Road, built between Waterbury and Cheshire through a corner of Prospect, was the only plank road ever completed in the State of Connecticut despite the fact that seven plank road companies were chartered by the General Assembly between 1851 and 1853. At least this was the conclusion of Frederic J. Wood in his book, *The Turnpikes of New England*, published in 1919. Wood listed six different companies which never succeeded in building such a road and then declared: "But one charter was granted which was not issued in vain." The author devoted a paragraph in his book to the Waterbury and Cheshire Plank Road, which extended from the Cheshire depot on the Northampton Railroad to the corner of East Main Street in Waterbury, where the entrance of Hamilton Park is located today. The route was about 8 miles long and was shown prominently on the 1855 map of New Haven County.

Ann Fennelly, a features writer for the Cheshire Herald, expressed surprise that the road was indeed constructed of timber planks. After hearing my presentation to the Cheshire Historical Society, she wrote: "Many are unaware that this bucolic byway was once a busy turnpike . . ."

Wood wrote that the first charter for a plank road in New England was granted in 1849 to the St. Albans and Richford Plank Road Company in Vermont. According to Wood, only a half dozen such roads were ever built in New England and all in Vermont except for this one in the Prospect area. The first plank roads ever built in North America were those constructed in Canada in the 1830s, but others followed, especially in New York State. There were those who argued that plank roads were better than the new macadam roads because they could carry heavier loads, offer less resistance, and cost less to build and maintain. The plank road was offered as a superior alternative since it was an all-weather road for every season. The main purpose of this kind of road was to connect industrial cities with the surrounding countryside and provide passage for farm produce, raw materials, and manufactured goods, thereby increasing commerce and communication for the homes and factories of the city.

Prior to the building of the Plank Road, there were two ways of travelling from the Cheshire railroad station to Waterbury. One was the Old Waterbury Road which was not direct and was hard to negotiate. The other was the Notch Road which was developed after the New Haven-Northampton Canal was built in 1827-28. This road ran from the Notch through Mixville and up a steep incline to Matthew Street, then up to Summit Road, and after a sharp corner, it veered to the left on what is now Old Scott Road. It followed this to the present Scott Road and then down the hill into Waterbury. There was another way west from Cheshire to Prospect and Naugatuck on what is now called Ives Row, then over a pass called Jacks Road, and then up Rag Hollow Road or Tucker Road and Mix Road to Prospect center.

When the New Haven-Northampton Railroad line replaced the canal after 1848, it opened up many possibilities for commerce and trade to New Haven harbor, to New York City, to Hartford, and to Boston. On May 5, 1852, a group of 58 merchants and others in the New Haven and Waterbury area petitioned the General Assembly, meeting in the old State House on New Haven Green, to build a plank road from Cheshire to Waterbury. Their petition began as follows:

That the public highways leading from the town of New Haven to the town of Waterbury are circuitous and hilly, and the transportation of freight between those towns, as well as the public travel, is attended with much expense and delay which might be avoided by the construction of a plank road from some point in the town of Cheshire to said town of Waterbury, and that the public accommodation would thereby be much promoted.

The petitioners asked for permission to take the necessary land and to locate and establish toll gates. Among the signers were such names as Ives, Leavenworth, Tuttle, Sperry, Lucius Hotchkiss, C.F. Hotchkiss, Lewis Mix, H.M. Upson, A. Sanford. There was also a petition supporting this plank road signed by 64 persons in Watertown. On June 22, 1852, the Joint Standing Committee on Roads and Bridges of the General Assembly recommended adoption of a resolution incorporating the Waterbury and Cheshire Plank Road Co. The incorporators were: William H. Scovill, William H. Ellis, John P. Elton, Arad Welton, William Johnson, John S. Griffing, Lucius R. Finch, Benjamin Noyes, and Lucius G. Peck. Capital stock amounted to $20,000 which could be increased to an amount not exceeding $40,000. Shares were sold at $50 each.

The company was given permission to erect one or more toll gates upon the road, but they had to be at least three miles apart. The toll was not to exceed: 3 cents per mile for any vehicle drawn by two animals; ½ cent per mile for every additional animal; 1½ cents per mile for every vehicle drawn by one animal; ¾ cents per mile for every horse and rider or led horse; and for mules, cattle, sheep, and swine 1 mill per mile for each; provided that no tollgate shall be erected as to obstruct or hinder free travel on any public highway. As with other turnpikes, people did not have to pay toll if they were travelling to church or to a funeral, or serving on a jury.

The town meeting in Cheshire on Oct. 4, 1852 voted to give the plank road the right of way to occupy the common road to the Waterbury line by giving the people free travel to the line or within the limits of the town. This included the road already in existence from the Cheshire RR station to the Notch, and the road from Matthew Street, crossing Summit Road up to where the Old Scott Road turns off to the left.

On March 9, 1853, a hearing was held on the proposed route at the office of Arad Welton near the RR station in Cheshire. During 1853 the land was surveyed and purchased for the plank road. The Town Clerk's office in Cheshire has on record 12 deeds conveying 14 parcels of land purchased in Cheshire and Prospect between May 13 and Dec. 2. Working our way west from the Notch, land was purchased from the John Humiston Estate, John Ives, Elias Brooks, Titus Mix, William Andrews, Erwin Mix, Lent Moss (Morse), Lois Blakeslee, George Hine, John Gillett, John and Ambrose Barnes. In each case the land for the road was 3 rods wide or 49½ feet. The pieces were sold for as low as $8.27 for 44½ rods and $10 for 51 rods, and as high as $475 for 140 rods from John Ives, probably because it was good farm land. The deed from Ives is unique because it specifies that a lead pipe running under the road shall not be disturbed, and the company is to build a cattle pass in a convenient place under the road. In several cases the seller is to build and maintain a fence on both sides of the road.

Building the plank road and grading up the mountain proved to be very difficult and expensive, and several swamps had to be filled in, all done by hand labor and teams. According to Charles Somers Miller (1858-1941), the planks were cut and sawn in the northern part of the state, primarily in Granby, and brought to Cheshire on the canal line, and then hauled over by oxen. In Miller's written recollection:

They were four inches thick and eight feet long, of hemlock. After the grading, chestnut stringers with the upper side hewed flat, were embedded in the road lengthwise, and to these the planks were spiked crossways. This all took two years, and it was not until 1854 that the planks were laid the whole length, from Silver Street in Waterbury to the Notch-in-the-Rocks in Cheshire. Then it was found so narrow that teams had trouble in passing each other on the planks. This called for widening each side with earth, which proved very expensive.

The original plan to earn money on the investment was to build tollgates on the Plank Road. One was to be in Cheshire, but at the town meeting on Oct. 3, 1853, the matter was tabled, as follows: "That the motion concerning erecting a tollgate on the plank road between the Railroad Depot and the Notch of the Mountains be laid on the table." One report was that a tollgate house was built in Cheshire near Tuckers Farm, at the intersection of Tress Road and Tucker Road, but there was no indication of this on the 1855 map. However, there is a tollhouse located on the 1868 map in Prospect at the present intersection of Plank Road and Cheshire Road (Fig 1). On Dec. 23, 1859, Titus Mix sold a small triangular piece of land to the company so the tollhouse could be built next to the wooden bridge over the Ten Mile River. The 1855 map does show a tollgate operating in Waterbury where the Plank

Road crossed Scott Road. These were the only two tollgates on the Plank Road, one in Prospect and one in Waterbury.

Fig 1 Plank Road gate house in Prospect.   Waterbury Republican, Dec. 8, 1935

Miller wrote that the tollgate consisted of a single straight pole that swung across the road and was held in place by a notch in a large post. The tollhouse was built with a large window facing the road, and at night a kerosene lamp shed its rays.

Long after the tollgate had ceased to function, the old tollhouse still stood in Prospect, *The New Haven Register* published an article with the incorrect title, "Old Cheshire Toll House Landmark of Bygone Days." One paragraph read as follows:

> *In those old days the old toll house on the Prospect road, located at the foot of a gently sloping hill, faced the north. In the front of the building there was a specially constructed window, built to extend out from the building itself to hold a lantern as a beacon for nocturnal travellers. Old Timers of that section, recalling the time when the road and toll gates were an important factor . . . say that this window always held a lantern at night as far back as they can remember, The house itself still stands, the same old structure as in those days, except for the fact that it now faces east.*

The evidence shows that the Plank Road opened up more commerce and travel between the Waterbury area and Cheshire and points north, east, and south. In 1858 there was a stage coach line from Waterbury to Meriden by way of Cheshire and the Plank Road, since this was found to be easier than the more direct route up or down Southington Mountain. There was also a report that the Plank Road took business away from the tavern at Prospect center, located north of the Green.

Jennie Beardsley Clapp, a long-time resident of Prospect, remembered living in the Prospect tollhouse with her mother and family. In a paper written about 1920 she recalled: "In October 1858 we moved to the Gate

House in Rag Hollow and lived there until the Fall of 1875 (or my mother did), when she broke up the home." She described the gate house as having a "mill by it and brook running a little east needing two bridges as the Prospect Road went one side and the Plank Road the other side of the little gate house." Further Mrs. Clapp remembered:

> For a number of years after we came to the gate to live, Col. Welton's stage coach with four horses went through the gate on its way to Meriden. I believe it was hung on leather springs or straps. It seemed to rock. There was a place in back to strap on trunks and a railing around the top. In the time of the war I've seen the top full of soldiers in their blue clothes.

The New Haven Register article added more information about this stage coach and its driver by the name of Thomas Welton:

> Every morning at 7 o'clock he would hitch up his team of black horses to the high coach, and drive out to collect his load. In the colder weather the passengers usually met him at the livery stables in Waterbury to insure a seat inside the vehicle. The coach itself was a large high affair such as is commonly seen in movies of the west. When the six seats inside were filled, the remainder of the travellers were forced to climb to the top of the old coach where there were 8 to 10 more seats. When these were filled the old hack would get under way and, as it trundled down the long plank road, could be heard miles away.

One can only imagine all of the other carriages, wagons, and carts pulled by horses or oxen which came by that gate house, carrying raw materials and manufactured goods, wood, hay and grain, farm produce, livestock — or the many single horses with riders going to a church meeting or town meeting or to call on a young lady, or to transact a business deal, or to go to work at the grist mill, the saw mill, the match factory, the blacksmith shop, the button factory. How many Yankee peddlers made their way along that road? How many pigs, goats, sheep, and cattle went to market? How many people missed the train in Cheshire because they were late getting down that road?

Not only did the Plank Road stimulate and facilitate trade and commerce, but it also opened up land outside the city of Waterbury in Prospect and Cheshire. For example, before the year 1853 was over, Erwin Mix had sold about 83 acres of land to Harry Moss and Harmon Payne, and the deed signed on Nov. 17 read that "The Waterbury and Cheshire Plank Road runs through said land in an Easterly and Westerly direction." Eleven years later that same piece of land was conveyed to the Benedict and Burnham Mfg. Co. of Waterbury. The deed indicated that it was bounded north "by the Plank Road so-called." The B. and B. Co. carted wood from its land by way of the Plank Road to Waterbury in order to fire its brass rolling mills. This company later became the American Brass Co.

The first house to be built on the Plank Road in Prospect, as far as the 1868 map is concerned, was by Andrew Oliver, who bought 3 acres from Erwin Mix in 1864. It is significant to note that Andrew Oliver was the first black landowner of record in Prospect. All that is left is the remains of a well between the former home of Frank Clyma and the Peaches.

The *Register* article mentioned one more notable character associated with the Plank Road, an elderly man by the name of Foster who was employed by the company to keep the road in repair and travelled about with a wheelbarrow. The article continued:

> *Each day the break of dawn would find this jolly old fellow out on the plank road, jogging along with his barrow of sand in his daily search for bad spots. This work of repairing the road was no small task, however, as the planks frequently split apart and slipped down into a swampy marshland. These breaks required instant repair, as it was not an uncommon thing for one of the horses on the stage coach to break a leg in them.*

As far as can be determined, the Waterbury-Cheshire Plank Road Co. gave up in 1875 after 23 years in existence. The road had apparently deteriorated and was not being maintained properly. On Oct. 5, 1874, there was a legal notice of a town meeting in Prospect "to take some action in regard to the plank road." At the meeting it was voted to repair the road described in the notice at a cost not to exceed forty dollars. There is no record of the road being turned over to the towns, but it was customary in those days for the towns to pick up where the turnpike company left off.

On Sept. 29, 1875, at the meeting of the Board of Directors of the Plank Road Co. held at the National Tradesman Bank in New Haven, it was voted to appoint Enoch Frost as agent of the corporation to sell and convey all real estate and other property which belonged to it. The gate house and ¼ acre of land in Prospect was sold to Titus Mix with the stipulation that the gate house was to be moved back and located upon the triangular piece of land at the expense of the corporation. The gate house in Waterbury with ½ acre of land was sold to Benjamin Wedge with the same kind of stipulation. Accounts differ as to whether the planks on the road were taken up or just covered with sand and gravel.

We may never know whether the Plank Road Co. made any profit from the turnpike. According to Miller, it was said that as an investment, the road never paid. The railroad up the Naugatuck River valley was opened several years before the Plank Road project, and the greater part of the freight was brought to Waterbury by that route. It was said, however, that the Waterbury manufacturers forced the railroad to reduce its rates by having some freight brought by the canal line and the Plank Road. Therefore, something was accomplished. Also, after the freight and stage traffic ceased, very little revenue was derived from the tolls at the gates. Local people found ways of getting around the tollhouse by taking what amounted to "shunpikes" or upper roads. The annual reports of the State of Connecticut listed the commissioners that were elected each year for the Plank Road Co. One such person was David R. Williams.

After the Plank Road Co. was dissolved, names of parts of the road were changed. In 1889 the Cheshire town meeting voted that the road from Maple Avenue past the RR station to the Notch be officially called West Main Street. From the Notch up to the Ten Mile River, it was called the Old Prospect Road or in Prospect, the Old Cheshire Road. The part of the road from the Townline Restaurant to Rolling Ridge Court behind the house at 260 Cheshire Road was not officially closed by the Town of Prospect until the early 1980s, long after Route 68 had been built through the area. In Waterbury not much is left of the Plank Road since it has been replaced by Capt. Neville Drive and I-84. At the very end near East Main Street it is called Hamilton Park Road.

Lou Mortison wrote humorously about the way that the new Interstate highway had turned the old Plank Road into a dead end as follows:

> I drove to where the road goes under the new highway, then took the first left. I was thinking what a fine entrance to the parkway or East Main St. This is when I found myself going around a circle down by the automobile graveyard and on my way back to where I came from. Why they built such a fine road just to reach the resting place of rusty, wrecked, and useless cars I can't figure out while they made the exits off the Plank Road and to the Main St. hardly wide enough for two cars to pass.

Yet, the Plank Road still exists in Prospect and runs through a corner of Cheshire to the Waterbury town line. People still use it to drive to Waterbury, using Austin Road to get onto I-84. Two other means of travel have been built, following much the same route as the Plank road, the railroad in 1888 and the trolley in 1904. But the last train ran in 1917 and the tracks were removed by 1924. The trolley gave in to the private automobile in 1935. Not much is left of the railroad and trolley lines, but the Plank Road still goes on with a different surface to be sure, and its name is a constant reminder of the only road ever built of planks in the State of Connecticut.

Whatever happened to the old tollhouse in Prospect? After it was sold to Titus Mix in 1875, it was moved to the back of a triangular lot and faced east toward the bridges on the Ten Mile River, rather than north up the Plank Road. In 1918 it was sold to John A. Chatfield and in 1920 to W.B. and Nellie Stone. A deed recorded on March 26, 1928 showed that the Stones sold the building and piece of land to the state of Connecticut for the building of State Highway 68. According to *The New Haven Register* article, a Mrs. George Kuehner was living in the building when it was "fast falling into decay." Bessie Mortison, who lived just west of the tollhouse, remembered that Mr. and Mrs. Babbitt lived in the tollhouse in 1919 before going to live at the Brookside Home in Waterbury.

MERIDEN, WATERBURY, AND CONN. RAILROAD

The story of the Waterbury and Cheshire Plank Road has not been told in much detail, but there have been several accounts of the railroad line that stretched from the Connecticut River in Cromwell all the way to Waterbury through Meriden, Cheshire, and Prospect. Glover A. Snow described the trials and tribulations of this railroad in the August 1953 publication of the Conn. Valley Chapter of the National Railway Historical Society. It has also been written up in newsletters of the New Haven Railroad Historical Society in 1982 and in an illustrated book of *Connecticut Railroads* by Gregg Turner and Melancthon W. Jacobus, published in 1986 by the Conn. Historical Society. On a personal note, I am indebted to my father-in-law, Herbert G. Clark of Cromwell, who has researched the material and also gathered a number of photographs from Col. C.B. McCoid of Middletown, who supplied the picture of the Prospect railroad station.

It was a group of businessmen and manufacturers in Meriden who conceived of a plan to build a railroad line to the Connecticut River and thereby find another way to move goods south to New York City and other Atlantic ports. For several decades the idea had germinated because of the feeling that the Consolidated Railroad (before it was called the New Haven Railroad) was charging unfair and discriminatory rates. The mere announcement of the proposed line stimulated Consolidated to lower the rates it charged to Meriden by 25%. Much credit goes to Horace C. Wilcox, president of a silverware company, prior to the International Silver Company, for taking leadership of the project with both energy and money.

Plans for the railroad were developed by September 1881 and sent to the state agencies for approval. It was to be called the Meriden and Cromwell Railroad, and the company was capitalized at $300,000, with $230,000 committed before the organizational meeting. At that meeting 150 leaders in the Meriden area received the project enthusiastically, as a result of which a board of directors was elected and Wilcox became President. By the following year the first equipment was purchased, consisting of an engine and five freight cars. Regular service began on the line on April 6, 1885.

The first years were filled with glowing reports. At one end of the line in Cromwell there were docks and coal-loading facilities, an engine house, turntable, and water tank. On the other end in Meriden, there were extensive railroad yards. Those people who got their freight to Meriden by 5 PM one day were assured of delivery in New York City by the next morning. Summer excursions were developed for vacationers on board the train to Cromwell and then on the steamers, "City of Springfield" and "Capital City" to Manhattan. Advertised in the Meriden papers in 1885 was a round trip from Meriden, leaving on Saturday and returning on Tuesday morning, as follows:

> *Excursion tickets, good for the trip only, for one passage and stateroom to New York and return, including use of a room three nights, giving excursionists an opportunity to visit seaside resorts in and around New York, Coney Island, Long Island, Rockaway, Glen Island, etc., Sunday and Monday . . .*

All for the cost of $4.25! In November it was reported to the stockholders that the line had earned 7% on their investment.

An extension of the railroad was considered to several places, including Wallingford, New Britain, and Bristol, but the most attractive site seemed to be the City of Waterbury. In his article Snow quoted a Waterbury newspaper in February 1887 which wrote about a revival of "the old railroad scheme." According to the newspaper account:

> *There is a movement on foot to build a railroad from Waterbury to Meriden to connect with the Meriden and Cromwell road. This would give Waterbury another tidewater connection for eight months of the year, increasing freighting facilities, and be a great convenience for passenger travel, as it would intercept the Canal, the Consolidated and Hartford and Connecticut Valley Railroad. Many of our business men look with favor on this project.*

The railroad directors approved the extension the following month, and plans went ahead. The Cromwell and Meriden Railroad Co. was not prepared for the problems and obstacles to be overcome to bring the line over the mountain to Waterbury. In the first place, in spite of a major campaign, Waterbury was unable to come up with the $200,000 which represented its share of the capital. Meriden had to contribute $75,000 toward the amount. Secondly, the grades were not difficult until the workers moved beyond West Cheshire. According to Snow: "The real climb began then. From West Cheshire station, a little beyond the Canal Road to Summit was three miles, with an elevation of about 549 feet." From the Canal line, this represented a climb of close to 300 feet. The steepest grade was 112 feet to the mile. In the third place, there was the difficulty of negotiating with over 200 landowners, and this proved to be a more expensive proposition than was anticipated.

Fig 2 Prospect wooden trestle.
Connecticut Railroads,
Connecticut Historical Society

Fourthly, there was vigorous opposition by other railroad lines to having the new railroad cross them. Again, Snow wrote that the New Haven Railroad, which controlled both the Canal line and the Naugatuck line, claimed they "owned the land under the railroad from the center of the earth to the stars above." There was a feeling that no railroad had the right to cross another one without a special act of the General Assembly. Finally, the weather caused some major delays when the line was being constructed through Prospect. The Blizzard of 1888 hit on March 12, and work could not resume until March 20 when the snow was finally shoveled off the road. In spite of all the problems, the line was completed, a distance of nearly 19 miles from Meriden to Waterbury. It might be called the story of "the little railroad that could!"

By May 1888 the new railroad was christened as the Meriden, Waterbury, and Connecticut River Railroad. The capital stock amounted to $500,000 plus bonds, and the company owned three locomotives, five Pullman-built passenger coaches, and 160 freight cars. Inside each passenger car there were 14 seats on each side. The seats had arms of carved cherry wood; there were racks for luggage; heating pipes ran the length of the car; lighting was supplied by three large and beautifully finished chandeliers; even the toilets were well furnished.

Five special cars carried stockholders from Waterbury to Meriden for a meeting in Meriden. The story was related by Snow of a Cheshire farmer in an old fashioned top carriage, who decided to race the train. He departed the Dublin Street station in Waterbury at the same time the train did and took already existing roads to Cheshire. Apparently, he reached Cheshire two minutes ahead of the train and "was happy as a clam."

The grand opening was on the Fourth of July 1888. The newspaper carried the story:

> *The formal and public opening happened auspiciously on the nation's 112th birthday . . . and four trips of the long and well-filled passenger trains were made without accident. The glorious Fourth could offer no more . . . opening the people's railroad . . . built by the people. There is not a rough spot on the whole road. Horseshoe Curve on the steepest grade of the mountain is well worth seeing, in Cheshire Notch.*

The reference in this newspaper account to "Horseshoe Curve" is the reporter's way of describing the loop that began on the trestle at the Notch and ended up at the corner in Prospect where the Peaches now live. The view must have been spectacular at that time with the Hanging Hills of Meriden in the distance and the farmland and pond on the Ten Mile River in the foreground with few trees to obscure the panorama. The article went on:

> *At 8:30 the train, hauled by new engine No. 4 started. A second engine hauled three open cars filled with seats, and in climbing the heavy grade assisted in pushing the first train over. The train ran slowly and gave plenty of time for inspecting the glorious scenery, arriving in Waterbury in an hour. Right on top of Cheshire Mountain, near Rag Hollow Ravine, Mr. Dunham of Cheshire has built up a beautiful picnic ground. At this point a flag station will be established.*

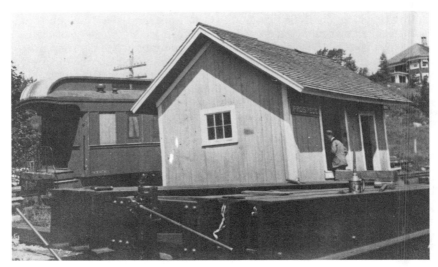

Fig 3 Prospect railroad station circa 1916.   Col. C.B. McCoid

Prospect residents may recognize that this grove was called Laurel Grove and was located in Prospect, south of the present Cheshire Road, near where the VFW Hall stands today. There was a large building which provided overnight accommodations and food. In succeeding years there were planned excursions by various groups and organizations to "Mr. Dunham's Grove." The Prospect railroad station (Fig 3) was built across the road where the Kathan's driveway is situated at the present time. It started as a "flag stop."

The roadbed of the line from West Cheshire through Prospect was engineered in such a way as to avoid grade crossings and to keep the gradient as low as possible. The result was a series of loops rather than a direct route up the mountain, and this part of the railroad was dubbed "The Loop" because of its twists and turns. It was said: "The engineer could lean out of the front window and shake hands with the breakman on the rear." The West Cheshire station was located at the Notch, up the slope from the entrance to present-day Quarry Village off West Main Street. The train left the station and travelled across a trestle at the Notch and ran up the hill on the eastern and southern side of the Plank Road, now Route 68. It crossed another small trestle over Jack's Road and proceeded to the Prospect town line where it veered left behind the present Townline Restaurant and went up the hill to Dunham's Grove (now the VFW Hall site). Here it crossed the ravine formed by the Ten Mile River and Rag Hollow Road (now Route 68) on a long wooden trestle (Fig 2). At the end of this was located the Prospect depot. The train proceeded north and west parallel to Plank Road, then crossed Plank Road and the Notch Road and looping west, it crossed Plank Road two more times. Before crossing Summit Road, north of Plank Road, there was another railroad stop. Then the train continued northwesterly to the Waterbury town line through the northwestern corner of Cheshire. The terminus was the Dublin Street station (Hamilton Avenue).

In the original 1888 timetable (Fig 4) there were three trains in each direction every day. Going to Waterbury the train would make a "flag" stop at Prospect at 11:52 AM, 5:57 PM, and 7:42 PM. Coming from Waterbury the train could stop at Prospect at 9:14 AM, 3:24 PM, and 7:08 PM. To make the 9 mile trip, the train was scheduled to take 24 minutes and the fare was 15¢.

By 1900 the schedule had been changed to two trains a day in each direction, but it seemed to be more convenient for "commuters." One train would leave Prospect at 7:28 AM and arrive in Waterbury at 7:50 AM, while at the end of the day it would leave Waterbury at 6:15 PM and arrive in Prospect at 6:35 PM. There was another important change: the stops at the Prospect station were no longer designated as "flag."

Meriden, Waterbury and Conn. River R. R.

....	....	P.M.	A.M.	P.M.	*Lv 8 6 88 Ar*	A.M.	P.M.	A.M.	P.M.	P.M.
....	....	.....	.....	4 00	.....New York.....	.....	.....	6 00	.....	.....
....	....	4 50	10 50	6 30	.....Cromwell.....	10 11	4 21	6 10	6 35	8 0[illegible]
....	....	4 56	10 56	6 37	.West Cromwell.f.	10 06	4 16	6 03	6 30	7 5[illegible]
....	....	4 58	10 58	6 40	....Westfield.f....	10 04	4 14	6 00	6 28	7 54
....	....	5 02	11 04	6 44	.....Smith'2.f.....	10 00	4 10	5 56	6 24	7 5[illegible]
....	....	5 06	11 08	6 48	....Highland.f....	9 56	4 06	5 50	6 20	7 4[illegible]
....	....	5 30	11 25	7 15	......Meriden.....	9 41	3 51	5 30	6 05	7 3[illegible]
....	....	5 38	11 33	7 23	..Hough's Mill.f..	9 33	3 43	.....		7 2[illegible]
....	....	5 50	11 45	7 35	..West Cheshire.f.	9 21	3 31	.....	.....	7 11
....	....	5 57	11 52	7 42	.....Prospect.f....	9 14	3 24	.....	.....	7 08
....	....	6 08	12 03	7 53	.....Summit.f.....	9 03	3 13	.....	.....	6 5[illegible]
....	....	6 12	12 07	7 57	...East Farms.f...	8 59	3 09	.....	.....	6 49
....	....	6 21	12 16	8 06	....Waterbury.....	8 50	3 00	4 30	.....	6 40

f. Flag Station.

HARTFORD DIVISION.
Meriden Branch.

.....	994	990	Ms	*June 10, 1900.*	991	995	.....	.....
.....	P. M.	A. M.	...	LEAVE] [ARRIVE	A. M.	P. M.	.....	.....
.....	†6 15	†8 50	0	...Waterbury...	7 50	4 00	.....	.....
.....	6 24	9 00	4	....East Farms....	7 40	3 50	.....	.....
.....	6 29	9 06	5	......Summit......	7 34	3 44	.....	.....
.....	6 35	9 12	7	.....Prospect.....	7 28	3 38	.....	.....
.....	6 40	9 18	8	...West Cheshire...	7 22	3 32	.....	.....
.....	6 45	9 24	10	Southington Road	7 16	3 26	.....	.....
.....	6 55	9 35	14	.....Hanover.....	7 05	3 16	.....	.....
.....	7 00	9 40	15	.....Meriden.....	7 00	3 10	.....	.....
.....	7 14	9 58	21	.....Highland.....	6 41	2 51	.....	.....
.....	7 23	10 08	25	.....Westfield.....	6 30	2 40	.....	.....
.....	7 26	10 12	28	.....Newfield.....	6 26	2 36	.....	.....
.....	7 31	10 18	29	...Middletown...	†6 20	†2 30	.....	.....
.....	P. M.	A. M.	...	ARRIVE] [LEAVE	A. M.	P. M.	.....	.....

Fig 4 Train schedules with Prospect stop in 1888 (l) and 1900 (r). NHRHS Newsletter

When the Prospect depot and railroad tracks were built, the Old Road (also called Mix Road) up the hill to Matthew Street was closed, and a new access road was built to the station from Rag Hollow Road. In addition, a railroad siding was built in Prospect in order to accommodate freight cars with a delivery of coal, lumber, or other supplies. There is no way of knowing how many people made use of the station; the largest number may have been tourists or vacationers going to Dunham's Grove. It is known that two high officials of the Shoe Hardware Company in Waterbury, James Crompton and Albert Field, moved to Prospect because of the railroad and built their homes near the Prospect depot. Dr. E. Irene Boardman, a later Prospect resident, remembered as a college student taking the Northampton line to Cheshire, changing to the Meriden-Waterbury line, and getting off in Prospect to be met by her older brother, Victor Boardman, with a horse and wagon.

Various stories have been told about the "Loop" line from West Cheshire through Prospect. This part of the railroad was dubbed the "Loop" because of its twists and turns. It was said, "The engineer could lean out of the front window and shake hands with the breakman on the rear." Nelson Tucker, who grew up on a farm in Mixville, remembered the sparks that would fly from the wheels of the train. Sometimes this would start small brush fires, and he and his friends and neighbors would put out the fires with water from the farm pond. He also recalled the passenger cars filled with weekend vacationers that would not be able to make it up the mountain without the help of a second engine. He remembered walking across the long wooden trestle at Rag Hollow. Clayton Walters told the story of a circus train heading to Waterbury which lost some cages of animals when it rounded the corner near where the Peaches live. Monkeys got loose in the woods, and the circus workers had to round them up. For some years that area was called "Monkey's Corner." No stories of accidents have been passed down from this section of the railroad, unlike the sections in the Meriden and Cromwell area. An interesting feature of the line was that scheduled passenger trains were always "mixed," with both passenger and freight cars on the same train when there was freight to haul.

In 1890 the company boasted in its annual report about its successful operations. In that year they carried: 74,439 passengers; 108,672 tons of freight. It had 107 employees, 5 locomotives, 10 passenger cars, and 154 freight cars. When the extension from Meriden to Waterbury had been opened, new coaches had been bought from Pullman, and the older coaches, made at the Wason shops in Springfield, Mass., were repainted to match the new coaches. The color was olive green with gold lettering with the name, "Meriden, Waterbury & Connecticut River Railroad."

Unfortunately, 1890 also marked a turn in the fortunes of the company. Horace Wilcox, president of the line, died that year. He was its main promoter and benefactor; it is reported that he may have invested one million dollars of his own money in the enterprise. After his death many changes took place. Financial problems plagued the operation. For one thing, much of the $125,000 pledged in Waterbury was never paid. Also, no one had anticipated the costs to extend the line and especially to carry it over the mountain to Waterbury and connect with the New England line. According to Snow: "If it had never gone over the hill to Waterbury it probably would have gotten along well enough and kept out of trouble."

In a few years the line had been leased to the New England Railroad, and then its chief rival, the New Haven, took control, and on December 1895 all special rates were ended. In other words, competition was ceasing and the New Haven line was gaining a virtual monopoly in Connecticut. For over two years, 1896-98, the railroad was shut down completely. When the trains started rolling again, the section between Westfield and Cromwell was abandoned, and traffic diverted to Middletown. The new corporation was called the Middletown, Meriden, and Waterbury Railroad Co. Already by the turn of the century the railroads were competing with the new electric trolleys for passengers. In 1909 the Meriden-Waterbury schedule had been cut to one train in the morning to Waterbury with the return to Meriden in the late afternoon. This part of the line was never electrified.

The last train on the MM&W ran on June 24, 1917, and the tracks were taken up in the Prospect area by 1924. All that was left were the wooden ties, some stone culverts, the rights-of-way, and lots of memories. Snow concludes his article:

> The need for freight facilities like the old Meriden, Waterbury, and Connecticut River Railroad largely passed with the advent of over-the-road trucking. But many of those who remember the old railroad find it rather sad to see most of the roadbed abandoned and overgrown with trees and bushes.

CHESHIRE STREET RAILWAY COMPANY

Unlike the railroad, little has been written about the trolley line which ran from Cheshire through the northeast edge of Prospect to Waterbury. There are more people living today who rode the trolley and who took it for granted, much as they would any public utility like the electric, gas, or telephone companies. Now, it is an era that is long-gone, and people look back with a trace of nostalgia. Somehow, the trolley has an almost romantic aura to it, which people try to preserve in trolley museums and the like.

It is fitting that the chief promoter of the Cheshire-to-Waterbury trolley line had the name, Walter Scott. Scott originated in Waterbury, but in 1896 he bought a large home on Maple Avenue in Cheshire, added a wing, converted it into a hotel, and called it Waverly Inn. In a booklet entitled *The Story of Waverly Inn*, published in 1952, it was stated:

> Ever mindful of the promotion of his inn, Scott was largely responsible for a trolley line trough Cheshire connecting the inn with such points as Hartford, New Haven, Waterbury, Meriden, and other towns. His efforts were rewarded because the trolley station, called Scott's Junction, was directly across from the inn.

One might add that the trolley line brought a lot of business to Scott's establishment. It is interesting to note that Waterbury businessmen predominated in the building of the Plank Road, that Meriden merchants instigated the railroad, but that it was this Cheshire inn-keeper who promoted the trolley line.

The era of the trolley car began in the so-called "Gay '90s," when electric power lines were strung along city streets, making it possible to replace horse-drawn railroad cars. In the cities of New Haven and Waterbury the trolley lines were extended; in the New Haven area as far as Mt. Carmel in Hamden; in Waterbury, as far east as East Farms. The Waterbury Traction Co. acquired its first electric car in 1894; five years later it was taken over by the Conn. Railway and Lighting Co. In 1903 the city of Waterbury was the locale of a long, bitter 210-day strike by motormen, resulting in several deaths, destruction of property and great economic hardship.

In the meantime, in 1901 a group of citizens, led by Walter Scott, had incorporated the Cheshire Street Railway Company and had applied through the Superior Court for the right to build the trolley line. A hearing was set on August 1, 1901 in New Haven to which were invited representatives of the railroads and all the towns affected, including the First Selectman of the Town of Prospect. In the application the Company stated that "public convenience and necessity require the construction and operation of said railway." The route was detailed in the application, summarized as follows:

Commencing at the terminus of the tracks of the Fair Haven and Westville Railway Company, at Mt. Carmel . . . along the Cheshire Turnpike . . . and Main Street, Cheshire, to Maple Avenue . . . thence along said Maple Avenue to a point nearly opposite the Waverly Inn . . . . Also, commencing at the intersection of Maple Avenue and West Main Street or the main highway leading to West Cheshire . . . or along private way northerly of said West Main Street . . . crossing the tracks of the Northampton (Line) . . . along the main highway leading to the West Cheshire station of the Middletown, Meriden, and Waterbury Railroad Company, crossing under the tracks of said Railroad Company; thence along the plank road so-called, or on private way adjacent to said highway, in the Towns of Cheshire and Prospect . . .

Fig 5 Trolley station on Prospect town line circa 1985.   Dick Caouette

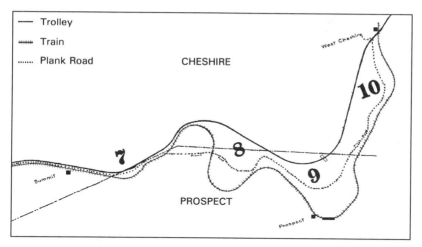

Fig 6   Map drawn by Albert E. Hill, Consulting Engineer, for the Cheshire Street Railway Co. Routes for Plank Road, Railroad, and Trolley through Prospect are shown. Large numerals are the miles from the start of the trolley line in Waterbury. The RR stations at Summit, Prospect, and West Cheshire are also marked. The trestle (Fig 2) is located just to the right of the Prospect station.

The description of the route continued with reference to travelling north of the Plank Road and north of the railroad line through the northwestern part of Cheshire into the City of Waterbury (Fig 6). At two places the trolley line touched Prospect: in the vicinity of the present Bow and Arrow Restaurant east of Plank Road; and for a short distance between Matthew Street and Summit Road just north of the Plank Road. A fieldstone trolley station (Fig 5) was built near this latter location, right on the Prospect town line. Another trolley stop was located down the hill from Prospect in Mixville.

The trolley line opened in 1904 and became a very popular means of transportation.   It was used by people going to work in the factories of Waterbury. Elsie Bens recalled the daily round trip to work at Scovill; she would walk over Jacks Road from Mountain Road in Cheshire and catch the trolley in Mixville in order to save 5¢. Students in Prospect took the trolley to attend high school in Waterbury. Nellie and Ruth Cowdell remembered the daily trips. People going to the shore for the weekend would catch the trolley in the Prospect area and change in Cheshire for the trip to Savin Rock and other places on Long Island Sound.

In the book, *Landmarks of Old Cheshire*, there are several references to the trolley: "Roland Pardee had vivid memories of trolley rides over the mountains from Waterbury. The big thrill came on the final plunge to Tucker Road. The motorman had planned perfectly when to release the brake and 'let her go.' The trolley fairly flew along, at times seemingly lifting one set of wheels off the tracks! But there were no fatal mishaps on this exciting run." This is a description of the downhill course from the present location of the Bow and Arrow Restaurant to the trolley stop at Mixville Road in the valley.

There was a time in the early 1900s when Connecticut was laced with a network of trolley lines, and you could travel as far away as New York State or Ohio by trolley. It wasn't long before the Cheshire Street Railway Co. was taken over by the Conn. Railway and Lighting Co.

Fig 7 Stone culvert that once carried trollies over Ten Mile River.   Boardman Kathan

By 1935 the trolleys ran for the last time, and they were replaced by buses of the Connecticut Co. All that is left in the vicinity of Prospect is the right-of-way that skirted Plank Road, the deteriorating trolley stop north of Matthew Street, beautifully constructed stone culverts over Ten Mile River (Fig 7) and other streams flowing into it, and the low stone overpass which still crosses a steep part of the Notch Road. For many years one could still see the trolley tracks in the asphalt at the Notch, the intersection of Routes 68 and 70.

~

Chapter Twelve

The Government

T he United States Constitution provides the basis for all laws for federal and state governments, but it never mentions cities nor towns. Their power to exist and govern comes from the states. In a sense, municipalities are children of their state. This is odd, considering that a number of towns in Connecticut were well established before the United States itself.

In Connecticut, municipalities may choose to operate under the state's general laws and statutes, or they may elect to adopt their own charter. Operating under a charter is known as "Home Rule." Under this plan each town can adopt its own laws and determine what form of government it wants to follow. This ability for municipalities to govern themselves has been allowed since 1919. The power for local control was strengthened by further legislation, including the 1957 Connecticut Home Rule Amendment which formally enabled the people of each town to govern themselves in local matters.

In the early days, the state set the laws which were applied uniformly to all towns. Each town had the same form of government, and the state determined the number and type of local officials required and how long they could serve for terms in office. When Prospect was incorporated in 1827, the first elections were held for town clerk, three selectmen, a team of grand jurors, a pound keeper, town agents, treasurer, a sealer of weights, a sealer of measures, fence viewers, assessors, surveyors of highways, tavern keeper, and other assorted positions (see Chapter 4). These positions were all part-time. Those elected to even the most important functions, like town clerk and selectmen, would meet only periodically to carry out their appointed duties. Most of their time was spent on the farm or earning a living at their trade.

The singular difference between town government and state or federal government is the degree of participation by the average citizen. A high percentage of town residents took an active role in local government. Women did not begin to play a role in politics until the middle of the 20th century. The number of men eligible to hold office in Prospect was not much more than one hundred for its first century. A good number of those men served in office, and those who did not took an active role in town meetings and other town functions.

The task of researching Prospect's history is hampered by the incomplete records available. Because the town officials were working only part-time with little or no monetary compensation, written records were not always kept for many transactions. Until 1961, when the town hall was built (Fig 1), records were kept in the homes of town officials. As individuals in office changed from year to year, the records were passed on. No doubt, some were lost or discarded in the process.

Fig 1 Dedication of the Prospect town hall in September of 1961.

Waterbury Republican-American

The annual town meeting was held the afternoon of election day. Other special meetings were held as needed. Town meetings were a form of local entertainment. They were sometimes wild, sometimes amusing, but always well attended. In the absence of a town hall, meetings were held in various buildings around town. The first gatherings were at the local tavern. Then, starting in 1841, the basement of the new Congregational Church building was used. Other meeting places included the Grange hall, Community School, and Center School on the Green.

> *When the old schoolhouse was the town hall, we would meet there in the evenings to write out checks and do town business. In the winter the first one to arrive would get a fire going in the stove so we could have some heat.*

> Carleton Benson, 1994

For two years the Prospect town hall was located in Oliver's Market. When Alva T. Cinq-Mars was elected first selectman in the fall of 1957, he put the town office in his restaurant at the rear of the supermarket. His secretary, Marion Bradford, dutifully carried her own typewriter from her home on Route 69, near the present town hall, to Cinq-Mars Restaurant each work day.

It wasn't a particularly good place to have an office, with the juke box going next door. But it was the only place available until the town hall was built. It was rather loud in there. There was a separate entrance to the office, but the door connecting the office to the restaurant was next to the men's room, which contributed to the noise.

Marion Bradford, Waterbury Republican, February 27, 1985

SELECTMEN

The selectmen were the main governing officials of the town. They were elected as first, second, and third selectmen. By tradition, the third selectman was usually from the opposing party to offer both major parties some share of representation. The pay was nominal for elected officials. In the year 1884-1885 all officers in town combined received $194.25. In 1922 Albert T. Allen was compensated $40.00 as first selectman while second and third selectmen each received $5.00 for their efforts.

ELECTED OFFICES	APPOINTED BY MAYOR	APPOINTED BY TOWN COUNCIL
Mayor	Fire Marshall	Economic Development Commission (5)
Town Council (9)	Regional Health District Representative	
Tax Collector		Civil Preparedness
Planning & Zoning Commission (5)	Director of Welfare	Inland/Wetlands Commission & Alternatives
	Town Attorney	
Zoning Board of Appeals (5)	Tree Warden	Library Board (9)
Town Clerk	Animal Control Officer	Water Pollution Control (5)
Treasurer	Assessor	Alternates to Planning & Zoning Board
Constables (6)	Civil Preparedness Director	
Board of Tax Review (3)	Building Inspector	
Board of Education (4)	Conservation Commission	
	Commission on Aging	
	Recreation Commission	
	Building Code Board of Appeals (5)	

Fig 2 Prospect Town Government after Charter Revision 3.

Beginning in the 1960s, Prospect amended its charter several times (Fig 2). The result was a new form of government which replaced the three selectman with one person. The title for this individual evolved from First Selectman to Chief Administrative Officer and then to Mayor. In the process, this position became a full time job. Raymond Peffers, who was first selectman from 1947 to 1953, and George Sabo, who served in the transition from first selectman to chief administrative officer to mayor between 1968 and 1977, recently gave their opinions on the top position in the town of Prospect.

There were no secretaries then. The first selectman had to do a lot, handling welfare cases and whatever else came along. It was supposed to be a part time job but it took a good deal of time. The pay was all of $150 per year.   Raymond L. Peffers, 1995

I always favored that Prospect should be run by elected officials. There were some people who wanted a town manager form of government. That's when the title "Chief Administrative Officer" was created. But then they realized that position could not be elected, so with the next charter revision it was changed to Mayor as it is today.

George A. Sabo, Jr., 1995

Because Prospect was growing rapidly in population during this period, it was thought that this new centralized structure would create more attention in Hartford and better serve the town. Most of the municipalities that adopt a mayoral system are larger cities. Even today, Prospect is the smallest town in Connecticut with this form of government.

TOWN CLERKS

The records kept by the town clerks are a major source of information about Prospect's history. In general, the town clerks held their terms of office for more consecutive years than did the selectmen. Most often the town clerk was also the registrar of vital statistics and the treasurer. Mildred Talmadge was the first women to hold the office of town clerk in Prospect. The clerk was the keeper of the town safe which was rather large and heavy. This may help to explain the longer terms in office because the safe was not something one wanted to haul around frequently. The town records have a number of entries about safe maintenance.

1889 - Repairing safe *$41.67*

1908 - New safe and moving same *$110.00*

1930 - Moving town safe & repairing safe *$24.25*

1949 - Blakeslee Co., Moving safe to town clerk's office . . *$30.00*

1954 - Safes, B.H. Riefe *$2,923.20*

While most of the power to create laws rested with the state government, municipalities did enact ordinances of local interest, such as problems associated with animal control, local roads, and liquor sales. The latter has always been a subject of heated discussion in Prospect. Many church members were opposed to the sale or consumption of alcoholic beverages in public places. The taverns were seen as a blot on the community. During the Civil War, liquor sales were banned in Prospect. When the issue of liquor permits was raised, it was defeated numerous times, most recently in 1934, 1946, and 1956. But in 1957 the sentiment of the majority shifted to allow the issuing of liquor permits.

From the annual town reports (Fig 3), one can learn a great deal about the events and the philosophy of townspeople at any given time. These documents contained the income and expenditures of the town along with reports by various town officials.   No doubt entries were made in complete seriousness at the time, but some might appear to be humorous today.

TOWN OF PROSPECT
EXPENSES

1880 - Damage done by dogs $5.00
1889 - Mowing grave yard $5.20
1891 - Voting booths $2.85
1900 - Survey Bethany-Prospect line $15.00
1900 - Printing town reports $8.50
1909 - Damage done by Ed Lewis' horse $30.00
1910 - Grass fertilizer for Green $9.50
1910 - Renting Grange hall $12.00
1918 - Telephoning .... $.75
1921 - Typewriter for probate office, town's share $6.63
1923 - Horse lawn mower $85.00
1927 - 2 keys for Grange hall .... $.70
1928 - Connecticut Light & Power Co. for street lights $102.20
1929 - T.B. Hotchkiss, use of car as assessor $10.00
1936 - The Ball & Socket Mfg. Co., buttons for Tercentenary $2.80
1936 - Halloween night duty: A.T. Allen $3.00
                                              Carl Canfield $2.00
                                              Arthur Hill $1.50
1941 - O.B. Maxwell, three sirens, defense $70.00
1945 - Paid for killing fox, Ralph Pratt $5.00
1948 - Time clock for Christmas tree $8.81
1951 - Davidson & McKirdy Co., Inc., 1000 books,
                          "Survival Under Atomic Attack" $50.00
1955 - Park Dept., City of Waterbury, Bandstand on Wheels $15.00
1957 - Hubbard-Hall Chemical Co., DDT $19.00

MISCELLANEOUS INCOME

1945 - Sale of outside toilet $25.00
1945 - Bingo permit $2.00
1945 - Scrap paper collected for Honor Roll $29.23

Fig 3 Entries from Prospect annual town reports.

REPRESENTATIVES

According to early state laws, Prospect was entitled to send one representative to the State Assembly.   This delegate to the Assembly was the town's voice in helping to govern the state. The pay allowance for representatives was $3 per day in 1867 for the 45 days that the assembly was in session. The old state registers offered instructions for travel between each town and Hartford. From Prospect the distance was 30 miles, and access for travelers to and from the Capitol was as follows:

> 1887   *Prospect is reached by stage from West Cheshire on the N.H. & Northhampton R.R. daily.*
>
> 1890   *. . . by Meriden, Waterbury & Connecticut River R.R., Prospect Station.*
>
> 1905   *. . . by the Meriden & Waterbury branch of the N.Y., N.H. & Hartford R.R.*
>
> 1920   *. . . by the Waterbury-Cheshire trolley line. Stops every ½ hour at Summit and Prospect stations.*
>
> 1921   *. . . stone roads under construction to Waterbury.*
>
> 1929   *stone roads to Waterbury & Naugatuck complete.*
>
> Connecticut State Registers

Bernice Buys was the first woman representative from Prospect. In 1967 state laws were changed so that each member of the Assembly would have a similar number of constituents. Prospect no longer had its own exclusive representative when District #83 was created by combining Cheshire and Prospect. During the period from 1967-1972, when this district was in effect, none of the representatives lived in Prospect.

In 1973 District #90 was formed, which included all of Bethany and Prospect and part of Cheshire. Richard E. Varis of Prospect served as the representative from this district from 1973-82. He was succeeded by Kenneth R. Tripp in 1982. Then the districts were changed again with Prospect split into two sections, #89 and #90, sharing representation with neighboring towns. Pros-

Fig 4 Representative George Cowdell at his desk in the General Assembly in Hartford.

Prospect Historical Society

pect's Carleton Benson was the representative for the 90th District in 1985-86, and in 1995 Vickie Nardello captured the assembly seat for the 89th District.

TOWN HEALTH

In the early years medicine was more of an art than a science, and cures were promised by many individuals with all sorts of pills (Fig 5) and contraptions. No sort of proof was offered, but there was always a long line of customers eager to try the latest fad.

> Dr. Bradeth's Pills can be obtained of the following agents in New Haven Co., who are duly authorized: Hobart C. Porter, Prospect . . . cure themselves of colds . . . small pox, measles.

Fig 5 The latest wonder pill.   Waterbury Republican, Feb 7, 1846

One of the major concerns of local government is the health of its citizens. Prospect had health officers who monitored the health and sanitary conditions in town. Their efforts were summarized in the annual town reports.

1893-94 Typhoid fever 0, Scarlet fever 4 (2 families), Measles none, Diphtheria 0, Malaria diseases - less than formerly.

1894-95 No infectious or contagious diseases. The town has been very healthy.

1895-96 Whooping cough 15-20 cases. None reported. If all were reported to me I could give a more satisfactory report.

Inspection of all the school buildings has been made. The number of schools, four. They have been fumigated with sulfur. The school buildings and houses are in good sanitary condition. There have been three complaints of nuisances, consisting of dead horses. They were abated.

1896-97 Scarlet fever - sixteen cases, three deaths; cannot trace the origin. Street quarantine was required. The houses were fumigated and disinfected. Garbage is disposed of in the pigpen mostly.

1897-98 We have no public provisions for the disposal of garbage or sewage. Nearly every house has the outdoor privy. There are no cesspools in town. Only one complaint of nuisance, a dead horse brought from Waterbury and left unburied.

1899-00 I recommend that the Board of Education build a privy or two at the East School House. I think the law requires two. The ice ponds are in fair condition. No ice is harvested here, except for private families.

John R. Platt
Town Health Officer

1908-1900 Recommend the West School to have a coat of white paint instead of the dark paint which is on it, as it is bad for the children's eyes.

1912-13 There is only one slaughter house in town.

Stephen A. Talmadge
Town Health Officer

1930-31 Our town is so small it seems as if everyone knew pretty much all that was going on, almost everything as well as the health of the town. In the past year the water from the new wells at the four schools and the church well was analyzed by the State Department of Health and found to be all right, although there was some color in some of it, probably due to the newness of the wells.

C.P. Wallace
Town Health Officer

1953-54   The building of homes on very narrow lots is increasing in this town; and it is an urgent recommendation that the town require at least a frontage of 110 feet for each house!

1955-56   Polio shots - 1,005. In August, when Prospect was host to evacuees from the flooded areas, Dr. Staneslow made daily calls on the evacuees at the school and gave two shots of typhoid vaccine to 108 people.

1955-56   A mosquito elimination program was held in March when 200 lbs. of granular DDT, supplied by the town, was distributed to 144 residents. Boy scouts under the direction of the scoutmaster treated the huge swamp lying between Matthew, Summit and Juggernaut Roads. Many reports this summer testify to the success of this program.

1957-58   Measles epidemic - 95 cases.

E. Irene Boardman, M.D.
Town Health Officer

In the later 1930s it was common practice to remove the tonsils of all children as a preventative treatment. On June 6, 1939, one room at Center School was set up as an operating room where seven children had their tonsils removed by Dr. John S. Staneslow. Mrs. John Riccardi, Mrs. John Miller, and Mrs. Susan Cocchiola were Prospect nurses who assisted in the operations. The patients were then moved to another schoolroom where they remained overnight on cots.

A memorable event in Prospect's medical history occurred in 1944, when Emma Hill of Prospect was one of the first of two patients in the Waterbury area to be given the new and scarce wonder drug Penicillin. Emma was admitted to St Mary's Hospital, suffering with a 105° fever from osteomyelitis, a bone infection in her leg. She did not respond to conventional treatment but was completely cured with this drug in a short period of time.

In 1975 the Prospect Town Council voted in favor of becoming part of a tri-town health district, known as the Chesprocott Health District, which includes Cheshire, Wolcott, and Prospect. A major reason for this decision was being able to receive matching state funds.

POLITICS

At the time of Prospect's founding, most influential townspeople were members of the Whig Party. When the Republican Party formed in 1854, it became the political movement of choice. The Republican platform's opposition to slavery very much fit the sentiment of the day in Prospect. Since that time, the politics of Prospect has been dominated by the Republican Party, the most popular party for small rural areas.

Fish markets in Waterbury could supply the seafood needed for special occasions. It was the custom in Prospect for the winner of the Republican caucus for Representative to put on an oyster supper for all. (In those days winning the Republican caucus was equivalent to the election.)   Prospect Pleasantries & Peculiarities

In the first census of the United States taken in 1774, Cheshire reported 13 slaves scattered among nine homes while Waterbury had 10 among four households. None of these lived within the bounds of Prospect. In the 1700s Samuel Hopkins of Waterbury was the first minister in New England to openly oppose slavery. In 1788 the General Association of Congregational ministers declared the slave trade to be unjust. By 1830 there were but nine slaves in the state of Connecticut. An active Underground Railroad transported escaped and freed slaves from the South to safety. New Haven was the port of arrival, and several routes headed north from there. One path left New Haven and passed through Waterbury on route to Torrington. It is likely that some slaves were escorted through Prospect on their journey to freedom.

In the United States presidential vote, Prospect favored the Republican candidate every year except 1932 (Roosevelt), 1960 (Kennedy), 1964 (Johnson), and 1968 (Humphrey), when Democrats received more votes. There have always been Democrats in town, and during most periods they have been an active and vocal minority party. Occasionally, this party has risen to the forefront and been a significant player.

> *The last full Democratic administration was elected in 1887 and went out in 1889 according to Albert Allen, unofficial historian, who served as first selectman in Prospect for 15 years. Allen said that the town was in partial control of the Democrats in 1921 and 1922, but that the party was unable to strengthen its position and the Republicans took over again.*
>
> *Town government here fell to the Democrats for the first time in 64 years today after a close-running election . . . When the count was in, Margaret G. Andrews, tax collector, stood as the lone Republican in office. For the rest, the Republicans were wiped out right down the line, including Mildred Talmadge, town clerk for 24 consecutive years. The Democratic sweep was led by Joseph McEvoy, new first selectmen.* Waterbury American, October 6, 1953

In recent years, with the influx of many new residents, Prospect is more balanced in its political position. Most citizens are inclined to vote for the principles and values of individual candidates rather than vote a straight party line as in the past. Finally, in small towns like Prospect, everyone has a greater opportunity to express their opinions and influence the governing of their town.

POPULATION

Prospect's ethnic mix has changed significantly over the years. The original founders were almost exclusively English. By 1840 the first group of immigrants from Ireland accounted for 29 people in town. The census of 1910 provided information on those born outside of the United States (Fig 6).

Fig 6 PROSPECT RESIDENTS BORN OUTSIDE THE UNITED STATES – 1910 U.S. CENSUS

Italy	36	Canada	7	Denmark	2	Russia (Lith.)	1
England	13	Russia (Polish)	6	Hungary (Slovak)	2	West Indies	1
Ireland	11	Switzerland	5	Lithuania	1	-------	
Germany	7	Sweden	3	Scotland	1	TOTAL	96

The population of Prospect remained fairly constant during the first eighty years after it was incorporated (Fig 7). But not everyone stayed in town. In fact, there was considerable migration away from Prospect, with many going to Connecticut's sister state, Ohio, in early years. A prime example of this flux is the Hotchkiss family. When Gideon Hotchkiss died in 1807, he had lived to see 105 grandchildren and 155 great-grandchildren — and yet, there is not one Hotchkiss descendent living in Prospect today.

After 1910 the population of Prospect underwent dramatic change (Fig 7). The number of residents was almost cut in half between 1910 and 1920. Then, the population approximately doubled each of the next four decades before slowing the pace of growth in the 1970s. This increase in the town population is due in part to the draw of Prospect living. The lure of a tranquil country lifestyle is more and more attractive to those weary of modern society's hectic pace. The reasonable land and housing costs offer further incentive. Prospect has consistently had low tax rates. The per capita tax for 1992-93 was $774.98, which ranked as one of the lowest (151th out of 169) of all towns in Connecticut. The amount of land still owned by the water companies and the strict zoning requirements combine to hold future growth at a modest rate.

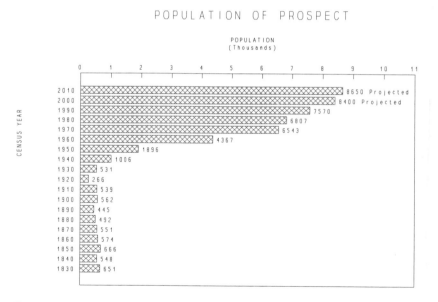

Fig 7   Prospect population from U.S. Census figures. Projections provided by the CT Department of Economic Development.

ELECTED TOWN OFFICIALS

The following list shows citizens who held the positions of selectman, representative, and town clerk from the founding of the town to the present. Of course, there have been many other positions and people who have served in governing Prospect. The information shown is based on data printed in the *Connecticut State Registers*. It should be noted that for the period 1827-1845, only the first selectman was listed. The positions of treasurer and collector are shown in the columns for second and third selectman for those years. The mark (---) denotes that no entry was provided for that position. This may mean the office was vacant, as was often the case with third selectman and occasionally second selectman. At other times the information may not have been submitted or received to be printed in a timely way. The incumbent may have continued in office for those unlisted years. The mark (") means the same person held office as the previous year. In Prospect the positions of second and third selectman were eliminated after 1965.

PROSPECT ELECTED OFFICIALS 1827-1995

	FIRST SELECTMAN	SECOND SELECTMAN	THIRD SELECTMAN	REPRESENTATIVE	TOWN CLERK
1827	Jared Burr	David Scott	Albert Hoppin	---	Edward Chittenden
1828	---	---	---	---	"
1829	---	---	---	Benjamin Bronson	"
1830	---	---	---	Benjamin Platt	"
1831	---	---	---	Lauren Platt	Franklin D. Benham
1832	William Mix	James Street	Vincent Tuttle	Joseph J. Doolittle	F.A. Berhan
1833	---	---	---	William Mix	---
1834	E. Chittenden	James Street	G.M. Hotchkiss	Samuel Peck	Ozra Collins
1835	Lauren Preston	A. Austin	"	Lauren Preston	"
1836	Joseph Payne	L. Hotchkiss	Vincent Tuttle	William Mix	Aaron Austin
1837	William Mix	"	Miles Payne	Joseph Payne	"
1838	"	James Street	Henry P. Platt	Libbeus M. Hatch	James Street
1839	"	C.M. Hatch	John Beecher	Benjamin Platt	"
1840	Benjamin Platt	---	Oliver Mitchell	Stephen H. Payne	"
1841	"	---	---	Ransom R. Russell	"
1842	Isaac Bradley	James Street	R. Tyler	Benjamin Platt	"
1843	"	"	"	---	Isaac Bradley
1844	---	---	---	---	---
1845	R.R. Russell	James Street	George C. Platt	Luther Morse	James Street
1846	---	---	---	Ransom R. Russell	"
1847	Thomas Wilmot	Isaac Bradley	G.C. Platt	Benjamin Doolittle	"
1848	George Platt	D.R. Williams	Lyman Smith	Ransom R. Russell	"
1849	R.R. Russell	Lucius Talmadge	---	George C. Platt	Samuel C. Bronson
1850	Garry B. Johnson	Aaron Austin	---	Reuben B. Hughes	"
1851	---	---	---	William J. Wilcox	---
1852	R.R. Russell	Aaron Austin	---	James Street	Samuel C. Bronson
1853	---	---	---	"	---
1854	Isaac Bradley	Aaron Austin	Benjamin Doolittle	---	Samuel C. Bronson
1855	"	David Hotchkiss	Merritt Clark	Asa M Train	"
1856	David Hotchkiss	---	---	John Gillett	"
1857	"	John Gillett	Merritt Clark, Jr.	"	"
1858	"	"	"	David Hotchkiss	"
1859	"	"	"	"	"

PROSPECT ELECTED OFFICIALS 1827-1995

	FIRST SELECTMAN	SECOND SELECTMAN	THIRD SELECTMAN	REPRESENTATIVE	TOWN CLERK
1860	John Gillett	Samuel Bronson	S.S. Clark	Samuel C. Bronson	Samuel C. Bronson
1861	"	D.M. Hotchkiss	Henry D. Russell	John Gillett	"
1862	"	Smith S. Clark	"	Merritt Clark, Jr.	"
1863	Smith S. Clark	H.D. Russell	George Payne	Edwin R. Tyler	Edwin R. Tyler
1864	David M. Hotchkiss	"	"	Henry D. Russell	William W. Atwater
1865	"	George Payne	Henry D. Russell	Benjamin B. Brown	"
1866	"	"	---	Richard Tyler	David Hawley
1867	"	"	Chas. E. Hine	"	Richard Tyler
1868	---	---	---	Charles E. Hine	---
1869	Hiram Ambler	Benjamin Brown	Merritt Clark	Richard Tyler	Richard Tyler
1870	David M. Hotchkiss	George Payne	"	John R. Platt	"
1871	Smith S. Clark	Algernon Plumb	"	George F. Tyler	"
1872	Algernon S. Plumb	Willis Ives	Horace Nettleton	Merritt Clark	"
1873	"	George Payne	George F. Tyler	Horace A. Nettleton	"
1874	Smith S. Clark	"	"	William Berkley	"
1875	"	George F. Tyler	Henry Judd	John Gillette	"
1876	"	Harris Platt	Merritt Clark	Henry Judd	"
1877	Algernon S. Plumb	David R. Williams	"	William Berkley	"
1878	John Gillette	"	Algernon S. Plumb	Harry Hotchkiss	"
1879	David R. Williams	Merritt Clark	Horatio N. Clark	"	"
1880	"	"	William E. Morris	William W. Phipps	"
1881	"	George F. Taylor	"	James Bottomly	David M. Plumb
1882	"	George D. Fenn	Harris Platt	George F. Tyler	Watson Hitchcock
1883	Smith S. Clark	Harris Platt	Algernon S. Plumb	Rufus M. Gillett	David B. Hotchkiss
1884	David R. Williams	John R. Platt	"	John R. Platt	David M. Plumb
1885	David B. Hotchkiss	"	"	George R. Morse	"
1886	James Bottomly	"	"	Edgar G. Wallace	"
1887	"	"	George D. Fenn	Halsey S. Clark	"
1888	"	"	"	"	"
1889	"	"	"	Byron L. Morse	"
1890	"	"	"	"	"
1891	David B. Hotchkiss	"	"	William A. Purdy	"
1892	George D. Fenn	"	David B. Hotchkiss	"	"
1893	Halsey S. Clark	Maurice Berger	William E. Clark	Minor Blackman	"
1894	William E. Clark	Frank R. Allen	Halsey S. Clark	"	"
1895	George R. Morse	William A. Purdy	Horatio N. Clark	George L. Talmadge	"
1896	Halsey S. Clark	"	William E. Clark	"	"
1897	"	"	"	Stephen Talmadge	"
1898	David B. Hotchkiss	"	"	"	"
1899	William E. Clark	Lavergne G. Clark	Horatio N. Clark	Edgar B. Jeralds	"
1900	"	"	David B. Hotchkiss	"	"
1901	"	George D. Fenn	Halsey S. Clark	Edgar G. Wallace	"
1902	Halsey S. Clark	"	Horatio N. Clark	"	"
1903	Stephen Talmadge	"	"	George D. Fenn	"
1904	"	"	William McDermott	"	"
1905	"	"	"	Lavergne G. Clark	"
1906	"	Elmer W. Griswold	---	"	"
1907	"	"	Frank H. Daley	David M. Plumb	"
1908	"	Lavergne G. Clark	"	"	"
1909	"	"	"	"	"

PROSPECT ELECTED OFFICIALS 1827-1995

	FIRST SELECTMAN	SECOND SELECTMAN	THIRD SELECTMAN	REPRESENTATIVE	TOWN CLERK
1910	Clifford P. Wallace	Lavergne G. Clark	Frank H. Daley	David M. Plumb	David M. Plumb
1911	Stephen Talmadge	"	"	Lavergne G. Clark	"
1912	"	"	"	"	"
1913	"	"	"	Elmer W. Griswold	"
1914	William E. Clark	"	Frank W. Burnham	"	"
1915	"	Geo. Rasmussen	Frank H. Daley	Stephen Talmadge	"
1916	"	Lavergne G. Clark	"	"	"
1917	Stephen Talmadge	"	"	Byron L. Morse	"
1918	Lavergne G. Clark	Albert T. Allen	"	"	"
1919	Albert T. Allen	Treat B. Hotchkiss	Benjamin E. Smith	Clifford P. Wallace	"
1920	"	Harry Talmadge	---	"	Clifford P. Wallace
1921	"	David M. Plumb	Frank W. Burnham	George Talmadge	"
1922	"	Frank Burnham	Merritt Walters	"	"
1923	Lavergne G. Clark	David M. Plumb	Frank W. Burnham	Lavergne G. Clark	"
1924	"	"	Arthur Harrington	"	"
1925	Albert T. Allen	Perle T. Beers	Frank W. Burnham	Edgar G. Wallace	"
1926	"	"	"	Albert T. Allen	"
1927	"	Merritt Walters	"	"	"
1928	"	"	Ross Duprey	"	"
1929	"	"	Harry Talmadge	Merritt Walters	"
1930	"	"	Michael Valasek	"	Mildred Talmadge
1931	"	"	"	"	"
1932	"	"	John Keiper	"	"
1933	"	"	Michael Valasek	George H. Cowdell	"
1934	Merritt Walters	Frank Plumb	John Keiper	"	"
1935	"	"	John Gayer	"	"
1936	"	"	---	Bernice T. Buys	"
1937	"	"	Daniel B. Conner	George H. Cowdell	"
1938	"	"	"	Bernice T. Buys	"
1939	"	"	Harold J. Shea	Thomas Plumb	"
1940	"	"	James Doyle	"	"
1941	"	"	Burton R. Hubbell	"	"
1942	"	"	Harry Coughlin	"	"
1943	"	"	Theodore Grieder	"	"
1944	"	"	"	"	"
1945	Lloyd E. Perry	"	John J. Griffin	George H. Cowdell	"
1946	"	Treat Hotchkiss	Dennis F. Murnane	"	"
1947	Raymond Peffers	"	John J. Griffin	"	"
1948	"	Robert S. Gray	Donald D. Brennan	"	"
1949	"	"	John Shea	John J. Griffin	"
1950	"	"	John L. Shieffer	"	"
1951	"	Carleton Benson	Edward Fanning, Jr	Robert F. Lee	"
1952	"	"	Joseph McEvoy	"	"
1953	"	Carl Canfield	Robert Sabo	"	"
1954	Joseph McEvoy	"	Carleton Benson	"	Melba R. Membrino
1955	"	"	"	John G. Miller	"
1956	"	"	Walter Voegeli	"	"
1957	"	"	"	Edward Harrison	"
1958	"	"	"	"	Marion P. Bradford
1959	Alva Cinq-Mars	Carleton Benson	Joseph McEvoy	Eraine L. Genest	"

PROSPECT ELECTED OFFICIALS 1827-1995

	FIRST SELECTMAN	SECOND SELECTMAN	THIRD SELECTMAN	REPRESENTATIVE	TOWN CLERK
1960	Michael Pugliese	Vincent Paolino	Carleton Benson	Eraine L. Genest	Mary Nolan
1961	"	"	"	Doris M. Sherlock	"
1962	George M. Cipriano	John G. Brundage	James A. Baker	"	Elmer G. Ericson
1963	"	"	"	Robert S. Gray	"
1964	"	Richard Varis	Frederick Green, Jr	"	"
1965	"	"	"	"	"
1966	"	--------------------	--------------------	"	Barbara Dubuque
1967	"	OFFICE OF	OFFICE OF	--------------------	"
1968	George A. Sabo, Jr	2nd SELECTMAN	3rd SELECTMAN	OFFICE OF	Marion P. Bradford
1969	"	DISCONTINUED	DISCONTINUED	PROSPECT	"
1970	"			REPRESENTATIVE	"
1971	"			DISCONTINUED	"
1972	"				Mary A. Handy
1973	"				"
1974	"				"
1975	"				"
1976	"				"
1977	"	← CHIEF ADMINISTRATIVE OFFICER			"
1978	Robert J. Chatfield	← MAYOR			Patricia Vaillancourt
1979	"				"
1980	"				"
1981	"				"
1982	"				"
1983	"				"
1984	"				"
1985	"				"
1986	"				"
1987	"				"
1988	"				"
1989	"				"
1990	"				"
1991	"				"
1992	"				"
1993	"				"
1994	"				"
1995	"				"

~

Chapter Thirteen

Town Services

POST OFFICE

One of the oldest services in Prospect, possibly predating the town itself, is the postal service. Although there is no direct documentation, the first post office was most likely in the general store, which opened in 1803 and was kept by Asahel Chittenden. It is recorded that his son Edward was the first postmaster in January of 1830. A post office continued serving Prospect for seventy-two years, operating out of stores, hotels, and businesses.

The post office in Waterbury was established in 1803 or a short time previous . . . Before this the post office at New Haven was chiefly used by the people of Waterbury, the mail being carried on horseback from New Haven to Litchfield.

History of Waterbury

As to Waterbury's mail facilities, I have heard my father say that before the present century [nineteenth] a weekly mail was brought on horseback from the more important town of Woodbury, the nearest point on the mail route . . . About 1820, the mail was brought in a four-horse coach, three days in a week, each way. "Bunnell" drove the stage and entered the town with a great flourish of whip and blast of horn, knowing well that he thus gave notice of the most important event of the week.

Horace Hotchkiss paper for the Mattatuck Historical Society

For many years a post office was maintained in Prospect Center. The town appropriated $25 a year toward its support, mail being trucked up hill, the long haul daily from the West Cheshire station on the Canal Road.

The New Haven Register, October 29, 1933

By 1888-89 the allotment for the Prospect postal service had risen to $52 per year. Luther Morse was postmaster, which was only a part-time job (Fig 2). He also ran a pocketbook factory near the center of town. At that time the cost to mail a letter was 3¢ for each half-ounce. Local delivery was 2¢. This was a real bargain compared to the rates in 1830 (Fig 1) when Prospect started its official post office.

Fig 1 1830 LETTER RATE	
DISTANCE	RATE
36 mi.	6¢
80	10
150	12½
400	18¾
400+	25

Connecticut Register 1830

Fig 2 POSTMASTERS OF THE PROSPECT POST OFFICE
1830-1902

	DATE APPOINTED		DATE APPOINTED
Edward Chittenden	January 19, 1830	Edwin R. Tyler	December 26, 1862
Aaron Austin	April 1, 1837	Luther Morse	July 23, 1864
Hobart C. Porter	May 21, 1841	Richard Tyler	November 14, 1871
Robert H. Platt	February 26, 1844	Henry Nettleton	November 19, 1880
Samuel C. Bronson	March 6, 1846	David B. Hotchkiss	November 1, 1881
Edwin R. Tyler	January 7, 1853	Sarah S. Talmadge	February 20, 1886
Samuel C. Bronson	April 21, 1862		

Fig 3 Charlie Hodges gets a cheery hello from Mrs. Joseph Neal as he delivers a batch of mail at the town drug store in Prospect.

Waterbury Republican, May 6, 1956

Sarah Talmadge was the only postmistress in Prospect (Fig 2) and she served the longest term — 16 years. She was also the last to hold that position as the post office in Prospect was closed on February 20, 1902. From that time until the current Waterbury branch office was opened in October of 1962, Prospect received its mail via rural delivery. Delivery was from three post offices: Waterbury, Naugatuck, and a small section from Cheshire.

Our postman, Bernard Kelly, helped spread local gossip from house to house. If you were standing by your mail box when he came, you could pick up the day's gossip as he passed it along. On a "good news day" it might be 6 P.M. before he finished his rounds.   Gloria Stieler, 1994

The rural carrier was a rolling post office who offered almost every service available, from selling stamps and collecting mail to making out money orders and registered letters. The first deliveries in town were made on horseback. Then, many postmen used their Model-T Fords. In the winter a buggy or sleigh might still be used if Prospect's weather was up to its usual tricks. In those days the mail carriers did more than just deliver mail. Mailmen, such as Charles Hodges (Fig 3) and Bernard Kelly, became well known figures in Prospect.

LIBRARIES

The first local library was in operation over 34 years before the incorporation of Prospect. The Cheshire Mountain Library was founded on Feb 19, 1793, by F. Hotchkiss. One of the library's books, *Goldsmith's Natural History*, dated 1804, is preserved by the Prospect Historical Society. This book was recorded as the 78th one in the collection of the Cheshire Mountain Library. Another early library in Prospect, located at the post office, was called the Oxford Circulating Library. The Cheshire Mountain and the Oxford Circulating Libraries, like other similar libraries, were not public institutions. Fees were charged to use these facilities. By 1892 the Cheshire Mountain Library had been open for a number of years and contained 220 volumes. It was established mainly through the efforts of Mrs. William H. Phipps, whose husband was the pastor of the Prospect Congregational Church from 1878-1906.

Fig 4 A library was at the Talmadge property on Center Street. The building was also used at various times as a tavern, post office, general store, private residence, and parsonage for the Congregational Church. It was razed in 1941.   Waterbury Republican, 1941

The Library Association was organized on August 18, 1886, with B.B. Hotchkiss as president. Existing record books are available, starting in 1896 with the secretary's record. Just prior to this time an act of the Connecticut Legislature provided state aid for libraries. There was a magazine club in town with members subscribing to magazines and exchanging copies among themselves. A Sunday School library also furnished reading material for young people.

Prior to the opening of the library building, Sarah Talmadge was the first librarian and kept the books in her home across the road (Fig 4) from the first permanent library. Her library was open twice per week, and she served for nine years with no compensation other than life membership in the Association. Later, the books were in the vestry of the Congregational Church with Mrs. W.E. Clark as librarian. The town made an appropriation of $25 per year then. The new building was completed at a cost of less than $5,000.

Fig 5 The Prospect Public Library from 1905-1991 was renamed the Meeting Place.
John Guevin

A canvas was made throughout the town to collect funds. A gift of $3 or a $1 gift for four consecutive years would constitute life membership in the association. Twenty-five cents gave the donor use of the library for one year. In 1895 the Library Association began loaning its books to the town and provided funds so that the library would be free to all who wished to make use of it.

The records of the treasurer begin in 1903, about the time efforts were being made to secure a building. The librarian was Mrs. W.E. Clark. The original Prospect Library building (Fig 5), now the Meeting Place, was completed in 1905 with much of the financial support coming from the Tuttle family of Naugatuck. Bronson B. Tuttle's pledge of $50 per year was the deciding factor to proceed with the building project.

A large number of people from Naugatuck, Waterbury and vicinity went to Prospect today, when the new Public Library Building was dedicated with appropriate exercises. The building, designed by F.E. Walters of this city, is a handsome structure, 30 x 39 feet in size, built of fieldstone with blue stone trimmings and a red tile roof. It contains three rooms, the largest a stack room is a very attractive place, 15 x 22 feet in size, finished in ash, with a tile fireplace, and ash mantel and beamed ceiling.

Waterbury Republican, May 25, 1905

Books that were not donated were purchased for less than 30¢ each. The magazine club gave some of their back volumes and these were bound. In the early days a grant from the state of $100 per year also helped purchase new books. The pay for the librarian was $50 per year when the library first opened. By 1944 the salary was $250.

The unsatisfactory heat received from $20 worth of wood is replaced by $150 worth of oil a year. The library was seldom open in the evening in years gone by. Then 50 cents for kerosene supplied light. Now electricity costs us $50, but none of the steady stream of Thursday evening patrons would question the success of evening hours. The noteworthy expenditures for library improvement were in cataloguing in 1927, the electric wiring in 1928 and the installation of an oil burner in 1935 . . . Some means for running water and toilet facilities remain to be found in the future.   Library Report 1945, Nellie Cowdell, Librarian

Fig 6 New Prospect Public Library with tools from the Petrauskas farm.   John Guevin

The dedication of the new Prospect Public Library (Fig 6) took place on June 16, 1991. This facility was built at the former site of the Petrauskas farm on Center Street. The construction of the new building was made possible through the generosity of the Boardman family trust, the Tress family, and many others who made donations for this project. The new structure provided much needed space for more books and a wide range of services. The population of Prospect has multiplied fifteen times since the first library was built.

LIBRARIANS

1886-01	Sarah Talmadge	1977-79	Joan Heller Errgong-Weider
1902-30	Nettie H. Clark	1980-81	Robert Gallucci
1931-34	Mrs. Elmer R. Main	1982-85	Jane E. Scully
1935-53	Nellie Cowdell	1986-88	Eva (Dolly) Anthony Nabors
1954-72	Miriam Levesque	1989-90	Brian Fitzgerald
1973-74	Judith Dreher	1990-91	Kathy Renna
1975-76	Miriam Levesque	1991-	Barbara Peterson

PUBLIC SAFETY

Public safety is a basic service provided by municipalities. From the early days of the town, the protection and safety of local citizens has always been a top priority. This function today includes three components: police, fire, and ambulance/emergency services. Traditionally, police department personnel are paid for their work; fire departments in small towns like Prospect are normally staffed with volunteers; and ambulance services are often a mixture of volunteers, paid municipal employees, and private firms.

◼ POLICE

Constables provided the local police protection from 1827 until about 1970, when the system of resident state troopers took effect. Constables were elected officials who enforced the local laws. They would arrest violators and turn them over to the justice system. Early offenses included:

> . . . *disturbing the peace "with loud noises in the night," or stealing honey from a hive of bees, or a woman's dress from the line. Some men did not pay their bills at the store, or their taxes. Some by "their idleness were in danger of coming to want and becoming town charges. "*
>
> Prospect - Primer of History

In later years the enforcement of motor vehicle laws was the most outward sign of the constables' presence. They would track down drivers who thought Prospect's country roads were a good place to burn the carbon out of their engine. Constables were a regular sight directing traffic at the intersection of the state roads where accidents were common (Fig 7).

Fig 7   One of many accidents at the intersection of the state roads, which led to the installation of a traffic light.   Waterbury Republican, 1941

Because of increasing traffic and accidents public pressure mounted to replace the constables with resident state police. In 1955 the subject was debated in a town meeting, but the vote was 95 to 63 against any change.

Discussion among the 160 voters preceding the vote on the trooper lasted more than an hour and together with the vote took up most of the meeting. Principal argument in favor of the resident trooper was that Prospect already has to summon troopers from Bethany Barracks in times of emergency. Rather than having to wait for dispatch and arrival of a cruiser, therefore, there should be a trooper always at hand nearby. A second argument in favor of the resident trooper was that since the town borders two state highways the motorists who travel through are not residents and would be more deterred from violations by the sight of the trooper than by the sight of the constables. Arguments against the trooper insisted that the benefit to be obtained does not balance the cost. If there is money to be spent on law enforcement, said the opponents in addition, it should be spent on increases to the existing constabulary.

Waterbury Republican, December 7, 1955

The constable system continued for a time, but the resident state trooper program was finally approved and has been in use for the last 25 years. Under this plan the town pays about 70% of the expenses for the trooper, and the state picks up the remaining 30%. The cost to the town is relatively constant, since extra state police for special emergencies are paid for by the state. In addition to one (or at times, two) troopers on duty in Prospect, local law enforcement officers are assigned for town duty. There are currently nine part-time officers. Since 1989 all local officers are required to complete a basic 2½ month training course. These officers are distinct from the elected constables who no longer perform the same law enforcement functions they did in the past. The constables can serve court papers but have no police powers.

Fig 8 The Prospect police station after expansion and remodeling in 1991.   John Guevin

In August 1978 the new Prospect police station was dedicated. This facility was expanded and remodeled in 1991 (Fig 8). Although Prospect is a small and peaceful town most of the time, it is not immune to the ravages of crime. Several from the Prospect Police Department have received certificates for bravery, including Trooper Raymond LaPalme and Constable Eugene Ober for their actions in 1980, when LaPalme was shot and wounded.

Besides dealing with the usual traffic, burglary, and other crimes, the police handle some situations that could only happen in a town like Prospect. One such example occurred in 1984 when police investigated the death of Nora Frederick's pig and piglets. It seems that a hot air balloonist was drifting over the Frederick farm on Matthew Street at a low altitude. A blast from the balloon engine frightened Mrs. Frederick's pregnant sow, causing her to slip on the ice and break her back. The pig and the dozen fetal piglets she was carrying had to be killed. The balloon pilot, learning of the mishap, was quite concerned and was able to have the damages covered by his insurance.

■ EMERGENCY SERVICES

For a number of years the Prospect Fire Department provided ambulance services to the town. They started with a used Packard ambulance purchased from the Waterbury Hospital. This vehicle was upgraded to an "almost new" 1966 Cadillac ambulance and then was supplemented by a 1974 Dodge van-type ambulance. Since the 1980s this function has been provided by Campion Ambulance Service of Waterbury with assistance from the fire department.

Prospect became the regional center for the coordination of 911 calls when the Northwest Connecticut Public Safety Communication Center opened on Cheshire Road on May 3, 1992. With new state-of-the-art equipment, response time for all emergencies has been cut to the minimum. No piece of equipment has yet to equal the quick response of Prospect's own mayor, Robert Chatfield. Mayor Bob displays the uncanny ability to be the first one to arrive at the scene of almost every accident or emergency in town — anytime day or night. Prospect was the focus of national attention when Ann Landers recognized Mayor Chatfield in her column (Fig 9).

Fig 9 ANN LANDERS COLUMN 11-15-94

Prospect, Conn.: I had to call 911 while baby-sitting my nephew. He had a seizure, and I was a nervous wreck. I called 911 immediately. While I was on the line, not only did one of our local policemen show up, but so did our mayor, Bob Chatfield. Three minutes later, the emergency squad arrived. Everyone was calm and reassuring, it was beautiful. It's OK to print my name. In fact, I hope you will.

Kathy Legere

■ FIRE DEPARTMENT

Few activities in a community capture the essence of small town life better than the volunteer fire department. The selfless giving by these dedicated men and women for the good of their town and its people makes Prospect the sort of place it is. This spirit is contagious, as many families are represented by several generations of service to the Prospect fire department.

Brush fires were handled by local citizens. The ringing of the Congregational Church bell signaled the need for fire fighters. If the need arose when school was in session, the older boys were dismissed to don back-pack water sprayers to tackle the brush fires. For 118 years Prospect was largely dependent on other towns for major fire protection. Because of the distances to travel and the hills to climb, this lack of self-reliance too often resulted in total losses to buildings and sometimes lives. There were measures taken to provide some protection. A town fire warden was responsible for seeing that buildings were in a safe condition and water buckets and ladders were available. These measures were effective for small fires caught quickly. Once a fire was beyond the initial stage, there was little that could be done.

Among the early fires was that of the Center School on Old School House Road in the 1850s. Students arrived for class to find their building reduced to glowing embers. Match factories were frequent victims of fire, as dis-cussed in the chapter on early industries. There were also numerous barn and house fires, but the greatest losses were the fires that destroyed two Congre-gational Church buildings, once in 1906 and again in 1941.

The second devastating fire (Fig 10) gave the final impetus to create a local fire department. Efforts to improve the fire protection in Prospect formally began with the organization of Hose Co. No. 1 on May 18, 1938. Eugene Lewis was elected captain. Fund raising was begun to acquire a piece of fire fighting apparatus. Not enough cash was collected to purchase some used equipment that was for sale, and the town would not approve funds for the fledgling fire department. The day of the church fire in 1941 a petition was started in Ed Chandler's store to hold a special meeting to purchase a fire truck. At the meeting the selectmen were given authority to purchase a fire truck and a supply of hose, which was stored in Carl Weyland's garage until a firehouse could be secured.

Fig 10 The stone Congregational Church destroyed by fire on Saturday morning, November 29, 1941.   Waterbury Republican

Fig 11 Prospect Hose Co. No.1 in front of the first fire house c. 1940s.
Waterbury Republican

Land was acquired from Rob Arrol, and the town voted to fund supplies for the first two-bay firehouse. With volunteer labor and some outside help the project was completed in 1942 (Fig 11). The first major test of the department came in February of 1943, when the Grange hall was extensively damaged. The 500 gallon tank of the only truck was not adequate, and the Cheshire fire department had to assist to prevent a total loss. The need for more equipment, more water, and more manpower was evident. The original Prospect Hose Co. No. 1 was expanded in 1945. Carl Canfield was appointed the temporary fire chief. A new company of 40 men, known as the Prospect Volunteer Fire Department, was formed that included many of the charter members from the hose company.

The town transferred ownership of the truck and building to the fire department for one dollar. Fund raising activities allowed the purchase of a truck to carry water. The siren, atop the old Center Schoolhouse and used by Civil Defence during WW II, was given to the fire department. Other sirens were added around town, and the system was supplemented with two phones manned 24 hours a day.

Over the years more and better equipment was added to the department. With no room to expand the fire house on the land available, a new lot at the intersection of Center Street and Route 69 was secured from the Water Company with the help of Carl Canfield in 1950. The sale of fireworks and other activities helped raise money for the construction of the five-bay fire-house at the present site (Fig 12).

Fig 12 Prospect Volunteer Fire Department, men, equipment, and four-bay fire house circa 1950s.
Mayor's Office

The true measure of a fire department's success should be the absence of need for their service. In reality, fire departments are remembered for the fires they have fought. A list of the major fires in Prospect in recent years includes a fire of a home on Plank Road in September 1952 where two men were killed, the Cedar Hill Dairy barn fire on Hydelor Avenue in 1971, and the Prospect Machine Products Company blaze in March 1977.

Foam Plastics of New England on New Haven Road was totally destroyed by a spectacular fire in 1983 (Fig 13). The smoke was visible for miles. The best efforts of fire fighters could not control the intensity of the blaze. After the fire, Foam Plastics owner, Gene Lewis, was determined to rebuild his factory in Prospect but knew there must be access to water lines for fire hydrants and sprinkler systems. With the assistance of Mayor Robert Chatfield, a state grant was awarded to bring water lines up Route 68 from Naugatuck to supply water to industrial parks in that end of town. The Foam Plastics plant on Gramar Avenue and many other companies have been able to build in Prospect with complete fire safety protection.

The most recent major fire was the total loss of Oliver's Market on February 25, 1985. A maximum effort was made, ferrying of tanker after tanker of water, but it was not enough to contain the inferno. The loss of Prospect's only supermarket, which had become an institution, was felt personally by all members of the town. In a short time and with much determination, Oliver's was rebuilt on the same location.

The most tragic loss of life occurred on Friday, July 22, 1977, when fire struck the Beaudoin home at the corner of Cedar Hill Drive and Route 68. Firemen brought the blaze under control within 30 minutes. When the smoke cleared enough to enter the house, firemen discovered the bodies of Cheryl Beaudoin and her seven children.

Fig 13 Foam Plastics building is destroyed in a spectacular blaze in April of 1983.

Waterbury Republican

Since 1950 the Ladies Auxiliary of the Prospect Volunteer Fire Department has supported the efforts of the firemen through fund raising, purchasing of equipment, and on-the-scene support with much needed food and refreshments. Ruth Chandler was the first president. In 1995 the Prospect Volunteer Fire Department celebrated its 50th year of service and dedication to the town.

Fig 14   FIRE CHIEFS
PROSPECT VOLUNTEER FIRE DEPARTMENT

1938-45 Eugene Lewis (Captain Hose Co. No. 1)	1963-70 John Gilmartin
1945-45 Carl Canfield (temporary Chief)	1970-86 Paul L. Murray
1945-46 Roy Burton Hubbell Sr.	1987-93 Donald Stankus
1946-59 Raymond Chandler	1994- Ronald Wislocki
1959-63 John L. Chatfield	

JUSTICE SYSTEM

In the early years of Prospect much more of the justice process was done locally than it is today. Serious offenses were still carried to state officials. Some Prospect citizens were elected grand jurors and they would swear out warrants. The function of the local constables was to make the arrests. Cases which were not of a serious nature were tried by the Prospect justices of the peace and often were done in the home of the justice. Typical crimes included petty theft, disturbing the peace, failure to pay bills, or compensation for damage done by someone's animals.

The western portion of Prospect was in the Woodbury probate district, and the eastern part was in the Wallingford probate district. These courts were for matters such as settling estates and caring for orphans. Today, all of Prospect is included in the Cheshire-Prospect probate district. Other cases are heard in Waterbury courts rather than by local justices, who now only perform functions such as witnessing signatures and performing marriages.

UTILITIES

Because of its sparse population Prospect lagged behind other towns in receiving many utility services. The first telephone was installed in town in 1904, although a line was run through the center of Prospect in November of 1898, connecting New Haven and Waterbury.

My grandfather, Joseph Grenier, had a telephone in his Prospect home in 1909. It was a pay phone. You would crank it to ring-up the operator, then deposit a coin (maybe 5¢ or 10¢) to be connected to your party. The phone company would come by once in a great while (maybe once a year) to pick up the coins in the phone.   Beulah Goggin (1994)

Ruth VanWagner remembers the phones when she moved to Prospect in 1939. The standard service then was an eight-party line. *Totalphone* came to Prospect in 1989, and many residents missed the convenience of dialing just 5 digits to reach another Prospect phone.

Electricity was extended to Prospect in 1929. It came up Route 69 as far as the center. The Grange hall, the Congregational Church, and three street lights made up the number of customers required by the company to establish service. There was power from Meriden by way of Cheshire for the trolley line. It also served lower Summit Road and the surrounding area.

It was exciting when we got electricity. It took awhile to run all the poles. Some power came from one direction and some from another. I think there were three power lines all together.   Bessie Mortison, 1995

I recall when electricity came. My mother went out and bought every-thing electric — radio, stove, etc. It seemed like the house became fully electric overnight. She must have been saving up for this day. Elmer Main was the first one in town to have an electric door bell. Kids just couldn't resist running up to his house, ringing the bell, running to hid, and then watching from the bushes. One Halloween night I was caught red-handed when I was putting a toothpick in the doorbell button just when Mr. Main came to the door.   Gloria Stieler, 1994

Residents of the East District of the town met at the East School Monday evening with a representative from the Waterbury branch of the Connecticut Light & Power Co. to discuss plans for a new extension from the center to that section. The East School is the only school house in the town where electric current is not available.

Waterbury Republican, September 17, 1930

Prospect has an abundance of water. Unfortunately, this water has been largely to the benefit of surrounding towns and cities who received their water supplies from the reservoirs of Prospect.   Only recently has pipeline water been available to portions of town.   In 1988 water begin flowing into the buildings along Industrial Road. On October 14, 1994, water service was extended to the center of Prospect for the first time in its history. This water not only supplies water to public buildings and private homes, but finally provides an abundance of water for fire protection in the center of a town which has seen more than its share of tragic fires.

Because of its altitude Prospect has been the site of two radio stations and one television station.   In 1934 the first radio transmitter in the area, WATR, was established near the Bethany line on Route 69 (Fig 14). Afterwards, the facility was moved to Waterbury. The road opposite the transmitter was renamed Radio Tower Road after the towers were removed.

Guy and Ralna of the Lawrence Welk television show were present for the grand opening of the new studios for W-104 FM on Waterbury Road. This country music format station was located on Waterbury Road, just south of Murphy Road in front of Turkey Hill, which was dubbed "Music Mountain."

Television Channel 20, providing the only non-cable television service in the Waterbury area, is located on Peach Orchard Road.

Fig 14 Sketch by Prospect's C.L. Mortison of the WATR radio station on Waterbury-Bethany Road.

Waterbury Republican, Oct. 28, 1934

~

Chapter Fourteen

Boundaries, Markers, and Monuments

B oundaries were the subject of many disputes among early settlers to Prospect. The Indians were the first to mark off borders defining their tribal territories and hunting grounds. Like the early white settlers to follow, the most frequent reference points were natural formations like rivers or trees. Sometimes a pile of rocks would be created if nature did not provide a distinctive marker in the right place.

Thirty-four years after the founding of the New Haven Colony, much of the outlying territory in that township was still considered to be wasteland and some parts had yet to be explored. On September 9, 1672, the townspeople expressed interest in surveying their northern borders.

> *Consider of and appoint some sutable persons to run the Line for a tryall to see how farre twelve miles will reach from the sea northward into the woods.* Republic of New Haven

Until this time the citizens of New Haven were not very curious about their northern property which they purchased from the Indians for some hoes, hatchets, and knives. The first record of carrying out the ancient custom of perambulation or walking along and marking property lines was on April 2, 1683. At that time Sergeant Winston was appointed to survey all common borders with Milford, Wallingford, and Branford. The landmarks were heaps of stones. The New Haven charter describes the northwest corner of the township to be defined by a clump of three chestnut trees growing from one root.

THE THREE BROTHERS TREE

The borders of Prospect may be traced back to the agreements made with the Indians. A document signed by eight Tunxis men and two Tunxis women on February 20, 1684, gave land rights to the Mattatuck settlement. One of the key markers in this deed and in almost all other land settlements in the region was the Three Brothers tree (Fig 1), sometimes known as the Three Sisters tree. This marker was the same clump of chestnut trees named in the New Haven charter and was a reference point used by the Indians for many years.

At one time or another, the Three Brothers tree has been the corner of nine different towns. In 1673 the "three chestnut trees growing from one root"

Fig 1   Three Brothers (Sisters) tree.
History of Waterbury

represented a boundary corner of New Haven and Milford townships. Later Waterbury and Wallingford met at the same spot. The southwest corner of Wallingford became the southwest corner of Cheshire. The north edge of Milford became Woodbridge. Eventually, the southwest part of Cheshire (and the southeast part of Waterbury) became Prospect. The northwest corner of New Haven became the town of Bethany. Then, the southeast corner of Waterbury and the northern part of Woodbridge became Naugatuck. The Three Brothers tree also grew in two counties, New Haven and Hartford, until Waterbury was transferred from Hartford county to New Haven county.

A RETURN TO THREE BROTHERS

After reading accounts about this historic clump of trees, I thought it would be interesting to visit the site. Reports indicated the trees had died from blight and were no longer standing by the 1920s. Still, it would be fascinating just to stand at this place that had been a marking point for so many years. A visit with Kathy Harvey in the land records office of the Prospect town hall revealed that the present owners of the land at Three Brothers were Benedict and Mary Pranulis.

A phone call to the residence was answered by Mary, who upon hearing the nature of my request, soon transferred the phone to Ben, who would become the enthusiastic tour guide. It was a warm summer day when my wife Betty and I met at Ben's home. He told us he bought the 30-acre property fifty years ago, not knowing any historical significance to the location. "I only wanted a place in the country to live and raise my family," he said. Ben had been living in the Brooklyn section of Waterbury. It was only after buying the property that its significance became apparent. A portion of the Pranulis property was in each of three towns: Bethany, Naugatuck, and Prospect (Fig 2).

Eager to get started, Ben began climbing the steep path to the Three Brothers site at the top of a hill. His pace defied his age of 78, as he led the way, causing us to catch up with him at intervals to the summit. As we ascended, Ben told us that none of the stumps were

Fig 2   Three Brothers - at the junction of Bethany, Naugatuck, and Prospect.

standing when he first saw them in the 1940s. One fallen trunk was still quite large and formed a shelter for his cub scout den camp-outs. My mind envisioned young scouts gathering around the camp fire in the darkness, listening to stories about Indian warriors as told to them by their cub leaders. I was moved by the notion that Indian children had huddled at this same spot for centuries, listening in awe at the tales of their elders.

We reached the site and found remnants of two of the three stumps. Each fell in a direction facing one of the towns. The trunk that fell toward Naugatuck was the largest. Another landing on Prospect soil was now much smaller. The third must have disintegrated years earlier and could not be seen. Two stone markers were at the base of the trees with the letters B N P, for Bethany, Naugatuck, and Prospect. One marker was surveyed in 1842 and 1856, while the other was inscribed in 1881 (Fig 3).

On the return from the summit, Ben told of two amazing coincidences about his property. He and Mary gave birth to and raised three sons (brothers) and those initials on the

Fig 3 Three Brothers marker from 1881.　　　　　　　John Guevin

marker — B N P — are the same as his name. Nearing the end of our descent, Ben talked about how he liked to ski down this slope. Betty, assuming he did this sport in his younger years, asked, "But you don't ski now?" "No, of course not!", Ben replied, "I did it last winter when there was snow here!" Our visit was complete when we were shown the collection of quartz Indian arrow points that Ben unearthed in the fifty years he farmed the land.　　　　　　　John Guevin, 1994

BOUNDARY DISPUTES

For some years conflicts kept cropping up between Wallingford and Waterbury as to the proper location of their common border. There were quarrels and some bloodshed until the *Generall Courte* took charge of the matter and called out surveyors to resolve the issue.

It was some of these boundary troubles that delayed the "laying out of their lands" to those who had received allotments in the Second Divisions. It frequently happened that after a "Lay out" had been made by one surveyor, the other surveyor would be asked to "lay out" some land for another planter. This last surveyor, not being aware that another surveyor had been over the ground, would run his lines sometimes so that his "lay out" would cut into, or surround the land laid out to the planter employing the first surveyor. It is not to be supposed that our ancestors were so rigidly moral as not to take advantage of their neighbor, indeed we find frequently to the contrary . . . then would follow a dispute settled either in town meeting or by a Committee.　　　History of Cheshire

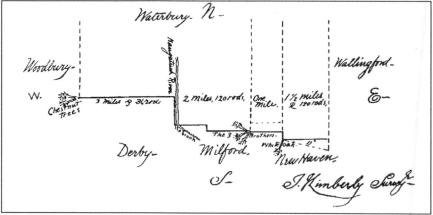

Fig 4 Map from 1715 survey of Waterbury & Wallingford. History of Waterbury

In 1715 the boundaries of Waterbury and Wallingford were surveyed to settle a dispute over the proper border line (Fig 4). A committee was appointed to resolve the matter. Both townships claimed ownership of the same land east of the Three Brothers marker. The final decision caused the proprietors of Waterbury to pay Wallingford the sum of four pounds, three shillings, and six pence. Also, they were required to relinquish their claim to the land lying east of the Three Brothers. This land was a section in the southeast corner of Waterbury, a little more than 1½ miles in width. Waterbury borrowed the money from Joseph Lewis and paid it back in 1720 with eighty acres of land.

REGIONS OF PROSPECT

The 1868 Beer's New Haven County Atlas shows Prospect (see Chapter 7, Fig 1) divided into the six regions that were used to designate school districts. These were: West, Centre, North East, East, South West, and South East. Part of northern Prospect was also included in the East Mountain District of Waterbury. Besides these districts there were also names for particular sections of town, such as *Sunnyside* in the Centre District; *Riverside* in the East District; *Shady Lawn*, also in the East District; and *Prospect View*, situated in the South East District. Two areas were called *Prospect Hill*, one in the Centre District and another in the South West District.

From other records we know of additional subsections within Prospect. In the chapter on early industries, *Rag Hollow* was discussed as the center of manufacturing activity. *Indian Farm* was the area set aside in 1731 as an Indian Reservation for the Quinnipiacs. The *Three Brothers* section was discussed earlier in this chapter. *Turkey Hill* is designated a point of high elevation in northern Prospect near the Waterbury line. *George's Hollow* was a depression at the head of Fulling Mill Brook near the Naugatuck line. *Indian Well,* near a meadow by the Naugatuck border, was another depression, circular in form, about thirty feet deep and flat on the bottom.

This depression no longer exists. *Log Town*, near George's Hollow, was east of Indian Well. Other names mentioned in the past were *Germantown*, *College Farm Bars*, and *Goat Lot Corners*. In the southeast corner of Prospect is a section of the *Naugatuck State Forest*.

Prospect has an abundance of water in the forms of rivers, ponds, and reservoirs. Most of the rivers existed for hundreds or even thousands of years. Some of the river's paths have been altered by dams and the creation of reservoirs in the nineteenth and twentieth centuries. Prospect never consumed any water from these reservoirs. They were built to supply Waterbury, Naugatuck, New Haven, and Cheshire with tap water. Several reservoirs in the eastern part of town, owned by the South Central Connecticut Regional Water Authority, have been placed in reserve, since Cheshire's current needs are met by two large well fields. The reservoir in the East Mountain area of town, owned by the Waterbury Water Department, has been discontinued and is for sale. Several reservoirs in the southwestern part of town are still owned by the Connecticut Water Company.

Fig 5 Site of early dam near the New Naugatuck Reservoir.   John Guevin

RIVERS	PONDS	RESERVOIRS
Roaring Brook	Juggernaut	West Brook
Fulling Mill Brook	Brook	New Naugatuck (Fig 7)
Ten Mile River	Beer's (Russell) Pond	Old Naugatuck (Fig 8)
East Mountain Brook		Cheshire
Millville Brook		East Mountain
West Brook		Waterbury #2
Marks Brook		
Mountain Brook		**PROSPECT'S WATER RESOURCES**

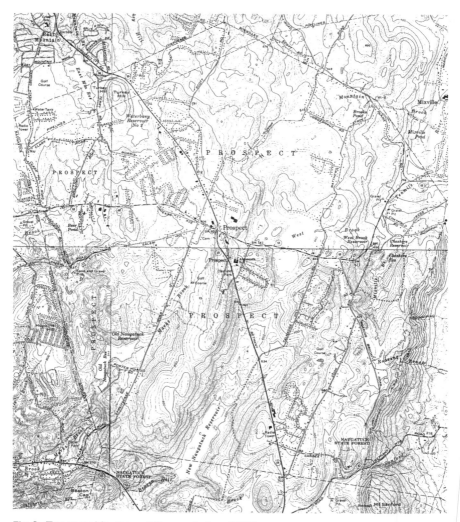

Fig 6 Topographic map of Prospect circa 1984.   U.S. Geological Survey

PROSPECT PARKS

Canfield Park   Located at the intersection of New Haven Road and Coer Road, this park is named for Carl Canfield, who was instrumental in acquiring this property for the town along with the land for the fire house. The fields are widely used for softball, baseball, and football. Tennis courts are available.

McGrath Park   Situated east of the town hall on Cheshire Road, the park (Fig 7) contains a fishing pond and has adjacent tennis courts.   This recreational area is in honor of William McGrath, who served for many years on the Board of Education and the Board of Recreation.

Fig 7   Fishing pond at McGrath Park.   John Guevin

Cipriano Park   George Cipriano was first selectman of Prospect from 1961-1967. This park, in his memory, is located on Matthew Street near Cheshire Road. It contains fields for soccer and other sports.

Hotchkiss Field   This field is located next to the Hotchkiss house on Waterbury Road.   It contains lighted basketball courts and a running track and is used for many town activities. The Hotchkiss family, for whom the field is named, contributed to the development of Prospect through the efforts of many family members.   They held numerous public offices, operated schools and businesses, and helped defend our country in times of war.

MONUMENTS ON THE GREEN

The focal point of the Prospect Green — at its very center — is the Soldier Monument. This location demonstrates Prospect's concern for honoring its servicemen and women who sacrificed so much for their town and country. The memorial is described in detail in the chapter on wars and soldiers. The flag pole next to the monument was erected in 1976 as a project of the Prospect Bicentennial Commission.

Across the Green to the south, on the east side of the Grange hall, is the first burial site in town. A stone memorial (Fig 8) was placed on the old burial grounds in 1987 by the Prospect Historical Society and the town of Prospect. No individual grave markers remain here. Most, if not all, of those interred in this original plot were moved to the larger cemetery located to the west across New Haven Road.

> **THIS IS THE RECORDED SITE**
> **OF THE FIRST BURYING**
> **GROUND**
> **IN COLUMBIA PARISH,**
> **NOW PROSPECT, 1765-1805.**
> PLACED BY THE TOWN OF PROSPECT &
> THE HISTORICAL SOCIETY MAY 1987

Fig 8   First burying ground marker.

Fig 9   Unspoiled beauty of the Old Naugatuck Reservoir.   John Guevin

To the west of the monument is a sign erected by the town of Prospect, the Prospect Historical Society, and the Connecticut Historical Society in 1980. It provides a capsule summary of the town's history. Included are descriptions of some of Prospect's famous citizens as well as industrial contributions and tributes to the town's military service. On the east side of the Green is a tree and memorial placed by MADD in honor of Karen R. Senese, who was injured on August 28, 1987.

In the northeast corner of the Green, next to the Meeting Place, is a scion of Connecticut's Charter Oak (Fig 10). The original Charter Oak tree was leveled by the hurricane of 1856. This tree was planted by the Prospect Historical Society in 1935 to observe the Connecticut Tercentenary. It was positioned at the same location as a sycamore or buttonball tree that had stood

> SCION OF
> THE CHARTER OAK WAS
> PLANTED HERE IN 1935
> TO OBSERVE THE CONN.
> TERCENTENARY
>
> PROSPECT HISTORICAL SOCIETY

Fig 10 Charter Oak scion marker.

at the crest of the hill for an estimated two hundred years. When it fell, a bayonet (now preserved by the Prospect Historical Society) was found in the crotch.

One memorial is missing from the Prospect Green. It can, however, be found across from the Green in Cheshire (Fig 11). The Rev. Phipps, in a historic address, referred to Cheshire as "The town with a stone in its heart" because the stone had been pilfered from the Prospect Green and taken to Cheshire in an ox cart by night. A group led by Robert Harvey, Sr. attempted to retrieve the stone in 1977, but their efforts were thwarted by Cheshire officials. The story of the stepping stone's disappearance is told on the plaque attached:

This old stone was brought from the center of Prospect early in 1800 by a group of Cheshire young men to serve as a "stepping stone" for those attending the church which then stood on the east edge of the present Green.

Fig 11 Prospect's old stepping stone now "on display" in Cheshire.   John Guevin

THE CEMETERIES

Cemeteries are sources of some of the earliest town records. Forty-four residents were buried before Prospect was incorporated. The following names were recorded as the burial records of Columbia Parish (Prospect) between 1762-1829 [name, age, year of death]:

Amos Atwater, 60, 1822	Minerva Hotchkiss, 23, 1822
Silas Barnes, 17,1829	Rhoda Hotchkiss, 47, 1814
Lambert Beecher, 2,1827	Robert Hotchkiss, 72, 1826
George Benham, 16 mos., 1829	Ruth Hotchkiss, 76, 1812
Polly Bronson, 35, 1816	Lydia Moss, 49, 1826
Samuel Castle, 49, 1826	David Payne, 76, 1825
Ashael Chittenden, 50, 1813	Edwin Payne, 2, 1813
Bradley Conkling, 25, 1817	Henrietta Payne, 3, 1813
Isaac Hine, 24, 1798	Joseph Payne, 45, 1822
Sally Hitchcock, 59, 1780	Lydia Peck, 46, 1822
Abraham Hotchkiss, 64, 1807	Ann Richardson, 39, 1818
Amos Hotchkiss, 70, 1820	John Sanford, 59, 1827
Anne Hotchkiss, 47, 1762	Sarah Wilmot Sanford, 73, 1818
Chloe Hotchkiss, 18, 1812	David Scott, 62, 1827
Ellen Hotchkiss, 15 wks., 1822	Martha A. Scott, 52, 1828
Gideon Hotchkiss, 91, 1807	Isaac Spencer, 33, 1803
Hannah Hotchkiss, 80, 1824	Josiah Terrill, 62, 1795
Jerusha Hotchkiss, 25, 1814	David Tyler, 58, 1826
Jerusha Hotchkiss, 65, 1824	Enos Tyler, 69, 1804
Laura Hotchkiss, 17, 1817	Mary Tyler, 72, 1806
Loly Hotchkiss, 8, 1794	---- Tyler, 30, 1826
Mabel Hotchkiss, 95, 1821	Samuel Williams, 77, 1813

Fig 12 PROSPECT
POPULATION
BY AGE
1840 U.S. CENSUS

AGE	COUNT
0-5	52
5-10	64
10-15	68
15-20	57
20-30	78
30-40	62
40-50	65
50-60	54
60-70	33
70-80	9
80-90	6
90+	0
TOTAL	548

As an indication of how tough life was during those early years, only ten of these 44 lived to be 70 years old. Their average life span was only 46 years. Many children succumbed to diseases, young women frequently died during childbirth, and young men were often casualties of war. The U.S. Census of 1840 (Fig 12) shows the age distribution among Prospect residents.

The first burial ground described earlier in this chapter was replaced by a larger ground at the southern end of the present "old" cemetery. The property was purchased from Asahel Chittenden in 1805, and most of those buried in the original small plots were moved to the new location. About 1860 the cemetery was enlarged toward the northern part of the "old" cemetery. Then, in 1896 land was purchased on the hill toward Route 69. This section became the "new" cemetery (Fig 13). Recently, the property was extended as far as Route 68.

In the beginning, maintenance of the grounds was the responsibility of the Congregational Church. The town of Prospect assumed this duty around 1860. The Cemetery Association, which is the current caretaker of the property, formed in 1921.

Fig 13 "New" Prospect cemetery.   Waterbury Republican-American

THE TOWN SEAL

In preparation for our nation's bicentennial celebration, a new town seal was adopted by the Town Council in June 1975. The designer for the seal was Jane Purdy Fowler, a fourth generation resident of Prospect. In creating the design, Jane made a number of sketches of the Civil War monument, which stands prominently on the Green as a silent reminder that Prospect sent more men into battle in proportion to the town's voter list than any other town in the state.

This veteran of the *Grand Army of the Republic* is pictured looking out over the hills in a pose that seems full of determination. He symbolizes the contribution of Prospect men and women to the history of the country. Other parts of the seal reflect aspects of the town's history. The waterwheel suggests the manufacturing that took place along the streams during the 1800s. The plow symbolizes the agriculture which was carried on for generations and still persists. The small cloud over the monument gives a hint of the town's extended view as well as a sense of future destiny. The scene is framed by the distinctive boundaries of Prospect.   ∎

Chapter Fifteen

Climate and Weather

O ne may rightfully ask what climate and weather have to do with the history of a town. In the case of Prospect, these factors have been significant in forming the character of the place. Prospect has the reputation of having *more* of whatever kind of weather is being dished out. That means more rain, more wind, more cold, more ice, and certainly more fog and more snow!

Climate refers to the long-term average meteorological conditions of a given area while weather concerns the day to day variations. Prospect also has a number of distinct microclimates. These are localized pockets that display differences in the temperature, precipitation, or fog level from the general region. Because of the hilly terrain the sun and winds strike sections of town at a variety of angles at different times of the day. This phenomena leads to more diverse weather patterns than experienced by a community on level ground.

Prospect is located approximately fifteen miles inland, close enough to Long Island Sound so that the extremes of temperature are somewhat modified. The Sound acts as a heat sink, releasing heat more slowly than land in winter, and absorbing heat from the land in summer. The mean annual temperature is 50°F, averaging 68°F in summer and 33°F in winter. The first frost usually occurs in mid-October and the last in mid-April, giving an average growing season of 180 days.

Total precipitation in the area averages 50 inches, including 32 inches of snow. An average of 6 inches more precipitation falls annually at Prospect than at Lake Whitney [Hamden], where regional climate is gauged. [Fig 1]. Prevailing winds are from the south and

southwest in the summer, as cool air flows north from the Sound. In the winter months, November through April, northwest winds prevail. Average wind velocity for the region is 7 mph.

Variations from these average figures can be extreme from season to season and year to year. Precipitation at Prospect, for example, was 72.5 inches in 1972 and only 36 inches in 1965. Changes like this are abrupt and patternless. The years of the early 1960s were very dry. The year 1965 saw less precipitation than any in the 93-year record of the U.S. Weather Bureau in New Haven, and most of the reservoirs in the New Haven Water Company system were severely overdrawn. Yet the draft at Prospect was above the estimated safe yield of the reservoir, and data show that excess water ran over the spillway for four months of the year. Prospect received about 8 more inches of rain than did the Lake Whitney area, and the lake levels in the Prospect Res- *ervoir remained relatively high, while other reservoirs in the system were severely depleted.*

Melissa Paly, *The Prospect Property, Prospect, Connecticut*

Fig 1   AVERAGE ANNUAL PRECIPITATION (Inches)

YEAR	PROSPECT	LAKE WHITNEY	YEAR	PROSPECT	LAKE WHITNEY
1960	57.70	41.65	1970	42.84	34.20
1961	46.65	41.28	1971	52.04	46.87
1962	44.09	36.64	1972	70.47	61.77
1963	42.70	38.20	1973	56.43	55.09
1964	38.16	33.52	1974	52.03	44.41
1965	36.18	27.67	1975	61.61	52.58
1966	40.16	32.06	1976	49.02	47.88
1967	47.87	40.63	1977	57.34	51.98
1968	51.85	40.11	1978	49.74	54.17
1969	54.26	49.83	1979	57.43	55.00
			AVERAGE (20 years)	50.43	44.28

MelissaPaly

CHRONOLOGY OF THE
MAJOR WEATHER EVENTS
IN PROSPECT'S HISTORY

1697-98   The hardest winter of the seventeenth century greeted the first land surveyors in Prospect.

1717   The "Great Snow" — four storms between February 27 and March 7 — deposited between three and five feet of snow throughout the region.

1740-41   Many called this winter worse than the 1697-98 winter. It left central Connecticut buried under three feet of snow.

1780   Troops in Connecticut during the Revolutionary War were immobilized during this winter. In southern parts of the state, snow was forty-two inches deep on level ground.

March 19, 1780   The "Dark Day" recorded by Yale president, Ezra Siles:

. . . there fell . . . a singular and very remarkable Darkness, which over spread the Hemisphere for about five hours . . . About Ten o'clock A.M. a Darkness came on, which by Eleven was perceived to be very unusual and extraordinary . . . and continued so intense from a little

> *before noon to near Two o'clock, as that a person could not read, and it became necessary to light candles. . . at Four P.M. the Heavens resumed their usual Light as in a cloudy day. . .* Connecticut - A Bicentennial History

Connecticuters were terrified and feared the end of the world was at hand. On this day the town of Cheshire became independent. Today, meteorologists have concluded that smoke from a western forest fire had obscured the sun's rays.

April 11, 1785   Though well into spring, Gideon Hotchkiss in Prospect recorded: *This day I measured the snow as it lies solid in the woods, and it is eighteen and half inches deep.*

Dec. 4-10, 1786   A spectacular series of snow and sleet storms that paralyzed the state was followed by temperatures falling to twelve below zero.

Jan. 19, 1810   "Cold Friday," when temperatures plummeted from a balmy 41° in the afternoon to -13° that evening.

Jan. 5, 1835   Temperature in Hartford recorded at -27°.

Dec. 22, 1839   *It began to snow Sunday night and it snowed until Tuesday morning and blew hard and drifted.*
                 Philemon Payne's account book

Mar. 27, 1843   *Monday night. It begun to rain about midnight and it rained very hard all day and there was a grate of snow on the ground and it raised the streams very high. Ozro Collins went to New Haven that day to take the benefit of the bankrupt account to check his creditors. Out of their trust and coming home 3 miles out of town, by carelessness or accident, he ran his horse off the road, got in to the stream, went down, and was drowned horse and all. Collins was found Tuesday of March 28.*
                 Philemon Payne's account book

Aug. 21, 1856   A hurricane called the "Charter Oak Storm" snapped off the trunk of Hartford's famous tree, six feet from the ground. A scion from the Charter Oak was planted on the northeast corner of the Prospect Green in 1935.

Mar. 11-14, 1888   The famous "Blizzard of '88" brought monumental snowfall, gale-force winds, and near zero temperatures. Snow accumulated on the ground at the rate of an inch an hour and fell for more than forty-eight hours. Work on laying down the railroad tracks through Prospect was halted for eight days.

William Purdy as a young boy remembered looking out the window of his Summit Road home shortly after the end of blizzard of 1888. He saw a long caravan of ox carts moving down the road toward Waterbury. That was the only way the Prospect residents could get their products to market and bring back needed supplies to their homes.

Jane Fowler (1994)

Feb. 25, 1898   *The ice storm in the center of Prospect is the severest ever known. The ice collected on the trees for two days and every twig and branch has a fringe of icicles besides a great body of ice around the branch itself. The accumulation of ice on some twigs varied from 6 to 16 inches in circumference. The telegraph wires looked like the fringe upon a lady's garment, but they were unable to endure so much adornment and broke down in many places rendering the roads impassable. The damage done by the ice is very great. Hardly a tree is left intact, and most of them are stripped of their branches. Large shade trees and apple trees as well as small peach and pear trees are torn to pieces.*   Waterbury Republican-American

1917-18   This winter, from December to January, was marked by bitter cold.

April 1924   A spring storm blanketed Prospect with eleven inches of snow. Three state snow plows were stuck on Waterbury Road, and men with shovels dug them out.

Feb. 19-20, 1934   A snowfall in Prospect resulted in a record number of snow removal charges for one month (65) as documented in the annual town report.

Residents of the Waterbury-Prospect road and the Naugatuck-Prospect roads who reside in Prospect are isolated. Little food has been brought into these sections since Feb. 20. Various appeals have been made by the residents to the state highway commissioner without success to plow the roads. There has been little suffering inasmuch as several children of the district skied into town to get provisions. Little or no mail has been received outside of the center in a week. The postman has made valiant efforts to deliver mail by carrying it through drifts on his back.   Waterbury Republican, February 28, 1934

February 1943   Temperature in New Haven dropped to -9°.

August 19, 1955   The "Black Friday Flood" ravaged the river towns, including Naugatuck and Waterbury. Prospect became a primary evacuation center. People left homeless were housed in Community School where they received medical attention. The course of Prospect's history was forever changed by this event. Those living in low lying areas began a migration to Prospect's higher and safer ground.

In the spring of 1955 I took a course in radio at the Civil Defense headquarters in the Waterbury Armory. I had always been interested in ham radio and this class, if I passed my examination, would lead to a ham license. On my 14th birthday in June I received my license in the mail. In the Town Hall at that time (the former one-room schoolhouse on the Green) there was a "radio shack" set up by Civil Defense in the southeast corner of the only room. It was set off from the rest of the room by wooden studs covered with chicken wire. It had a door that was always locked. Inside there was a 10-meter transceiver as *well as a 2-meter Gonset. Kenneth MacLeod of Talmadge Hill Road was responsible for the station but I could get to use it when I wanted to. My license allowed use of the 2-meter Gonset which, due mainly to the location, had a range of about 250 miles. I spent quite a bit of time there learning the ropes and talking with other "hams" in the New York, New Jersey, and New England areas.*

I don't remember how my sister, brother, and I learned on the morning of August 19th that something was wrong because our mother failed to come home from work. She was a private duty nurse at Waterbury Hospital on the overnight shift. Somehow word came to our neighbors that she was stranded on the other side of the Naugatuck River at the hospital and all bridges were down. After three days she was given a pass by the National Guard to cross the river at West Main Street. She still has the pass.

The high ground at the center of Prospect soon turned into an evacuation center with the homeless families from up and down the valley being put up at Community School and the National Guard encamped on the Green. Meals and typhoid shots were served at the Grange. I was assigned to the radio shack and soon began relaying information to and from similar stations concerning evacuees and supplies. The whole scene was somewhat chaotic with the constant generator noise, people wandering around, military vehicles in and out, children trying to play everywhere, and once in a while food would appear out of nowhere, and people would gather around to grab a sandwich. I believe the emergency lasted about a week at which point people began to move to more permanent housing, temporary bridges were deployed, and the cleanup began. My most vivid experience occurred one afternoon when Bob Sabo and I installed the Gonset in his car (no small feat!) and headed down toward Beacon Falls/Seymour to pick up some supplies and actually see what the flood had done. Up to that point, I had seen only the small issues that the Waterbury paper had been able to publish and talked to the troops on the Green and other radio operators. The devastation was beyond words but I can still see to this day in my mind the damage to the cemetery along the river south of Beacon Falls. The flood had floated the vaults to the surface and, as the water receded, they fell on their sides and their contents were dumped on the mud and debris.

Dick Caouette

1963-66	This period covered the worst drought in Connecticut's recorded history. Prospect fared better than most towns and provided much needed water from its reservoirs to other communities as described earlier in this chapter.
Feb. 6, 1969	This Sunday snowstorm forced many to abandon their cars as the roads were no longer passable. The next day school was cancelled, and cars were still stuck all around Prospect. People had to walk everywhere until the plows made it through town about 5 P.M.
Dec. 1972	An ice storm, the most intense to hit Prospect since 1944, caused extensive damage.

August 2, 1975	The hottest day on record in Connecticut. The mercury reached 107° in Hartford.
July 22, 1977	A day to remember in Prospect, when the outdoor thermometer on the Connecticut National Bank sign rose to 102° at two o'clock in the afternoon.
Feb. 6-7, 1978	A major blizzard led Governor Grasso to close the state highways for three days.
July 28, 1982	A tornado crossed through Prospect, nearly striking Michael Nachin's home on New Haven Road. Trees in his yard, as tall as 50 feet, were snapped off. Next-door neighbor, Lucien Fortier, also lost the tops of his trees. On Candee Road a tall oak tree belonging to James McKeow was uprooted as well.
July 10, 1989	A major tornado ripped through the state from Litchfield to New Haven. Widespread damage was caused in Prospect. Many trees were knocked down, and five utility poles had to be replaced.
Dec. 12, 1992	The Blizzard of '92 reminded many in Prospect of the winters of old. The average snow depth in town was 21 inches, and drifts reached as high as seven feet from the windswept snow. Church Street was impassable for several days after the storm.

Since the earliest years Prospect has been resourceful in dealing with the ravages that storms brought to town. Often residents would wait out the storm, letting nature take its course to clear the roads. With plenty of horses and oxen available, there was always a way to get needed supplies. In later years the state plows would clear the main roads, but Prospect was not usually their first priority. Today, Prospect boasts a road clearing system for its local roads that is second to none. Out of necessity, this hilltop community prepares for the worst weather — and usually it is not disappointed.

Prospect residents have developed a sense of pride in their ability to deal with the adverse weather conditions. Almost everyone has experienced traveling home from a neighboring town, like Cheshire or Waterbury, only to enter a winter wonderland upon crossing the town line. How often Prospect is on the edge — just that much colder — to make the difference in the type of precipitation. As with its rocky and hilly terrain, the challenging weather in Prospect has helped to mold the town's image. Its people are independent and self-reliant and are not afraid to face adversity — in the weather — or any other obstacle that may cross their path. Over one hundred years ago a visiting minister at the Congregational Church spoke of:

Nature being in her misty, moisty mood . . . Prospect is a place where every prospect pleases and only the weather is vile.

Pleasantries and Peculiarities of Prospect

~

Chapter Sixteen

Organizations

I n the early days of Prospect, social organizations were few in number. Long work hours left little time for leisure activities. Most of the social life was centered around the home and the church. Those groups that did form were often concerned with particular social, political, or religious views. Some organizations, like the **Grange**, were extensions of the members' occupations — in this case, farming. Still, others were created purely for artistic, dramatic, or musical expression and pleasure.

One of the most active and largest groups, with over 300 members, was the **Prospect Total Abstinence Society**, which began in 1840. In their records are lists of those who "fell from grace." Many town residents were opposed to the sale or public use of alcohol. Through the diligent efforts of this society, Prospect became a "dry" town, beginning around the Civil War and continuing into the middle of the twentieth century. **The Prospect Cornet Band** was a group of men who marched in parades and played at local dances from 1858-1882. The band was very active at the start, but interest diminished when many members enlisted for service during the Civil War.

PROSPECT GRANGE

In September 1894, 27 Grange members from surrounding towns circulated a petition in Prospect to establish a local chapter. Having obtained the required number of signatures and approval of their application, the first meeting was held December 10, 1894, in the vestry of the Congregational Church. Prospect Grange #144 was organized with 22 charter members — 13 sisters and 9 brothers. There is one Grange idea that was unique and far ahead of its time — giving equal opportunity to both men and women members. Almost all other organizations at that time were single-sex. The first officers were: George Cowdell (master), Katherine Bingham (lecturer), Sara Talmadge (secretary), and Rev. William Phipps was the first chaplain. In February 1897 the first Grange hall (Fig 1) was built on property donated by Mathilde Peterson. The building was 25x43 feet and made mostly with North Carolina pine. A well was dug next to the hall in 1900 that was shared by the town for many years.

Fig 1 The first Grange hall building (left), constructed in 1897, which was destroyed heavily by fire in 1944. Center School is to the right.   Prospect Historical Society

The Grange began its fairs in 1927, the year of Prospect's centennial. Admission was 10¢ to see exhibits of flowers, fruits, and vegetables. Electricity came to the center of town just in time for the 35th anniversary in 1928. A **Dirt Road Association** was formed, and Grangers enthusiastically worked for the paving of roads in Prospect. **Prospect Juvenile Grange #31,** which prospered for many years, was organized in 1938.

Fig 2 MASTERS OF PROSPECT GRANGE #144			
1894-95	George Cowdell	1937-38	Ruth Hotchkiss
1896-97	Stephen Talmadge	1939	Howard Hodges
1898-99	David Hotchkiss	1940	Carl Canfield
1900	John R. Platt	1941	Charles Hodges
1901	Albert Talmadge	1942	Carl Canfield
1902	David Hotchkiss	1943-44	J. Russell Putnam
1903-04	Ernest Wooding	1945-48	John Davies
1905	Elmer Griswold	1949-50	Edmond Morin Sr.
1906-07	Charles Fenn	1951-52	Henry T. Holihan
1908	Albert Talmadge	1953-54	Adolf Bender
1910-11	William Bottomley	1955-56	Carl Canfield
1912-13	William B. Clark	1957-58	Edmund Allard
1914-16	Clifford Wallace	1959-62	Edmond Morin Sr.
1917	Harold Pierpoint	1963-64	Edmund Allard*
1918	Stephen Talmadge	1964	Adolf Bender*
1919-20	Albert Talmadge	1965-66	Edith Canfield
1921	George Cowdell	1967-73	James Bramhall
1922	Clifford Wallace	1974	Alvah Hamilton
1923-26	Charles Hodges	1975-87	Leona Miller
1927	Edward Ward	1988	Mae Clark
1928-29	Charles Hodges	1989-90	Leona Miller
1930-32	Josephine Stieler	1991-92	Patricia Tataranowicz
1933-36	Carl Canfield	1993-94	Richard Kuhn
			* split year

Prospect Grange #144 Celebrates 100th Anniversary

When I joined, the Prospect Grange was in the wooden buildin' that burned down a few years ago and dues were 10¢ a month. How that wooden buildin' would creak when the wind blew on winter meetin' nights. Seemed as if it didn't make any difference how much wood we threw in the ole wood burnin' stove. With the wind blowin' unobstructed all the way from England the heat would disappear under the doorjams an' between the windows like magic. . .

If I remember right the pipes, both up an' down stairs, ran the length of the buildin' from the stove to the chimney an' it was a poor night when we couldn't collect a quart or two of creosote which leaked out through the joints in the stove pipe. . .

Joinin' the Grange meant a lot to the boys an' girls in those days. Outside of the church it was the only social organization in the town.

Lester Green (C.L. Mortison), Waterbury Republican, Nov. 18, 1951

Fig 3 The second Grange hall building in 1994.   John Guevin

On a meeting night in 1944, fire ravaged the Grange building. Members were able to save the Bible, altar, staves, and a few pieces of furniture. The hall was rebuilt at the same location (Fig 3) from money raised from dances, suppers, and other fund raisers. These activities were held in the new basement portion of the Congregational Church, which had also been destroyed by fire a few years earlier.

Community service was always a prime mission of the Prospect Grange.

When a hurricane brought floods and destruction to the Naugatuck River valley, the Grange was opened for those in need of food, clothing, and a place to sleep. Prospect Grange #144 has been among the top four winners of the Community Service Contest sponsored by the State and National Granges for the past ten years. The Grange just celebrated its 100th anniversary of continuous service to Prospect. This organization has 150 members and 24 of them have over 50 years service.

Excerpts from
100TH ANNIVERSARY
BY MATHILDE BENDER & JEAN MEEHAN

ONE HUNDRED YEARS HAVE BROUGHT MANY A CHANGE
ALL OVER OUR TOWN AND IN PROSPECT GRANGE.
IT WAS A SNOW-COVERED NIGHT DECEMBER TENTH
EIGHTEEN HUNDRED NINETY-FOUR
WHEN 13 SISTERS AND 9 BROTHERS CAME KNOCKING ON THE DOOR.

THE BUILDING WAS TWENTY-FIVE FEET BY FORTY-THREE FEET IN SIZE
SHEATHED AND CLAPBOARDED FROM SIDE TO SIDE.
FLOORED AND CEILED WITH NORTH CAROLINA PINE
THIS SURELY WAS A VERY GOOD SIGN.

A PATH WAS WELL SHOVELED FROM VESTRY FOR ALL
TO MARCH WITH LIT CANDLES INTO THE NEW HALL
WITH SNOW BANKED-UP SHOULDER HIGH ON EITHER SIDE.
DO YOU 'SPOSE ASHES WERE SCATTERED SO NO ONE WOULD SLIDE?

COMMUNITY SERVICE ON EVERY OCCASION
AND CHURCH SERVICES TOO OF EACH PERSUASION.
RED CROSS AND FARM BUREAU AND 4-K AND SCOUTS
THE GRANGE HALL WAS USED AND SUPPORTED DON'T HAVE ANY DOUBTS.

THE CHURCH HAD A BAD FIRE IN NINETEEN HUNDRED FORTY-ONE
SO MET IN GRANGE HALL, PLANS WERE SCARE BEGUN
WHEN THE GRANGE CAUGHT FIRE IN FEBRUARY NINETEEN HUNDRED
FORTY FOUR ON A MEETING NIGHT.
THIS SENT US TO THE LIBRARY TO ASSESS OUR PLIGHT.

TORE DOWN THE OLD, SAVING EACH BOARD AND NAIL
WITH HEARTS SET ON A NEW HALL WE COULD NOT FAIL.
'GAINST PROBLEMS OF SHORTAGES AND WAR-TIME RATION
IN NINETEEN HUNDRED FORTY NINE WE HAD A NEW DEDICATION.

MANY WE'VE LOST OVER THE YEARS.
WE HAVE SHED MANY A TEARS
AS THE GRANGE HISTORY COMES TO MIND.
IT IS GREAT TO BE A GRANGER IN THIS PLACE IN TIME.

~   ~   ~

CHURCH ORGANIZATIONS

Many early organizations were centered in the churches. The women of the Congregational Church (Fig 4) had a social group in some form from the early years.

We would respectfully call attention of the reader to the **Ladies' Fair**, *to be held in Prospect, on Friday the 13th. Their purpose is laudable, and we hope, will be crowned with success.*   Waterbury Republican, February 7, 1846

In August 1850 the **Union Benevolent Society** was organized. The members of this group made articles to sell or give to the needy. Dues were 12½¢ and some of the money was given to the Methodist Society. Most meetings were held in private homes. In 1868 it was known as the **Ladies Sewing Society**, and dues were only 5¢. Money earned was used to improve the furnishings for the house of worship. According to records in 1907, meetings were held in the dining room of the Grange hall after the second church burned. Meetings continued here until December 1908, when the group moved to the new chapel room.

The entire town took part in these church activities. The school teachers and students put on some of the programs. Catholic residents worked along side their Protestant sisters. In 1942 the **Evening Woman's Association** was formed in addition to the original **Woman's Association**. This new group accommodated women who worked during the war and could not meet during the daytime.

Fig 4   Prospect Historical Society

St. Anthony Church has had an active women's group since its days as a mission church. Starting as a card club, the **Altar Society** was a forerunner of today's **Ladies Guild**. In both cases the women were responsible for much of the fund raising that was applied toward construction and improvements in the church over the years.

All the churches in town had men's groups. **Knights of King Arthur** at the Congregational Church was active around the turn of the century. The **Knights of Columbus** at St. Anthony Church and the **Laymen's Association** of the Congregational Church were more recent examples of fellowship groups for men. Organizations for children were very popular as well, filling the recreational and spiritual needs of the community. For the most part though, it has been the women who have consistently been the cohesive force in promoting and maintaining church social activities.

TWENTIETH CENTURY ORGANIZATIONS

The **Farm Bureau** or Extension Service started during WW I. The **Red Cross Sewing** group was active in the early years of this century until the 1940s. It was supported by many woman from the town. A group known as the **Lycium Society** started in 1923. It offered programs that were well received, including a home talent play. **Boy Scout** (Fig 5) and latter **Girl Scout** troops have been active in Prospect for a long time.

Fig 5   Prospect Boy Scouts circa 1923.   Prospect Historical Society

Rear row (L-R): Carl Welton, Philip Wallace, Alden Yaegar, Nelson Fenn; middle row: Thomas Kritzman, Raymond Fournier, Rev. Oscar Locke (Scoutmaster), Clark Wallace (Assistant), George Kritzman, George Keiper; seated: Carl Keiper, Milton Fournier.

The **Parent Teachers Association** started around 1930, and Myrtle Chatfield was the first president. A number of new programs were started in Prospect because of the PTA: school nurse (1932); school physician (1934); hot lunch program (1947); dental clinic (1948); fife and drum corp (1949); playground (after a pupil, Pauline Brown, died outside Community School in 1956); Kindergarten (1963, although the PTA first petitioned to start a Kindergarten in 1940-41); arts programs; swimming classes; room mothers; and fund-raising for scholarships and other projects, such as the Prospect Spring Festival held in 1946 at St. Anthony's Parish Hall to raise money for a movie projector for Community School.

In 1945 the **Prospect Historical Society** was incorporated although it existed for some time before then. This organization is dedicated to the study and preservation of information, artifacts, and buildings of historic significance to Prospect. The group has the use of two town owned buildings. The one-room Center Schoolhouse on the Green is open during many town celebrations with displays appropriate to the occasion. The Hotchkiss farmhouse is the headquarters for the organization. Meetings, open to the public, are held there at 7:30 P.M. the first Monday of each month. The gala affair of the year is the December open house when all rooms of the Hotchkiss farmhouse are gaily decorated for the holiday season.

Fig 6 The Prospect Homemaking Club circa 1945.   Prospect Historical Society

Rear (L-R): Mae Clark, Annie Plumb, Myrtle Davis, Mrs. Erskine Russell; Front: Edna Cinq-Mars, Nellie Cowdell, Josephine Steiler, Lillian Miller, Ruth Van Wagner.

The **Prospect Drum Corps** began in 1949 by members of the Parent Teachers Association (Fig 7). Dorothy Harlow is a founding member and the current corps president. She indicated that the original idea was to provide a group of students to march to the cemetery with the firemen on Memorial Day. It was to be a one time event. After 45 years the Prospect Drum Corps has grown into one of the most successful organizations of its kind. The 55 or so members travel throughout the Northeast as well as places like the New York World's Fair and Disney World in Florida. During its years of competition, the corps has accumulated an astounding number of awards. For nine consecutive years the Prospect Drum Corps took home the New York

State Hudson Valley championship, the Northeast regional championship, and the Connecticut Fifers and Drummers Association championship. Members have also won countless individual awards over the years. Membership is open to anyone aged 8 to 18 in the Greater Waterbury area. No experience is necessary. Besides performing in about 30 parades each year, the corps practices each Friday at Community School.

Fig 7 The Prospect Drum Corps 1950.   Dorothy Harlow

Front (L-R): __?__ , Elaine Marino, Elaine Cocchiola, Dubie Santos, Nancy Minor, Judy Chapin, Louise Ann Schieffer, Edna Chapman, Kathie Angelicola, Carole Krong, Marion Stanton, Charlotte ?__, Peggy Holley, Margot Galvin, Ann Jones, Jean Schieffer, William Lee, David Young, Ann Blanchard.

Back: Peggy Bosco, Pat Hubbell, Jean Albanese, Barbara Root, Jean Cocchiola, Dorothy Brundage, Joan Sanbuy, Pat Doyle, Bill Jones, Jim Schweizer, Ed Poudim, Barry Fanning, Robert Tyler, Bill McCasland, Jack Fanning, Willard Lee, Bob Schweizer, Paul McLean, Francis Duigan, Kay Fanning, Noberta Carvalho, Margie Schnerr, Ilda Santos, Verna Dorne, Lorainne Hill, Richard Gonneville, Alice Fanning, Shirley Chandler, Randall Saunders, Henry Rigoulot, Norman Curtis.

Veterans groups included **The Grand Army of the Republic**, which was superseded by the **Veterans of Foreign Wars** and the **American Legion**. The **Prospect Lions Club** began in 1952. During the Lion Club's 25th anniversary in 1979, the backstop for Fusco Field was dedicated in their honor.

The **Prospect Chamber of Commerce** is dedicated to the promotion of commerce in the Prospect area and for the betterment of the community at large. The Chamber of Commerce, which began in 1958, represents over 100 local businesses engaged in a wide range of manufacturing and service industries. The Chamber publishes the much used Prospect phone directory. Other recent activities include the town beautification project and participation in the Prospect town picnic. The Prospect Chamber of Commerce Scholarship Program provides college scholarships each year to outstanding high school seniors living in Prospect.

The **Prospect Jaycees** began on February 11, 1972. Initially for men between the ages of 21-36, the organization became co-ed in the early 1980s, and the age limit was extended to age 40. The group's philosophy remained the same — providing members with the opportunity to grow in the areas of management, community development, and individual development. To that end, the Jaycees hold seminars and town-wide activities throughout the year. For the past five years, the Jaycees have selected a person to receive their Distinguished Community Service Award. The recipients have been: Bill Sereduck - 1990, Evelyn Kiley - 1991, Ruby DeCosta - 1992, Lucy Smegielski - 1993, and Gwenn Fischer - 1994.

The **Prospect Senior Citizens** began on January 27, 1970, when a group of Prospect residents met at the American Legion hall on Salem Road. Joseph Ciarcia of Clark Hill Road was elected the first president. Other officers included Louise Gomez of New Haven Road (1st vice president), John Miller of Clark Hill Road (2nd vice president), Adella C. Williamson of Clark Hill Road (secretary), and James Baker of New Haven Road (treasurer). Later, meetings were held at the town hall basement until the Senior Center was established in the Chapel School in 1974.

The inside of the chapel was extensively remodeled in 1976. Most of the cost was covered by a grant from the Connecticut Department of Aging. The twentieth anniversary of the group was held in 1990 at the Prospect firehouse. Those on hand included charter members Nellie Cowdell, Ruth Cowdell, Louise Gomez, and Gertrude Lindsay. Invited but unable to attend were Edith Canfield and Effie Willits. In addition to the **Chapel Senior Center**, many residents are also involved in the **Prospect Chapter AARP #2845.**

SPORTS AND RECREATION

The participation in sports has become an increasingly popular pastime in town. Organized sports of all types are offered for adults and children. Some are presented by the town's recreation department while others are sponsored by independent organizations. Examples of the latter type are the **Prospect Little League, Prospect Pop Warner Football,** and **Prospect-Bethany Youth Soccer.** The Little League plays baseball on Fusco Field off Talmadge Hill Road. The field was constructed in 1976 on land leased from the Water Company. Youth Soccer is played at Cipriano Park on Matthew Street on land leased from the New Haven Water Company since 1977. Pop Warner Football takes place on the field at Canfield Park between Coer Road and Route 69.

The **Prospect Board of Recreation** monitors and provides some assistance to private organized sports. The town offers a wide range of community recreational services. Senior citizens programs complement the activities of AARP and Chapel Senior Center. Arts and crafts, quilting, crocheting, and line dancing are among the current topics.

Youth programs include: boys'/girls' basketball (grades 4,5), boys' basketball (grades 6,7,8), girls' basketball (grades 6,7,8), girls' softball, horseback riding, swimming, as well as baby-sitting, golf, karate, and tennis instruction. These programs are offered for students through the eighth grade.

Current adult activities are golf, men's and women's baseball, men's and women's volleyball, horseback riding, and aerobics. The Prospect Board of

Recreation participates in town-wide activities, such as the Winterfest and long-range planning to develop future recreational areas. Efforts now are focused on the expansion of services at Hotchkiss Field while retaining the scenic and historic values of that property. The town of Prospect does not currently have any enclosed recreational areas. It is dependent on the use of schools and other independent facilities for indoor programs.

Among the outdoor facilities, Canfield Park provides fields for softball and baseball plus lighted tennis courts. McGrath Park has more lighted tennis courts and a fishing pond. Cipriano Park offers fields for soccer and other programs while another diamond is available for use behind the town hall. Hotchkiss Field has a half-mile run/jog track, a 20-station exercise area, lighted basketball, volleyball, and soccer facilities. New this year is a lighted 80'x100' ice skating rink that makes use of natural water on the site.

SPECIAL OLYMPIC WORLD GAMES

In 1995 Prospect was honored to host the Special Olympic athletes from Portugal. The Portuguese Olympinas arrived in Propect for the World Games on June 26, 1995. They joined the community in events over the next four days including receptions, dinners, concerts, games, and a parade. The athletes then competed in their respective sports at the World Games in venues throughout the greater New Haven area from July 1-9.

INTERSPORT USA

Intersport USA was founded in March of 1988 by Rev. Philip J. Cascia of Prospect. It provides international and educational exchange programs between young people of the United States and young people of foreign countries. Emphasis is on those nations with the poorest U.S. relations and the least common understanding. Encouraged by former President Ronald Reagan and subsequent administrations, Intersport USA has brought much recognition to the little town of Prospect in many foreign countries. Over the past several years athletic, cultural, and educational exchanges have been organized with Russia, Armenia, the Ukraine, China, Vietnam, Sweden, Italy, Poland, Cuba, and South Africa.

Prospect's Intersport USA hosted athletes from Russia, Vietnam, and Cuba. They were housed by families in town during their stay. To these young people, Prospect *is* what they know about the real America in contrast to what they see in their media. Coverage of these events was featured in *People* magazine and was broadcast on the ESPN network.

In November 1989 Nguyen Can, the Vietnamese ambassador to the U.N., was allowed to visit Prospect. This was the first time the U.S. State Department permitted him to venture outside of the United Nation's zone. He spoke to the congregation at St. Anthony Church. Another "first" occurred in July 1993, when Alcebyadies Heloago, the ambassador from Cuba, came to Prospect. The ambassador was involved in the Intersport USA baseball event here. Since 1961 Cuban officials had not been permitted to travel to any place in the United States except the U.N. zone.

Fig 8   Visitors to Prospect through the efforts of Intersport USA.   Fr. Philip J. Cascia

Top (L): (September 1991) The Hanoi High School soccer team was the first sports delegation from Vietnam to visit the U.S. (R): Garnik Nanagoulian, the First Secretary to the Armenian Embassy in Washington, D.C., Julia Tashjian, and Fr. Cascia with members of St. Anthony's Ladies Guild in 1990.

Middle (L): The first visit to Connecticut of the Cuban Sports Committee. To the left of Fr. Cascia are Jorge Lusson, Albert Juantoreno, and Ernesto Luna. Alberto Juantoreno is a member of Parliament and was the Gold Medal winner in the 400 and 800 meter track events at the 1972 Olympics in Rome. (R): Vietnamese Ambassador Nguyen Can with Fr. Cascia on his first visit outside the United Nations zone.

Bottom (L): Cuban Boxer Teofilo Stevenson enjoys barbecue in August 1994 at St. Anthony Church with Fr. Cascia. Stevenson is the only person to hold four Olympic Gold Medals in heavyweight boxing and is listed as the top amateur boxing champion of all time. (R): In 1994 this soccer team was the first to visit to the United States from the New Republic of Nagorno Karabagh.

Below is a partial list of organizations that have flourished in Prospect over the years. When available, the starting year for the group is shown.

These organizations were registered at the Prospect town hall for 1995.

Aerobics
Boy Scouts of America, Long Rivers Council
Chapel Senior Center
Concerned Parents Association
Friends of the Library
Girl Scouts of America, CT Trails Council
Prospect-Bethany Youth Soccer Association
Prospect Board of Recreation:
Prospect Boy's Basketball 6,7,8
Prospect Boy's/Girl's Basketball 4,5
Prospect Girl's Basketball 6,7,8
Prospect Men's Volleyball
Prospect Tennis Club
Prospect Women's Basketball
Prospect Women's Soccer
Prospect Women's Softball
Prospect Women's Volleyball
Prospect Car Owners Association (1986)
Prospect Chamber of Commerce (1958)
Prospect Chapter, AARP No. 2845
P.C.C., Evening Women's Association (1942)
P.C.C., Women's Association

P.C.C., Laymen's Association
Prospect Democratic Town Committee
Prospect Drum Corps (1949)
Prospect Grange (1894)
Prospect Gun Club (1975)
Prospect Historical Society (1945)
Prospect Jaycees (1972)
Prospect Land Trust (1994)
Prospect Little League
Prospect Pop Warner Football
Prospect Public Library(1905)
Prospect Republican Town Committee
Prospect Running Club
Prospect Senior Citizens (1970)
Prospect Tax Payers Association (1993)
Prospect Volunteer Fire Department (1941)
P.V.F.D. Ladies Auxiliary
PTO, Algonquin-Community School
PTO, Long River Middle School
St. Anthony Church, Ladies Guild
T.O.P.S. - Take Off Pounds Sensibly
Tough Love
Town Hall Quilters

The following organizations served Prospect over the last few decades. Some are still active today.

American Legion Post 194 Baseball (1969)
B-Tweens
Babe Ruth Team
Bicentennial Prospect Chapter A.A.R.P.
Boy Scouts:
    Cub Pack 27
    Cub Pack 127
    Boy Scout Troop 27 (1940)
    Boy Scout Troop 194
    Boy Scout Troop 130 (1968)
    Explorer Post 27
Community Chorus
Democratic Women's Club of Prospect
5-Mile Run
Girl Scouts:
    Brownie Troop 4178
    Brownie Troop 4018
    Brownie Troop 4185
    Brownie Troop 4126
    Girl Scouts (Senior) 4039
    Girl Scouts (Junior) 4121
    Girl Scouts (Junior) 4103
    Girl Scouts (Junior) 4225
    Girl Scouts (Junior) 4307
    Girl Scouts (Cadette) 4122
Mayer Stable Riding Club
Miss Prospect Scholarship Pageant (1962)
Mom's Soccer (1987)
Pioneer Squares (1965 - square dancing club)

Prospect 4-H Club (1969)
Prospect Arts Association
Prospect Auto Club
Prospect Country Club
Prospect Democrats
Prospect Football Association
Prospect Horsemen's Club
Prospect Lions Club (1952)
Prospect Mobile Home Association (1969)
Prospect Mother's Group (1987)
Prospect Photography Club
Prospect P.T.A.
Prospect Proettes Girls Softball (1973)
Prospect Republican Women's Club
Prospect Stamp Club (196.)
Prospect Young Republicans Club
Prospect Youth Advisory Committee
Prospectors (1964)
Region 16 Special Olympics
Rodeo Association
Senior Citizens Club (1970)
Skyview Country Club
Sing For Joy Singers
Third Wednesday Club
Tommy Merrimam American Legion Post # 914
Tommy Merrimam American Legion Auxiliary
Town Chorus
VFW Mattatuck Post No. 8075
Welcome Wagon
Woman's Club of Prospect (1965)
Women's Softball League
Young Democrats of Prospect   ■

Chapter Seventeen

Celebrations

P rospect is a quiet peaceful town most of the time. But on the occasions when a celebration is in order, the residents know how to throw a party. Most of these festivities have taken place around historical anniversaries of the town, state, or nation. One of the first recorded events of this type occurred on July 4, 1826 — one year before Prospect was incorporated. A document preserved at Plumb Farms lists the honored military guests in uniform at the 50th celebration of our nation's independence. Those who signed the roll of the military were most likely members of the local militia. At this time, Harris Smith was the owner of what is now the Plumb property, and he was the first to sign the list. The signatures include Henry Judd, Hiram Beecher, and Harmon Payne, who were young boys at the time. It was not uncommon for the militia to have boys in the ranks as mascots.

Harris Smith	Amos Austin	Harmon Payne
Reuben B. Hughes	Sherman Blakeslee	Harry Moss
John Wallace	Hiram Beecher	Lucius A Russell
Geo. S. Sloper	Ira G. Farrels	Fremon Sanford
Henry S. Stevens	Asa Farrels	Lucius Merriams
Lauren P. Blakeslee	John Gilles	Isaac Spencer
Bela E. Hotchkiss	Dimon Hitchcock	Richard Tyler
Chas. Preston	Phila Hitchcock	Spencer Tyler
Henry Judd	Seldon Hotchkiss	

Fig 1   Roll of the military in uniform July 4, 1826.   Plumb Farms manuscript

Along with the roll of the military was a series of thirteen toasts that were drafted for the occasion. As is often the case with handwritten documents, reading the names correctly was difficult. There were more names than shown above on the original document, but a portion of the paper had disintegrated, cutting off some names.

TOASTS FOR THE 50TH ANNIVERSARY OF THE UNITED STATES

1st   The 50th Anniversary of American Independence — while we celebrate this day let us sympathize with those who are now struggling with liberty.

2nd   The Declaration of Independence — the first . . . sound of the trumpet of freedom.

3rd   The principles of 76 — The pillar of cloud by day and of fire by night, to lead our country to the pinnacle of glory.

4th   Washington, his farewell address the catechism of Civil Liberty and American Union.

5th   Revolutionary officers — The need of praise bestowed on them — ought to satisfy their cravings.

6th   The United States — Palsied by the tongue and mitten, the hand which attempts to divide them.

7th   The President of the United States.

8th   The State Governments — The lifeguard of the national constitution.

9th   A well disciplined militia, with our Army & Navy — a nation of free men in arms . . .

10th   Agriculture, Commerce & Manufacturing, may the one never be shackled for the benefit of the other.

11th   Public Officers — Servants be obedient to your masters.

12th   The State of Connecticut — Her literary Institutions . . . secure an influence far beyond her territorial limits.

13th   The American Fair — Civil Liberty elevates female character.

When our nation celebrated its 100th anniversary, Prospect was nearing its 50th year. The separation of only one year between these events prompted many future Prospect celebrations to revolve around the national holiday. A number of prominent Prospect residents traveled to the Centennial Exhibition in Philadelphia during the exposition of 1876 (Fig 2). Exhibits displayed a wide range of industrial and agricultural products. Over 40,000 visitors registered at the Connecticut "Cottage" which featured typical goods from the state, such as Britannia ware, sewing machines, brass ware, and buttons. Willis Ives, Prospect's representative to the General Assembly, went in June as part of the legislative excursion party.

On May 7, 1919, Connecticut celebrated the one-hundredth anniversary

PROSPECT VISITORS TO THE CONNECTICUT COTTAGE AT THE 1876 PHILADELPHIA EXPOSITION	
VISITOR	DATE
B.B. Brown	Sep. 6
D.B. Hotchkiss	Sep. 5
Julia Hotchkiss	Sep. 5
David Hotchkiss	Sep. 5
W.C. Hitchcock & wife	Oct. 3
Willis Ives	Jun. 3
E.H. Mix	Nov. 8
Mrs. E.J. Nash	Oct. 3
A.M. Payne	Oct. 4
Lydia A. Payne	Oct. 4
David Plumb	Sep. 5
D.M. Plumb	Sep. 5
Mrs. Wm. W. Scoville	Oct. 5

Fig 2 Souvenir of the Centennial Exhibition.

of the first meeting of the General Assembly. Clifford P. Wallace, a grocer and farmer, was Prospect's representative for the special festivities. Also present were former representatives George L. Talmadge, Stephen A. Talmadge, and Edgar G. Wallace.

PROSPECT CENTENNIAL CELEBRATION

Fig 3 EXPENSES FOR THE PROSPECT CENTENNIAL CELEBRATION IN 1927	
Puritan All Ginger Ale	$ 25.84
Fulton American Band	85.00
Mattatuck Drum Corps	30.00
Butler Printing Co.	18.80
Sachsenhauser's Inc. for frankfurters	11.39
R.F. Worden, ice cream	62.45
Rapid Awning & Decorating Co.	50.00
Postage	8.20

	$ 291.68
1928 PROSPECT TOWN REPORT	

The town report of 1928 itemized the expenses for the Prospect centennial in 1927 (Fig 3). The celebration was the largest event to date in the town's history and cost the taxpayers a total of $291.68. Some of the participants lived long enough to take part in the sesquicentennial celebration, fifty years later. Activities and events were centered on the Prospect Green (Figs 4-6).

Fig 4 Noted citizens of Prospect gather in front of Soldiers Monument during the Centennial Celebration in 1927. Among them are M/M William A. Purdy, Mrs. W.A. Matthews, M/M Dwight W. French, Mrs. F.A. Willets, Mrs. Fannie Wallace, M/M Edgar Wallace, Mrs. D.B. Hotchkiss, Mrs. E. Nettleton, M/M William Chandler, Mrs. Ellen Allen, Lavergne G. Clark, Theodore Allen, and Duncan Gibbud.   Waterbury Republican

Fig 5   A sextet of war nurses pose for the Centennial Celebration in 1927.
Waterbury Republican

Fig 6   Four honored guests representing the Civil War and World War eras at Prospect's centennial. (L-R) Fred Hager, World War veteran; Miss Myrtle Riggs, war nurse; Duncan Gilbert, Civil War veteran; and Mrs. Halsey Clark.
Waterbury Republican

The Prospect centennial celebration lasted three days. There were parades, historical presentations, and a wide variety of games and races. Women had a chance to compete in the nail driving contest while the unmarried men defeated the married men (8-0) in a game of baseball. Many of the activities honored the men and women who served in military service from the Civil War and the World War (I).

CONNECTICUT TERCENTENARY CELEBRATION — 1935

Fig 7 Those taking prom-
inent parts in Prospect's
celebration of the state's
tercentenary.

top row left to right:
Lavergne Clark, Rep.
George Cowdell, Halsey
S. Clark.

middle row: Miss Mabel
Hotchkiss, Mrs. Clifford
Clark, Mrs. Harold Bun-
nell, Mrs. Bernice Buys,
Miss Nellie Cowdell,
Charles Fenn

front row: Selectman Mer-
ritt Walters, State Sen.
H.M. Bradley, of Derby,
Miss Bessie Moshier,
Mrs. Halsey Clark

Waterbury Republican, 11-25-1935

Prospect, Oct 12 — Eight hundred and seventy-five attended the local observance of the State Tercentenary Saturday. The program opened at 10 o'clock with the flag raising exercises conducted by the school children under the direction of Miss Catherine I. Cooke, Miss Eleanor Leahy, Miss Mary Roach, and Miss Helen Hartnett. Miss Kae Ellen Hotchkiss, music supervisor, conducted the singing.

The first episode in Connecticut history was presented by the children of Center School I, a colorful representation of Pilgrims going to church. "The Connecticut Peddler" was portrayed by the Summit School children with music, "Grandfather's Clock." A square dance was given by the East School children, "Pop Goes the Weasel." Ralph Pratt played accompaniment on his harmonica. The story of the Charter Oak was given by the children of Center II School. The song, "Connecticut," closed the feature. The West School pupils gave a parade of famous Connecticut persons, featuring Thomas Hooker, Harriet Beecher Stowe, Joseph Wadsworth and others.

A scene of the Charter Oak given by Rep. George Cowdell was dedicated. Dinner was served by the Ladies' Aid Society of the Congregational Church, with Mrs. Joseph Buckley in charge. The afternoon program opened with a welcome from First Selectman Merritt Walters. A chorus sang. "Connecticut" was one of the songs, the verses being written by Mrs. Halsey S. Clark, one of the oldest residents of the town. She read poems and other selections which she composed for the tercentenary celebration.

Tells Of Towns' Histories

The main address was given by Sen. Henry Bradley, Jr., of Derby. Sen. Bradley spoke of the origin of .the different names of the 169 towns in Connecticut mentioning how well the name Prospect suited the town because of its beautiful view. He also named several famous persons from Connecticut and made special mention of those who came from Prospect and the surrounding districts.

Miss Kae Ellen Hotchkiss sang. Miss Mabel Hotchkiss read a paper describing the early days of Prospect, the important historical events. Vocal selections were given by Evelyn Walker Fenn.

"A Half Hour in the Town Clerk's Office in 1835" was portrayed by descendants of the original town officers with Gregory Lines as Aaron Austin, the town clerk; Merritt Walters as William Mix; Halsey S. Clark as Isaac Doolittle, and George Cowdell as Joseph Paine. Others participating were Lavergne G. Clark, John Kay, and Clifford P. Clark. To close the afternoon program a concert was given on the Green by the Cheshire Band.

Waterbury Republican, 11-25-1935

UNITED STATES BICENTENNIAL

The tradition of joint Prospect-U.S. celebrations continued when the national bicentennial, observed in 1976, was followed by Prospect's sesquicentennial in 1977. An early event was a Ben Franklin Ball at St. Anthony Church on Jan 17, 1976, with most guests in costumes of the colonial period. The 200th anniversary of our country climaxed on July 4, 1976, with activities on the Green and at Canfield Park. Events included old-fashioned games, a nationwide bell ringing at 2 P.M., dancing, musical entertainment, and fireworks. A town crier announced events throughout the day. Rev. John Beck, Bob Chatfield, Boardman Kathan, and Mayor George Sabo, Jr. took part in the opening ceremonies.

Judy Fiengo directed the community chorus in the singing of the anthem "Chester" which was written during the Revolutionary War. Prospect State Representative Richard Varis spoke about hiding the first Connecticut constitution in the Charter Oak. Varis and Mayor Sabo then planted a seedling from the Charter Oak on the Prospect Green. A town guest book, first used in 1927 and brought by Nellie Cowdell, was on display at the Bicentennial Commission booth and was signed by over 1,300 persons during the day. Each signer received a button with the new town seal on it, the words "I'm from Prospect," and the dates, 1827-1977.

PROSPECT SESQUICENTENNIAL

The following year Prospect marked its 150th anniversary. Most of the activities were concentrated between May 21-30, 1977. On May 21 there was an art exhibit at Long River Middle School featuring thirty-six artists and crafts persons. The Sesquicentennial Ball was held at St. Anthony Church hall with music by Dick Cyr and his orchestra. A program entitled "Historical Roots of Prospect" was presented on Sunday evening, May 22, at the Congregational Church. Another event was a concert by the Sesquicentennial Chorus directed by Judy Fiengo with Joan Heller as pianist. Music included selections sung at Prospect's Centennial celebration fifty years earlier. A special highlight of the concert was the introduction of Mrs. Adella Clark Williamson and Mr. Gould Clark, who had sung in a quartet during the 1927 celebration.

"Homecoming Weekend" was May 28-29, 1977. There were open houses at the Historical Society, library, churches, town hall, and Grange where an old-fashioned bean supper and square dance was held. Twelve "Sesquicentennial House" plaques were presented to some of the homes known to be built before 1827. Other activities that week included the inauguration of the nature trail in the town park by the Woman's Club. Ted Hanson premiered a film entitled "Prospect Celebrates." The Prospect Historical Society dedicated a monument in the cemetery to soldiers buried in unmarked graves. Babette Strumpf unveiled a new monument and honor roll to veterans of WW II, the Korean War, and the Vietnam War. A sesquicentennial minstrel show played to capacity audiences at Long River School in June.

On July 4, 1977, residents witnessed the largest parade to date in Prospect's history, with over forty floats and marching units. A town picnic followed in Canfield Park where there were games and activities throughout the day. The Prospect Drum Corps and other groups entertained those gathered. Fireworks at dusk climaxed Prospect's 150th birthday party.

OTHER CELEBRATIONS

Fig 8 Christmas 1986 on Williams Drive.   John Guevin

The next major celebration for Prospect will be the 200th anniversary of the Congregational Church in 1998. This will be followed by the town's 175th birthday in 2002. Meanwhile, there are festivities every year. Prospect celebrates the holidays in a variety of ways. In January or February there is the annual Christmas tree burning where residents have an opportunity to dispose of their trees and enjoy hot chocolate and a marshmallow roast.

Other regular events include the Easter egg hunt, a classic car show, the Memorial Day parade, town picnics, carnivals, band concerts, dances, and open houses. The Winterfest sponsored by the Jaycees caps off the year.

Private citizens also got involved. Over the years there have been neighborhood block parties and picnics. In June 1976, 140 people from 32 families enjoyed singing, dancing, and food at a block party on Woodcrest Drive. Neighborhood picnics were annual events on Nancy Mae Avenue and in other parts of town.

Many homes have been decorated in the spirit of the various holidays throughout the year. Christmas decorations were done on a grand scale on Williams Drive (Fig 8) during the 1970s and 80s. Cars came from all over Connecticut and neighboring states to view the amazing displays of lights and decorations on homes along the street. Traffic backed up on Route 69 as cars waited their turn to see Christmas in Prospect. Peter and Lucy Smegielski outfit their Morris Road home with distinctive decorations for as many as five holidays each year. Occasions include Valentine's Day, St. Patrick Day, Memorial Day/July 4th, Halloween (Fig 9), and of course, Christmas.

Fig 9 Halloween 1994 at the Smegielski home.   John Guevin

Another citizen with a flair for decoration is Nancy Mulcahey, whom Mayor Chatfield has named the "queen of yard decorations." Her home on Waterbury Road is visible to many who pass by. Viewers might see a gigantic, seven-foot Halloween pumpkin sign, an Indian tepee at Thanksgiving, or snow sculptures in the winter in the form of dinosaurs or other creatures.

~

Chapter Eighteen

Wars and Soldiers

The contributions Prospect made over the years to defend our nation in times of war has been a distinguishing feature of the town since its early beginnings. It is a paradox that the people who settled on these hills over the past two centuries were peaceful people. They were content to do their work, attend their churches, and enjoy the simple pleasures of life. The conflicts that raged around the world or in other parts of America could have seemed far removed and unimportant to the citizens of Prospect. Yet, they rose to the occasion, time and time again, to support this nation and the principles they so firmly believed. Prospect never turned its back when there was a need for soldiers to fight in war.

Peter Gilkey, better known for his counterfeiting operation in Prospect, was involved in the 1762 campaign in Cuba. Gilkey was one of two thousand men sent by King George III as part of the French Wars. They went in two ships, and those that survived the stormy voyage took part in the storming of Havana. Between 1754 and 1763, some early settlers fought in the French and Indian War over the boundaries of Acadia (Canada). Among them were Gideon Hotchkiss, his son Jesse, and Enos Tyler. These men came to the aid of England because the colonies were still under British rule. Two decades later, these same individuals fought against England in our struggle for independence.

REVOLUTIONARY WAR

During the American Revolution the men living on the land that would become Prospect enlisted to become *Minutemen* for independence. Those living on the western third of town joined forces with Waterbury, while those to the East went to Wallingford/Cheshire. The monument on the Prospect Green lists twenty-two soldiers from this area who served in the war, but many names were omitted. A Roll of Honor published in Waterbury on May 30, 1895, lists only nineteen. A more complete list of Prospect soldiers (Fig 1) is offered in the Bicentennial Booklet #4, *Prospect Soldiers 1775-1783*, researched by Dick Caouette. Some of these soldiers are discussed in the biographies chapter of this book. The reader is invited to consult the Prospect soldiers booklet for more details.

PROSPECT SOLDIERS 1775-1783

Amos Atwater	Robert Hotchkiss	Selden Spencer
Maj. Samuel Bronson	Titus Hotchkiss	Elihu Spencer
Hezekiah Beecher Sr.	Stephen Ives	Ansel Spencer
Jared Burr	William Jones	Enoch Terrell
Asahel Chittenden	Walter Judd	Josiah Terrell
Peter Gilkey	Philemon Payne	Isaac Terrell
Ambrose Hine	Riverius Russell	Oliver Terrell
Isaac Hine	Elmore Russell	Moses Tuttle
Daniel Hitchcock	Aaron Russell	Phineas Tyler
Gideon Hotchkiss	Archibald Sanford	Abraham Tyler
Abram Hotchkiss	John W. Sanford	Enos Tyler
Amos Hotchkiss	Ephraim Smith	Nathaniel Tyler
Asahel Hotchkiss	Ira Smith	Reuben Tyler
David Hotchkiss	Ephraim Smith Jr.	Levi Tyler
Eben Hotchkiss	Josiah Smith	Amos Wilmot
Eldad Hotchkiss	Daniel Smith	Elisha Wilmot
Jesse Hotchkiss	Isaac Spencer	

Fig 1   Prospect Soldiers 1775-1783, Booklet #4

In May 1798, after Columbia Society was formed, the residents of this area petitioned the State Assembly for the right to form their own militia rather than continue to join militia of surrounding towns.

Upon the Petition of John Cook Hotchkiss and Frederick Hotchkiss of Columbia Society in New Haven County for themselves and their Associates shewing that the Inhabitants of said Society subject to Military Duty are about sixty five in number, and belong in part to the 10th Regiment and Second Brigade of Militia, and in part to the 26th Regiment and Eighth Brigade praying to be incorporated with the usual privileges into one Military Company and that the bounds of said Society shall be the Bounds of said Company as per Petition on file.

Resolved by this Assembly that the Inhabitants living within the limits of said Society who are subject to Military Duty be, and they are hereby incorporated into one Military Company with the privileges and immunities by Law appertaining to other Military Companies in this State and that the Bounds and Limits of said Society be the limits of said Company, and that the said Company be annexed to the Tenth Regiment of Militia in this State.

And Be it further Resolved that the Commanding Officer of the said Tenth Regiment be directed as soon as may be to Issue his Orders to some suitable person to warn the members of said Company to meet and choose their Officers and make Return.

Public Records of the State of Connecticut, 1798

PROSPECT'S MINUTE MEN

On the Cedar Hill Farm, on the Union City Road, is a flat meadow of 10 acres, between the Union City Rd. and Salem Rd. George Payne donated the use of that 10 acre meadow for the Prospect volunteer soldiers to do all their training on. This was the old Civil War training ground, now the Cedar Hill dairy farm.

Amos Hotchkiss, A Revolutionary War soldier, one of Gideon Hotchkiss' nineteen children, owned Clark Hill, 320 acres, before the six generations of Clarks lived there. He built the first plastered house in Prospect with sand from the sea shore, a round trip of 50 miles, and brought with oxen. My grandfather built the first hog house. Both of these items can be found on the Prospect town records.

A school teacher of mine in the West District of Prospect, who is still living, wrote an essay for Prospect Grange 60

years ago, "History of Prospect", and told me that she won a prize and still has the prize in her possession. In that essay she said, "There lived a man in the west side of Prospect, by the name of Amos Hotchkiss; and when the British came into New Haven Harbor, with forty vessels after the regicides that were hiding in Judges Cave and who had chopped off the head of Charles the First, and when they were burning up the houses of the Naugatuck Valley, and when the light was flashing from West Rock to Beacon Hill to Litchfield, the county seat, Mr. Hotchkiss left his plow in the field and went." Mr. Hotchkiss has been considered by different ones as one of the Revolutionary War Minute Men. Hurrah for Amos Hotchkiss, a "Minute Man" in the Revolutionary war, from the town of Columbia, versus Prospect!

Clifford Clark, May 30, 1957

CIVIL WAR

It is not known if men from Prospect fought in the War of 1812 or the Mexican War. The next major confrontation which would involve wartime soldiers was the Civil War. This war of American against American established Prospect as a town willing to stand up for its principles. The abolitionist movement and the belief that slavery was inherently wrong were strong convictions for most of the residents in town. When asked to join the cause and defend the Union, Prospect did not hesitate, and men volunteered in large numbers. At least seventeen Prospect men lost their lives in the Civil War.

PROSPECT'S CIVIL WAR SOLDIERS

Stephen Talmadge, a Civil War volunteer, not only marched 300 miles with Gen. Sherman through Georgia, but he fought in every [many] battle of the Civil War and came back unscratched. Stephen Talmadge served the town of Prospect for more than 40 years, with high honors after he came back from the Civil War.

John Platt, a Civil War volunteer, who lived on Straitsville Rd., marched in a parade with the most dignity of any man that I have ever seen. I have been told that he held a record of chopping and piling six cords of wood in one day. Mrs. Platt went to New Haven to meet a Prospect volunteer whom she was soon to marry, but all that came back was his body for he was killed in action. [Asaph] Tyler, a volunteer from

Prospect, lived on the Straitsville Rd. He was very popular as an orator at a good many occasions. William Morris, a volunteer from Prospect, owned Mr. Kinsella's farm on the Union City Rd.

William Morris plastered all the house I live in, ten rooms, in one day. Elmer Smith, a volunteer from Prospect, lived on the Union City Rd. Elmer Smith was the son of Leveritt Smith that lived on the Bronson Rd. 150 years ago. I remember Elmer Smith. He was way over six feet tall with tremendous strength. He carried on his back an enormous sack of medicine. My father told me that it weighed a good deal more than a hundred pounds. Hurrah for Elmer Smith, a medicine man in the Civil War! and from Prospect!

Clifford Clark, May 30, 1957

PROSPECT CIVIL WAR SOLDIERS

Lafayette P. Anthony	Edward H. Hotchkiss	Edward B. Royce
George L. Austin	Evans B. Hotchkiss	Philander Royce
Luzerne Baldwin	George H. Hotchkiss	Charles B. Russell
Bennett Benham	Lester L. Hotchkiss	Lester Russell
Jehiel Benham	Philo D. Hotchkiss	Seymour Russell
Lewis Benham	Henry Hull	Spencer L. Sanford
Robert Benham	Joseph W. Jewitt	William Sanford
William Berkeley	Henry Judd	Albert Sherman
James J. Blakesley	David Karrmann	Elmon E. Smith
Spencer Bronson	George Karrmann	George H. Smith
Joel Brooks	Henry Lewis	George L. Smith
Charles Carman	Pierre Marie	Samuel S. Smith
David Carman	Franklin N. Marvin	Samuel Spencer
George Carman	Harvey L. Matthews	William Stump
Almon E. Chandler	John F. Matthews	Frederick A. Talmadge
John W. Chandler	Augustus Morse	John Talmadge
Edward H. Clark	Edward L. Morse	John W. Talmadge
James E. Clarke	Burton H. Payne	Stephen A. Talmadge
Henry P. Daley	James Payne	James Taylor
William H. Dougal	Nelson Payne	Aseph R. Tyler
Theodore G. Durand	Sheldon F. Payne	George R. Tyler
Levi Elton	Willis E. Payne	Myron E. Tyrell
Ira G. Farrell	Homer G. Perkins	Franklin Wallace
Lauren J. Farrell	John H. Platt	Frederick H. Williams
Porter L. Gardiner	John R. Platt	John Williams
Charles E. Hine	Giles Robinson	Miles Williams
Watson C. Hitchcock	Charles B. Royce	

Fig 2   Consolidated list of Civil War soldiers on Monument and Honor Roll.

From letters written home by Prospect soldiers during the Civil War, we can gain insight into the feelings that must have weighed on their minds. The following letters were written by Watson C. Hitchcock to his parents, Icabod and Lucy Emeline (Hotchkiss) Hitchcock. Watson was a clerk in the Commissary Department of the 20th Regiment, Connecticut Infantry. His comments cover news from the battlefield, his thoughts on war, fear of mail theft, local politics, and concern for his animals at home.

**Excerpts from manuscripts of
Watson C. Hitchcock**
Connecticut Historical Society

My dear Parents,   May 7/63

. . . I will tell you that on Sunday last, was fought the hardest battle of this war & our forces were compelled to <u>withdraw</u>. <u>In other words we are whipped</u>. There is no use trying to disguise this. The 12th Corps stood the blunt of the fight. The 20th Regt. was in the hottest of it & <u>stood to the rack like men</u>. But Co. A suffered greatly. I

have been to the Regt. tonight & seen the boys. Those missing from Prospect are Fred, Johnny, Jim, Frank & Joel J. Brooks. Frank was shot through the calf of his leg [while he] stood close by Lieut. Basssett. It is supposed all of these were taken prisoners, still no one knows. The boys say Fred fought like a tiger. Of the rest nothing is known. 18 men of our Co. are missing.

. . . It seems hard that so many men should be killed & wounded & all to no purpose. I for one have seen enough of

this kind of work, but of course more men must be raised & more killed & finally the last mile conquer. I feel this & I also feel for the friends of those who are gone. . .

Love to all, Watson

My dear Parents,   April 13th, 1863

. . . I was over to the Regt. yesterday to get "Mustered" & sign the Pay Roll. . . we shall get 4 months pay $52 . . . I don't want to send it right away after we are paid off, for the agents and clerks in the Post Office know when the Army is paid & are generally on the lookout for money.

. . . As for Prospect I have nothing to say, only that every man who voted for H.D. Russell, is a coward. & I wish I was there to say it.

He is a mean, contemptible, sneaking, straddle-of-the-fence office seeker. That is my opinion. He has not the least particle of principle or honesty & the man who nominated him is another of the same class . . . I hope father did not vote for H.D.R. If he did, I shall begin to think he is really losing his mind.

I am glad to hear so favorable an account of the animals. I hope as the spring advances & roads become settled, Father will get time to take the colt out once in a while, only he must remember horses are weaker in the spring when they are shedding their coats & more liable to take cold than at any other time. So if he uses the colt & he gets sweaty, he must not neglect to give him a good rubbing down. . .

From your affectionate son, Watson

Soldiers Monument on the Green was constructed in part by a grant from the State Legislature because of Prospect's sacrifice in the Civil War. Prospect men enlisted at a higher percentage in relation to the 145 registered voters than any other town in Connecticut. The plaque on the monument lists 70 men. A published Honor Roll with 75 names includes ten men not listed on the monument, so there may have been 80 or more who served.

It was a bright and clear day when the monument was dedicated on May 30, 1907. Canvas was draped over the statue, and the base was covered with wild-flowers, apple blossoms, and lilacs. Adella Clark, the ten year old daughter of Representative Lavergne Clark, had the unveiling honor. About 1,300 people gathered for the event. There were performances by the Cheshire Band and the Naugatuck Fife and Drum Corps. Among the speakers, Judge Cowell spoke about Capt. Gideon Hotchkiss and his Minutemen. The singing of the Skilton Quartet received applause from the crowd, which included veterans of the Civil War and the Spanish-American War.

How the town of Prospect received a State Grant to put the Soldiers Monument on the Prospect Green

My uncle Lavergne Clark when he was a representative at Hartford in 1906 got a bill passed that enabled Prospect to receive a state grant of $2,500 to place the monument on the Prospect Green. There are very few people today that know why Prospect received that grant. I will tell you.

In Connecticut there are 169 towns. Prospect sent the most men in the Civil War in proportion to the voting popula-

tion than any of the 168 towns. 76 men out of 145 voters, over half and I understand they volunteered when Lincoln called on the people to save the country.

. . . When they dug down six feet to grout for the monument, they came upon the stump of the Revolutionary flagpole. It was a big chestnut tree. Not always did the stars and stripes float from that pole. One night a Tory flag hung there. In the morning when the people of the town found out, a poor barefoot boy climbed the pole and tore the flag down. Stephen Talmadge, a Civil War volun-

teer, said to me it was a miracle the boy was not shot down right on the flagpole, feeling was so high in Prospect.

71 years ago I sang to 3 seats full of soldiers in the old white church, "Marching Through Georgia", all 6 verses. My mother played the piano. I can see her now as she turned and rais-

ed her hand for the chorus. Those Civil War volunteers, all dressed in blue, arose like one man and how they did sing. They drowned all the other voices. A good many years after they told me that the top of my head was just level with the keyboard of the piano . . .

Clifford P. Clark, 1955

WARS OF THE TWENTIETH CENTURY

PROSPECT SOLDIERS OF THE FIRST WORLD WAR

Harry J. Beers	W. Ronald Morse	Umberto S. Pivirotto
Reuben W. Berglund	Charles C. Moshier	Victor J. Pivirotto
Reuben W. Blanning	Charles Neumaier	Frank Powell
Henry D. Boardman	Robert H.H. Nichols	Marinus D. Scovill
Henry N. Burnham	Russell B. Nichols	Emil C. Sporbert
Richard W. Coer	John J. Nichols	Clifford Waters
Fred Hager	Edward A. Nichols Jr.	Charles L. White
Edward D. Hotchkiss	Arthur J. Odgers	
Raymond F. Huckins	Albert Pawasaris	

Fig 3   WW I veterans listed on Soldiers Monument.

WORLD WAR II VETERANS

Arthur H. Alsdorf	Richard Coer	William Jones	Alex Rozum
Harvey Atwood	Peter Collins	Arthur Kathan, Jr.	Andrew Rozum
Edward T. Ayotte	Daniel Connor	John J. Kiesel	Joseph Ryan
Frank Baker	Roger Connor	Thomas Kinsella	George Sabo, Jr.
Frederick Berger	Montague Donston	Donald D. Krell	Robert Sabo
Louis Bernier	Frank Doyle	Sam Lodarska	Francis W. Salvatore
Wilfred Berube	Wilfred Dupre	Jerry Mascoli, Jr.	John L. Salvatore
John W. Brundage	James J. Dupreay	Richard Mascoli	Joseph S. Scholan
Robert Brundage	Chester Frederick	Walter Miller	Howard Sills, Jr.
Albert Buddzinowski	James Fusco	Robert Milton	John S. Staneslow
Harvey Bullis	Louis Giordano	Leroy Noble	Harry Talmadge, Jr.
Walter Bullis	Henry Girouard	Joseph C. Nocera	Edwina Thatcher
John W. Burke	Raymond Girouard	Cecil O'bar	Joseph Tress
Henry Burnham, Jr.	Leo Gonneville	Thomas F. O'Brien Jr	Kenneth Tuckey
George Caine	Marcel Gonneville	John W. Parry	Richard Tuckey
Francis Carroll	Charles J. Griffin	Charles Peach	Robert Utenner
James J. Carroll	John F. Griffin, Jr.	John A. Peach	William Vining, Jr.
David Chatfield	John J. Griffin, Jr.	Raymond Peach	Fred Voegeli
Myrtle Chatfield	Arthur Hill	Jane E. Perry	Edward H. Wallace
William Chatfield	Franklin Hill	Frank J. Plumb	Miriam Weik
W. Dean Clarke	Frederick T. Hill	Ralph N. Pratt	Ernest Weir
James F. Cleary	James Ives	Benjamin Rachas	Joseph Welton
Frank Clyma	Armand Jolly	Branna Rachas	Robert Young
Louis A. Cocchiola	Maurice Jolly	John Raudis	

Fig 4   WW II Honor Roll compiled by Babette Strumpf

KOREAN WAR VETERANS

George Brewster	Henry Fiengo	Thomas Merriman*	Robert Schweizer
Domenic Briglia, Sr.	Charles Finke	James Mulvey	Richard Spellman
Richard Brundage	Richard Finke	Charles M. O'Brien	Robert Spellman
Harold Chapman	Alfred Gonsalves	George Pavlik, Jr.	Alfred Strumpf
Robert Cipriano	Robert Harvey	Alfred Peach, Jr.	John J. Sullivan
Robert Connor	John S. Holley	Eugene Sabo	David Young
Harry Coughlan, Jr.	Charles Kathan	Harold Schnerr, Jr.	
Walter Crandall, Jr.	Joseph Lee	James K. Schweizer	
Phillip Eastman	Eugene Lewis	John E. Schweizer	

Fig 5   Korean War Honor Roll compiled by Babette Strumpf

VIETNAM WAR VETERANS

Patrick Acquin	Anthony Ciminera	Thomas Hartnett	Paul Moneta
Harvey Alborn	Frank Clyma, Jr.	Frederick Hill, Jr.	William Moneta
Michael Alix	Anthony Cocchiola	Archie Holloway	Raymond Moniz
Arthur Alsdorf	Edward Cocchiola	Thomas Howson	Paul J. Murray
Gerald Antworth	David Cooper	James Hubbell	Edward Nelson
Dale Ashwood	Leodore Cote	Ronald Humphrey	Philip Noble
Norman Ayotte, Jr.	Robert Crane	Peter Iosa	James Nolan, Jr.
Robert Ayotte	Mark Dorais	Frederick Jones	Eugene Ober
Mark Baker	Robert Dorn	David Kluge	Robert O'Donnel
Francis Baker	Anthony Dorso, Jr.	Randall Korn	Nicholas Palchick, Jr.
Peter Baltrush	John F. Doyle*	Arthur Lagasse	Joseph Paolino
Gary A. Barrere	Jack Drelichowski	Joseph LaMadeleine	John Paparazzo
Keith Bassett	Jack Dupreay	Robert L. Lampron	Donald Paradis
Anthony Bell	Joseph E. Dyson	Anthony Lanesey	Lendor Parent, Jr.
Susan Bell	Dominic Farina, Jr.	Thomas Lavorgna, Jr.	Don Peach
Stephen Bradford	Alan A. Fazi	Daniel LeFrancois	Claude Pelkey
Raymond Bresnahan	Thomas Feero, Jr.	Steven Lieber	David Pelletier
Roy Breton	Cecile Fortier	Joseph Lokis	Gary Petrauskas
Walter Breton	Charles Fortier	Franklin Lombardi	David Pettinicchi
David Brewster	Leo J. Fortier	Ernest Lubenskas	George Pilkington
Frank Briglia	Maurice Fortier	Robert Lukas	Robert Pinto
James Briglia	Robert Fowler	John Lusas	Ernest Pizzuto
Richard Brown	Peter Genova, Jr.	Frances Magnavice	Gregory Ploski
David Burke	Charles Gionet	Walter Magnavice, Jr.	Evan Plourde
John M. Burke, Jr.	Thomas Giordano	David Marino	Joseph Polletta
John D. Burns	Wayne Green	Roger Masone	Arthur Pratt
William D. Canale	Raymond Greenwood	John Matthews	Edward Pratt
Keith Carroll	George Griffin	John E. Mikishko	James Pratt, Jr.
Kenneth Carroll	Edward J. Hankey	Bernard Mikletonas	Robert Pratt
Conrad Carvalho	James Hancock	Anthony Milton, Jr.	William Rek
Charles A. Case	Donald Hansen	Bradley Milton	Dennis Russell
Michael O. Cass	Thomas Hanson	Brian Modrow	Robert Rzewuski
Donald Chatfield	Fred Harkins	David Modrow	Stephen Satkunas
Robert Chatfield	Charles Harrison	Robert Modrow	David Saunders

Fig 6   Vietnam War Honor Roll compiled by Babette Strumpf

Joseph Saveriano	John Streich	Norman Violette	Curtis Wheeler
John Schieffer, Jr.	Frederick Strumpf	Victor Visockis, Jr.	Daniel Wheeler
Edward Schweizer	Edward Sullivan	Frederick Voegeli	James Wilson
Robert Scriver	Alfred Sweeney	Frederick Volmar	Kenneth Wilson
Laurence Sereduck	Konrad Tauber, Jr.	Patrick Walsh	John Wioncek
Richard Soden	Robert Theroux	George Watterworth	Jerry Wright
William Soden	John Thompson	George Walters	
Robert Spino	James Vander Eyk	Charles Wentworth	
Harry A. Streich	Steven R. Veilleux	William J. Wentworth	

Fig 6 Continued   Vietnam Honor Roll compiled by Babette Strumpf

GULF WAR VETERANS

Darren T. Besse	John M. Geary	James Parker
Linda Bluette	Dane J. Hassan	Sue Patterson
Paul Dubay	John L. Hastings	Trisha Ross
Darren Evans	Michael Malm	Michael Trotman

Fig 7   Prospect Town Hall

Many other citizens from Prospect served in the armed forces during peacetime. Those listed in Figures 6-9 qualified as veterans by serving during the prescribed periods for each war. The following individuals were also veterans from Prospect during one of the wars of the twentieth century. The available records for those shown below did not specify the particular war for each soldier.

ADDITIONAL VETERANS OF WW II, KOREA, OR VIETNAM

William Alencynowicz	Kent Carroll	Frederick Gross	Basil W. Schwarz
Harry Alsdorf	Reginald Crocco	Christopher Grudzien	Arthur Shattuck
Louis Benson	Carla F. Dunford	Douglas King	Edwon Sperry
Harry Benson	Victor Fusco	Andrew O'Leary	Adam Stanulis
William Berzinskas	Joseph Goggin	Edward Pakus	Emanuel Umberto
Kenneth Blake	George F.A. Goodwin	Robert Phelan	Joseph Wolyniec
Joseph Blinstrubus	Thomas P. Griffin	John T. Pivirotto	Peter Wolyniec

Prospect is currently home for two WW II prisoners of war. Charles G. Lizauskas served in 17 Army Artillery in the invasion of North Africa. He was captured in February 1943 at Kassarine Pass and flown from Tunis, Tunisia to Naples, Italy. During his confinement he was forced to construct prefabricated officers' quarters. He was moved by boxcar through Austria to Stalag 7A in Bavaria, Germany. After movement to other prison camps in Germany, Charles Lizauskas was part of a forced march on December 28, 1944, to another stalag in Luckenwald. Under the threat of being shot, he and his comrades were without food or water during the march. In April 1945 the Russians liberated Charlie from the stalag after he had spent fourteen months in captivity. He was then flown from Germany to Rheims, France.

James Cavallo was a member of the 15th Air Force and became a POW as a result of a bomber mission over Germany during WW II. His plane was attacked by enemy fighters, and he was severely wounded. Jim managed to parachute from the bomber but was captured by the Germans as soon as he hit the ground. He was a prisoner for thirteen months and was confined to a prison hospital where he received limited care for his injuries. Liberation came for Jim when the 26th Yankee Division reached his location in Germany.

Below are tributes to the last two servicemen from Prospect to be killed in action while defending their country. Thomas Merriman served during the Korean War, and John Doyle was in the Vietnam War.

R. THOMAS MERRIMAN
PFC
Thomas Merriman was killed in action in Korea on Sept. 7, 1950. He entered the service in March of 1949 and first served in Japan. He had been in Korea only 3 weeks.

Tommy was the son of Mr. and Mrs. Roy V. Merriman of Summit Road. Prospect's American Legion Post 194 was renamed in his honor.

JOHN F. DOYLE
Army Spec. 4th/Class
John Doyle died of shrapnel wounds from hostile fire August 15, 1966 while trying to retrieve wounded in Binh Doung province, Vietnam.

John was "born on the Fourth of July" in 1947. He enlisted in 1964 and was stationed in Germany before volunteering for Vietnam duty.

Fig 8 Memorial Day services in 1971 at the old memorial next to the fieldstone library for World War II, Korea, and Vietnam era veterans.   Babette Strumpf

In honoring the servicemen and servicewomen of our nation, no town in Connecticut does it better or more often than Prospect. Beginning in 1970, the American Legion Post 194 began sunrise flag-raising ceremonies on the Prospect Green for Memorial Day. These annual events were reported to be the only of their kind in the country. For special occasions like the return of our soldiers from the Gulf War, Prospect went all out with yellow ribbons, decorated trees, and parades. Every year respect has been paid to the members of our armed forces, past and present. On Memorial Day and other military events — including Pearl Harbor Day — services were offered to honor our fighting men and women. In 1995 Prospect was one of the few towns in Connecticut selected to commemorate the 50th anniversary marking the end of World War II. Veterans of that war, both living and deceased, were honored with a parade and special events at the town picnic.

The author is grateful to Babette Strumpf, who provided much of the information about Prospect veterans of World War II, Korea, and Vietnam. Babette was the author of the column "Military Corner," which appeared in the *Prospect Reminder* in the 1960s and 70s. Over the years she has been very active in supporting the men and women from Prospect in the armed forces.

~

Chapter Nineteen

Myths, Legends, Stories, and Prospect's Personality

T he creation of myths is inevitable in the evolution of any town's story. This is especially true in early history accounts when much of the information was passed on by word of mouth. Very little was written down. In the process of transferring historic accounts in this way, there is a natural tendency to "embellish" the truth, even if ever so slightly, by each storyteller. Over a period of time, the compounding of minor changes can lead to major distortions of facts. If one of these untruths finds its way into print, it "becomes true" and is very hard to disprove in the future.

PROSPECT MYTHS

MYTH #1 . . . At one time Waterbury was a suburb of Prospect.

> *Strange as it now may seem, this little contented town [Prospect] was a thriving industrial center of which Waterbury was a suburb. These turning wheels and pumping arms of bustling manufactories turned out immense amounts of pins and needles, hoes, matches, britannia ware and gay umbrella trimmings. And men from Waterbury commuted to assist this active trade.*

Hyways & Byways of Connecticut

The above paragraph overstates the magnitude of Prospect's manufacturing contribution. Even at its peak, factories represented only about half the towns economic base, and Prospect's total output was relatively small. Manufacturing in Waterbury, Naugatuck, and Cheshire was always greater. It may be true that some people commuted to work here, but it was more likely that workers from Prospect walked down the hills to jobs in neighboring communities.

MYTH #2 . . . More people were engaged in industry than in agriculture at one time in Prospect.

This fallacy begins with statistics that show the number of people employed in the factories of Prospect. While the figures may be accurate, they fail to reflect that most factory employees worked on a part-time basis. They helped in the factories during the winter (off-season) months when not engaged in farming. Many held two or more factory jobs, so they were counted more than once. The central fact remains that Prospect was primarily an agricultural community.

MYTH #3 . . . Waterburians shopped in Prospect.

The records are clear that very few stores existed in Prospect in the early days. Most of the time there was only a general store for the daily necessities — hardly the sort of shop that people from Waterbury would climb the hills to reach. For special shopping, Waterbury was most often the place Prospect residents patronized. Some goods made in Prospect were sold in New York, and no doubt, some residents of Waterbury may have purchased them there.

MYTH #4 . . . More than the registered number of voters in Prospect fought in the Civil War.

The Civil War took many of Prospect's men, its percentage of 75 out of 145 voters being the largest of any town in the state. The often repeated statement that more than the registered number of voters went to the war from Prospect is just as mistaken as the first day it was spoken. Nellie Cowdell, 1947

MYTH #5 . . . By law, every municipality in Connecticut must have a street named Prospect in honor of Prospect's sacrifice during the Civil War.

While it seems to be true that many towns do have streets named Prospect, there is no law to require this. An interesting project for someone with the time or resources would be to see if every town does indeed have a Prospect Street (except Prospect, of course!).

LEGENDS AND STORIES

Legends, on the other hand, are most likely based on fact. They may even be 100% true. Legends are often very colorful, giving the hint that there may be some exaggeration in the events they portray. In many cases it is difficult or impossible to prove or disprove legends. But then, maybe we shouldn't even try. History is more than facts and dates. It is really about people and the stories they tell.

To a great extent the art of storytelling has been lost. In the early days the telling of stories was the principal form of entertainment. Families, relatives, and friends would gather in the evening and swap stories. Storytelling was the newspaper, radio, television, movies, and the electronic highway all in one. Let's relax and join the residents of Prospect — past and present — as they entertain us with their stories.

MY FIRST DAY TEACHING AT PROSPECT WEST SCHOOL

It was such a new adventure and such a lovely day on which to start. The wayside was rich with goldenrod as I came up to the schoolhouse. At my first glimpse of it I was astonished. It was such a beautiful spot. We had a little bit of a space for the school, surrounded by tumbledown walls of fieldstone on three sides. The fourth side was the road. A large flat stone that had evidently been brought in from the field served as a step. There was just a footpath going up to this step. The door itself seemed very slight but it had an enormous key. I put it in the lock and opened the door. There was a large entry where the children hung their clothing, each on a wrought-iron nail with their name below it, with girls on one side and boys on the other. There was an old table in the entry — oh, so old that it was probably worth money but nobody knew it — and I didn't either. On this table was a water pail, a dipper and a basin. Since the boys had to bring water from quite a distance, and you didn't want to waste their time sending them for water too often, you were very careful not to waste it. Also, since any water left in the pail would freeze overnight in winter, you had to be sure it was emptied every night.

I didn't know whether I looked forward to the opening of school or whether I dreaded it — probably a mixture of both. Here I was, at fifteen, starting to teach a class, in which I later discovered, there were children almost as old as I was. Well, I walked into the schoolroom and looked around. There were desks (doubles) all around the outside of the room on either side, pushed against the wall. This meant the child who sat beside the wall was unable to get out unless his partner on the outside moved out for him. The blackboard, not very large, was a pine board painted and when I wrote on it the chalk often slipped. Now this was all I had to illustrate the children's lessons, and all

they had to show me what they could do. The only place I could put anything was a crate brought in from a store. The stove stood on a piece of zinc; in case sparks flew out (we burned mostly chestnut wood) they would not hit the splintery wooden floor and set the place on fire. Flies buzzed in the windows, bees, too, and spiders waved on the outside. The panes of glass were very small and if you looked outward they seemed to have many different colors in them. Everything was distorted when you looked through those panes of glass. There were no fixtures at all on the windows to open them; you pushed them up and held them in place with a stick. It was so primitive it is hard to believe it was as it was. This was in the 1890s in the West Prospect School in Prospect, Connecticut.

My supplies had arrived — they stood on the teacher's desk. They were: a tall bottle of ink and a box of chalk. There was no dictionary, no sign of a book, no paper and no pencils. The books in each family were passed on from one child to the next, as was their slate. Each child had one with a pencil tied to it, and very often a big piece of the slate was missing. If they were unfortunate enough (and they often were) to break these pencils, it often caused tears to fall. Luckily my family had a large assortment of books and I used to drag the dictionary with me to teach the children how to look up words such as "library" which was not in their vocabulary at all.

I would have to get to school very early to start the fire, empty the ashes and gather my own kindling. The wood for the stove was brought in great loads by a farmer who would dump it in the yard. It was all sawed to the right size for the stove, which was of cast iron with a long pipe. This pipe gave as much heat as the stove which was fortunate as the room was so hard to heat.

Children would arrive on cold winter mornings actually crying — they were so cold their feet hurt and to their embarrassment, the teacher had to remove their shoes, and found both shoes and stockings in need of mending. The furniture was often so cold the children couldn't sit at their desks so each would take a log and all sit around the stove. This we liked as it made us feel very close to each other. When the wood came, the boys all worked very hard to get their lessons done so they could bring in the wood. No matter how deep the snow was, we either walked over it, through it or around it. Getting through it often made us gasp for breath but we finally got a path worn down.

Most of the families were German immigrants and the parents were not masters of the English Language. They could make themselves understood with very few words. Actually the children who attended the school came from only four families. From one family alone there were five girls and two boys. Our supervisor was always the minister who came about twice a year, shortly before it ended. There were two chairs in the classroom, one with a back and the other without. When the minister came he always sat in the chair with the back so I usually ended up standing. He always shook hands, then sat down, and had nothing to say. The pupils were frustrated because they were frightened by him. I wanted to show him what we had done, so we followed the usual procedure — I rang a bell, the children stood up, the bell again, they turned and marched to the front of the room and placed their toes on the mark on the floor. We had been taught to memorize when I went to school and that is what I taught my class to do. However I had one boy, Forrest, who could never get his lessons. It was poor Forrest whom the minister chose to question. He asked, "What did the Spanish plant on the ground as they got out of their ship?" Forrest just couldn't get it — he couldn't think what it could be, so one very helpful friend whispered to him, "How did Christ die?" and happily came to his answer. "Someone shot him with a bow and arrow!" During

the mathematics class he read a problem from a book he had with him. It was, "What is a half of four cups?" They gave all kinds of answers but the right one. Finally this cute little girl wiggled her hand frantically so I said, "Do you know the answer, Maggie? Tell us what it is." Her answer, "the saucers."

We began each day with a hymn and a Bible reading chosen by one of the children who had to give the reason for choosing that one. The children came to school barefoot but always wore a hat for they believed they would get sunstroke without it. If a child had new shoes, you could forget about teaching anything that day. The children were dressed alike as mothers usually purchased a bolt of cloth and made their dresses all alike. They were very respectful and as the year passed an affection developed between us that made me want to bring out the very best they had to give. It was a very rewarding experience.

Mathilda Blanchard

MOVING TO THE "BIG CITY"

From the West Prospect School in Prospect, Connecticut, I went to the East Mountain School in Waterbury. (Remember this was in the 1890s.) The change there was so great it almost frightened me. The school was brand new and we had plenty of supplies and books. We had a nice library and each year we were allowed to select new books to add to this library. There were two classrooms here — I had fifty-two children in mine. We still had to build the fire but there was a cellar here — and a snow shovel — that was an improvement. I had only been teaching three years but what a difference here in supplies and books.

The brook from the reservoir ran through our school yard. This reservoir provided us with drinking water and more! Once when they were cleaning it, all the fish came down into our school yard. It furnished the whole neighborhood with bushels of delicious fresh fish. I took some home for myself.

We had three elements of nature to contend with — snow, rain and mud. The rains were dreadful but the mud was the worst of all. We just couldn't get out of the mud — it was everywhere. What difficulty we had trying to keep our room clean when the mud season was upon us!

When we saw the snow coming we had to use our own judgment. If it began to get deep and blowy I had to dismiss school. I had to be very careful to see that the older children supervised the younger ones on the way home — whether they were related or not. If there was a severe storm, we had no way of knowing whether school was to be held. There were no whistles, no telephones, and no radio announcements. When the road was broken through, we went to school and the children would know that the teacher could get through so they came to school too.

Supervision here was on a much higher plane than previously — there was absolutely no comparison. One morning we were having a grammar lesson when the supervisor arrived. We were working on sentences, so he put one on the board and asked them to give him the subject which they did. (I was very proud of my grammar classes.) He often did this — he had a way of endearing himself to the children and we were all glad to see him.

Mathilda Blanchard

LAVERGNE CLARK'S TRAGIC EVENT

Lavergne and Will were hunting on the Roberts farm in Union City. They were standing on opposite sides of a bridge which crossed a wooden ravine. They both spotted a partridge and fired at the same time. The shot from one gun hit Lavergne in the head, shoulder, and arm, and riddled the gun stock. If it had not riddled the gun stock, it would have killed him instantly. His wounds immediately began to swell and Will did not know the way home. They finally pried one of Lavergne's eyes open so he could give directions. They went a distance of two miles. When they came down the road, I was standing out in front of the old Clark homestead. This happened in 1887, yet it is as clear in my mind now as it was that tragic afternoon.

Lavergne was totally red. He went into the house and sat down because he could not lie down. His mother met him at the door. She called out, "They have killed my boy", but she did not faint. As they sat there, they talked about what to do. They finally decided on a Dr. Cormalt in New Haven.

Lavergne Clark owned a very beautiful dark bay horse with four white feet. They told me that he was 16 hands high, weighed about 1100 pounds, and was exceedingly fast. No horse ever went past him when once he was stirred up a little in the 25 years Lavergne owned him. Lavergne could call that horse from anywhere on the big 325 acre farm and he would come right to him. If anyone else called him, he would not raise his head. The horse's name was Major.

While they sat there, Lavergne said, "Will, can you drive Major to New Haven?" He responded, "Yes, Lavergne, I think I can." My father and Will went out to put the harness on that horse. They said that they experienced great difficulty in getting the harness on for he was uncooperative. It seemed as if that horse sensed trouble and there was. They finally got the harness on and he came out by the stepping block at the gate that was hewed out of solid rock by the first Merritt Clark 146 years ago. I have found out that he and I are exactly the same height and weight after four generations. The horse stopped as quietly as he always did when he came out there.

As Lavergne was getting into the wagon, he said, "Will, don't spare the horse for I never expect to come back here alive." Will picked up the reins and the horse started down the road at a brisk trot. As they went around the bend, a cloud of dust rose higher than the wagon and they were gone. That horse was running and Will could not hold him.

Two days passed and Will came back. Will said that when he reached the New Haven Green that dark brown horse Major was pure white, every bit of him. I never saw such a sight in my life. Major had run right straight down the Carrington hills through Bethany, Woodbridge, and Westville to the New Haven Green on a dead run nearly all the way. Will said he had no control over that horse until we got way below Woodbridge.

Lavergne Clark did come back and carried with him 26 of the 48 shot that hit him. That did not inconvenience him during the remaining 56 years of his life.

About twelve years after, he had a horse race with a man that lived not far from the Prospect center. He stirred up Major a little and he went past that other horse as if it were standing still. That man followed Lavergne home and pulled out a roll of bills. Lavergne told me it was the biggest roll of bills he ever saw. He offered more than twice what the horse was worth. Lavergne said, "No, I will not sell that horse. He saved my life once. He has done his share and will always stay on Clark hill." The man with the roll of bills was no other man than Martin Dalton.

Clifford Clark, June 28, 1952

THE STORY OF MAD DOG HILL

A true story about something that happened on the Bronson and Union City Roads about 150 years ago. This story was told to me by my father and Alonzo Bronson who was next to the last of the family for which the road is named. This story has thrilled me for more than 70 years.

It started about half way up the Bronson Road on the west side. There lived a man by the name of Leveritt Smith who was standing in his yard with his big ugly vicious bull dog. Down the road came a great big dog who promptly jumped on the bull dog. They told me there was a terrible fight and the bull dog drove off the other dog who went down the road. Mr. Smith called the bull dog and patted him on the head and neck praising him for driving the other dog. A few minutes latter a gang of men with guns came down the road. They said someone's big dog had gone mad and had bitten pigs.

The mad dog went to the corner of Bronson and Union City Roads. There on the west side was a house with children playing in the dooryard making mud pies. The dog turned toward them. One child had a dish of water and threw it at the dog. The dog turned and went down Union City Road. Mad dogs were called water-shy dogs in those days.

The dog went to the corner of Clark Hill and Union City Roads. There another Mr. Smith lived who was not a relative of Leveritt Smith of Bronson Road. His name was Lymon Smith, the brother of my great grandmother, Katurah Smith Clark. Across the road from Lymon Smith's house was a pig pen. The mad dog jumped in the pen after the pigs. There the gang of men caught up with him and shot the dog as it was biting Lymon Smith's pigs. They took the dog back to the Bronson farm. About 100 feet from the corner of Bronson and Union City Roads there is a hill. There they buried the dog and that hill has been called Mad Dog Hill ever since.

One day my father, who was first selectman in Prospect, was digging gravel in Mad Dog Hill to put on the road. As he was digging he came to those bones. He placed a few of the bones in a piece of paper. When he came home to dinner, he brought those bones and showed them to me — the bones from that mad dog that had been buried more than 85 years earlier.

Now I am going to take you with me up the Bronson Road to Mr. Leveritt Smith — the hero of this story and the bull dog. Mr. Leveritt Smith was a giant. I don't mean maybe! He was the strongest man that ever lived in Prospect if not all of the United States. It was reported to me that he was so strong that he could bend a horseshoe with his bare hands. I studied ancient history at Mt. Hermon School. I came across a clipping that said a man in the ranks of the ancient Roman ruler, Tiberius Gracci, could bend a horseshoe with his bare hands.

Mr. Smith was a blacksmith and had scratched his hand with a horseshoe nail before he patted the bull dog's head and neck where the mad dog had chewed. Mr. Smith knew that if he was stricken by the mad-dog infection, nobody could hold him down. So he welded a pair of bracelets to his own wrists then welded the bracelets to a chain which he welded to a ring in the kitchen floor. Mr Smith made an iron spoon with a handle three feet long. Then he waited.

Mr. Smith went mad and frothed at the mouth. He was terribly sick for a long time. His family fed him with the iron spoon. But then he got well. Everybody knew about the case and all credited his superhuman strength for saving him from the mad-dog infection. Mr. Smith lived to be 67 years old. His wife was Betsy Pardee Smith. A Smith family Bible in the hands of Mrs. Peter Slater, the 4th generation down, verifies the fact.

Clifford Clark, August 11, 1960

MOVING TO PROSPECT

My husband and I moved to Prospect when the snow was as "high as an ele-

phant's eye." We both came from big cities, he from West Haven and I from Toronto. At that time (1950) the population was about 700 and everyone knew one another. We thought we were moving into the dark ages. A constable in town was directing traffic at the intersection of Routes 68 & 69. He was dressed like a keystone cop, complete with puttees and looking very important (he thought).

When we were made voters we were sent to a tiny building with a pot belly stove, hardly big enough to turn around in. Town meetings, which were dutifully attended, were a riot. More laughs than a movie comedy, residents screaming at each other over unimportant things. One night they had to take a vote by ballot and had forgotten to bring the ballot box. One of the constables went backstage for a so-called ballot box and came back with a huge Kotex box. This brought down the house.

We also found that my husband had a first cousin living in town that he didn't even know existed. She also told us that the Wilmot family was one of the first settlers in Prospect. We've loved every minute of living in Prospect and will continue to live here to the end. My daughter Paula was the first "Miss Prospect" and also a member of the Prospect Drum Corps as a baton twirler and was State Champion.

Tillie Wilmot (1994)

PROSPECT BEGINNINGS

Walt's father, Fred Hintz, gave us seven acres on the corner of Talmadge Hill and Cheshire Roads. My father-in-law came here earlier and had a chicken farm on Cook Road. I think he bought the property from Chandler. We built a house and brought all four children here. All of them joined the Prospect Drum Corps. Karen, at 12, was first in the Northeast Fife Competition.

Myrtle B. Hintz (1994)

OUR PROSPECT HOME

In building our house, believe you me, I found out what was what in tools. Digging ditches by hand — I did it. Lucky that I didn't fall in because I'm just a "little kid". Mud! Rocks! Unbelievable!! I said, "Wow, what am I getting myself into?" I was always a "city girl" but now I'm a "country girl" on the rodeo — no horse yet though!

One day I was cooking in the kitchen and doing dishes on Country Brook Road when all of a sudden a whole herd of cattle shot across our lawn. I watched them cut across our path and laughed. They were lost and broke off from their farm (Frederick's I think).

At the 9ᵗʰ birthday party for our son Raymond Jr., my sister-in-law had an accident while riding her bike. One call for help and sure enough "Thank God" Bob Chatfield was promptly on the scene. He brought her to St. Mary's hospital for medical attention.

Cecile Tanquay (1994)

THE PROSPECT CURE

While Marge was on the Library Board, Albert Allen (a real gentleman and "old timer") was also on the Board. We had a daughter who had a case of croup and Albert brought in some skunk oil to put on her chest. It worked — and NO SMELL!

Marjorie C. Bell (1994)

SCOUT TRAINING
HELPS NEIGHBOR

One snowy night, Mr. Albert Wilmot of Buckley Lane was taken to the hospital in the Prospect ambulance. After spending a long, worried night at the hospital, Mrs. Wilmot was taken home in the daylight hours with the dreadful thought of coming home to a driveway filled with snow. To her surprise, four scouts, who heard the ambulance take

Mr. Wilmot to the hospital, had gotten up early and proceeded to completely remove all the heavy snow from the driveway. When the boy scouts, Christopher Supra, John Brewster, John Petro, and George Petro were offered a reward, all they answered was, "No thank you, this was one of our good deeds for today."

Prospect Reminder, April 1968

HELP WHEN YOU NEED IT

My husband John and I have been here since 1949. Our house was the only one on Talmadge Road besides the Talmadge Farm. The pavement ended at our place and it was dirt the rest of the way. In 1961 we had a fire in our home. Everyone in town was great. For six weeks, while we were rebuilding, we never knew where our clothes (or even our girls) were. Someone took care of them and all were returned in tip-top shape — children as well as clothes. There is no other town that was so great and could be counted on.

Marjorie C. Bell (1994)

THE RAILROAD

I heard stories about boys putting lard on the rails of the train tracks. Then they would hide and watch as the train engine would spin its wheels trying to get up the hills of Prospect.

Lillian Walters (1994)

SCHOOLS

I remember going to the one-room schoolhouse. On certain days two or three students would be selected to go up to the library. One day on my way back from the library, I dropped a history book in the brook that ran along the road. I tried to dry off the book as best I could on my way back to the school.

I remember that the older boys would be excused from class when brush fires broke out. The ringing of the church bell would summon them to the scene of the fire. Using portable backpack water sprayers, the boys would assist in putting out the fires.

Lillian Walters (1994)

APPLE PICKING

Plumb Farm was well known for its apples. I remember being eager to earn money, so I was hired to pick drops. At age 12, five cents a bushel sounded pretty good to me. Grandpa and Uncle Tom would be up in the trees picking as I fought off bees and tried to avoid touching a rotten apple on the ground. Only the good drops were to be picked up. I was proud to have earned $13.00 that fall. Twelve years later my cousin, Tom Wheeler, was earning ten cents a bushel — that's inflation for ya!

Lorraine (Plumb) Centrella, 1995

FAVORITE SAYINGS

One of Uncle Tom's favorite sayings was "Watch your pennies and your dollars will take care of themselves." Grandpa and Uncle Tom always wore their clothes until they were patched, threadbare and ready for the rag bag. They really did have nice new flannel shirts, hats, and pants; but their frugal nature caused them to look ragged. They were honest, hard working people. Pure Yankee. They saved everything because you never know when you'll need it. Repair it if you can. Use something else (ingenuity). Make do or do without.

They lived and worked by the sweat of their brow and what the Good Lord provided. No sense complaining about the weather. "If you don't like the weather, wait a minute." After all, this is New England!

Liquor and tobacco had no part in their lives. "They're no good for ya.

They'll kill ya," was their advice. The "old gent" (their father) and the Mrs. (their mother) gave gold watches to Grandpa, Uncle Tom, and their brothers & sisters (George, Ed, Fred, Florence, and Lena) as gifts when they were 21 for abstaining from liquor and tobacco.

My grandma wouldn't mince words. You knew just where she stood. She was straightforward, to the point and at times, I felt, too blunt. But that's the way she was.

All three were very generous, giving people. That was their nature. My grandpa would say, "One hand washes the other."

Much of our family history is oral. I do remember my grandpa telling a story of when he was young, someone stole a pig from the farm. No one said a word until one day a person asked the "old gent" (that's what his father was called) if they ever found the culprit who stole the pig. The "old gent" replied, "Yes, and I'm talking to him now!"

The morning's work started before dawn with milking cows and continued non-stop until noon. Grandpa and Uncle Tom took care of all the chores related to running a vegetable and dairy farm. After dinner and afternoon break, it was back to work until sunset.

My grandma's domain was the house. She was an excellent baker. There was always pie, cookies, or cake to sneak out of the pantry. Her specialty was home-made bread. She used the wood stove during the winter and electric stove during the warm weather. She was a font of knowledge pertaining to canning, preserving, cooking, baking, cleaning, and sewing.

Dinner was always at noon. A full course meal with plenty of meat and potatoes. My favorite and most memorable meals were suppers. Whatever the seasonal crop was we'd eat that exclusively: fresh strawberry shortcake with real whipped cream, fresh peas in cream, corn-on-the-cob, watermelon, blueberries, or succotash.

I don't want people to think that their lives were all work and no play. They knew the art of relaxation. After the noontime meal, Grandpa and Uncle Tom would listen to the baseball game or take a nap on the couch or in a favorite chair. Grandma would use the afternoon to braid of hook wool rugs. She also created quilts, crocheted delicate lace doilies, or just sat and mended.

Part of the afternoon was also spent with old friends who would stop by for a bit to chat and enjoy the breeze under the big maple tree that is in front of the farmhouse. Mr. John Chatfield (Mayor Bob' father), Mr. James Bramhall, Mr. Ed Morin, and Mr. Bill Dalleywater were the main people I remember. Being lifelong Grange members also provided social and community involvement.

Lorraine (Plumb) Centrella, 1995

CHRISTMAS TREE BONFIRE

In the early 1960s, my grandpa and Uncle Tom dammed up a small brook that ran through a field. The field flooded, froze over, and made an ideal skating rink for family and friends. We kids would skate until dark and Uncle Tom would unlace my skates. Fingers were too frozen and numb to function. Then he would take a broom and sweep my back to dust off the ice and snow I had collected while sliding across the pond. Grandpa and Uncle Tom wanted us to enjoy the winter so they built a shed and bench for shelter by the pond.

One winter soon after creating the pond, my friends, Tom Milton, Len Parent, and I had an idea to have a Christmas tree bonfire. My grandparents and Uncle Tom gave us permission. So we put up a sign along the roadside for people to dump their Christmas trees here at the farm. The date was the first weekend in January. Friends and family were invited and we had a huge bonfire. I ran back and

forth between the pond and farmhouse, making sure refreshments were plentiful. My grandma was busy at the wood stove making hot chocolate and supplying us with homemade cookies. After a few winters, the crowd and bonfire got too big to handle, so we discontinued the tradition at Plumb farm. Now the town of Prospect has the Christmas tree burning at Hotchkiss Field.

Many other precious memories include: Uncle Tom tending his flower garden (especially his favorite flowers - gladioli), haying in the field, riding on top of a truckload of hay and barely beating a pending thunderstorm back to the cover of the barn, watermelon eating and seed-spitting contests with grandpa, learning how to sew and bake from grandma, family picnics, and wonderful Christmas Eve family gatherings at the Farm.

My life has truly been blessed to have known these three dear people.

Lorraine (Plumb) Centrella, 1995

THE TYLER FAMILY

For many years there was a Tyler Reunion, often held in Prospect, for the descendants of Spencer Tyler. There were some years ago a number of Tyler families in Prospect, none of the name now remain. The history of Waterbury tells us that Spencer Tyler, son of Ichabod, m. Sarah Farrell, dau. of Zebah, both of Prospect, 7 Nov. 1727.

We know that Enos Tyler was one of the first to donate to the Columbia Company, before the church was formed. He was m. 3 times and had at least 6 sons; one Levi, "died in camp," June 1777. Another, Abraham was in the Rev. and is buried in Prospect Cem., who had a large family, inc. Ichabod, d. 1848, ae. 69. I do not know the names of all the children, but one was Spencer. There were cousins of all degrees all over as Tylers intermarried with Tylers, Clarks,

Hotchkisses, Pecks, and others.

Spencer died 2 Dec. 1858, ae. 50, and his wife Sally, 1859, ae. 57, in our cem. In the 1850 census, Spencer is listed as 43, Sally's age not given, in household, Mary 21, George 18, Sarah 12, Fanny 9, and Luke 19. Ichabod apparently lived in the house he sold to Charles Adams, (to Ross Dupre, to Tom Marino.) George Payne m. Achsa Adams, and that house is now Mabel Johns'. Spencer Tyler lived nearer the center, on the same road (the original Naugatuck road), now Hydelor Ave.

For the 50th anniversary of the Spencer Tyler family reunion, August 1921, Fannie wrote a paper of her memories. She would have been 80. We have some other papers written by old people, and the descriptions of houses, who lived there, are very helpful, but there is always a possibility of error. Fannie married William Berkley, a Civil War soldier. She died in 1922. Her daughter, Bessie Berkley, copied this paper, *Reminiscences of the Little Town of Prospect*, in June 1932 for me.

Nellie Cowdell

REMINISCENCES OF THE LITTLE TOWN OF PROSPECT

My memories of Prospect and what happened there in the days of my girlhood and of my early married life are very vivid. I was born in a little house that stood about one-half mile north of Prospect Center, opposite the Icabod Hitchcock House which is now owned by ? (Nichols, Buckmiller). Nothing remains today of the little house but the cellar and the well. The home which I best remember, however, is a little cottage which is still standing about a mile west of the center, on the Naugatuck road. (owned by Mr. Fournier when the paper was written, torn down by Mark Dana Guastaferri and now ?) That is where my brothers and sisters and myself grew to manhood and womanhood and from there we were married and went into homes of

our own. There were no old maids or bachelors in our family, which consisted of two boys and four girls. There my father Spencer and mother Sally died while they were still young. Father died Dec. 2, 1858, and mother died Sept. 13, 1859, when my first baby, Eva, was a few days old, only one of my children to have a living grandparent. My grandfather, Icabod Tyler, lived in the old house still standing on the other side of the road just west of our home. It is as old, if not the oldest of any house in town. This house is opposite the George Payne house and was in recent years owned by Charles Adams. My grandfather died Nov. 13, 1848, in his 75th year. My grandmother died three years later, Oct. 5, 1851, age 77.

We attended the Congregational Church in Prospect, but Mother, often against Father's wishes, often went to the little Methodist Church to prayer meetings. That little church stood where the Grange hall now stands. The Congregational Church was in the same location as it now is today, although at that time it was the old fashioned church with the high steeple, typical of those days and which we still see in old towns throughout New England. Some years ago that church burned down but was rebuilt, and they have the same beautiful church which we see today. (Stone church, 1907).

My sisters, Mary and Charlotte, and my two brothers, Luke and George, sang in the choir. At that time there was a large choir and a number of pretty girls in it. They had a melodian which was played by Anna Train and at times by Edwin Tyler, our cousin and son of Richard Tyler. There was also a number of musical instruments in the choir. Luke played the cello; Evans Hotchkiss, a violin; Rufus Gillette, a flute. This was before any of my brothers or sisters were married. I can think now how pretty my sister Charlotte used to look in her blue dress and bonnet as she sat there in the choir. I am sure the choir of today can boast of nothing better than we had sixty five years ago (about 1856 NHC). Frances Tyler, daughter of Richard, owned the first melodian brought into the town of Prospect.

In my earliest remembrances of Prospect, the general store was located on the same ground as that on which the school now stands. This store was stocked with clothing, dry goods, shoes, groceries, etc. Everything needed could be bought in the town. It is said that at one time Waterbury used to come to Prospect to do some shopping. I remember buying a black silk mantilla for my mother in this store, which I now have. Over this store was a dance hall, where the young people of the town used to go for their good times. The schoolhouse was located on the road which branches off from the Waterbury Road at a point just north of the Icabod Hitchcock place and running southwesterly to the Naugatuck road, reaching it at a point just west of the Luther Morse place.

There was a hotel standing at the top of the hill opposite where the Library now stands, on the road leading to Cheshire. They sold liquor in this hotel, which was the only blot on the fair name of Prospect. The proprietor of this hotel was George Payne. There was also a bowling alley in the rear of the hotel.

There were a number of match factories in Prospect in those days. One was on the Bethany Road under the management of Ezra Kimball, and (1855) my brother, Luke Tyler, had a match factory on the Salem Rd., which was previously owned by Zebah Farrell, his grandfather. There was one on the Straightsville Rd. owned by Brooks Hotchkiss, and in 1850 Richard Tyler and Samuel Bronson had a match factory opposite the cemetery and near the center of the town. The boxes for these different matches were taken to the different homes in the town and made by the women and children, and in this way many comforts were enjoyed in the homes that would not have been only for the money they earned in that way.

On the Naugatuck Road, Ransom Russell had a button factory. This was also in operation about the year 1850 and after. Ransom Russell was a brother of Lewis Russell, Dr. Will Russell's grandfather.

There was a family of Smiths who had a factory on the road going east from Prospect towards Cheshire, but I do not remember what they manufactured. At one time there were pocketbooks and other novelties manufactured by Luther Morse in the center of town. There was a small factory on Matthews Street where they made match sticks, which supplied the factories in that locality.

Farther east was the Capt. Wm. Mix place (Henry Mix's father) where Capt. Mix had a grist mill, and I think he also had a spoon shop there. This was a large house in which Capt. Mix lived. At one time we lived in this house, and my daughter Bessie was born there. In later years, say between fifty and sixty years ago (1860-70 ? NHC), there was a needle factory in Rag Hollow, and in the same building they made hoe ferrules. These ferrules were carried to Naugatuck to a factory owned by Eben Tuttle, and which in later years developed into what is now known as the Naugatuck Malleable Iron Company. My brother George and my husband used to work in this ferrule factory. Near the Needle and Ferrule factory (which was owned by the Jeralds and Lawton Company) was a button factory owned by Henry Judd.

Mr. Wilcox started a match factory in Rag Hollow of which my brother Luke had a share after Mr. Wilcox died. Mr. Wilcox built the house in Laurel Grove, where for several years we had our family reunion. Edwin Tyler was also associated with Luke in this match business, and I worked for him during the Civil War. Later this match factory was taken over by the Ives and Judd Co., where for a number of years my husband was employed.

Finally it was taken over by the Diamond Match Company and the business was taken to other towns.

At the time of the Civil War, 75 of the Prospect boys enlisted out of a population of something over five hundred - among them being my George and my husband.

All of my children with the exception of Eva were born in Prospect. Arthur, Charlie, and Eleanor Beecher, Elsie, Georgianna, and Elmer Tyler, Emma Tyler, Lilla Mix, Lewis Russell, Dr. W.S. Russell, all children of Tylers.

The first reunion was held in Matthews Grove, about one mile east of Prospect, fifty tears ago. This was a grove of large chestnut trees, and I doubt if they are still standing.

Written by Fannie Tyler Berkley (1921)
and copied by Bessie Berkley (1932)

LIVING IN PROSPECT

I was born in 1897 in a house at the top of Summit Road. We had a small garden, but my father worked as a helper at another farm. Later we moved farther down on Summit Road to where the Cowdells later lived.

When I went to Center School, girls went longer than boys who had to help out on the farms. I sat on a bench in the front row with two other girls. We would sometimes fool around, and one girl would push me with her hip and send me to the floor. The teacher would scold us and we would be good — for a little while! There was a woman who worked at the library on Wednesday afternoons. She was very helpful to the children and would answer any questions.

I liked to go ice skating around the Plumb farm. They had one pond right behind the house, but there was a better one down the road a little. In those days we wore flat skates which strapped onto your regular boots. I was having trouble putting on my skates one day when a boy came over and helped me. Then we skated around for a couple of hours. His name was Bill Mortison, my future husband. Mrs. Plumb would always have a big kettle of hot chocolate and other treats waiting for us after skating. Besides skating we would go sledding. But that wasn't as much fun because it was more work to walk back up the hill.

We would go to Waterbury to buy shoes and to shop. Everyone went to church, and almost all the functions were there. Children walked to church but often would get a ride from someone going or coming. Everyone was very friendly and would gladly share a ride.

During the war it was hard to get a minister for the church. They couldn't afford to pay much, and ministers wouldn't stay long. I remember when I was young, there was a pastor [Rev. Phipps] who was old but had been there 25 years or more. I remember when the church burned down in 1906. My father came home and told my mother about it. I can remember more about the stone church. I got married there when I was twenty. My father told me when I was younger that I couldn't get married because I had to watch out for my siblings. But later he changed his mind.

I didn't attend many town meetings. My husband would go and tell me what went on afterwards. It was exciting when we got electricity. It took awhile to run all the poles. Some of the power came from one direction and some from another. I think there were three power lines altogether. I only took one trip on the train that stopped at the Prospect station. I took it and went to Maryland. It was a big adventure — like taking a plane today!   Bessie Mortison, 1995

WHAT PROSPECT MEANS TO ME CONTEST

Prospect Pages, January 1988

. . . Granted it's not the biggest town, but come to think of it, and knowing what I know now, I'd rather live here than anywhere else in the world . . . I can't put my finger on it, but there's something about this town that makes it more special, and in a way bigger, than other towns.
Melissa Mentus

To me, Prospect means many things — a great little town to live in and to bring up your children in. . . Prospect has always been such a friendly town and I'm grateful for good neighbors and friends. . . With a town like Prospect, who would ever want to live anywhere else? So you see, to me, Prospect means love and happiness, thankfulness and many happy memories.
Peg Iannantuoni

The true sons and daughters of Prospect revel in their countryism and hold it forth as a model for others to emulate. Prospect natives have cultivated the skill of arguing with one another, yet still respecting the other's point of view. From the early beginnings Prospect was a sort of multicultural town. There were different opinions about religion, politics, and running the town. These conflicts exist today and will no doubt continue in the future. But this is good — this is true democracy.

Humor is certainly a part of Prospect, and many of its citizens try not to take life too seriously. In his cartoons and newspaper articles, C.L. Mortison (Lester Green) made people laugh with Prospect and not at Prospect. Another example of Prospect's sense of humor is evident in the small ad placed in the Waterbury Republican in 1952 by Prospect resident Howard C. Sills (Fig 1). Among his other talents, Howard claimed success at the use of divining rods to locate underground water.

1939 PACKARD SEDAN — Only running on 5 cylinders but will beat police car up East Mt. or will swap for 1949 Cadillac.   Howard C. Sills, Prospect, Conn.

Fig 1   Waterbury Republican

THE PERSONALITY OF PROSPECT

Some may argue that the personality of a town is simply the sum total of the individual personalities of its citizens. If people were randomly distributed among towns, then all municipalities would have a similar character. In reality, people do not settle in towns on a random basis. They are attracted by what is already present there: the people and institutions that define the town. As a result, communities do develop distinct personalities. What's more, these personalities are not stagnant. They are in a constant state of redefinition. Let us examine the personality of Prospect.

Prospect, in many ways, is the typical New England town. Space and privacy are afforded to its people. No one is overwhelmed by zealous neighbors trying to become "new best friends." Yet, there is a sense that people are present — but at a distance — on the fringe — ready and waiting — if and when they are needed.

> *But after being in a town for almost 70 years, it seems a little late for me to be asking what I like about the place. I was born here and I've never been away for more than a few weeks at a time, and I probably wouldn't have gone away at all except that I like to catch fish when I go fishing and they bite a lot better in Maine and Vermont than they do in these parts . . . We have always had good people in Prospect — I mean honest, reliable and kindly neighbors. They look after their affairs and let you look after yours. That is until you've got trouble. Then they're swarming around to see what they can do to help. That's what I call good people and good neighbors, and that's the kind of people that have made Prospect a pleasant town to live in.*

Albert T. Allen, The New Haven Register, July 13. 1952

While everyone may have a different definition as to just what this town's personality is, there are some basic characteristics to which most should agree. First and foremost, the people of Prospect are countryfolk — not city-folk. This fact has made Prospect the brunt of jesting over the years from its city cousins. Sometimes this kidding was in fun, but at other times with a feeling of disdain. From the writer's perspective, Prospect accepts these attacks by turning lemons into lemonade.

Fig 2   The residents of Prospect assemble on the Green in 1993 for a town photograph.   Waterbury Republican-American

In 1993 Connecticut Magazine published its ranking of the quality of life in small towns. When Prospect was ranked 39th out of 39, a collective nerve was touched, and town pride reached a new high. Bumper stickers for the occasion soon appeared, and events were staged to demonstrate the unanimous disagreement with Connecticut Magazine's survey and to show everyone that Prospect has pride (Fig 2). To the natives, Prospect is the "best small town in Connecticut."

PROSPECT — THE DEFINITION

Prospect's main charms have always been residential, and they remain so today as the town has become home to a large number of single-family residences meant largely for those who earn their wages in Waterbury, New Haven, or elsewhere.

And Prospect became, as it remains today, a quiet and pleasant place to buy or build a house and raise a family. And a popular place as well. In 1987, of all the towns of the region, only Waterbury, Naugatuck, Watertown, and Cheshire (all far larger in population) built more housing units than did Prospect. It appears that its "in between" location is at last to its advantage. It remains removed from the crowds of the cities, yet close enough for an early commute. As a result, Prospect has never had it so good.

Charles Monagan, Greater Waterbury - A Region Reborn

Isn't it great, that we live in a world, country and great little town where people allow one another space and freedom to have different opinions. Yea, right!

Now, you'll notice I didn't say anything about being able to express that opinion in public without the concern of retribution.

Unfortunately, too many residents and taxpayers all, have become complacent about important issues at hand. This will change.

And things are changing rapidly! Prospect is changing, its needs and direction. You are an important part of this movement and should become an active participant.

Attending meetings of the various boards that govern our town and addressing your feelings and concerns either verbally there, or in writing are positive ways you can express your legitimate opinion.

Robert A. Marcella, *Prospect Pages*, October 1994

One of the better aspects of living in the Best Little Town in Connecticut is the ability to agree to disagree while respecting one another's opinions.

Robert Chatfield, Mayor

When I was tracing my ancestral roots a few years back, my family and I went to the home town my paternal grandfather in St. Léonard d' Aston, Québec. At once we were struck by the peace and tranquility of the place. Everyone seemed so friendly and got along so well during our brief stay. Upon closer examination, I began to realize why this was so. Almost everyone had the same beliefs and customs. They had common ancestry. Most went to the one school in town and attended the only church. They were all "family." But is this really a good thing? Does this way of living prepare people to live in the real world? I think not. If all people are to learn to live in peace, they must first learn to understand and accept their differences. This is not to say they should compromise their beliefs. Not at all. They should just be able to appre-ciate the diversity of human values and traditions. While this concept may be idealistic and a bit naive, in a place like Prospect, achieving this dream is a real possibility. John Guevin

~

Chapter Twenty

Twentieth Century Businesses

T he bustling factories of the 1800s grew silent in Prospect with the dawn of the twentieth century. This town was unable to compete with the attractions for industry found in neighboring cities and towns. These municipalities offered a network of transportation, abundant electric power, and a pool of immigrant labor. As a result, Prospect returned to its agricultural roots.

FARMING

Vegetable and fruit farming were important to the economy as were the dairy and cattle industries. Sheep grazing for wool was popular. Other crops included flax, corn, rye, barley, oats, flowers, and hay (Fig 1). Most homes did some farming for their own consumption if not as the primary source of family income.

Prospect was a supplier to Waterbury and other towns of produce from its farms. Poultry and egg farms grew in importance. Doyle's Double A Farm on Cook Road was started in 1939 and is still in operation. When it began, it was one of many egg producers in Prospect. Farms were in all parts of town, even the center. The Clifford Wallace farm was located at the present site of the town hall and Long River School.

Fig 1 Frank M. Plumb and grand-daughter Lorraine haying in the field in 1951.

Lorraine Plumb Centrella

Fig 2 The Wallace Barn near Cheshire Reservoir.   John Guevin

The new library on Center Street was built on land that had been farmed since the founding of Prospect.   Ephraim Nettleton purchased 22½ acres in the center of town in 1826.   The Nettletons had ten children in the original one-room house.   A sleeping loft was above.   Later owners were the Petersons from Denmark and most recently, the Petrauskas family, who sold the property to the town (see drawing by Jane Fowler, page 6).

BEEKEEPING

Beekeeping was another industry that was common in Prospect. Most farms had a colony or two for pollination of fruit trees and as a source of honey for food and sale. One of the town's most famous authorities on bees was First Selectman Albert T. Allen. His specialty was in bee hunting or the establishment of new colonies.

The old church in Prospect that burned down in 1906 or thereabouts had a famous bee hive in its belfry. This ecclesiastical honey was gathered each year by some kind of feudal right by a citizen named Philo Delos Hotchkiss who had this prerogative in recognition of certain services rendered the church.

Mr. Allen goes hunting purely in the spirit of a collector of locations, not the collector of honey. He has been bee hunting for 31 years, and each year has found five to 27 swarms, depending principally on the amount of time that he devotes to

the pastime . . . A. Ralph Driver of Prospect, now 81 years old taught him the craft of bee hunting when Mr. Allen was 15.

Connecticut, or this section of it, is a great bee country. Some centuries ago the Indians and the bears used to hunt wild bees here as a source of food. The honey they found was made by native black bees; and occasionally swarms of those bees are still discovered.

A generation ago practically every farmer had several swarms of bees, and swarming time was a big event in farm life . . . It provided a welcome interlude in the labor of a hot June day, and the operation was an important one, because honey was a necessary element in the yearly food supply of the farm. One of the rites was that the proprietor of the farm and master of ceremonies of swarming, usually washed his face and hands in some good hard liquor kept for that purpose, and he was

privileged to have a good hearty drink in accordance to the ancient custom.   This external coating was to prevent bee stings, and the drink was taken, presumably, in case one of the bees should be swallowed.   Waterbury Republican, 1936

LOGGING

Logging and lumber production were frequent by-products from clearing property of trees for farming (Fig 3).   The area around Old Logtown Road was noted for this industry although almost every farm offered some of its surplus timber for sale.

Fig 3   Truck with logs going to saw mill in 1951.   Boards cut from this load were used for flooring in the Frank J. Plumb house.   Lorraine Plumb Centrella

MERCHANTS

Retail stores in Prospect slowly increased in number during the first half of the century, then multiplied rapidly beginning in the 1950s.   In the earlier years the general store was the source for almost all necessities.   For many years Chandler's General Store, located in the center of town, was *the* place to buy everything.   The town records are filled with purchases from Chandler's for all sorts of supplies.   It was more than a store — it was the unofficial meeting place for residents.   When the Congregational Church burned in 1941, townspeople signed a petition in Chandler's that authorized the town to purchase fire fighting equipment.

Stores began to specialize more.   Clifford Wallace had a small store in his house where the town hall is presently located.   Wallace carried staple food items like flour and sugar.   In 1948 Oliver's opened and today is Prospect's only supermarket. Another small grocery store was Mr. Fusco's Market on Rt. 68. Keenan's was the local gasoline station and candy store on Route 69, just over the line from Waterbury into Prospect. An article by Jane Stanwich gives a sense of life in Prospect when there were places like Keenan's.

Mr. and Mrs. Keenan lived behind the garage in a Quonset hut. Nestled quietly among the trees, barely noticeable, it looked untouched and secretly hidden from most of the world — and in a way I guess it was. But the whole place was clearly a home, the kind that made the kids want to go there. I wonder now just how many people over the years stopped in there to fill up, and how many kids bought candy and just how many young and old remember the Keenans as I do.

Mr. Keenan, better known to the kids as Tom, was a tall brawny, gray-headed man, bearded and a bit bent over at times, depending on the hour of the day. Mrs. Keenan (and we called her "Mrs. Keenan" for some reason), was short and stout; her hair was cut close and it too was gray, but it had a more lady-like, soft color to it as I recall. She was always somewhere close by to Tom just to be there and to help out if needed; I can still hear her comfortable slippers and the slow steps she took with them as she'd come in from the back of the store.

When we'd all pop in they'd smile at us, say things to make us giggle and ask us all about school and stuff and you knew they really wanted to know. And Tom would fix our bikes and tell us to be careful riding the highway; and it was more than once I saw them holding hands as they stood behind the candy counter waiting for us, oh! so patiently, to make the big decision of the day — whether to buy a Peter & Paul Mounds bar or a Three Musketeers. And I can hear that

cash register ring and flash the numbers and remember the time Mr. Keenan let me do it!

I miss the Keenan's and I miss those days. I was 9 years old then and I'm 29 now. I drove by Keenan's a short while ago; I'd been away and come back. I'd grown up with seeing Mr. Keenan and his dog, King (we can't forget King), servicing a car or talking to a kid leaning up against his bike and spotting Mrs. Keenan a few steps away watching them from behind. That whole scene was always there — cozy and quiet, friendly and peaceful; a warm sight and fond memory you could depend on.

Yet, I think we took Keenan's for granted like most of the good, simple things in life are taken when you're all "grown up". I know I did . . . This day I drove by was peculiar. I'd actually planned for a mile or so to take a good look over — to simply remember and smile hello.

. . . The buildings were still there but they stood buried in a cold silence. It was empty and dark and the gas pumps were gone and snow had piled up against the doors. I felt strange, lonely perhaps — suddenly abandoned.

Tom and Mrs. Keenan had died. And I think something in those days and times died with them; that is, if we don't take that moment to look back and smile and somehow forget to remember.

Prospect Reminder, March 1, 1975

According to Nellie Cowdell, the first two gas stations were built in 1934. Other stores brought a greater variety of goods, saving trips to Waterbury or other towns. Tony Cretella opened his barber shop in 1951 inside the Shell gas station on Route 68 (Fig 4). Joseph J. Neal opened his Pharmacy on Waterbury Road in 1954 and had filled nearly 350,000 prescriptions by the store's 25th anniversary in 1979. In 1957 the first two liquor stores began operations after Prospect repealed the nearly century-long ban on alcholic beverage sales. Town Spirit Shop was followed within three months by LoCascio Liquors.

Fig 4 Shell gas station (now Sunoco) at intersection of Old Schoolhouse Road and Route 68 circa 1950s.   Prospect Service Center & Towing

Starting in the 1950s and continuing to the present, Prospect businesses began to attract customers from Waterbury and other towns. By capitalizing on easy access and convenient parking, shopping plazas were developed along Routes 68 and 69. Stores sold products of every description and offered a wide range of services (Fig 5). In Prospect one could now obtain shoes, gowns, cleaning services, televisions, auto body repair, furniture, hardware, ice cream, real estate, building supplies, beauty salons, flowers, and gifts to name but a few. Banks also opened offices along Route 69.

SOME PROSPECT BUSINESSES OF THE RECENT PAST

Macary Shoes	Betty's Flowers & Gifts	Prospect House of Charm
Prospect Hardware Co.	Drew-Albert Furniture Co.	Hilda's Beauty Shop
Custom Caterers	Daren's Cash 'N Carry	Farm House Foods
Genvieve Shoppe	Gerry's Grocery Barn	Silver Moon Clothing Shop
Carvel	Pet Town	Prospect Sports Center
Prospect Meat Market	Rivendell Books	Gloria's Flowers & Gifts
Ed Cass' Boot & Shoe Shop	Carroll Furniture Store	Hayes Hardware
Bella Coiffures	J & L Family Shoes	
Toga Shoppe	Health & Beauty Aids etc.	

Fig 5   Businesses of the 60s and 70s from the *Prospect Reminder*

RESTAURANTS

In the 1800s, meals for guests were available at the taverns in town. Of the modern restaurants, Russell's was one of the earliest.

I remembers stopping there for supper en route from West Haven to Waterbury on Sunday evenings prior to moving to Prospect in 1948. They served great food with occasional French-Canadian dishes like pea soup, yellow whole peas, and home-made pies. Many a day my mother sent me down (we lived on Radio Tower Road) to buy a loaf of bread. They had a real soda fountain with stools. A specialty of the house was vanilla Cokes (cost an extra nickel — 15¢). The Merriman's ran a great restaurant (very fancy) for some years (60s?) where there are now office buildings behind Buckmiller's.   Dick Caouette

Fig 6 The Prospect Country Club in 1975 was also the Fieldstone Restaurant. A WW II communications tower is visible to the left. The property off of New Haven Road is now the private residence of designer Louis Nichole.

Waterbury Republican-American

In 1953 Vincent and Olive Visockis opened the Dairy Bar, which is Prospect's oldest restaurant in continuous service. The original idea was to sell the ice cream and dairy products from their family farm down the street. It was a seasonal business, closing for the winter months. Forty-two years later the restaurant is still in business under the direction of Carol and John Jones. Neal's drug store had a fountain where coffee, soda, and sandwiches were served from 1954 until that service was discontinued in the mid 80s. In 1956 the Bow 'N Arrow restaurant was built on ten acres overlooking the

Mixville Pond. Many dining establishments followed, including the Fieldstone Restaurant (Fig 7), Lou-Ann's Luncheonette, The Fort Restaurant, Richard's Luncheonette, and Prospect Pizza Palace among others.

RECREATION

When better roads made access to Prospect easier, it became a destination for people looking to relax. City dwellers found peace and tranquility in the country living of Prospect. One of the earliest attractions was Laurel Grove, near the site of the present VFW. Laurel Grove was a stop along the railroad through Prospect and offered dining and overnight accommodations.

Today, several riding stables provide services for people wanting to ride horses or be driven in horse drawn carriages or wagons. Volmar's Grove, off Cook Road, and Holiday Hill, on Candee Road, offer outings for families and groups. When Highland Green's golf course opened in 1967, it was the first lighted course in the area. The addition of the Prospect Golf Driving Range & Miniature Golf helped to make Prospect a pleasant place to spend leisure time.

THE INDUSTRIAL REBIRTH

In the middle of the twentieth century, manufacturing began to emerge as an alternative to agriculture in Prospect. Tala-Bal Company was started in 1942 by Harry "Bud" Talmadge, Jr. and operated until his death in 1978. The facility was located in a building on Route 69 across from St. Anthony Church. In this factory foam plastic products, such as packaging material and styrofoam snowballs for Christmas decorations, were manufactured. Tala-Bal was a family business. Bud Talmadge also worked with Gene Lewis in developing plastic foam backer board for the aluminum siding industry. Under Gene's direction this product line led to the formation of Foam Plastics of New England discussed later in this chapter.

The Salem Manufacturing Company was another early industrial operation. Rudolph Strumpf used his years of experience as a toolmaker working around the Waterbury area to design equipment for his own factory on Salem Road in Prospect. He ran this family enterprise from 1945 until he died in 1967. Salem Manufacturing produced a variety of small hardware items, such as the pull chains for electric lights. The factory is most famous for the jingle bells that were sold to companies all over the world.

With the development of industrial parks in the last few decades, Prospect's manufacturing base expanded greatly. The reasonable land prices and low tax rates were attractive incentives for industry. Easy access and its central location to major highways made Prospect the town of choice for many emerging companies. A host of support service companies joined the manufacturing renewal. Insurance, real estate, marketing, advertising, consulting, and computer services are among those who have found that the view from the top is an asset to their bottom line.

CURRENT PROSPECT BUSINESSES

The following list provides a good indication of the diverse nature of commerce in this town today. Nearly two hundred businesses call Prospect home. Most are small to medium size operations providing specialized services and products. During the 1990s an increasing number of entrepreneurs abandoned the daily commute to work by starting home-based businesses. Enterprises are listed in alphabetical order, showing company name, address, phone number, year started in Prospect, and a brief description of products or services. Anecdotes, company histories, and reasons for locating in Prospect are shown when information was available.

Accurate Secondary Products Co.
80 Scott Road ▪ 758-6243   1981
Milling, drilling, tapping, slotting, and reaming secondary processes.

Dr. Nick Forte
Advanced Chiropractic Offices of Prospect
16 Waterbury Road
P.O Box 7143 ▪ 758-3391
Complete family practice of chiropractic services for accident, athletic, or work related injuries. Also nutritional and wellness counseling, physical therapy, and X-ray facilities.

All American Electric Company
22 Colonial Drive ▪ 758-5821
Electrical services.

All State Construction Company
41 Talmadge Road ▪ 758-3888
Construction services.

Allstate Insurance Companies
33 Union City Road ▪ 758-6683   1989
Home and automobile insurance.

Artistic Construction
54 Scott Road ▪ 758-4844
Construction services.

Atlantic Pavement Marking Co.
Industrial Road ▪ 758-0800
Pavement marking systems for parking lots and roads.

Ayotte Machine Products, Inc.
13 Gramar Avenue ▪ 758-6400   1964
Screw machine products.

B&R Riding Stables
Roaring Brook Road ▪ 758-5031
Trail rides and horse drawn hay rides.

Baker's Dozen
47 Waterbury Road ▪ 758-6962   1980

Tom Santos offers a complete line of bakery products.

Peter Baltrush Electrical, Incorporated
20 Prospect Industrial Park ▪ 758-3515 1987
Commercial, industrial, and residential electrical services.
    The business started in Naugatuck in 1983, then moved to Prospect in 1987. Peter Baltrush grew up in Prospect and all of his staff members are from within the town. The company has been supportive of town programs, including the Little League, fire department, police station, and new library.

Barbara Ann's Hair Care
44 Waterbury Road ▪ 758-3794   1987
Hair styling and haircutting services.

Chris Barrere Trucking
95 Clark Hill Road ▪ 758-5338   1980
Construction material hauling.

Ben-Art Manufacturing Co., Inc.
109 Waterbury Road ▪ 758-4435   1952
Eyelet manufacturing - metal stampings.

Benny's Gun Shop
52 Waterbury Road
P.O. Box 7256 ▪ 758-4995   1977
Complete line of equipment for hunting and fishing. Guns bought and sold. Archery equipment and fishing tackle. Video rentals. The original location was opened in 1977 on Old Schoolhouse Road.

Big Dipper Ice Cream & Yogurt Factory
91 Waterbury Road ▪ 758-3200   1986
Production of homemade ice cream made to be served in our retail store.
    The Big Dipper started as a dream and was fulfilled with the opening of the retail ice cream store in November of 1986. Barbara and Harry Rowe of Prospect had spent the prior 5 years before opening, researching ice cream stores from Maine to

Florida, from Maryland to California, often revisiting many stores they felt were of the best quality.

The Rowes developed a working scale to judge ice cream quality, and they used that scale to judge the ice cream from the stores they visited. The scale rated a list of qualities for taste, texture, creaminess, melting point, and other factors that affect the quality of ice cream. This list was used to find the style of ice cream the Rowes wanted to produce.

Once the decision was made to open an ice cream store, Harry Rowe enrolled at Rutgers University in New Jersey for their commercial ice cream course. This world famous course accepts only 25 students a year and is considered one of the best ice cream manufacturing schools. After finishing school at Rutgers, the Rowes spent much time attending seminars and trade shows to find the very best quality ingredients to produce ice cream of top ranking. After all the work and time spent, it was now time to open The Big Dipper.

With the opening of The Big Dipper, the Rowes fast developed a following for their ice cream. Word of mouth brought ice cream connoisseurs from across the state to Prospect to taste and enjoy Big Dipper ice cream. The Big Dipper's ice cream has set the standards for quality ice cream, winning national awards for the last five years. At the Big Dipper a smile with every scoop is as important as using the freshest and finest ingredients.

The Big Dipper home made ice cream is freshly made on the premises in small batches to insure the finest product. In their search to bring you the finest gourmet ice cream, The Big Dipper brings you the world's best vanilla from the island of Madagascar and the best cocoa made brought from Holland. The Big Dipper combines a farm fresh dairy cream from one of New England's best dairies with choice chocolates, nuts, berries, and the purest flavors and extracts. The fruits of the Big Dipper's labors brings you an award winning quality ice cream.

Biographical Publishing Company
35 Clark Hill Road ▪ 758-3661   1991
Book publishing, historical and biographical.

Branson Ultrasonics Corporation
4 George Street ▪ 758-0601   1991
Ultrasonic cleaning systems for industry. Prospect is a satellite operation for the home office in Danbury, CT.

Building Technologies, Inc.
7 Gramar Avenue ▪ 758-6607
General contractor, construction management.

Buckmiller Brothers Funeral Home, Inc.
Waterbury Road ▪ 729-4334   1974
Funeral Services

C F D Engineering Co.
194 Cook Road ▪ 758-4148
Metal stampings.

Caruso's Remodeling Service, Inc.
Waterbury Road ▪ 758-6122   1965
Residential and commercial remodeling. Over 30 years of service to Prospect.

Centerbank
Waterbury Road ▪ 758-5778
Full service financial institution.

The Chimney Doctor
220 Cook Road ▪ 758-6595   1979
Complete chimney maintenance and restoration for residential and commercial accounts.

Cipriano Agency - The Prudential
6 New Haven Road ▪ 758-6546   1992
Insurance and financial services.

Converse Cabinets
Gramar Avenue ▪ 758-4406   1976
Residential and commercial cabinets.

Country Fare Restaurant
Waterbury Road ▪ 758-4353   1984
Lunch and dinners featuring good, wholesome, inexpensive fare.

Custom Printing
6 New Haven Road ▪ 758-5748   1992
All types of commercial printing, specializing in small custom jobs.

Cyr Associates
43 Scott Road ▪ 758-6804
Vinyl siding, seamless gutters and leaders, vinyl replacement windows.

D&L Transportation Inc
Gramar Avenue ▪ 758-5989
Bus transportation for schools, churches, seniors, clubs, or organizations.

Dairy Mart
22 Union City Road ▪ 758-6092
Convenience store and deli.

Dan Dixon's Carpets
New Haven Road ▪ 758-5910   1976
Residential and commercial carpeting. 19 years of service in Prospect.

Dance Theatre & The Arts
9 Schoolhouse Road ▪ 758-5644   1976
Dance, tap & ballet instruction.
Dance Theatre & The Arts started its studio in 1976 as the Prospect Dance & Karate Center on the corner of Rte. 68 and Old Schoolhouse Rd. The school's director and choreographer was Miss Susan Sullivan who developed the studio into its present size of 300+ students. In 1985 the school moved to its present location on 9 Old Schoolhouse Rd. and changed its name to Dance Theatre & The Arts.
Miss Susan is now sharing teaching responsibilities with her daughter, Miss Nefra, who spent two years studying with New York's great dance masters, such as: Phil Black, Luigi, Linda Gaché, Frank Hatchett, Gus Giordano, and many more.
Dance Theatre's motto is "Our students perform better because we care." Over the years the students and dance teams have won numerous awards and competitions.

Dart Building Systems
P.O. Box 7273
13 Morris Road ▪ 758-3420   1989
General contractors specializing in pre-engineered steel and construction management. Design/build projects.

Dataset Business Graphics
63 Melissa Lane ▪ 758-4284   1990
Industrial printing distributor. Design and production of all types of commercial printing.

Harry M. Davis Equipment Corp.
210 Cheshire Road ▪ 758-6454   1971
General contracting, mostly for utilities. Construction equipment sales.
Business founded in 1969 by James and Lillian Davis. Moved to Prospect in 1971. Auctions, offering a wide range of products for bid, are conducted periodically.

Dependable Fuel
Division of Noble H.V.A/C Systems, Inc.
17 Gramar Avenue
P.O. Box 7187 ▪ 758-5831   1994
Oil delivery and service.
[see Noble H.V.A/C Systems, Inc.]

Pete Doyle
Doyle's Double A Farm
40 Cook Road ▪ 758-4491   1939

Farm fresh eggs.

Doyon's Mobil Mart
New Haven Road ▪ 758-4846   1983
Gas service, convenience store with Dunkin Donuts.
There has been a gas station at this location, the junction of 68 & 69, since the 1960s, owned then by Richard A. Dibeneditto. The Doyons took over the station in 1983 and maintained it as a traditional garage bay service station until it was recently remodeled by Mobil, eliminating the service bays and adding the store and Dunkin Donuts branch.

Dry Cleaners of Prospect
28 Waterbury Road ▪ 758-5872   1991
Dry cleaning, shirts drapes, blankets, rugs & most household items. We also have an excellent tailor for alterations.
Larry Shea purchased the first lot on Rosewood Drive. He opened the business in town because, "I live in Prospect and believe in Prospect."

Bill Dunn Sanitation
209 Straitsville Road ▪ 758-0223   1986
Cleaning and disposal of sewage.
Bill Dunn is a lifetime resident of Prospect and his company is family owned.

Duracore Radiator of Prospect, Inc.
150 Waterbury Road ▪ 758-6886   1982
Complete automotive cooling and heating system service specialists. Engine repairs for cars and trucks.

ESI Electronic Products, Inc.
11 Industrial Road ▪ 758-4401   1988
Design and manufacture of wide range of electronic controls. Primary business is microprocessor-based electronics for healthclub exercise equipment.
Located in Prospect because the primary owner, Frank Sundermeyer, lives in town and wants to work in town and support town with local taxes. ESI Electronic Products was incorporated in 1982. The company employs 30 people and had sales of $2.4 million in 1994.

E-Z Way Products
9 Gramar Avenue ▪ 758-6621   1973
Distributor for janitorial and maintenance supplies.
The company was originally founded in 1941 by Harry Coughlin. The first product was a commercial dishwashing compound. During the flood of 1955, E-Z Way Products came to the aid of rescue centers who were set up for the flood victims. Because the

Waterbury distributors were under water, E-Z Way was able to supply disinfectants and other needed supplies. The current owners, Fletcher and Gregory Ostrander, purchased the company in 1973.

The Edwards Printing Company
16 Waterbury Road ▪ 758-4433   1985
Complete printing services.
    Edwards Printing began in Cheshire in 1983, then moved to Prospect in 1985. Specialties include computer generated and enhanced graphics and five color printing.

Equipment Maintenance Co.
42 Scott Road ▪ 758-5766   1960
Fork lift repairs and service. Work also on tractors, air compressors, wood chippers, and all kinds of off-road motorized equipment.

Explorations of Education Inc.
18 Salem Road ▪ 758-0486   1993
An organization dedicated to the practices and principles of living naturally. Founder Robert A. Hubbell offers children's field trips and training in vocational skills for the less fortunate and publishes a quarterly newsletter.

Eye Care Associates, P.C.
67 Waterbury Road ▪ 758-6644   1968
Complete line of fashion eyeglasses. Eye examinations. Contact lenses.
    Dr. Lawrence N. Kline began his practice out of his home/office in 1968.

Falcone Art Studio
181 New Haven Road ▪ 758-6729   1977
Custom fine arts.
    Owner Tony Falcone creates custom fine art on a commission basis. Artworks include portraits, landscapes, murals and backdrops. He also teaches art and gives presentations. In 1977, while searching for a studio, Tony came upon the barn owned by the Visokis family. It was — and still is — the perfect art studio!

Farm On Wheels
9 Spring Road ▪ 758-4203   1991
Traveling farm - Fence enclosure 15' x 15' with cow, pig, sheep, goats, ducks, geese, rabbits, miniature horses, and llama. Visits birthday parties, convalescent homes, nursery schools, fairs, etc.

Feero Consulting
34 Nancy Mae Avenue ▪ 758-0343
Computer solutions for business and educational needs. Pre-purchase recommendations, software/hardware sales, point of sale

systems, custom programming.

Attorney John W. Fertig, Jr.
20 Waterbury Road ▪ 758-4414   1982
Law office
    I chose to re-locate my office to Prospect due to its small town charm and friendly citizens and proximity to the highways and cities. I have thoroughly enjoyed my fourteen years in Prospect.

Fine Arts Security Transport
45 Sherwood Drive ▪ 758-3247   1987
Packing, crating, transportation of fine arts and antiques.
    A climate controlled storage warehouse is available for art objects. The business serves most major museums and private collections from Maine to Washington, DC. The owner, Daniel J. Heery, has lived in Prospect since 1969.

First Federal Bank, FSB
45 Waterbury Road ▪ 758-6691   1988
Full service financial institution.

The Flower Farm
50 Scott Road ▪ 758-6788   1989
Retail store and greenhouses with bedding plants, hanging baskets, vegetable plants, and geraniums.

Foam Plastics of New England, Inc.
Gramar Avenue ▪ 758-4961   1970
Manufacturer of wide range of foam plastic products.
    Eugene Lewis, the company founder, was born and raised in Prospect. He graduated from the University of Connecticut in 1952 and was accepted in the Officer Candidate School of the U.S. Navy during the Korean War and served 4½ years as Chief Engineer aboard a destroyer. This valuable experience and training eventually led to the manufacture of expanded polystyrene foam. Gene founded Lewis Construction Company, a residential remodeling and siding contracting business, after his discharge from active duty. He saw at a home show that Dow Chemical's Styrofoam products were being used as insulated backing for siding products. Gene's friend, Harry "Bud" Talmadge, owner of Tala-Bal Company, had been cutting Styrofoam for packaging and display applications since the 1940s. Together they tried cutting some Styrofoam first with a band saw and then with a commercial bread slicer after seeing one during lunch at the Handy Kitchen Luncheonette next to Oliver's Supermarket. Eugene Lewis Sr., a mason who retired due to rheumatism, revamped the cutting blades to increase production to

24 pieces at a time.

The small foam fabrication company purchased foam blocks from Plastifoam Corporation in Rockville, Connecticut, and sold insulation panels to various siding manufacturers until production was scaled back after one major account began making the backerboard themselves. In 1965, a 5000 square-foot building was erected on Rte. 69 to house the construction company's warehouse and showroom. Doris Lewis managed the office, Eugene Sr. supervised the warehouse and Eugene continued to sell remodeling jobs and help his crew with siding installations. A small amount of foam fabrication was done here to supply local siding products distributors.

In 1968 Eugene designed the first foam backer configured to the shape of the siding panel and called it "Double-Four" Backerboard. Hot-wire cutting machines designed by Eugene and his father increased the production while allowing for different shapes to be cut from the foam blocks. Sales of this unique product soared and Foam Plastics of New England was incorporated to manufacture and market this product for nationwide distribution. Due to the great increase in need for foam blocks and to increase quality control, Foam Plastics of N.E. bought its first expanded polystyrene block molding equipment in 1975. A second clock mold was added in 1978. It was 20 feet long and the largest in the country at that time. From this point on, Foam Plastics of New England has been an incubator for several new companies while maintaining its position as a leader in the polystyrene insulation products market.

The Route 69 building was expanded with the addition of each block mold and David Lewis joined the company in 1977 after graduating from the University of Connecticut. David had ideas to expand product lines by adding a new fan-fold, foil-faced leveling board and he incorporated Insulation Technologies in 1978 and began manufacturing Insul-wrap leveling board. David added a patented grid design onto foil facers to the Insul-Wrap product which helps the siding contractor to install the product more easily. Eugene and David kept redesigning the molding, cutting and laminated processes to increase plant efficiency. Mellisa Lewis Tweedie joined the company in May 1992 after graduating from Boston College.

On April 7, 1983, a fire that started in the mold area swept through the Route 69 plant and destroyed the entire building. David had been working on two prototype laminating machines in a garage on the site,

and production commenced out of the garage within 10 days of the fire. Eugene directed the construction of the new plant and offices which were fully operational by December 1983. Another plant was built at the Gramar Ave. site in 1985 with a complete duplication of production facilities. With the help of Mayor Bob Chatfield, a state grant was obtained to bring water lines for fire protection up Route 68 to the Gramar Ave. industrial park.

In 1985 David and Melissa incorporated Technicut, Inc. to serve the packaging, display and specialty foam markets. David incorporated Glacier Cooler Company in 1991 to further diversify the organization into non-building industry related markets. Glacier Cooler serves the beverage industry with unique point of purchase display coolers.

Foam Plastics of New England and its related companies are well positioned to succeed in these trying economic times. Innovation combined with foresight and conservative business management give these companies a great advantage over the competition. Eugene Lewis and his family are proud of the team they have built and look forward to taking these companies into the next century.

Four Corners Restaurant & Pizza
19 Waterbury Road ▪ 758-6044   1975
Full service restaurant and pizza parlor.

The current owners, Nick and Bill, purchased the restaurant in 1980 from the original owner, George, who had started it on August 4, 1975. When they outgrew the building on the east side of Waterbury Road, they built a new facility on the west side, which opened for business on Mother's Day, 1989.

The Furniture Gallery
Waterbury Road ▪ 758-6666   1975
Quality furniture at affordable prices. Fine furniture, bedding, and accessories.

General Construction & Design
P.O. Box 7196 ▪ 758-6140
Custom homes. Residential and commercial construction. Framing specialists.

Get the Picture Studio
93 Waterbury Road ▪ 758-6315
Professional photography and video production. Custom wedding photography and storybook wedding videos. Complete line of wedding invitations and accessories.

Goldenrod Corporation
100 Union City Road ▪ 758-0100   1994

Manufacturers of pneumatic air shafts and chucks. Goldenrod was attracted to Prospect by the available skilled labor force.

Dr. Gordon M. Goodrich
2 Birchwood Terrace ▪ 758-5310
Practice in general dentistry.

Great Lengths & Short Cuts
105 Waterbury Road ▪ 758-5191   1993
Hair styling and nail salon. Professionals experienced in all phases of hairstyling, haircutting, coloring, permanent waving, and nail care.

Dorene E. Carpentier started this business in Prospect for three reasons: *(1) A very close friend, whom I met in dance class at Prospect Dance and Karate, was a cousin of the previous owner, P.J. Lawless. My girl friend, Carla Gerest, had been convincing me to buy the shop. Finally, after considerations in many aspects, I decided why not! (2) My husband's family is from Prospect - most of whom still live in town. (3) Its a reasonably safe, quiet town with friendly people, good schools, and a country atmosphere. Eventually, my family may move here.*

Gugliotti, Peterson & Palombia Advertising
16 Waterbury Road ▪ 758-3311   1985
Full service marketing communications company.

The company produces print, broadcast, and direct mail advertising. They consult with regional and national companies to produce marketing strategies and complete digital pre-press through production facilities. Prospect was chosen as the site for the business because of the relationship with the landlord and the location.

Halim General Contractors
5 Roy Mountain Road ▪ 758-4923   1977
General contractors specializing in residential remodeling and additions.

Hat Trick Darts
33 Union City Road ▪ 758-6600
Dart supplies including soft tip, steel tip, electronic, and non-electonic boards and accessories. Owners Doreen and Joe Folio have added a catalog/mail division to their retail store.

Hometown Automotive
69 Waterbury Road ▪ 758-4444   1992
General automobile repairs and used car sales. Business was previously called Suburban Automotive for many years.

Hometown Luncheonette
44 Waterbury Road ▪ 758-0661   1993
Restaurant serving breakfast, lunch, dinner, and pizza. There has been a restaurant at this location for about thirty years under various names and ownership.

Hughes Agency
27-A Waterbury Road ▪ 758-6647   1980
Group and business insurance; auto, boat and home insurance; individual health and life insurance; both personal & business insurance counseling.

The business was established 4/6/80. During a conversation with the mayor of Prospect, it was suggested that we might establish a much needed insurance agency here in Prospect. From those humble beginnings, the business of Catherine Montagano Hughes, a life long resident, and Peter Hughes has grown substantially in 15 years. The Hughes Agency was the first agency and continues to serve Prospect as one of the two independent agencies and three direct writing agents.

Hunter Associates
15 Stonefield Drive ▪ 758-3522
Comprehensive financial planning services, including estate planning, asset, allocation, retirement planning, and income and investment management.

J/C Stained Glass Art
P.O.Box 7163 ▪ 758-4710   1994
Custom works of art in stained glass. Also, sand blasting and etching. Instructions and repairs

J & R Auto Supply, Inc. & Power Equipment
35 Union City Road ▪ 758-6623   1962
Quality parts for all makes and models foreign and domestic. Also, servicing and repair of mowers, snow blowers, saws, and trimmers. Propane filling station.

Knapp Engineering
20 Industrial Road ▪ 758-3503   1989
Instrumentation and control systems. Control system design, control panel fabrication, and instrument calibration services for industrial, waste water, and water treatment applications.

The owner, Greg Knapp, started the business in Prospect which is his home town. The operation was moved to its present location on Industrial Road in 1993.

William M. Lanese Associates
139 Salem Road ▪ 758-5625   1978
Real Estate Appraiser.

The owner, William Lanese, has been a

Prospect resident since 1973. The property at 139 Salem Road was the last West Schoolhouse, which served that part of Prospect in the early 1900s.

Lardie, Wazorko & Clark, P.C.
37 Waterbury Road ▪ 758-4479   1993
Certified Public Accountants. Financial statement preparation, income tax preparation, computer consulting and retirement, estate and trust planning.

This organization purchased the accounting practice of John Garrity, CPA.

Lehigh-Noble Heat & Fuel
Gramar Avenue ▪ 758-6344   1946
High quality heating fuel delivery. Oil burner, boiler and furnace installation and service.

LoCascio Liquors
22 Union City Road ▪ 758-4533   1957
Complete line of liquors plus holiday and custom gift packages, party planning, food & wine recommendations, friendly service.

Antonio R. Macatol, M.D., D.A.B.S.
4 Summit Road ▪ 758-5286   1984
Medical; general and vascular surgery.

Main Moon Chinese Restaurant
14 Waterbury Road ▪ 758-4205
Restaurant featuring Chinese food for take-out or eat-in.

Margot's Flowers, Gifts & Candles
52 Waterbury Road ▪ 758-3393   1987
Florist carrying large variety of silk flowers, wall items, centerpieces, plus a nice selection of Yankee candles. They also do fruit and gift baskets.

The owner was born and raised in town. Margot Foster came from a family very active in Prospect and wanted to serve the people in town - all friends and neighbors - with quality flowers and services.

Mauriello's Hot Dogs
Waterbury Road ▪   1987
Hot dogs with all the trimmings.

You won't find Guy Mauriello's Hot Dogs in the phone book - but then, Guy doesn't have a phone. And you won't see his restaurant outside Hotchkiss Field either - unless you drive by between the beginning of April and the first week in October. That is when Guy parks his hot dog stand along busy Route 69. Patrons, including UCONN coach Jim Calhoun and Governor John Rowland, have sampled his wieners. Many loyal customers declare Mauriello's hot dogs to be the best in the world.

Dom Moffo Trucking
152 Waterbury Road ▪ 758-6655
Rock, sand, gravel, asphalt pavement, heavy hauling, snow removal and flat bed services.

Moffo's Universal Martial Arts
105 Waterbury Road ▪ 758-3165
Affiliated member of United Fighting Arts Federation. Karate, Kenpo, Judo, and self-defense for men, women, and children.

Mower Repair of Prospect
14 Waterbury Road ▪ 758-0324   1978
Service and sales of mowers, blowers, trimmers, chain saws, and snow blowers. Log splitter rentals.

The owner grew-up in Prospect and this is a family-owned business.

Murphy's Auto Service Inc
56 Cheshire Road ▪ 758-4640   1981
Complete auto service, including computer diagnostics and wheel alignment as well as front end, exhaust, and brake service. 24-hour towing service.

Murray's Hardware
22 Union City Road ▪ 758-5437
Complete line of hardware products featuring sharpening service and screen & window repair.

Neal Pharmacy
34 Waterbury Road ▪ 758-3316   1954
Your family health care center with a complete line of prescription and non-prescription drugs and medical, health, and beauty supplies. Cards and gifts are also offered.

The original owner, Joseph J. Neal, opened the pharmacy on July 22, 1954. The store had filled nearly 350,000 prescriptions when it celebrated its silver anniversary in 1979.

Neri Sand & Gravel, Inc.
17-A Terry Road ▪ 758-3532
Fill, gravel, sand, stone, loam. Trucking. Payloader rental.

New England Visa Services, Inc.
4 Summit Road ▪ 758-6636   1993
We process and then hand deliver paperwork to foreign embassies and consulates in NYC and Washington DC for the purpose of obtaining passports and visa needed to travel to many countries worldwide.

Visa and passport services are usually located in big cities where there are consulates or embassies. Being located in Connecticut offers companies and travel agencies in CT and surrounding states a closer and more personal service than dealing with agencies in the bigger cities.

Many people, who don't generally travel internationally, confuse us with a credit card company. When I advised a first time traveler that he was required to have a visa to travel to Australia, he innocently replied, "Don't they accept Mastercard there?"!

Noble H.V.A/C Systems, Inc.
Gramar Avenue
P.O. Box 7187 ▪ 758-5831   1946
Heating and air conditioning installation, replacement, and repair.

Located in Prospect because the family business originated here with grandfather. It is a very community oriented town that looks out for the people.

It all began back in 1938 when Glenn and Elizabeth Noble decided to make their home in Prospect. Glenn worked for Naugatuck Fuel almost 8 years, then became manager of the service department of D.L.&W. Coal Company in Waterbury. After two years of servicing oil burners for them, he began his own business in 1946, installing and servicing stokers.

Both Glenn and Betty were involved with their community; she raised funds for a new parsonage. Glenn was one of the founders of the Lions Club and a member of both the Zoning Board of Appeals and Citizen's Advisory Committee for the Board of Education. Life took its course, as it many times does, and the second generation arrived. Steve lived in Prospect all of his life, attending local schools, and deciding to become involved in his father's business on a full-time basis in 1963. Glenn A. Noble & Son became the new name of the company in 1964.

Totally on his own, Steve expanded the business in 1970 and formed an oil company, Noble Heat and Fuel. This kept him very busy servicing and installing heating equipment along with delivering oil.

Another expansion took place in 1983 when he decided to purchase an oil company in Naugatuck. At about the same time, the third generation made his appearance, and Steve's son Glenn came on board part-time while attending W.F. Kaynor Technical School.

After his graduation in 1984, Glenn continued as his dad had before him and became involved full-time with his father. The business grew at such a rapid pace from that point that in 1988 Steve made the decision to sell his business. They formed their new and present company, Noble H.V.A/C Systems, which stands for "Heating, Ventilating, and Air Conditioning." As their logo states, they are now a "Total

Comfort Company." Together they work to install the best heating and air conditioning systems, not only in brand new homes, but in older homes which need to be updated. They specialize in Hydro-Air systems which is a relatively new concept in this business.

In 1994, Glenn took over the business from his father. He decided to open an oil company as an added service to the heating and air conditioning business. Dependable Fuel, a division of H.V.A/C Systems Inc., offers high quality fuel oil, 24-hour service and a commitment to the highest level of satisfaction to its customers.

Nolin Aluminum Products, Inc.
16 Lakeview Road
P.O. Box 7095 ▪ 758-4527   1975
Vinyl and aluminum siding, replacement windows, gutters, and leaders.

Norm's Pony Rides
Roaring Brook Road ▪ 758-5284
Pony and hay rides for birthday parties, outings, or fairs. Your place or ours.

Northwest Connecticut Public Safety Communication Center, Inc.
28 Cheshire Road ▪ 758-0050   1991
Emergency 9-1-1 communications center. Northwest Connecticut Public Safety Communication Center, Inc. has been providing emergency communications in the area since 1976. The center moved to Prospect in December of 1991 from Waterbury City Hall.

The center provides 9-1-1 service to 7 communities and U.H.F. medical communications to an additional 14 towns and cities. This facility handles over 60,000 calls for assistance annually. Tours of the facility are always available.

Nutmeg Pantry
28 Waterbury Road ▪ 758-6137
Convenience store and gasoline service.

Oakridge Associates, LLC
P.O. Box 7031 ▪ 758-5574   1994
Forestridge Rd. - Oakridge Subdivision. Twelve lots, framing, new construction, and alterations. Steve Satkunas and Jeff Slapikas, partners.

Occupational Therapy Associates
7 Summit Road ▪ 758-0315   1987
Agency providing occupational therapy services to individuals, extended care facilities, school systems, and home care agencies. Located in Prospect because the owners live in town and love its rural, small town flavor - but convenient location.

Oliver's Supermarket
75 Waterbury Road ▪ 758-4009   1948
Supermarket convenience and economy with personal service.

George Oliver started his supermarket in Prospect in 1948. From the beginning, service and quality were the unwavering standards. From free carry-out service to your care to custom cuts of beef, the desire of the customer was always first.

Noted for the individual attention he would give to each customer, George Oliver was always willing to help those in the community. Through donations of food, students' tuitions, or simply letting any organization in town use his store as a magnet to promote their fund raising activities, Oliver's never turned anyone away.

In 1980 Ken Gnazzo and Len Noble took over Oliver's Market, with George Oliver in semi-retirement. The store has faithfully maintained the same personal service that has been Oliver's trademark for almost fifty years.

W.J. Opusynski & Sons, Inc.
19 Industrial Road ▪ 758-0660
Industrial construction and municipal supplies.

Oxford General Industries, Inc.
Union City Road
P.O. Box 7033 ▪ 758-4467
Precision C.N.C., production machining, tools, dies, and fixtures.

Packard Specialties, Inc.
6 Industrial Road ▪ 758-6219   1980
Designers and builders of specialized machinery.

In 1980 John F. Jones began his business in his 560-square-foot garage. He started by restoring early automobiles and making machine parts. The company name comes from his love of antique cars.

The focus of the operation was on the design and creation of custom machinery. With diverse projects, such as equipment for Friendly's "Harbor Bars" production and a machine to make raviolis, the business grew steadily. By 1983 he put up a 1,200 square foot building on his property which was expanded by another 800 square feet a few years later.
By 1990 property was purchased in the Prospect Industrial Center. John elected to stay in Prospect because, "We've lived here for 22 years and it's a no-hassle town." Along with his wife Carol, he also runs the Prospect Dairy Bar.

Much of the success of Packard Specialties is attributed to good employees. Much

of the equipment is made from scratch without using other contracted parts. Previously all work was done in response to specific customer needs. Now the company is marketing its own line of packaging machinery called *Intermittent Motion Cartoners*.

Pavlik Real Estate Agency
1 Union City Road ▪ 758-4416
Complete residential, commercial, and industrial real estate services. Also appraisals, property management, rentals, and relocation services.

Pavlik Real Estate is located in the oldest historic building in Prospect.

Peck Electric
89 Scott Road ▪ 758-3137
Quality electrical service and construction.

Plastic Mold Design & Service
55 Straitsville Road ▪ 758-6984   1980
Mold designs, plastic molding systems.
A home town business.

Plumb Farms
61 Cheshire Road ▪ 758-5590   1993
Retail nursery and flowers. Wide selection of annuals and perennials, artistically arranged fresh and dried flowers, top quality Christmas trees and wreathes.

For over 100 years, the Plumb family has been supplying agricultural products to residents of Prospect and surrounding communities. It made sense to us to continue that tradition. Plenty of land available for growing plants, a highly visible location, a "rural-like" setting in which to work and live, a good support system of family and friends and a community with strong appreciation for history and tradition, all made Plumb Farm an ideal location for our dream business. [see business history in Chapter 9]

Prestige Photography
15 Stonefield Drive ▪ 758-3522
Portrait photography.

Prospect Barber Shop
Old Schoolhouse Rd. ▪ 758-5007   1951
Family haircuts and styling. Since starting his barbering trade in Prospect, Tony Cretella has been in three locations, none of them very far apart. The first was at the gas station (now Sunoco) on Union City Road. Then he moved to the group of stores just west of the gas station. Finally, Tony set up his permanent barber shop on Old Schoolhouse Road in a converted house garage. When asked if his antique cash register was original to the start of his business, Tony replied, "Yes, and it was old then."

Prospect Continuing Care
170 Scott Road ▪ 758-5491
Residential nursing home care.

Prospect Dairy Bar & Restaurant
29 Waterbury Road ▪ 758-5651   1953
Breakfast, lunch, dinner, and ice cream served in an authentic 1950s atmosphere. The oldest restaurant in Prospect still in operation.

The Dairy Bar opened in 1953, selling ice cream and dairy products from the family farm of owners, Vincent and Olive Visockis. Besides the dairy items there were soups and sandwiches cooked on the grill. The Dairy Bar closed for the winter months then. In 1955 the Visockis' built an apartment in back of the restaurant where they still live. During the Waterbury flood of 1955, the Dairy Bar was the only business in town with electric power, thanks to their standby generator. The rescue workers were kept well fed with hot soup.

The current owners, Carol and John Jones, leased the restaurant for 10 years from the Visockis before purchasing this Prospect landmark. They had gained experience working with Curtis Blake, the co-founder of Friendly's Restaurants. John was designing equipment for Friendly's new ice cream line through his other Prospect enterprise, Packard Specialties. In 1984 the Prospect Dairy Bar became a year-round business but will always retain its traditional fifties flavor.

Prospect Dental Associates
16 Waterbury Road ▪ 758-6637   1981
To provide quality family dentistry in a relaxing environment.

In 1981 there was the need for caring dental providers in this town. Doctors Estra, D'Agostino, and Brennan wanted to provide the town with dental service so the residents would not need to travel to a larger city.

Prospect Development, Inc.
17 Gramar Avenue ▪ 758-5150
Excavating Contractor.

Prospect Electric Services
105 Waterbury Road ▪ 758-6842
Complete residential, commercial, and industrial electrical service.

Prospect Excavating
91 Cook Road
P.O. Box 7114 ▪ 758-6481
Septic systems installed and repaired.

Prospect Flooring
30 Union City Road ▪ 758-4207
All types of flooring, including carpets, no-wax, area rugs, tile, and wood. Carpet repairs and cleaning.

Prospect Golf Driving Range & Miniature Golf
144 Waterbury Road ▪ 758-4121
Outdoor golf driving range and miniature golf course.

Prospect Grocery Stop
34 Waterbury Road ▪ 758-4265
Convenience/grocery store with take-out food and beverages.

Prospect Liquor Cabinet
Prospect Country Plaza ▪ 758-6494
Full selection of liquor products.

Prospect Machine Products, Inc.
139 Union City Road ▪ 758-4448   1949
Contract manufacturers of eyelet, automatic screw machine, and CNC turning center components.

Prospect Machine Products was founded by Michael A. Pugliese, Sr., a former first selectman of Prospect.

Prospect Nursery & Florist
246 New Haven Road ▪ 758-4909   1967
Nursery stock (evergreens, etc.), greenhouses (annuals & perennials), and a full service florist.

Since David T. Kluge was born in Prospect, he decided to open his business here. He has been at the present location on New Haven Road for over 20 years. Dave's parents moved to Prospect in 1936 and settled on Kluge Road. Since they were the first to build on the street, they got to pick the name. Dave and his family now reside there.

Prospect Nursery School, Inc.
25 Center Street ▪ 758-5001   1972
Preschool for children ages 3-5.

Prospect Oil
103 Union City Road ▪ 758-4734
Heating fuel oil delivery. Automatic service, volume and senior citizen discounts.

Prospect Pizza
34 Waterbury Road ▪ 758-3264   1992
Pizza take-out (no sit-down). Delicious "New Haven Style" pizza - the first of its kind in Prospect! Delicious grinders (hot or cold), calzones, salads, and buffalo wings.

A town resident for 26 years when the

business opened, Bill Lawson and his wife Lynn liked the people of this town well enough to introduce this delicious product to them, so they wouldn't have to go very far!

Prospect Pools
33 Union City Road ▪ 758-0524   1991
In ground and above ground pools at reasonable, not seasonable, rates. Complete installation service. Repairs, replacement parts, and pool openings and closings.
Family run business by Prospect residents Chris and Anna Keeler.

Prospect Printing
105 Waterbury Road ▪ 758-6007   1988
Full service printing and copy center including offset printing, copy service, typesetting, business cards, letterheads, envelopes, wedding invitations, tickets, and Christmas cards.

Prospect Service Center & Towing
20 Union City Road ▪ 758-6069   1991
General mechanical, electrical, and body repairs for foreign and domestic vehicles. Long distance and heavy duty towing. Prospect's only full service gas and repair station.

Prospect Sunoco
Waterbury Road ▪ 758-6069   1971
Gasoline service station.

Prospect Video
44 Waterbury Road ▪ 758-5959
Video tapes and discs rental. Over 4,000 titles. Services include rental reservations, fax service, and copies.

Prospect-Wolcott Veterinary Hospital
93 Waterbury Road ▪ 758-6601   1986
Total personalized health care for small animals. Surgical facilities. As an addition to their animal health care facility, Prospect Boarding & Grooming provides boarding facilities, all types of bathing and grooming and a complete line of dog and cat food and supplies, as well as obedience and training classes.

Quality Truck Repair
103 Union City Road ▪ 758-4286
Truck repair service.

Reilly Management Associates
40 Center Street
P.O. Box 7376 ▪ 758-3321   1992
Community association management and management consulting services.
Prospect was selected for the business location because it is centrally located to the market area. The owners are also Prospect residents.

Rivard Jewelers Ltd.
27 Waterbury Road ▪ 758-6888
Excellent jewelry at affordable prices.

Robert J Rogoz, CPA
33 Union City Road ▪ 758-6225
Full range of accounting and tax services for businesses and individuals.

Martin J. Rutt, DDS &
Leonard J. Fusco, DMD
44 Center Street ▪ 758-6639
Full range of dental services.

Santoro's Plumbing & Well Service
5 Porter Hill Road ▪ 758-3066
Residential and commercial plumbing, heating & boiler service, water heaters, well pumps and tanks, fire protection, and installation of underground oil tanks.

Scarpati Electric Service of Prospect
23 Bayberry Drive ▪ 758-6767   1983
Residential and commercial electrical repairs of all types.

Schiavo Sheet Metal, Inc.
9 Gramar Avenue ▪ 758-0233   1963
Custom sheet metal fabrication.

Scovill Fasteners, Inc.
121 Union City Road ▪ 758-5545
Fasteners for clothing.

Shawmut Bank
Waterbury Road ▪ 758-3939   1967
Full range of financial banking services. Opened as Connecticut National Bank in 1967.

Sheldon Precision Co., Inc.
106 Union City Road ▪ 758-4441   1969
Manufacturer of precision screw machine parts.
Prospect was selected for its good location to labor, roads, and suppliers.

Site-Tech, Inc.
7 Gramar Avenue ▪ 758-6629   1983
General excavating contractors.
Prospect offers a great location, reasonable land opportunities, and great tax rates. Best small town in Connecticut.
Site-Tech was incorporated in 1973 while in Wolcott. The company moved to Prospect in 1983. The owners are: Jack Crumb, President; James Crumb, Vice Presi-

dent; Mary Magee, Treasurer/Secretary; and Kerry Lynn Arnold, Office Manager. The business deals primarily in commercial or high volume residential property construction projects, with specialty in roadways, water, and sewer piping.

Skrip's Auto Body, Inc.
104 Cheshire Road ▪ 758-6605   1978
Complete auto body repair service, including the handling of insurance appraiser and paperwork. State-of-the-art equipment operated by certified technicians. Perfect color matching and only original equipment parts used.

Smart Designs, Inc.
4 Summit Road
P.O. Box 7100 ▪ 758-6934   1986
Printing and publishing: monthly community newspapers - *The Prospect Pages*, *Wolcott Community News* & *Naugy-talk Newz*.

Prospect is the home/residence of President & Treasurer, Robert A. Marcella.

Smedes Realty
37 Waterbury Road ▪ 758-5744   1976
Real estate sales, rentals, and appraisals.

The owners are lifelong residents of Prospect with strong ties to the community.

Stanley's Centerless Grinding
Gramar Avenue ▪ 758-5577   1969
Centerless grinding.

Summit Physical Therapy Services
4 Summit Road ▪ 758-4278   1985
Physical therapy services by registered physical therapist.

The owner, Kathy Doyle, has lived in Prospect since 1957. She wanted a location close to home when she began the therapy service in 1985.

T & T Home Improvements
Roy Mountain Road ▪ 758-4372   1989
Vinyl siding installation, replacement windows, and general remodeling.

Thermo Conductor Services, Inc.
7 Industrial Road ▪ 758-6611   1971
Specializes in providing solid and stranded thermocouple conductors to wire and cable manufacturers for temperature measurement and control in aerospace, power-generating, manufacturing, agriculture, military, medical, and other applications. Also makes bare and tinned copper strand for communications, computers, shipboard, and military applications

The company's founders and owners, Mark and Arlene Baker, have lived in Prospect for over 40 years.

Townline Seafood & Pizza Restaurant
280 Cheshire Road ▪ 758-3303
Family dining for lunch and dinner 7 days a week. Private banquet facilities. Off premises catering.

Town Spirit Shop, Inc.
Baker's Dozen Plaza
47 Waterbury Road ▪ 758-5118   1957
Complete beverage line plus custom gift baskets, party planning, and monthly specials.

Triple Stitch Sportswear
6 New Haven Road ▪ 758-6303   1984
Embroidery, screen printing, and advertising specialties. The owner resides in Prospect.

Tyler Equipment Corporation
94 Union City Road ▪ 758-3925   1992
Sales, service, and product support of heavy construction equipment.

The Used Car Company
232 New Haven Road ▪ 758-4963
Sales and purchase of used cars and trucks. Towing and snow plowing services.

V C Construction
246 Matthew Street ▪ 758-4548
New construction, remodeling, and general contracting services.

Bob Van Delft Plumbing & Heating
45 Morris Road ▪ 758-6343
Residential and commercial plumbing and heating; new construction and remodeling.

Wescor Building & Remodeling, Inc.
P.O. Box 7031 ▪ 758-5574   1985
Specializing in new construction and framing, also. President: Jeff Slapikas.

Maria S.P. Wozniak, MD
6 New Haven Road ▪ 758-3343   1985
Medical office.

Young Cleaners
52 Waterbury Road ▪ 758-0577
Professional dry cleaning. Fast service. Shirts laundered and alterations.

~

Chapter Twenty-One

The Biographies

T he biographies contained within this chapter represent a cross-section of individuals who played a role in the development of Prospect. Some of the people are famous, but many are not. Some held positions of great influence, while others led simple lives. Some were born here, others moved here, and still others were here for a time and then left. These Prospect residents from the past (for they have all gone to their just reward) did share one thing in common — a love for the simple country life that can be found in a town like this.

The decision to include the persons listed below was based on the information available to the writer at the time of publication. This list is in no way complete, but rather a sampling of some who have lived and worked on this hill. For the many other interesting personal histories to be told, there will be other books and other writers. The notation (?) indicates that dates or information was unavailable or uncertain. The spelling for many names differed from one source to another. The spelling used in this list of biographies was the one most commonly found in the available sources.

Albert T. Allen (1883-1956)

Born in Prospect, the son of Theodore and Grace (Goodspeed) Allen, who were farmers who moved here from Orange. After attending the one-room schoolhouse, Albert began working on his father's farm at the age of fourteen. He continued to farm until after World War I.

He became sexton of the Prospect Cemetery Association in 1918. He was custodian of the Congregational Church for 20 years, custodian of the Prospect Community School for 8 years, and custodian for St. Anthony Church, 2 years. Albert also did road maintenance work for the town. He was considered an authority on bees and did bee hunting for 58 years while selling honey from his beehives.

Albert married Florence Wooster of Naugatuck, who was a direct descendant of John Quincy Adams. They had one daughter, Hazel. In 1904, the year he cast his first vote, Albert began his long record of public service. He served Prospect in many positions, including constable for 45 years, dog warden, second selectman, first selectman, school board member, grand juror, chairman of the library board, and state representative in the General Assembly from 1926-1928.

He was also the State game warden for 15 years.

Albert Allen helped found and served as president of the Prospect Historical Society. Mr. and Mrs. Allen donated the Society's incorporation cost in memory of their daughter, Hazel Allen Beers. In his spare time he collected funds for the Red Cross and March of Dimes campaigns. At the time of his death, he was the oldest member of the Prospect Volunteer Fire Department.

Even I know there must be something about Prospect that isn't perfect — but up to now I've never been able to find out what it is. — Albert Allen

The New Haven Register 7-13-1952

Edward Allen

Operated a wire factory on Clark Hill Road.

Dr. Aaron Austin (1803?-?)

Medical doctor who held town office in 1844.

Benjamin Dutton Beecher (1791-1866)

Invented and patented the first fanning mill (grain winnowing machine) and the screw propeller for steamboats. He lived in Prospect in an old-fashioned eight-sided house, which he also invented himself. No vestige of the house remains today.

Fredus Benham

Partner with Julius Hotchkiss in store business.

Sherman Blakeslee

Took over business from Smith & Wallace making britannia spoons and other items.

Dr. E. Irene Boardman (Mrs. Arthur W. Kathan, Sr.) (1889-1980)

Emma Irene Boardman, the tenth of eleven children, graduated from elementary school in Springfield, MA and from the Nyack Academy in Nyack, NY. She received a B.A. degree from Smith College in 1915, being the first student to finish the four-year course in three years, and the M.D. degree from Cornell University Medical School in 1920. She also taught for one year at Smith College in the Zoology Department and worked in the women's suffrage movement. After interning for a year at the Woman's Hospital in Philadelphia, Dr. Boardman practiced medicine in New Haven and served as a school physician from 1924 to 1953. She was also medical examiner for the New Have State Normal School from 1922 to 1936 and worked as the health officer of Prospect from 1944 to 1965. Having suffered from polio as a girl, one of her greatest satisfactions was in administering the Salk anti-polio vaccine to hundreds of school children and many adults in her home town. In New Haven Dr. Boardman was the first woman on the governing board of the First Methodist Church and was active in the YWCA and the County, State and American Medical Associations.

After having lived in a summer place on Cook Road since 1923, she moved with her family permanently to Prospect in 1936, purchasing the former Field home called "The Ledges." She taught Sunday school for many years at the Prospect Congregational Church and served on the church building committee, securing the funds to build a steeple on the new church building. She was also elected an honorary deacon of the church. Dr. Boardman was director of health and medical temperance of the National WCTU, a life member of the State WCTU, and an adviser to both local and state Youth Temperance Councils. She was a former president of the Conn. Huguenot Society, a regent of the Cheshire DAR, a member of the Mayflower Descendants, and a member of the Waterbury branch of the American Association of University Women.

She married Arthur W. Kathan in 1928 and raised seven children, including three from his first marriage. In her years as health officer of Prospect, she introduced zoning to the town and persisted in getting it adopted.

When she retired from the Department of Public Health of the City of New Haven after 29 years of service, she was cited for her role in the eradication of the diseases of diphtheria in the *Waterbury American* stated in part: Her absolute insistence upon compliance with health regulations in new housing developments got her into controversy with Prospect real estate developers who were more interested in the profit motive. Dr. Boardman could set an example today for officials who are not adequately concerned with proper health safeguards before they authorize homes to be built or occupied."

Isaac Bradley (1794-1855)

Isaac, who died at the age of 61, had five wives. He buried four of them, and one of them buried him. His widow must have chosen to be buried two year later in a different plot in the Prospect cemetery, away from Issac and his four other wives.

James Bramhall (1905-1994)

Jim moved to Prospect in 1948 on a "temporary" leave of absence from Scovill Manufacturing. The School Board offered him a job as head custodian at Community School — a position he would hold for thirty years. He never did go back to Scovill. Their loss was Prospect's gain.

Jim was the son of William and Augusta (Nichols) Bramhall. He and his wife, Inez (Zeller), had no children, but he felt that the hundreds of students who called him "Uncle Jim" were "all the children he would ever need." Besides his service to the town as custodian, Jim was a member of the Prospect Grange where he was master for eight years. He was also a member of the Pomona, State, and National Grange. He was president of the Litchfield County Fairs for four years, a familiar figure in his position of parade marshal in the Memorial Day parades, member of the Lions Club, Congregational Church member, member of the Republican Town Committee, Prospect volunteer fireman, Prospect constable, and Justice of the Peace.

John Bronson

Owned match factory.

Samuel C. Bronson

Owned match factory.

Benjamin Brewster Brown (1815-1900)

At the age of thirty, Benjamin Brown moved to Prospect from Windsor, NY and located on a farm he would occupy until his death. Through the summer months he engaged in agricultural pursuits, while during the winter he was employed as a teacher in the Prospect and Cheshire district schools. He was considered one of the most popular educators of his time. Benjamin married Emily B. Hotchkiss and they had two children.

In earlier years Mr. Brown was identified with the Whig party but in 1864 was elected on the Republican ticket to the State Legislature. Later in life he cast votes with the Prohibition party because of his views on the temperance question. He served as a member of the school committee, justice of the peace, and selectman in Prospect. Active in the Congregational Church, he was superintendent in the Sunday school and Deacon for 40 years. Before his death at home, Benjamin Brown was the oldest living resident in town.

John G. Brundage (1897-1986)

John was born in Waterbury, the son of Marcus and Mary (Gribble) Brundage. He was a resident of Prospect for 55 years and was active in the Republican Party. Brundage served the town as foreman and as second selectman and was a member of the Congregational Church. At the time of his death, he was the oldest charter member of the Prospect Volunteer Fire Department of which he was a member for over 50 years.

Dr. Hiram Bunce

Medical doctor who lived here in the early 1830s.

Jared Burr (1759-1829)

Born to Joseph and Rebecca Burr of Wallingford, Jared played an active role in Columbia Society. He lived in a modest dwelling on Cheshire Road opposite Coer Road with his wife Anna. The foundation still exists on a small parcel of Water Authority property. Of his three known children, a daughter, Rebecca, married Jesse Ford of Prospect. Jared is listed on the Prospect Soldiers Monument as having served in the local militia.

Bernice Talmadge Buys (1893-1963)

Bernice was born in Prospect, the daughter of George and Ella (Caroll) Talmadge. She married Orville Buys. At the Prospect Congregational Church, she was a member of the standing committee and held the office of treasurer in the Women's Association.

Mrs. Buys was auditor for the town of Prospect and a member of the Library Board, the Board of Assessors, and the Board of Tax Review, where she served as chair. She served as state representative from Prospect during the 1937-1938 term and was a chair of the Republican Town Committee. Other memberships included National Order of Women Legislators of the United States, Prospect Grange, the state and national Grange, the New Haven County Farm Bureau, and Crescent Chapter, Eastern Star, Cheshire.

Frederick Catlin Candee (1854-?)

Frederick was educated in the district schools of his native Oxford, CT, and attended Lovell's Lanchaterian School in New Haven. He then purchased a valuable farm in Prospect and pursued a career in agriculture.

Carl Canfield (1891-1971)

Carl was the son of Frederick and Clara (Bell) Canfield and played a key role in the history of the Prospect Volunteer Fire Department. He laid one of the cinder blocks for the first fire department, which was completed in 1942. The property had belonged to Rob Arrol. Carl Canfield was appointed temporary chief in 1945.

Carl came to the rescue of the fire department when storage space was needed for a ladder truck purchased from Naugatuck. He was project manager for the New Haven Water Company, where he was employed for 40 years and arranged for the use of the Edgar Wallace barn near the Cheshire Reservoir for this purpose. Again in 1950 Carl was able to secure land from the water company — this time at the intersection of Center Street and New Haven Road for the construction of the new fire house and later Algonquin School and Canfield Park.

Canfield also served Prospect as selectman, assessor, and fire marshall. He was a member of the Congregational Church and a seventh-degree member of the Prospect Grange. His wife was Edith Boardman Canfield, who was a Republican registrar of voters.

Samuel & Hannah Castle

Owned and operated the first recorded tavern in Prospect. They had two daughters, Emeline and Loly, and one son, Samuel A.

Samuel Augustus Castle (1822-1887)

Born in Prospect, the son of Samuel and Hannah (Hotchkiss) Castle, Samuel moved to Waterbury at the age of fifteen. There, as well as in Cheshire and New York City, he carried on the business of harness and saddle making. He married Mary Ann Steele, the daughter of Elisha Steele; they had a daughter, Elizabeth.

John L. Chatfield (1918-1975)

Born in Prospect, the son of John A. and Myrtle (Carley) Chatfield, John served the Prospect Volunteer Fire Department since the mid-1940s, where he was department head from 1959-1963. He also was treasurer of the fire department.

John L. Chatfield was employed as foreman at the Waterbury Rolling Mills for 35 years. He was a member of the Board of Finance, the New Haven County Fire Chiefs Association, and the Prospect Congregational Church.

Asahel Chittenden (1763-1813)

Asahel lived in the house still standing near the cemetery gate. He and later his son Edward operated what may have been the first store in town. As a young man, he enlisted in Col. Beecher's Infantry Regiment, where he saw action at White Plains, Horseneck, and other areas. Asahel married Anna, who was the daughter of John Lewis, an early minister. They had nine children. After Asahel's death at the age of 50, Anna married Robert Hotchkiss, who died a year later. Her third husband was Richard McFarland. They relocated to Ohio. After Richard died, Anna applied for widow's pension and bounty land from Asahel's war service. She then returned to Waterbury and lived with her son Edward.

Edward Chittenden (1801-1893)

The son of Asahel and Anna Chittenden, Edward worked in the Prospect store his father had begun. In 1828 he married Emeline, daughter of Samuel Castle, who was Prospect's hotel keeper. At the age of thirty-eight, he moved to the center of Waterbury to become proprietor of the Mansion House. He also was a manufacturer of small brass articles.

Alva T. Cinq-Mars (1910-1982)

Alva Cinq-Mars was born in Hartford, the son of Leon and Lillian (Countenmanch) Cinq-Mars. He and his wife Edna lived in Prospect many years before moving to Ormand Beach, Florida.

Alva was first selectman in Prospect from 1957-1959. He was owner of the Handy Kitchen Bakery and the Cinq-Mars Restaurant in Prospect and served on the advisory committee of the Prospect branch of Connecticut Bank and Trust Co. The Cinq-Mars were members of the Prospect Congregational Church, and he served in the Laymen's Fellowship.

George Cipriano (1907-1983)

George Cipriano served as first selectman of Prospect from 1961-1967. During his three terms of office, the town constructed two additions to the Algonquin School and purchased land off Plank road for the town's landfill. He considered a run for the state Senate in 1964 but later decided against it. He told his constituents, "My place is right here in our town." He was active in the Republican Party and was a delegate to the 1966 State Republican Convention.

For many years he and his wife Helen owned and operated the Prospect Hardware Store on Waterbury Road. Cipriano was also owner of the Green Acres Driving Range of Prospect and Cipriano and Cipriano Real Estate.

George was born in Waterbury, the son of Louis and Marie (Bergamo) Cipriano. He was a member of St. Anthony Church, the Tommy Merriman American Legion Post Nº 94, the Prospect Social Club, the National Police Officers' Association of America, AARP, and the Prospect Grange.

Smith S. Clark (1822-1906)

Born in Milford, CT, the son of Celah and Hannah Stone (Smith) Clark, S.S. Clark moved with his family to Prospect at an early age. He went to the district schools, then learned the painting trade. Later in life he turned his attention to farming near the old family homestead. His farm consisted of 200 valuable acres upon which he made many improvements. His first wife, Abigail Williams of Cheshire, bore no children before her death. He then married Sarah E. Thomas, a native of Woodbridge. This union produced two children. Their second child, Adelbert, remained in Prospect and later ran the family farm.

The Clarks were members of the Congregational Church where Smith was clerk and treasurer. He was on the society committee for 25 years. In town politics he was a Republican and served as tax collector. He was selectman for twelve years. Mr. and Mrs Clark and their son Adelbert were active members in the Grange.

Miles S. Clark (1824-1906)

Born in Prospect June 8, 1824, Miles began learning the carpenter trade at age sixteen. Two years latter he went to Naugatuck and finished his trade with Amos Hotchkiss. Afterwards, he began to work in the hoe shop of Eben C. Tuttle. In 1861 Miles went to Canada and helped Mr. Tuttle put the machinery in a shop there. Returning from Canada, Miles located in Naugatuck and Union City.

Halsey Steele Clark (1855-1941)
Fannie (Phipps) Clark (? -1937)

Halsey was born in Prospect, the son of Merritt and Mary (Skilton) Clark. Until his marriage to Fannie Phipps in 1881, he lived on the Clark Hill Road farm built by his grandfather. The couple moved into their new home on another part of the family homestead. They had one son, Clifford Clark, born in 1883.

As a young woman, Fannie Clark taught in the East district school, making her home on Matthew Street with Mrs. Frank Matthews. Her brother William was pastor at the Prospect Congregational Church for nearly 30 years. It was Rev. Phipps who persuaded Fannie to come to Prospect and become acquainted with Halsey, who would become her husband.

For many years Fanny and Halsey conducted a butter, egg, and vegetable business. They peddled their wares in the Willow Street section of Waterbury. Everyone in that part of the city knew the Clark horse and wagon. The Clarks were among the last to abandon old Dobbin as a means of transportation.

Halsey served his town as first select-man for two terms in the 1880s. Mr. Clark was also a second selectman, member of the Union school district for 26 years (mostly as chairman), member of the board of relief for 48 years, and Prospect's representative to the State Legislature for a number of years.

Halsey Clark was active in the Congregational Church. He was part of the building committee for the 1908 church structure. Halsey also served as Sunday school teacher for 60 years, deacon for 40 years, and was made honorary deacon in 1939. Halsey Clark was fatally injured by an automobile August 2, 1941, while crossing Union City Road. Prior to his death he was the oldest member of the Congregational Church, having joined at the age of nine. He was also the oldest man in Prospect.

In Prospect no one thinks that anyone is old because at 60 and 70, the folks there are as active as striplings.

Halsey Clark, Waterbury American, 3-20-1938

Lavergne Grant Clark (1863-1945)

The son of Merritt Clark, Lavergne Grant was born in Prospect at Clark Hill. His mother, Mary Skilton Clark, sister of Henry Bennett Skilton, saw a clipping in the paper indicating Fort Lavergne, Kentucky, had just fallen into the hands of Lincoln's soldiers. Thus the name Lavergne. His middle name was for Grant, the war time general and President.

Lavergne was a member of the Prospect Congregational Church for 65 years. He served several terms as deacon and was treasurer the last 37 years of his life. An active member of the Prospect Grange, he received his 50 year Gold Sheaf. Lavergne married Katherine Bingham and they had one son, Gould, and two daughters, Adella and Sylvia. He died in his home at the age of 82.

Katherine Bingham Clark (1866-1960)

The wife of Lavergne Clark, Katherine was born in Port Elizabeth, New Jersey, and the daughter of William E. and Anna

(Gilbert) Bingham. She was a resident of Prospect for 64 years.

Mrs. Clark was a member of the Prospect Congregational Church, a charter member of the Prospect Grange, and a graduate of Northfield Seminary Class of 1886. She was a teacher in the Prospect schools and served as treasurer of the Prospect School Board. Katherine was very active in civic and educational activities in town and during World War I and played a major role in Red Cross work for Prospect.

Clifford P. Clark (1883-1969)

Clifford was the only child of Halsey and Fannie (Phipps) Clark. He was a farmer on Clark Hill. Clifford married Clarabel Shepard of Simsbury, and they had three children: Josephine, Alfred, and Gertrude. He was a member and honorary deacon of the Prospect Congregational Church. He held many offices in the Prospect Grange, where he was the oldest member with 69 years service.

Clifford Clark compiled many stories in letter format about life in Prospect and some of the more colorful residents of this town. A number of his works are contained in this book.

Selah Clarke (1795-1880)

Selah came to Prospect in 1823 and located on the Platt farm — a tract of 115 acres in the southern part of town — where he spent the remainder of his life. He was a man noted for his industry, and despite a limited education, he was well versed in the issues of his time. Selah was a faithful member of the Congregational Church. His wife, Hannah (Stone), was a descendent of Rev. Samuel Stone, the first Stone in America.

Horatio Nelson Clarke (1841-?)

Horatio was the youngest of eight children in the family of Selah and Hannah Clarke. As a boy he attended the district schools of Prospect Mills, a preparatory school in New Haven, and Naugatuck High School.

At the age of eighteen, he took charge of his father's farm and cared for his parents during their declining years. In 1864 he married Laura De Ette Perkins. She was born in the Bethany hotel of her grandfather, Archibald Perkins.

The Clarke family located on the Hotchkiss farm where Horatio made extensive improvements. After the death of his parents, he bought the old homestead and other lands owned by his father. This acquisition made him one of the largest landholders in Prospect, with an aggregate of 600 acres. He was involved in general farming, ran a dairy with Jersey stock, and found a ready market in Waterbury for the wood cleared from his property.

Politically, Horatio was a life-long Democrat, but at local elections he voted for those he considered best qualified, regardless of party lines. He was assessor for five years and tax collector, nine years. In Prospect he was justice of the peace, grand juror, member of the board of relief, and member of the board of selectmen. Horatio was instrumental in securing rural free delivery to Prospect. His memberships included the Beacon Valley Grange and the Episcopal Church.

Daniel Bryan Conner (1899-1955)

Daniel Conner lived on New Haven Road after moving to Prospect in 1934. He was the son of Daniel L. and Mary (Shea) Conner of Waterbury. Daniel served as deputy sheriff from 1937-1947 and again from 1951-1954. He and his wife, Theresa (Lynch), had four sons and a daughter. Daniel was a member of St. Anthony Church, the parish Holy Name Society, and the Knights of Columbus. He was active in Prospect Democratic politics.

Harry F. Coughlan (1901-1987)

Harry Coughlan was born in Waterbury, the son of Terrance and Mary (Cahill) Coughlan. He married Catherine Kelley and resided on Morris Road. Harry owned and operated E-Z WAY Products of Prospect. He served as selectman for the town and was a chief of the Prospect Volunteer Fire Department. A member of St. Anthony Church, he was also a member of Sheridan Council, 3rd Degree, Knights of Columbus.

George H. Cowdell (1870-1961)

Born in England, the son of Samuel and Ruth (Melling) Cowdell, George attended private schools. He came to the United States in 1888 and became a resident of Prospect in 1892. A machinist by trade, he served in the Connecticut House in 1933, 1935, and 1945, with membership on the education and labor committees.

George was active in the Prospect Grange, serving as the first master from 1894-1895 and again in 1921. He also participated in several other civic organizations. He and his wife, Luella Hotchkiss, had two daughters, Ruth and Nellie. [see photograph in Chapter 12]

Nellie Cowdell (1908-1993)

The second daughter born to George and Luella Cowdell, Nellie played an active part in many Prospect activities. She was a life member and deacon emeritus of the Prospect Congregational Church. She was also a member of the Women's Association of the Prospect Congregational Church. She was a member of numerous organizations, including the Prospect and Connecticut Historical Societies, Prospect and Connecticut Grange, Connecticut Chapter of the National Society of Daughters of Founders and Patriots of America, Lady Fenwick Chapter of the Daughters of the American Revolution, Order of Easter Star, National Society of New England Women, Connecticut Society of Genealogists, AARP, and Prospect Senior Citizens.

Nellie worked in the dietary department of the Waterbury Hospital and was librarian for the Prospect Library for many years. She served as the historian of both her church and the town. She wrote or edited numerous publications about the history and life in Prospect as well as the Congregational Church. A list of her works may be found in the bibliography.

Her challenges have been many
But always without frown
She's contributed her whole life long
To our church, our community, and our town.

For many years our Historian
Both church and town as well
To relate the many tales
That Prospect had to tell.

From *Our Tribute* by Gwenn Talmadge Fischer

Joseph Doolittle (?-1892)

As a young man Joseph Doolittle became a Prospect farmer, speculator, and manufacturer of buttons. Later, he engaged in the hotel business in Naugatuck, Waterbury, and Milford.

Dr. Henry Ducachet (1820-?)

A medical doctor who was in Prospect as noted on the U.S. census of 1850. By 1865 he had moved to Guyana, Puerto Rico.

Elmer Gustaf Ericson (1899-1979)

Born the son of Theodore and Louise (Strom) Ericson, Elmer attended local schools and graduated from Brown University in 1925. He was employed as an accountant with Anaconda American Brass for 30 years. He was a member of Prospect Congregational Church and Phi Gamma Delta fraternity.

Mr. Ericson was active in town activities and served as town clerk, town treasurer, and trial justice. He also served on many town boards, including the school transportation committee.

Albert Daniel Field (1853-1923)

Albert D. Field was educated in a private elementary school taught by his mother, and graduated from a public high school in Columbus, Ohio. He started his career in a sign painting business with his brothers, but his inventive skills and managerial ability took him to many other places. After inventing an extension curtain rod and an extension stair rod, he organized the Globe Curtain Pole Co. in New York City in 1885. Two years later he moved the business to Waterbury, CT. Between 1891 and 1897 he was involved in the Manufacturers Supply Co. of Buffalo, NY and the Metal Goods Manufactory Co. in Bridgeport. His invention in 1897 of the metal buckle for arctic boots and firemen's raincoats led to the creation of the Shoe Hardware Co. in Waterbury. He served as Secretary-Treasurer and later as President of the company. In addition, he opened a rubber reclaiming plant for the U.S. Rubber Co. in Naugatuck and had financial interest in mines in California, Montana, and Idaho.

Rev. Alida B. Wolfe

In 1906 he purchased the Erwin Mix farm and land in Prospect and built a large country home, which he called "The Ledges." When built, the house was equipped with a powerhouse generating electricity, a burglar alarm system, and a gravity-fed spring water line. Although at first dependent on the Meriden-Waterbury railroad to commute to work (the depot was down the hill from his home), he purchased one the first automobiles in Prospect in 1916 and hired a chauffeur to drive it. Field was a member of the First Baptist Church of Waterbury and served

as chairman of the Finance Committee and of the Building Committee for the new church office.

He married Ella Clara Clapp in 1885, and they had one daughter, Delia (Mrs. Alonzo J. Bloodgood), who served as a member and treasurer of the Prospect Board of Education. In the National Cyclopedia of American Biography, Vol. 20, published in 1929, he was described as "a man of genial nature, impulsive and generous, with a combination of vision and practical ability."

Leonard John Fusco, Sr. (1929-1973)

The son of Lorenzo and Maria Mancini Fusco, Leonard was the owner of Fusco Construction Co. He was born in Waterbury but spent his last 13 years in Prospect. He was a veteran of the Korean War, serving in the U.S. Navy Sea Bees. Leonard was a member of St. Anthony Church and the president of the Prospect Horsemen's Club.

Roland Henry Gelinas (1922-1979)

Roland, better known as Pat, was the son of Maxime and Regina (Matteau) Gelinas of Maurice Province, Quebec, Canada. At the age of nine months, he and his family settled in Waterbury, where he went to school. He served in the armed forces and then married Helen Tora. They had a daughter Barbara.

Pat began working in watch repair and jewelry sales. Eighteen years later he made a career change to advertising. He owned and operated the Clark Specialty Company on Morris Road. Two years later Pat published the first Prospect telephone guide and directory. In 1963 he launched the monthly *Prospect Reminder* — the first local news media in town.

Pat was an active member of the Prospect Chamber of Commerce and served as director. He was involved in the Miss Prospect Pageant, Zoning Board, Prospect Little League, and a host of other activities. His friends described him as "a man everyone should have known."

Peter Gilkey (?-?)

Peter Gilkey was perhaps Prospect's most notorious character of the 1700s. Our first record of Gilkey's life begins in 1762. Peter was one of a thousand men sent in two ships on an expedition against the French in Havana, Cuba, toward the end of the French Wars by King George III. The American settlers were still expected to support England and its missions at this point in history. Peter Gilkey was one of a handful of men who survived the losses from sickness and shipwreck.

After completing the mission and storming the castle at Havana, Peter stayed on in Cuba for an extra year. He learned the die-making trade and the forging process to manufacture Spanish coins.

Gilkey returned to the part of Wallingford that is now Cheshire. Now on the side of the Militia, he fought battles in New York during the Revolutionary War. Mustered out in 1776, he returned to Cheshire. In 1782 he purchased land about one-half mile in from the current end of Peter Gilkey Road in what is now Prospect. With partners Isaac Hine and Abraham Tyler, he constructed a house on the site.

The building was unusual in that it had a second lower basement with a chimney connection. This structure would become their counterfeiting factory. Hine was an expert die maker while Tyler was knowledgeable about the furnace required to forge coins. Another accomplice, whose name is unknown, served in distributing and exchanging the coins in New York for good currency as they were produced. Peter Gilkey himself never passed the counterfeit coins.

This operation went on for some time. Then one day a man from Prospect Centre was hunting around the Gilkey property. He was puzzled by a hammering sound. The next day the hunter returned to the same location with a friend, and they both heard the noise. They summoned the sheriff, who came with three or four men. They entered and searched Gilkey's house but could find nothing out of the ordinary.

Upon leaving the house the sheriff looked back and saw smoke coming from the chimney. He did not remember seeing any fires burning in the house, so he went back inside to take another look. This time he detected a hollow sound to the floor. A trap door was discovered leading to the cellar, and the counterfeiting operation was exposed.

Gilkey was fined thirty pounds plus seventeen pounds court costs. Not having the money to pay, Peter was sent to the underground prison at Newgate. Because he could not support his family, his wife and children went to prison with him. After two years Gilkey was released. Returning to Prospect, he found his home in such a state of disrepair that they could not live there. He then moved to the East Farms section of Waterbury where he practiced the cobbler trade.

Peter Gilkey always seemed to be well off financially in his new life — better than the low wages of a cobbler would warrant. The legend persists that Peter would periodically return to his old property and dig up some of the coins he was rumored to have buried there. We only know that Peter and his family later returned to Cheshire, and no further records of his life or death can be found.

Garret Gillette (1788-1874)

Originally from Milford, CT, Garret married Nancy Platt and shortly thereafter moved to Prospect and located on a farm where he would spend the remainder of his life. Of their eleven children, Abigail married Lucius Talmadge, who farmed in Prospect; Johnathan and Bennett remained in Prospect as carpenters; Mary wed Harry Smith, a Prospect manufacturer; Sarah Ann married another local farmer, Harry Morse; and Garret became a farmer in Prospect.

Rufus M. Gillette (1829-1906)

A carpenter and joiner by trade, he latter engaged in farming. Born in Prospect March 31, 1829, Rufus was educated in the common schools. He was identified with the Republican Party, served as Treasurer of the Town Deposit Fund, and was a member of the Society and Church Committee. In 1888 he was a Connecticut Lower House representative. Rufus married Abigail Payne, the daughter of Steven and Abigail (Doolittle) Payne. They had three children and were influential members of the Congregational Church.

John C. Gilmartin (?-1970)

Born in Waterville, the son of John and Elizabeth Gilmartin, John was an organizer and charter member of the Prospect Volunteer Fire Department. He served as Fire Marshall from 1959 until his death and was fire chief for seven years. He was also drill instructor for the department. John was a state instructor for emergency first aid and a former auxiliary State Trooper. He was a member of the New Haven County Fire Chiefs Association and the Connecticut Fire Marshals Association. He was a Prospect resident for more than 30 years along with his wife Florence and two daughters.

Robert E. Harvey Sr. (1929-1979)

Born in Waterbury, the son of Milton and Evelyn (Niess) Harvey, Robert Harvey was a 25-year member and captain in the Prospect Volunteer Fire Department. He also was the town's fire marshall and a member of the Prospect Ambulance Corps, where he served as emergency medical technician.

Mr. Harvey married Jean (Lambert) Williams. He was an assistant foreman at Sikorsky Aircraft in Stratford and a lieutenant of the fire Brigade there. He was a member of the Prospect Historical Society, treasurer of the Whirleybirds Camping Association, president of the Flying Square Dancing Club, and a member of the Prospect Congregational Church.

Ambrose Hine (1726-1794)

Ambrose Hine was the first owner and probably builder of George Sabo's house.

He bought the lot in 1755. Ambrose served as a Lieutenant of the 1st Company of Wadsworth's Brigade when he enlisted for three years in 1777. Being an officer he probably had seen previous service.

Ambrose had two wives, Sarah Terril and Betsey Ford. Of his children, Ambrose Jr. may have served in his father's company, and Sarah married Amos Wilmot.

Isaac Hine (1743-1807)

Isaac was a cousin of Ambrose Hine. He served as a Captain in Col. Beardsley's Regiment of Militia that fought in New Haven, Fairfield, Bedford, and Norwalk. He married Eunice Wilmot. Isaac's will of 1804 mentions his children: Chloe, Freemen B., and Susanna. Isaac and Eunice were interred in the old Prospect burial grounds at the south end of the green.

Daniel Hitchcock (1763-1839)

Daniel was born in Cheshire. Both he and his family were buried in Prospect. He served in the military from 1778 to 1783, when he was discharged at West Point. He was present at the capture of Cornwallis. Daniel may have been disabled as he and later his widow, Lydia (Ives), received a larger than normal pension.

Charles Edward Hodges (1896-1981)

This Clark Hill Road resident was a postal carrier for 35 years. Active in the Prospect Grange, he served as master three times. He was state secretary for the Connecticut Rural Letter Carriers Association and chairman of the Board of Deacons (Deacon Emeritus) of the Prospect Congregational Church. He served as the superintendent of the Prospect cemetery. During his retirement he raised miniature trees in his greenhouse.

Charlie, as he was known by all, was very popular with the youth in town. In 1957 he was chosen as the first *Citizen of the Year* by the Juvenile Grange.

When asked why "Charlie" was chosen, Bruce Folmar, master of the Juvenile Grange, quickly responded, "he lives on our road and is a wonderful neighbor and friend. All the kids love him. He's delivered our valentines and birthday presents and things. My mother says he even delivered all our birth announcements when me and my brothers were born." Roger Folmar, Bruce's younger brother, piped in, "and even our bad report cards!"

Waterbury American 7-11-57

Gideon Hotchkiss (1716-1807)

In 1736 Gideon Hotchkiss settled on a parcel of land, located on Straitsville Road, given to him by his father, Stephen Hotchkiss. He married Anna Brocket, who died after bearing thirteen children. His second wife was Mabel, daughter of Isaac Stiles of Southbury, who gave Gideon another seven children.

Gideon was an ensign, then promoted to lieutenant in the French and Indian War under Captain Edward Lewis. During the Revolutionary War, he was captain of a Continental Army company. Several of Gideon's sons fought in the Revolution as well. His first born son, Jesse, fought in the French and Indian war. A young soldier of nineteen, Jesse returned home from that war, but lost his life in the Revolution in 1776.

When Gideon Hotchkiss heard of the attack on New Haven, July 5, 1779, he was working on his farm . . . he mounted his horse in the field, and with a hired boy galloped to the Elm City. He encountered the enemy at Westville, where there was a ford. Arriving at the scene of the battle, he dismounted and was about to send the boy home with the steed. Just then a shell struck the boy, and killed him instantly. There was no time to show sorrow or sentiment. The old soldier picked up the body, and laid it by a concealed place beside the road. Fastening the reins to the saddle, he started the horse back to the farm, and remained to take part in the fray.

Connecticut Magazine article by Rev. Sherrod Soule 1907

Aaron Russell was listed as killed in the attack and is most likely the hired boy in the article.

When the Society of Salem was organized, Gideon was made deacon of the church. He was also one of the founders and active supporters of the church and Society of Columbia (now Prospect). He served his town as selectman and its State Legislature representative.

He was the father of nineteen children, all living to be over 21 years. Gideon Hotchkiss owned 1000 acres of land between the Salem Rd., the Straightsville Rd., and the Porter Hill Rd. The Logtown Rd. went straight through it. This was known as the "South Farms." Gideon Hotchkiss transferred large gangs of men from the town house in Naugatuck to the South Farms in Prospect to hoe turnips. Gideon Hotchkiss was the first to be buried out there beside the Grange Hall in the "old Glebe" cemetery, and later down under the hill. Clifford Clark, May 30, 1957

Before his death September 3, 1807, Gideon lived to see 105 grandchildren, 155 great-grandchildren, and 4 from the fifth generation. On his Prospect Cemetery tombstone is written:

A citizen of worth & influence in his community.
A Godly and faithful man.

Amos Hotchkiss (1751-1820)

Amos was a son of Gideon Hotchkiss. He evoked the anger of his father when he embraced the beliefs of Methodism. Gideon was a strict Congregationalist and threatened to disinherit Amos for his heresy when Amos became active in the political movement to sweep away all connections with the church and the civil order of the commonwealth. Fortunately for Amos, Gideon was too forgiving to carry out his threat.

Amos was the main organizer in the construction of a Methodist meetinghouse. Nearby was his spacious farmhouse, which would later become the residence of Merritt Clark. His house was a frequent stopping place for itinerant preachers, including the famous Bishop Asbury. It was also the gathering place on "quarterly meeting" occasions for Methodists from all around the region.

Abigail, his wife, lived to the age of 92 and bore three sons and a daughter. The daughter, Molly, married Joseph Bronson of Prospect and with her husband united with the Baptists. Amos is buried in Prospect cemetery.

Robert Hotchkiss (1755-1826)

Robert was the son of Asa and Mary Hotchkiss. He served in Capt. Bunnell's company in 1776. *The History of Waterbury* identifies Robert as one "who went over to the enemy."

Robert Hotchkiss . . . Jail by a military warrant for some supposed crime . . . committee reported nothing criminal . . . so were released without cost or charge.
1782 Records of the State of Connecticut

He was later made lieutenant in the militia and is buried in the Prospect Cemetery.

Eldad Hotchkiss (1756-1832)

Born in Bethany, the son of Joel Hotchkiss, Eldad spent the last fifty years of his life in Prospect. He enlisted in the regiment under the command of Capt. Johnson. After being discharged he became a privateer, and for two months he was taken prisoner and detained aboard a gun ship and then a prison ship. His son Eldad Jr. was an early town clerk who died of typhoid. At a young age, Eldad 3rd also died of this disease a few years later.

Eben Hotchkiss (1757-1853)

A son of Gideon Hotchkiss, Eben served in the Waterbury militia and the State Troops commanded by Capt. John Lewis of Waterbury. In 1776 he became sick and got his brother Titus to complete his tour. Later, he saw action with Captain Norton's company of Durham in New London and Providence, Rhode Island.

On his pension application he indicated he lived on the Waterbury side [of Straitsville Road] until fifteen years ago and then moved 40 rods across the street to Cheshire. Prospect records indicate he died at the age of 95 from a broken hip and old age. He must have been the oldest Revolutionary veteran in town at the time of his death.

Asahel Hotchkiss (1760-1841)

Asahel was the son of Jesse Hotchkiss and the grandson of Gideon. He was drafted in 1777 at the age of seventeen into the militia for six months until the regular army could be organized. In June 1788 he took the place of his uncle Jonah Mallery. Jonah's wife had just given birth to triplets, and he was needed at home. In 1780 Asahel joined the regular army and served a colorful tour under General Lafayette.

Asahel lived with his father on Clark Hill Road before and after his return from the war. Some of the time he lived with his grandfather on Straitsville Road. Asahel's fourth wife, Ruhana Wakeman, drew his pension from his military service.

Polly (Castle) Hotchkiss (1770-1870)

Polly Castle was an East Farms Methodist. She was remarkable for her intelligence and piety and was a highly respected Prospect citizen. She married Woodward Hochkiss of Prospect, the son of Amos and Abigail Hotchkiss. Polly was the mother of Julius Hotchkiss, the first mayor of Waterbury.

Benjamin Hotchkiss (1786-1842)

Reared and educated in Prospect, Benjamin was the youngest son of Abraham and Hannah (Weed) Hotchkiss. Abraham was a landowner and farmer who spent his entire life in Prospect. Benjamin married Hannah Beecher. Both he and his wife were active and influential members of the Congregational Church. They were among the first Sunday school teachers in the town of Prospect. Benjamin was laid to rest in the Prospect cemetery.

David Miles Hotchkiss (1797-1878)

David M. Hotchkiss was born in Prospect, the son of Frederick Hotchkiss. Gideon Hotchkiss was his great-grandfather. As a member of the committee, David secured the name of Prospect when it was incorporated as a town in 1827. David Hotchkiss was appointed captain of the militia of Waterbury and Salem (now Naugatuck) and afterwards was called by this title.

David married twice. His first wife was Zeruah Stevens of Naugatuck. His second, Hannah Doolittle Bristol, was a widow from Cheshire.

The well on the D.M. Hotchkiss farm was dug in the autumn of 1819. The following spring the house was erected with lumber and timber prepared in the preceding winter. David kept detailed records of the expenses for building his house. The completed house cost $660.99.

David was a man of considerable education. Soon after the house was completed in 1820, he opened a school, known as the Select Academy, on the second floor of his home. This floor was designed with a large room for this purpose.

Hotchkiss was prominent in civic affairs. He served the town as selectman and twice was sent as representative to the State Legislature. He was the first man to advocate the formation of the Free-Soil party in Connecticut at a convention in Hartford. An advocate of both total abstinence and abolition, David voted the Free-Soil ticket alone in his town for several years, when it was difficult to go against public opinion. Those opposed to his views went so far as to cut down his fruit trees and girdle his shade trees. They even destroyed his fences, tools, and farm implements.

David Hotchkiss is buried in Prospect. The house which David built on Waterbury Road is still standing and serves as the home for the Prospect Historical Society.

Julius Hotchkiss (1810-1878)

History of Waterbury

One of Prospect's most recognized citizens, Julius Hotchkiss was a remarkable example of the self-made man. He was the son of Woodward and Polly Hotchkiss, farmers in Prospect. From his humble beginning, he rose to positions of wealth, influence, and honor.

At age seventeen Julius began teaching in the Prospect district schools. Next, he became a traveling salesman for two or three years. He then moved to Derby where he opened a store and developed a successful business. He returned to Waterbury and was involved in another store and a factory that made cotton webbing and suspenders.

In 1853, when Waterbury became a city, Julius Hotchkiss was nominated by both parties to be the first mayor and received a nearly unanimous vote. In politics he was an old line Whig, but when that party dissolved, he joined the Democratic ranks and was an active partisan. He served two terms in the State Legislature (1851 and 1858). In 1867, during President Andrew Johnson's administration, he was elected representative from the Second Congressional District of Connecticut and sat on the 40th Congress. In 1870 he was chosen as the Lieutenant Governor of Connecticut. This closed his public career, and he devoted the remainder of his life to reading and study.

During the better part of his life, Julius was a zealous member of the New Church (consisting of those who accept the teachings of Emanuel Swedenborg). He frequently lent a helping hand to the poor and unfortunate. In 1823 he married Melissa Perkins of Oxford, and they had five children.

Harry Hotchkiss (1814-1883)

The son of Gideon M. and Arvilla (Brooks) Hotchkiss, Harry was born in Prospect and became a farmer. In politics Harry was a Republican serving as representative in the State Legislature. He also was an assessor for a number of years. Harry and his wife, Sarah (Hoppin), were faithful members of the Congregational Church. One of their three children, Elizabeth, married John R. Platt of Prospect.

Hervey Dwight Hotchkiss (1822-1896)

Reared in Prospect, Hervey engaged in the manufacture of spoons near his home with his partner, Robert Wallace, in the factory they named Hotchkiss & Wallace. After a time he sold the patent for a device that strengthened britannia spoons with a wire in the center. The plant then moved to Yalesville. Hervey was superintendent of the factory. He subsequently moved to Meriden.

Berkeley S. Hotchkiss (1826-?)

Born in Prospect, the son of David M. and Zeruah Hotchkiss, Berkeley began his adult life by teaching school in Cheshire for several winters. Next he taught in Prospect Centre School both winter and summer for a year and a half.

Berkeley then formed a partnership with Howard C. Ives in the grocery business. This enterprise was so prosperous after two years that Berkeley sought the broader market of Waterbury in 1861. He continued this grocery operation there for 23 years.

Commemorative Biographical Record of New Haven County

Gilbert Benjamin Hotchkiss (1833-1906)

Gilbert was the son of Benjamin and Hannah Hotchkiss. As a boy, Gilbert attended the district schools of Prospect and a public school of Naugatuck. At age fourteen he went to the town of Union Mills, Indiana, the birthplace of his mother. He practiced farming there until 1856. Returning to the Waterbury area, he located on the Stephen Hotchkiss farm where he engaged in dairy farming and stock raising. Also, in 1856 Gilbert married Emma Chatfield, who was a Waterbury native. He remained a member of the Prospect Congregational Church where he served as deacon and superintendent of the Sunday school for many years.

Commemorative Biographical Record of New Haven County

Henry D. Hotchkiss (1850-1932)

Raised on the Prospect homestead of his parents, Harry and Sarah Hotchkiss, Henry was educated in the district school. In 1879 he moved to Waterbury where he began a career in contracting and building roads. He probably was responsible for more miles of road being built than any other man in Waterbury. Real estate was his chief and most lucrative occupation. He was instrumental in developing much of North Waterbury. Henry and his wife Ella are interred in the Prospect Cemetery.

G. Mills Hotchkiss (1784-1864)

G. Mills was prominent in community and religious affairs. He owned a match factory on Straitsville Road.

Brooks Hotchkiss

Ran the match factory of his father, G. Mills Hotchkiss.

Mabel Hotchkiss (1882-1966)

Mabel was born in Prospect, the daughter of David Bryan and Nellie (Hupman) Hotchkiss. She studied in Prospect grammar school and graduated from Crosby High School and Mt. Holyoke College. Before attending college, Miss Hotchkiss taught school in area towns for four years. After college she taught in New York State before returning to Crosby High School where she taught Latin, French, and English for over 35 years. She was a third generation teacher as her grandfather operated a private school in his home. Both her parents were teachers.

Mabel joined the Prospect Congregational Church in 1896 and was a member of the Prospect Grange for 70 years. She was also a member of the Excelsior State and National Grange. Miss Hotchkiss was an "honorary founder" of the Waterbury Branch of the American Association of University Women, member of the Mt. Holyoke Club of Waterbury, member of the Naugatuck and Cheshire Chapters of the DAR, Eastern Star member, and member of the Connecticut Historical Society. Miss Hotchkiss was instrumental in getting electrical service to Prospect as well as bus service to the town.

Ruth Hotchkiss (1885-1978)

Ruth was the fourth child of David B. and Nellie (Hupman) Hotchkiss. Many from her long line of ancestors moved away from town — but one or more Hotchkiss males always stayed in Prospect. The chain of succession at the property on Waterbury Road was finally broken. Ruth became the last Hotchkiss to reside there.

"Aunt Ruth," as towns people called her, even if not related, attended Prospect Center School. She with her sisters drove a horse to high school in Waterbury, leaving the horse in a livery stable during the day. Then Ruth went on to normal school in New Britain and eventually taught at Webster School in Waterbury. There she took an early retirement to help her aging mother. Her brother Treat was a forest fire warden, and she became involved in the telephone communications to help him. With the advent of Civil Defense during World War II, she began dispatching for fires and alerts from her home.

She attended the "old" wooden church that burned in 1906. She saw the stone church that replaced it burn in 1941 and helped in building the new present structure. Her dedication was to the Congregational Church, and she was the oldest member at the time of her death.

Miss Hotchkiss was a member of the D.A.R., Society of Daughters of Founders, Huguenot Society, Prospect Historical Society, Naturalist Club of Waterbury, Prospect Grange, Eastern Star, A.A.R.P., and the Prospect Senior Citizens.

She gave freely the use of her property for civic purposes. The Prospect Volunteer Fire Department showed their appreciation for her dedication and generosity by making her an Honorary Chief, a recognition she frequently remarked on. Her casket was escorted to its final resting place by the fire department members and equipment.

Treat Hotchkiss (1888-1957)

A lifelong resident of Prospect, Treat was the son of David B. and Nellie (Hupman) Hotchkiss. He was a descendant of Robert Treat, Colonial governor of Connecticut. Treat attended Crosby High School in Waterbury and the School of Agriculture, Cornell University.

Treat Hotchkiss managed the home farm for many years but was involved in the development and sale of the property in later years. A member of the Prospect Congregational Church, he was also a 50-year member of the Prospect Grange. Treat belonged to the New Haven County Farm Bureau and the Waterbury Fish and Game Association. He was a forest fire warden in Prospect for over 25 years. Treat held several town offices, including second selectman, assessor, and member of the Board of Tax Review.

Reuben Beecher Hughes (1820-?)

Born in Southbury, Massachusetts, Reuben moved to a farm in Prospect, which he worked for nine years before moving to New Haven. During this period he practiced shoemaking and carpentry. He was sent to the State Legislature from Prospect for the 1849-50 session. Locally, Reuben served as justice of the peace, tax collector, and member of the school board.

A natural mechanic, Reuben Hughes learned the trade of toolmaker and became an expert engineer. Subsequent to the Civil War, he made tools for manufacturing pistols, cutlery, clocks, guns, carriage springs, and many other articles. He served as a lieutenant in the military.

His greatest accomplishments were in the field of music. Reuben was a master of the cello, trombone, string bass, ophicleide, violin, and other instruments. He was a member of the Union City and Wheeler & Wilson male quartet, the Wheeler & Wilson Band, and the Second Company Governor's Foot Guards Band. After he was seventy-five years old, he still played in bands and marched as far as fifteen miles. In 1877 he organized an orchestra for the benefit of the New Haven City Missions, conducting it free of charge for twenty years.

Reuben married Harriet M. Sloper in 1840, and their son George was born in Prospect.

John Isbell

Continued the operation of the A. Smith needle factory with partner, S.E. Jeralds.

S.E. Jeralds

See John Isbell.

Mabel Johns (1895-1988)

Mabel and her three sisters and six brothers came from England and settled in the Platts Mill area of Waterbury. The group decided to purchase a parcel of 100+ acres in Prospect to allow ample pasture for grazing, haying, and growing vegetables.

In 1920 Mabel and her family made the move to Prospect. They waited until midnight to start the caravan, so that any traffic would be off the road. With lanterns in hand, it took seven hours to walk the 60 or so milking cattle from Platts Mill to their Cedar Hill Farm on Hydelor Avenue. When they arrived that morning, Mabel fixed breakfast for the workers on a cook stove. She then watched as everyone lay down and went to sleep in the field.

On their farm all equipment was horse drawn, including the buggies used on the two milk routes in Union City and Waterbury. By 1988 Mabel was the only living member of the original family. At the age of 92, she still tended to the farm although the size of the herd diminished to eleven (including Mabel's pet cow, Mabel). Mabel had a poem she would recite every day:

When the golden sun is sinking
and your thoughts and cares are free

when of others you're not thinking
will you sometimes think of me?

Walter Judd (1758-1833)
Walter was the son of Isaac Judd of Salem and served as a sergeant in the Revolutionary War in Capt. Martin's company. He married Margaret Terrell. Walter's name is found on early Congregational Church records, but in 1805 he signed a declaration that he was a Baptist and would no longer support the Columbia Congregational Society. His brother, Chauncey Judd, operated a sawmill in Prospect near the Naugatuck Reservoir dam.

Henry Judd
Operated a metal button factory across the street from his brother-in-law, Elais Mix. His products were taken to Beachport (West Cheshire) where they were loaded on canal boats destined for New York.

Thomas J. Keenan (?-1973)
Tom was the son of William and Bridget (Kelley) Keenan of Waterbury. He was a resident of Prospect for over 40 years and operated a Texaco gas station and candy store on the Waterbury Road. Previously he attended Yale University and had his pharmaceutical license. He practiced as a pharmacist until 1930. Thomas was a member of St. Anthony Church. He married Gertrude Davis and they had two daughters.

Gertrude Keenan (?-1970)
Gertrude was born in Brooklyn, NY, the daughter of Thomas and Margaret (Kastle) Davis. She moved to Prospect in 1947 and was very active in Republican politics. Gertrude was the president of the Prospect Republican Women's Club and a member of the Republican State Committee. She was known in Prospect as "Mrs. Republican."

For four years she was a police dispatcher in Prospect and she was also proprietor of a restaurant. Gertrude was a member of the Prospect Grange, Women's Auxiliary of St. Mary's Hospital, Burma Mission Club, St. Anthony Church, and the Ladies Guild of the parish.

Ezra Kimball
Ran a store opposite the old library. Also had a match factory on New Haven Road.

E.R. Lawton
In partnership with Nettleton, manufactured ferrules, hollow steel handles for button hooks, tableware, and bicycle wrenches. He was the last manufacturer in Rag Hollow.

Wooster Martin (1790-1862)
Wooster was born within the current boundaries of Prospect, the son of Samuel Martin. Samuel Martin was originally from England and a sea captain by occupation. He died while in command of a vessel in the West Indies but was the first representative of this branch of the Martin family in America. In the early days Wooster was a wagon maker. From 1832 onward, he ran a wagon shop at North Farms, Wallingford.

Joseph J. McEvoy (?-1965)
Joseph McEvoy was the son of James and Frances (Horan) McEvoy of Waterbury. He was employed at Anaconda American Brass for 44 years and was secretary of Local 1251, UAW. Mr. McEvoy was active in Democratic politics in Prospect. He served as first selectman for two terms in the 1950s.

Joseph married Helen Sullivan and was a resident of Coer Road. A member of the Connecticut Probation and Parole Association, he was on the Board of Directors of the Cheshire Reformatory and served there as secretary. He was also a member of the advisory board of the Diocesan Bureau of Waterbury, Holy Family Laymen's Retreat, and St. Anthony Church.

William McGrath (1896-1974)
William McGrath was born in Waterbury, the son of Michael and Margaret (Maher) McGrath. He retired as a foreman at Scovill after 45 years of service. He married Grace Cary, and they had one

daughter, Sister Roberta McGrath.

William served for many years on the local Board of Education and for almost ten years on the Board of Recreation during the administration of Mayor George Sabo, Jr. He was a charter member of the Prospect Senior Citizens organization. He was a treasurer of the Democratic Town Committee. William was a member of St. Anthony Church, Knights of Columbus, and chairman of the March of Dimes in Prospect. McGrath Park was dedicated to recognize his volunteer work on behalf of youth programs.

Arthur H. Merriman (1866-1935)

Arthur was born in Plantsville, the son of John and Philinda (Humiston) Merriman. At the time of his death in Prospect, he was survived by his wife Sarah (Knapp); four sons: Warren, Irving, Walter, and Roy; as well as a step-daughter, Mrs. George Taylor, and ten grandchildren.

Arthur Merriman entered the dairy business in 1898. He founded the Merriman Dairy Co. in Waterbury in 1917, which developed into one of the leading milk businesses of the area. Upon his retirement from active involvement, the firm became known as Fernwood Farms.

John G. Miller (1900-1978)

Born in Waterbury, the son of Henry and Jennie (Gough) Miller, John Miller served two terms in the state legislature from Prospect in the early 1940s. He was also Republican town chairman.

Jack was the owner of a Goodyear franchise in Waterbury as well as Jack G. Miller Real Estate. He married Christine Quilter and they had two daughters. Mr. Miller was a member of the Elks and Masons of Waterbury, Lafayette Consistory of Bridgeport, Shrine Temple of Hartford, and the Prospect Congregational Church.

Edwin T. Mix (1843-?)

Edwin was born in Cheshire, the son of Titus Mix, who came from Wallingford and settled in Prospect. He engaged in making boxes for the Ives & Judd Match Company. Edwin had a factory with good water power in Rag Hollow where he manufactured wagons and did a successful repair business.

William Mix

Invented (but failed to patent) the rag wheel which revolutionized the metal polishing industries. He ran a fishery and operated factories that produced pewter spoons and tea pots. Another operation made clay buttons and knobs.

Elias Mix

Elias had a blacksmith shop on Cheshire Road in 1812.

Carl Louis Mortison (1889-1963)

C.L. Mortison was also known as Lester Green or just plain Mort. He was born in Waterbury to John and Caroline (Hylander) Mortison. When Carl was fourteen his father died, and the family moved to a farm in Prospect. He worked as a factory errand boy, then became a watchmaker and toolmaker at the Waterbury Clock Co., where he eventually became a foreman.

Carl then took up poultry farming. He became a member and then director of the Connecticut Poultry Association. He was also a member of the Prospect Grange and the Prospect Congregational Church and served the town as tax collector. He was a Mason and a Shriner.

C.L. Mortison's greatest accomplishments were in cartooning and story telling. In 1912 he "walked around the block three times" with eight cartoons clutched under his arm, getting up the nerve to approach W.J. Pape, the publisher of the Waterbury Republican and the Waterbury American. Mr. Pape paid him $2 for one cartoon depicting municipal departments in tree houses. Thus began a five decade career in the press.

Under the pen name Lester Green, Mort became the Prospect correspondent. He was the creator of columns, such as "Lester Green" stories, "Kowless Farm" and "A New Worry Every Day." For forty years his humor and vivid imagination appeared in the Waterbury newspapers and others across the country. His favorite topics were farm life and politics. Lester loved to poke fun at politicians and the government.

Did you ever notice how the minute some folks git a job workin' for the city they spend the whole day figurin' how they can duck work. An' before they got the job they spent 12 hours o' the day trapsin' around lookin' for work to do.

Sunday Republican 9/15/1935.

His cartoons and "tall stories" earned him national acclaim. During the 1950s Mort entertained our military forces on a number of tours throughout the world. Some of his works were presented to Presidents Eisenhower, Truman, and Kennedy.

Luther Morse (1809-1888)

Commemorative Biographical Record of New Haven County

Born and reared on the farm in Prospect, Luther was the son of Lent Moss (Morse) and his first wife, Lydia Doolittle. As an adult he became a manufacturer of pocketbooks, but later in life he returned to farming. A man of note, Luther served in the General Assembly, filled several local positions from time to time, and was selectman for many years. His remains are interred in the Prospect Cemetery.

Harry Morse (1815-1879)

Harry, another son of Lent Morse, was born in Prospect Centre and received a district school education. He married Sarah Ann Gillette, who was born in Prospect in 1824. She was a daughter of Garret and Nancy (Platt) Gillette. Harry and Sarah located on the Thomas farm, where Harry did general farming and stock raising until 1859, when he was afflicted with a type of paralysis. He was first a supporter of the Whigs, then later the Republicans. Harry was liberal in his religious views.

George Morse (1852-1895)

George Morse was born in Prospect, the son of Harry and Sarah (Gillette) Morse. A graduate of the local common schools, he served Prospect as constable for some time. George was a Republican and held the 1885 term in the legislature.

Walter G. Morse (1857-1950)

Another son of Harry and Sarah Morse, Walter was a deacon at the Second Congregational Church in Waterbury for more than 50 years. Walter had the distinction of being one of the oldest active licensed automobile drivers in Connecticut when he died in his Matthew Street home at the age of 93.

Byron Luther Morse (1859-1933)

A brother of George Morse, Byron was educated in Prospect's common schools. Due to his father's illness, Byron took charge of the farm at an early age. It comprised 150 acres — much of which devoted to fruit production. He shipped large quantities of apples annually and had some interest in the wood business. Besides his vocation as a farmer, he was a stanch Republican and was elected to the legislature in 1889, serving on the committee of forfeited rights. Byron was treasurer of the Prospect Grange for three years.

Lent Moss (1780-1845)

Lent Moss' grandfather was John Moss, one of the original settlers at the New Haven Colony from England about 1638. As a young man, Lent Moss moved to Prospect from his Cheshire birthplace. A land owner and farmer, he chose the Whig party and filled many prominent positions. He died October 12, 1845, and was buried in Prospect Centre. After his death the family name was changed from Moss to Morse.

Hattie Chandler Nichols (1875-1962)
Hattie was born in Prospect, the daughter of William and Evalina (Peck) Chandler. She married Samuel G. Nichols and they lived on Waterbury Road. She was a member of the Prospect Congregational Church and a Golden Sheaf member of the Prospect Grange. For about 20 years Hattie served Prospect as tax collector.

Rev. Floyd Allen Pascall (1926-1984)
Rev. Mr. Pascall was born in Washington, GA, the son of Thomas Allen and Clara (Lewis) Pascall. He founded the Bethel Baptist Church in Naugatuck in 1976 with 27 members. In 1981 the church erected a new building on Union City Road and moved to Prospect. The church has since grown to a congregation of over 500. Rev. Mr. Pascall was also credited with starting about 30 churches in New England.

He graduated from Fruitland Bible Institute and spent nearly three decades in the ministry. Besides pastoral assignments in North Carolina and South Carolina, Rev. Mr. Pascall was one of the founders of the Baptist Bible College East in Shrub Oak, NY., where he served as professor of homiletics for five years. He was held the offices of president and vice president of the Connecticut and Rhode Island Baptist Bible Fellowship.

Rev. Mr. Pascall resided on Bronson Road with his wife, Elizabeth (Klingman) Pascall. They had one son and three daughters. He was a member of the I.B.E.W Electrical Workers' Union and was a veteran of World War II, serving in the U.S. Navy as an electrician first class.

Joseph Payne (1751-1805)
Joseph is the first Payne found in the records of New Haven county. He lived in Prospect when it was part of Water-

bury. He owned a farm and was engaged in milling. In 1796 Joseph owned a mill, known as Hough's, on the Mad River. At one time he ran a small shop on Turkey Hill Brook near the Waterbury Reservoir.

He outlived his first three wives: Hulda Hotchkiss, Esther Hotchkiss, and Abigail Olcott. His fourth wife, Lois Hotchkiss, lived 37 years after Joseph was laid to rest. In the custom of that time, the coffin was borne to the grave on men's shoulders, in some cases for two or three miles or more.

In April 1805 Joseph Payne's coffin was brought to this [Grand Street] cemetery on neighbors' shoulders from Columbia (now Prospect), for burial beside his kindred. A violent thunder-shower came up as they neared a large barn standing on present Dublin Street, the only shelter within reach, and all took refuge in it until the shower had passed over.

History of Waterbury

Silas Payne
Silas was a resident of Prospect all his life, a farmer and a soldier in the Revolutionary War. He married Lois Farrell of Wolcott. They had four children, including J.F., a wheelwright in Prospect.

Joseph Payne, Jr. (1776-1855)
The son of Joseph and Esther operated a farm in Prospect near the Waterbury Reservoir. He was a member of the Congregational Church and had two wives: Ruth Beecher and Rebecca Barnes.

Col. Stephen Hotchkiss Payne (1805-?)
The son of Joseph Payne, Jr., Stephen married Abigail Doolittle, the daughter of Joseph I. Doolittle. Stephen was a manufacturer of buttons and matches and ran a general mercantile business. In 1838 he was commissioned a Lieutenant Colonel for Waterbury's 22nd Regiment.

Because it was peacetime, the military had lost some of its enthusiasm. When assembled for parades, the soldiers wore an assortment of mismatched uniforms and carried a wide range of weapons of all sorts. Only the officers maintained a degree of spit and polish. There were few regular drills in those days; once a year the regiments met for parade and inspection. The 22nd regiment usually met in Cheshire, Meriden, or Waterbury, with headquarters at some tavern or inn.

Stephen married his second wife, the widow of Ransom S. Todd. Together as Payne & Todd, they ran the Scovill House in Waterbury from 1870-1874, which the *Waterbury American* described as "a splendid hotel." Col. Payne later moved to Milford and died there.

Edwin B. Payne (1816-1894)

Born in Prospect to Joseph Jr. and Rebecca Payne, Edwin was reared on the farm and educated in the district schools. After his marriage, he moved to Bristol where he followed teaming for a while. He returned to Prospect where he ran a hotel. He was also one of the first in this area to manufacture matches. In 1855 he moved to Cheshire.

Joseph Doolittle Payne (1829-?)

Commemorative Biographical Record of New Haven County

Joseph was a child when his parents, Stephen and Abigail Payne, moved from Cheshire to Prospect. He attended the public schools and was later a student in the Everest Academy. At the age of nineteen, he relocated to the Westville section of New Haven where he pursued a career as a merchant.

Miles E. Payne (1846-?)

A son of Edwin Payne, Miles attended public schools in Cheshire, Prospect, and Waterbury and also a select school. He worked at farming and teaming. In 1880 he married Mrs. Martha E. Scovill, a sister of George L. Talmadge of Prospect. Miles was a Democrat, active on the school committee, and a member of the Prospect Congregational Church.

Edward Payne (?-1889)

The son of Silas Payne, Edward was born and raised on the farm in Prospect. In early life he was a carriage-spring maker but later was a rubber worker in Naugatuck. His son, J. Frederick, was born in Prospect in 1858 and became a foreman at the Goodyear India Rubber Shoe Company in Naugatuck for a number of years.

Capt. Benjamin Platt (1782-1870)

Benjamin descended from Richard Platt, who arrived in New Haven Colony from England in 1639. Born in Milford, Capt. Platt later moved to Prospect where he was a farmer and drover. He was well known throughout Connecticut for his miliary affairs. He married Nancy Bristol. Of their twelve children, Harris and John remained in Prospect as farmers. His daughter Adelia married Luther Morse.

Benjamin was a prominent member of the Prospect Congregational Church. For three terms he represented his town in the State Legislature. Locally, he served as selectman, assessor, and other positions.

John R. Platt (1824-1904)

John, the son of Capt. Platt, was a common school graduate. He left home at the age of seventeen to work in a clock shop in Plymouth for a short time. He then took up the trade of carpentry until the Civil War broke out. John served three years in the 20th C.V. under Col. Ross and Capt. Timothy Gilford. He participated in the battle of Gettysburg and was with Sherman on the celebrated march to the sea and all through the Atlanta campaign. For meritorious service on the field of battle, he was promoted to the rank of Lieutenant.

Returning to Prospect, John purchased the Hughes farm of 87 acres and made many improvement while engaged in general farming and fruit production. He held the town office of constable for forty years and was also registrar of voters. This Republican was Prospect's representative in the Lower House in 1869 and 1889.

John Platt had two children by his first wife, Augusta Carrinton. After her death he married Elizabeth Hotchkiss, a daughter of Harry and Sarah (Hoppin) Hotchkiss of Prospect. Mr. and Mrs. Platt were members of the Prospect Congregational Church and the Prospect Grange.

Henry P. Platt (1813-1879)

A son of Capt. Platt, Henry lived all his life in Prospect where he was a carpenter and joiner. A stanch Whig in his earlier years, he later became an active Republican and served the town as deputy sheriff for many years. He and his wife Rebecca were members of the Prospect Congregational Church.

John H. Platt (1842-?)

The son of Henry P. Platt, John grew up in Prospect. He was eighteen years old at the outbreak of the civil war. In 1861 he enlisted in Co. A, 20th Conn. V.I. and fought in the battles of Chancellorsville, Fredericksburg, and Gettysburg. After a transfer to the Western Division, he joined Gen. Sherman on his journey to the sea. A wound he received at Bentonville, NC, caused him to return to Prospect. By 1866 his injured arm had improved, and he moved to New Haven where he pursued a career as merchant of interior decorations.

Thomas D. Plumb (1894-1976)

Born in Prospect, the son of David and Addie (Matthews) Plumb, Thomas served Prospect as legislator from 1939-1945. He was a member of the Prospect Congregational Church, Prospect Grange, Townsend Lodge of Odd Fellows, and an hon-

orary member of the Prospect Volunteer Fire Department.

The family farm on Cheshire Road contained 300 acres when it was purchased in 1859. Thomas and his brother Frank operated the farm, which now contained only 90 acres when taken over by Frank's daughter, Florine Wheeler, in 1959.

Frank M. Plumb (1897-1989)

He was born in Prospect, the son of David and Addie (Matthews) Plumb. Frank Plumb was a member of the Prospect Grange for 76 years, joining at the age of 16. The Plumb family's ties to the Grange extend back to the association's founding in 1898. Frank's grandfather, Algernon Signey Plumb, made donations and loans that helped pay for the original building. When the building was de-stroyed by fire in 1943, Frank was among a group of men who constructed the new hall. During his more than three-quarters of a century with the Prospect Grange, he held every position in the organization except master.

He married Annie Bird, and they had two daughters, Florine and Sylvia. Frank Plumb was a member of Excelsior Pomona Grange 7, Connecticut State Grange, and a 50-year member of Townsend Lodge IOOF of Waterbury. At the time of his death, he was the longest continued resident of Prospect.

Robert C. Pouliot (1921-1984)

Robert Pouliot was born in Waterbury, the son of Oliver and Aurora (Chevette) Pouliot. He was a U.S. Army World War II veteran and served during the Normandy invasion with the 234th Combat Engineering Division. He received three Purple Hearts and five battle stars.

Robert owned the Prospect Hardware store on Union City Road. He and his wife Olga, who died in 1977, raised more than 135 foster children in addition to three of their own. They were twice cited by the state as "Foster Parents of the Year."

Mr. Pouliot was a member of the Prospect VFW, Prospect Volunteer Fire Department, Inland-Wetlands Commission, Prospect Chamber of Commerce, National Riflemen's Association, and St. Anthony Church.

John Wesley Rowland (1918-1984)
John was born in Dexter, GA, the son of Charles and Mary (Johnson) Rowland. He was the president of the Meloria Children's Nursery of Prospect and also worked for the U.S. Postal Service in Waterbury.

John Rowland was active in town affairs. He was president of the Prospect Lions Club, member and zone chairman of the Waterbury Lions Club, honorary member of the Prospect Volunteer Fire Department, member of the Prospect Veterans of Foreign Wars, member of the board of directors of the Federal Credit Union of the Waterbury Post Office, and member of the Prospect Chamber of Commerce where he was chairman of the annual Scotch Foursome Golf Tournament. He was a member of the Prospect Congregational Church where he served as deacon and was a member of the church choir.

Mr. Rowland was a U.S. Army veteran of World War II. He served under General Patton in the 761st, 3rd Division, tank battalion, in campaigns of Northern France, Central Europe, the Ardennes, and the Rhineland. In 1979 he was awarded the presidential unit citation by President Jimmy Carter. In 1981 he was a representative to France where he received the Croix de Guerre. He also served in the Korean War.

Elmore Russell (1761-1835)
Elmore was the son of Nicholas and Charity (Hotchkiss) Russell. At the age of sixteen, he enlisted for three years and joined Capt. Brown's company. After his three-year service, he applied for discharge, but was told he had enlisted for the duration of the war. Rather than leave without a discharge, he served five more months and then left unable to secure a lawful discharge. He then went to sea and

served faithfully. He was listed as a deserter, but in time he was able to clear his records and received his just pay. Elmore was married to Asenath Hotchkiss, the daughter of David Hotchkiss.

Aaron Russell (1766-1779)
Another son of Nicholas and Charity (Hotchkiss) Russell, Aaron was only 13½ years old when he was killed by the enemy in the Revolution. He is almost certainly the boy killed by the British in the attack on New Haven. A detailed account is given under Gideon Hotchkiss.

H.D. Russell (?-?)
Operated a factory near the Naugatuck line, producing metal buttons as well as harness and carriage trimmings.

Rev. Henry Alanson Russell (1826-1911)
The first person to be "raised up" for the ministry by the Prospect Congregational Church was the Rev. Henry A. Russell. He graduated from Yale University Divinity School in 1853, did graduate study there the following year, and received an honorary M.A. degree from Yale in 1855. For over 40 years he served pastorates in three different states: Winsted, East Hampton, Centerbrook, and Colebrook, CT; Mooers, NY; and Calbot, VT. He retired and lived in Winsted the rest of his life.

Archibald Sanford (1759-1844)
Archibald, the brother of Gideon Sanford, lived in the southern part of town. He had several short enlistments in the military. Part of the time he lived in Woodbridge (Bethany), Salem Society of Waterbury, and Cheshire — but always within four miles of where he was born. Several of his children remained in Prospect and his daughter Anna married Lauren Preston, an early town officer.

Louise (Deschenes) Schieffer (1915-1983)
Born in Prospect, the daughter of Joseph and Louise (Blanchard) Deschenes, Louise married John L. Schieffer. They resided on Cook Road and raised five daughters

and four sons.

Mrs. Schieffer was employed at Uniroyal for 22 years. She served Prospect as the Democratic registrar of voters. She was a member and president of the Prospect Senior Citizens, a member of the Uniroyal Girls' Club, a charter member of St. Anthony's Ladies Guild, and a graduate of Waterbury Catholic High School.

Ephraim Smith (1733-1806)

Ephraim and his wife, Thankful (Tyler), were two of the original sixteen original members organizing the Congregational Church in Prospect on May 14, 1798. He served in the Revolutionary War and was enrolled in Col. Douglas' company. Ephraim was a farmer and son of Jonathan Smith, who settled in the Hop Brook section of Mattatuck. Ephraim lived on what is now the Plumb farm.

Ira Smith (1757-1835)

The son of Ephraim and Thankful Smith, Ira was a farmer in Prospect. In the spring of 1777 Ephraim was drafted for military service, but Ira went in his place. As a private he served for eight months in Capt. Jesse Kimball's company, commanded by Col. John Chandler. Ira's military application states that he was born within 40 rods of where he now lives. In 1779 he married Elizabeth, the daughter of Isaac Judson. They had seven children. Ira served as a deacon in the Prospect Congregational Church.

Josiah Smith (1757-1833)

Josiah lived on the Cheshire side of town. He was a teamster and also served in the military under Col. Hooker. At Horseneck he was wounded for which he received a lifetime pension. In 1815 he had declared that he belonged to the church of England and would not support the Congregational Church. No stone marks his grave.

Andrew Smith (1796-1878)

Born the son of Ira and Elizabeth Smith, Andrew remained a lifelong resident of Prospect as a farmer. He built a dam on Beaver Dam Brook, leasing land from Rebecca Ford in 1843. On this site he constructed a water wheel and foundry.

Andrew was a Whig, a man of strong political and social convictions. Along with his friend, William Lloyd Garrison, he made tours of the schoolhouses where he advocated the cause of anti-slavery at a time when that view was unpopular in New England. He was a strong advocate of temperance and a member of the Congregational Church. In 1818 Andrew married Rachel Tuttle, the daughter of Obed Tuttle. They had seven children.

Lyman Smith (1800-1862)

Born in Orange, Connecticut, Lyman moved to Prospect (then Columbia) at the age of eighteen. He moved in with Merritt Clark, who married his sister. He met and married Rebecca Wooster of Salem in 1821. They immediately settled on a farm adjoining that of his employer. Among their children, Eli lived on the farm until the age of sixteen.

Lyman worked for Hopkins & Wheeler, a button manufacturer in Naugatuck. Here, he advanced step by step until he was admitted to a partnership in the company and was elected secretary and general manager of the factory, a position he held for 30 years.

"Uncle Lyman," as he was called by everyone, was stricken during the latter part of his life with a malady called "Lo Po," which was manifest in various kinds of hallucinations. He was committed to an asylum in Middletown where he died.

Sidney Smith (1828-?)

Sidney, the second son of Lyman Smith, lived at home on the farm until 1864. In 1850 he married Polly Morgan of Warren.

An incident of Sidney's early married life will remind many of the older residents of Prospect of the time of his return home with his bride. The "Boys of the Hill," many of whom were singers in the same church choir with Sidney, thought they would serenade him. So old flint-lock muskets, cannon, shotguns, bells, and

everything and anything that would make a noise were enlisted into service by scores of his former mates. Sidney was importuned, implored and teased to show his bride, but from the second-story window he flatly refused. Such a noise caused by the bombardment of old cans, stones, kettles, etc., at that south spare guests' chamber was seldom heard in that usually peaceful home. The old cider barrel was tapped, and the cider with cake, etc., passed. The over-enthusiastic party withdrew, but not till the house had been more or less defaced and some shots fired at the risk of lives. Such actions in the earlier days were common as the rice and slipper act at the present writing.
Commemorative Biographical Record of New Haven County

Sidney and his wife Polly settled down at his father's home for a number of years, but in 1864 he purchased the Hoppin farm, one mile south of the Lyman Smith residence.

Andrew H. Smith (1840-?)

Commemorative Biographical Record of New Haven County

Andrew H. Smith was born in Prospect, the son of Andrew and Rachel Smith. He spent his boyhood days on the farm and attended the district schools until he was seventeen. Andrew went to high school in Watertown and later attended boarding school in Charlottesville, NY. He taught school in Prospect, Cheshire, and Bethany. At the age of twenty-one, Andrew joined his brother in the manufacture of needles in Prospect. They were the first in the nation to have a factory entirely devoted to making sewing machine needles. The three Smith brothers (Ira, Julius, and Andrew) formed a needle manufacturing company in Hamden in 1864.

Harris Smith

Operated an umbrella trimmings factory.

Isaac Spencer (1723-1787)

Isaac Spencer, son of Isaac and Mary (Seldon) Spencer, was a lay preacher of the Separatists and a very devout man. To his marriage with Temperance Goodspeed were born eight children, of whom Seldon, Elihu, and Ansel served in the Revolutionary War. Ansel was also one of the town's earliest school teachers. Isaac's death occurred in Prospect in 1787.

Willard Spencer (1801-1890)

History of Waterbury

Born and raised in Prospect, Willard Spencer moved to Waterbury in 1826 where he was involved in the manufacture of gilt buttons. He was active in politics and served as selectman for seventeen years. He held numerous other offices. Those who knew him well recognized him as a man of ability and excellent judgement. A lifelong friend said of him:

"If I could pass out of this world as he did, respected by all and against whom naught could be said, I would feel that I had successfully lived and died." History of Waterbury

William Henry Strong (1839-1881)

William Strong's roots go back to England in 1545, when a Strong married the heiress of Griffin in Caerarnonshire, Wales. Richard Strong, according to tradition, a Roman Catholic, was a member of this family branch. His son John was part of the Warham company which settled in Dorchester, MA. William H. Strong located in Prospect from New York in 1870 and became a farmer. He was a member of the Adventist Church and a Republican by political choice. William served in the 13th Connecticut Volunteer Infantry, Company D. He married Rhoda M. Hotchkiss of Cheshire.

William Seymour Strong (1865-?)

William S. Strong, the son of William H. and Rhoda Strong, grew up in Prospect and attended its district schools. He began his business career in agriculture and practiced dairying on a small scale. At the same time he was in charge of the Waterbury reservoir.

Energetic and enterprising, William became the largest dairy farmer of his time in Prospect. He had thoroughbred stock which yielded the highest market price. He owned a 65 acre tract with one of the finest homes in town. In 1887 William married Hattie R. Hotchkiss of Waterbury. Affiliated with the Republican party, he was a member of the Grange and the Adventist Church.

Lucius Talmadge (1807-1896)

A resident of Cheshire, Oxford, and New Haven, Lucius finally came to Prospect where he spent the remainder of his years in general farming. He gave his support to the Whig party. In later years he favored the Republicans. He married Abigail Platt Gillette, and both became active members of the Congregational Church. They had eleven children, including Frederick and John, who died in the Civil War. The family name has been also recorded as Tamag, Talmage and Tamage.

George L. Talmadge (1855-1930)

The youngest child of Lucius and Abigail

Talmadge, George attended the district schools of Prospect while living on his parents' farm. He then traveled extensively through the western states and returned to Prospect in 1885. George located on the Garret Gillette farm, a tract of 100 acres, to which he added 50 acres. He followed general farming, dairying, stock raising, and selling wood from his property.

Ella Carrell of Cheshire became his bride in 1880. They had two daughters: Daisy and Bernice. Daisy, the older daughter, graduated from Cheshire High School and New Britain Normal School, then taught for a short time. George Talmadge was a member of the Prospect Grange and a staunch supporter of the Republican party. He served Prospect on the board of relief and as a grand juror. In 1894 and again in 1922, he was elected to the State Legislature.

Mildred A. Talmadge (1894-1987)

Mildred was the daughter of Richard and Lena (Sloane) Heckel of Meriden. She was a Prospect resident for more than 65 years. Mildred served as town clerk, registrar of vital statistics, and treasurer for Prospect from 1929-1953. A 1937 survey revealed many records she kept, including the Bee Register. Because of the many orchards in Prospect, bees were used to pollinate the fruit. Mildred kept track of the beekeepers and their colonies, frames and hives.

Prospect has no town hall and most of the town records are kept in a fire-proof safe in the residence of the town clerk and registrar of vital statistics who is also treasurer. Records of the selectmen, tax collector, board of education and other agencies are kept in the homes of the various officials.   Historical Record Survey - 1937

Mildred married Harry W. Talmadge and made her home with her daughter, Mrs. Harry (Barbara) LaFage of Watertown, in later years. After her death at the age of 92, Mayor Bob Chatfield ordered the town flags flown at half-mast in her honor. "She was a great, great lady," Chatfield said, "she will be missed."

Isaac Terrell (~ 1735-1817)
Isaac lived in Prospect and served the Revolution in the expedition against Crown Point in 1756 and in the Connecticut Line 1779-1781.

Enoch Terrell (1742-1804)
Enoch was a sergeant in Col. Douglas's company in 1776. He married Experience Wilmot. Enoch was among those whose bodies were moved to the oldest part of the present cemetery in 1805. There is no record of his grave, but records show the death of "Enoch Terrell, a Baptist."

Josiah Terrell (1742-1795)
Josiah, the brother of Isaac, married Eunice Hoadley. He was a captain of the Alarm List Company of Salem and served in the defense of New Haven. His grave stone, having been moved from the old cemetery, is one of the oldest in the present cemetery.

George E. Terry (1856-?)
George Terry moved to Waterbury from Sag Harbor, Long Island in 1881 and worked in a watch factory until coming to Prospect in 1892. He took up residence on the John Swartz farm, which was the property of his wife, Emelie Adaline Kyser. During the winter months he continued to work at his watchmaking trade in Waterbury. Mr. Terry was a member of the Democratic party.

Katherine I. Tress (1894-1981)
"Katie," as she was known to her friends and neighbors, was born in Prospect to John and Vincenza Tress. She was an excellent student and graduated from normal school at age 17. She was offered a teaching position in Prospect, but declined because many of the students were close to her age. After teaching in Wolcott, Suffield, and Meriden, she began a teaching career in New York City in 1924. In 1928 she graduated cum laude with a B.S. degree from NYU.
   During WW II she worked part-time as society editor for the *Waterbury Republican-American*. After a teaching career of more than 50 years, she retired to the family farm in Prospect. Her last teaching position was at Erasmus Hall High School in Brooklyn, NY.

John V. Tress (1898-1989)
Born the son of John and Vincenza (Delfavero) Tress, John V. was a lifelong resident of Prospect. He was a member of St. Anthony Church and was a self-employed carpenter for many years.

Moses Tuttle (1753-1835)
Moses married Damaris Hitchcock, a sister of Rev. Oliver Hitchcock. Under Capt. Nathaniel Bunnell, Moses was engaged in the retreat to New York. He also served under Col. Douglas at Kips Bay. He became sick and left his tour of duty before his term expired. Among his children were Wooster Tuttle and the future Mrs. Benjamin Dutton Beecher.

Obed Tuttle (1776-1856)
Obed was the son of Reuben Tuttle of North Haven. He married Lucretia Clark of West Haven, then moved to Prospect where he engaged in farming. They had four children. He worked as a blacksmith, making scythes and axes on the Waterbury Road opposite Maria Hotchkiss Road. Other manufacturing activities included a factory producing iron ferrules, hoes, forks, rakes, and shovels. On Matthew Street near the Walter Morse house, he had a third business making bone buttons.

Eben C. Tuttle
Tuttle was the son of Obed Tuttle and a true entrepreneur and early pioneer in Prospect manufacturing. He perfected methods for making garden hoes of unsurpassed quality. His reputation was widespread, and he soon had to expand his operation by moving to Naugatuck and forming the Tuttle Manufacturing Company in 1851. He later started another company that produced malleable iron and employed hundreds of people.

Enos Tyler (1735-1804)
Enos served in the French and Indian War and may have seen service during the Revolution. His home was where St. Anthony Church now stands. He is buried in Prospect with his third wife Mary. Enos was the first man to donate to the formation of the Columbia Society Company. His gift of $100.00 was a most generous offering for that time.

Abraham Tyler (1738-1823)
Abraham served as a sergeant in the company of Capt. John Lewis in 1777. He also fought in the war in 1780. Years later Abraham's son Lyman would write:
When 14 years of age, I ploughed the land (rough it was and hard soil), and sowed rye and harvested it, and planted corn and potatoes and worked the farm with only the help of brother, David, age 12, while father Abraham was away in the army.

George Franklin Tyler (1833-?)
George was born in Prospect, the son of Spencer and Sally (Ferrell) Tyler, who were both lifelong Prospect residents. He attended school and learned the watchmaker's trade, which he followed for some time. Later he worked at brazing in a hoe and fork factory before and after the Civil War. During the conflict he enlisted in Company A, 20th Conn. V.I., for three years. While stationed at Arlington Heights, George became ill and was honorably discharged in 1862. He continued to make his home in Prospect until moving to Cheshire in 1893.

George Tyler married Emily A. Mix, and they had one daughter. He was a member of the State Legislature from Prospect in 1870 and again in 1882; was doorkeeper of the house in 1887, 1889, and 1894; and doorkeeper of the Senate in 1897. He served as selectman, justice of the peace, and various other local positions in Prospect.

Luke Tyler
Ran a match factory on Salem Road.

Richard Tyler
Ran a match factory opposite the cemetery on Naugatuck Road. He married Flora Taylor in 1830.

Daniel Upson (1769-1854)

History of Waterbury

Daniel's father died eighteen days after his birth. The youngest of eight children, Daniel was educated by his mother and the common schools. In 1796 he married Mary Adams, the daughter of Samuel Adams, and together they had nine children. Starting as a farmer in the Town Plot district of Waterbury, Upson went on to be selectman for Prospect (then Columbia), Naugatuck (then Salem), and Waterbury for many years.

Gertrude (Keenan) VanderEyk (? -1979)
Born in Waterbury, the daughter of Thomas J. and Gertrude (Davis) Keenan, Trudy, as she was known, was the Treasurer for the town of Prospect from 1955-1960 and from 1965-1966. She married Louis VanderEyk. They lived on Maria Hotchkiss Road and raised a son, James, and a daughter, Nancy.

Mrs. VanderEyk was an employee of the State Department of Labor. She was a president of the Parent-Teacher Association, founder of the Pauline Brown Scholarship Fund, neighborhood chairwoman of the Girl Scouts, Cub Scout and Girl Scout leader, merit badge counselor, director and treasurer of the seals campaign for the Connecticut Lung Association, one of the founders of the Wily High School Football Parents Club, and member of the Ladies Auxiliary of the Prospect Volunteer Fire Department. She was also chairwoman of many financial drives for the Lions Club, March of Dimes, and Boy Scouts. She was a member of St. Anthony Church.

Franklin Wallace (1827-?)

In Prospect's founding year, Franklin was born, one of nine children to James and Urainie Wallace from Massachusetts. Franklin followed farming and teaming from Waterbury to Wallingford while living in Prospect. He enlisted in Company A, 20th Regiment Connecticut Volunteers. After serving seven months he was discharged for disability and moved to Cheshire.

John Wallace

Operated a match factory near his home.

Edgar Wallace (1852-1935)

Edgar died at the home in Prospect where he had lived his entire life. He was the son of John Edward and Nancy Ann (Tuttle) Wallace. Edgar was a member of the Prospect Congregational Church and the Prospect Grange. He was elected to serve as Representative to the General Assembly three times and held many local offices. He had two sons, Edward P. and Clifford P., and a daughter, Leila Augusta. In 1906 he sold 96 acres of his land to the New Haven Water Company.

Robert Wallace

Son of Edgar. In partnership with his cousin John, they produced the first German silver spoons by Prospect residents.

Clifford P. Wallace (1879-1971)

Clifford was born in Prospect, the son of Edgar and Leila (Platt) Wallace. He was a member and Deacon Emeritus of the Prospect Congregational Church and a 50-year member of the Prospect Grange. He served as first selectman in 1910, judge and prosecutor, assessor, and town clerk from 1920-1929. Clifford was a chairman of the Republican Town Committee.

Merritt Walters (1890-1962)

The son of Edward and Rose Walters, Merritt was the first selectman of Prospect for many years. He was a poultry farmer and electrician, living on Plank Road. He and his wife, Bessie (Haynor) Walters, had one son, Clayton.

Besides his service as fist selectman, Merritt was active on several town committees and served as justice of the peace and town judge. He was credited with the establishment of the Prospect Volunteer Fire Department. During the 1930s Mr. Walters was the town's road foreman. He was instrumental in building several local roads under the Federal Government's WPA project.

Merritt Walters was a member of the Prospect Congregational Church, the Evening Men's Club of the church, Townsend Lodge of Odd Fellows, Prospect Grange, and the Prospect Volunteer Fire Department.

Albert S. Wilmot (1915-1982)

Albert was born in West Haven, the son of Nelson and Lucy (Maurer) Wilmot. He married Tillie Schwarz and they had one daughter, Paula. He was an insurance agent for Allstate. Mr. Wilmot was vice president of the Senior Citizens of Prospect, treasurer of the Prospect Chamber of Commerce, and a member of Harmony Lodge of Masons.

~

BIBLIOGRAPHY

1

Paly, Melissa. *The Prospect Property, Prospect, Connecticut*, 1982.
Regional Water Authority. *Land Use Plan Update*, 1994.

2

Anderson, Joseph, D.D. *History of Waterbury*, 1896.
DeForest, John W. *History of the Indians of Connecticut*, 1964.
Hirschfilder, Arlene. *The Native American Almanac*.
Kagan, Mayna. *Vision in the Sky*.
Mills, Lewis Sprague. *The Story of Connecticut*, 1932.
Spiess, Mathia. *The Indians of Connecticut*.
Sturtevant, William C. *Handbook of North American Indians (Vol 15)*.
Van Dusen, Albert E. *Connecticut*, 1961.
Whipple, Chandler. *The Indians and the White Man in Connecticut*.

3

Anderson, Joseph, D.D. *History of Waterbury*, 1896.
Beach, Joseph Perkins. *History of Cheshire, Connecticut*, 1912.
Bickford, Chrsitopher P. *Farmington in Connecticut*, 1982.
Blakely, Quincy. *Farmington, One of the Mother Towns of Connecticut*.
Connecticut, Federal Writers' Project, 1938.
Green, Constance Mc L. *History of Naugatuck, Connecticut*, 1948.
Landmarks of Old Cheshire, The Cheshire Bicentennial Committee, 1976.
Mills, Lewis Sprague. *The Story of Connecticut*, 1932.
Rockey, J.L. *History of New Haven County*, 1892.
Van Dusen, Albert E. *Connecticut, 1961*.

4

Beach, Joseph Perkins. *History of Cheshire, Connecticut*, 1912.
Cowdell, Nellie. *Prospect Primer of History*, 1977.
Prospect Grand Lists. Manuscripts, The Prospect Historical Society.
Prospect Reminder.
Waterbury Republican-American.

5

Caouette, Dick. *Sesquicentennial House Research and Other Notes*.
Clapp, Jennie Beardsley. *Some of the Houses in Prospect, Connecticut*, c.1920.
Cowdell, Nellie. *Prospect Soldiers 1775-1783*, 1976.
Cowdell, Nellie. *Prospect Primer of History*, 1977.
Cowdell, Nellie. *A History of the Congregational Church, Prospect Conn.*, 1973.
Guevin, Mark. *A Guide to Historic Buildings in Prospect, Connecticut*, 1988.
Sabo, Shirley M. *Captain Ambrose Hine House c. 1759 As Compared to Other Dwellings in Prospect, The Guide to Historic CT*, 1984.
Walk Around Our Town, A (pamphlet)
Waterbury Republican-American.

6

Anderson, Joseph, D.D. *History of Waterbury*, 1896.
Barber, John Warner. *Connecticut Historical Collections*, 1838
Beach, Joseph Perkins. *History of Cheshire,*

Connecticut, 1912.
Cowdell, Nellie. *A History of the Congregational Church, Prospect Conn.*, 1973.
Cowdell, Nellie. *Prospect Primer of History*, 1977.
Highways & Byways of Connecticut, G. Fox & Co.
Lee, W. Storrs. *The Yankees of Connecticut*, 1957.
New Haven Register, The.
Prospect Reminder.
Prospect Pages.
Rockey, J.L. *History of New Haven County*, 1892.
Roth, David M. *Connecticut A Bicentennial History*, 1979.
St. Anthony Church, 50th Anniversary, 1994.
Waterbury Republican-American.

7 & 8

Clapp, Jennie Beardsley. *Some of the Houses in Prospect, Connecticut*, c.1920.
Cowdell, Nellie (1976), and Boardman Kathan (1995). *Education in the Town of Prospect*, manuscript.
Education for Prospect, report by University of Connecticut, 1906.
Education Under Double Jeopardy: Report on Region 16 School District, report by Connecticut Education Association, 1976.
Final Report, Temporary School Study Committee, Prospect-Beacon Falls, 1969.
Report of Fact-Finding Committee to the Board of Education, Prospect, 1953.
Rockey, J.L. *History of New Haven County*, 1892.
Ward, William. *The Early School of Naugatuck*, 1906.

9

Anderson, Joseph, D.D. *History of Waterbury*, 1896.
Barber, John Warner. *Connecticut Historical Collections*, 1838
Beach, Joseph Perkins. *History of Cheshire, Connecticut*, 1912.
Clark, George L. *A History of Connecticut*, 1914.
Cowdell, Nellie. *Prospect Primer of History*, 1977.
Cowdell, Nellie. *A History of the Congregational Church, Prospect Conn.*, 1973.
Cowdell, Nellie. *Old Prospect Factories [paper]*, 1947
Grant, Ellsworth S. *Yankee Dreamers and Doers*.
Green, Constance Mc L. *History of Naugatuck, Connecticut*, 1948.
Landmarks of Old Cheshire, The Cheshire Historical Society.
New Haven Register, The.
Paly, Melissa. *The Prospect Property, Prospect, Connecticut*, 1982.
Rockey, J.L. *History of New Haven County*, 1892.
Roth, David M. *Connecticut A Bicentennial History*, 1979.
Tyler, Daniel P. *Branches of Industry in Connecticut*, 1846.
Waterbury Republican-American.

10

Anderson, Joseph, D.D. *History of Waterbury*, 1896.
Beach, Joseph Perkins. *History of Cheshire, Connecticut*, 1912.
Connecticut State Register & Manual.
Cowdell, Nellie. *Prospect Primer of History*, 1977.
New Haven Register, The.
Records of the Prospect Historical Society.
Waterbury Republican-American.

11

Clapp, Jennie Beardsley. *Some of the Houses in Prospect, Connecticut*, c.1920.

Clark, Herbert G. *History of the Cromwell, Meriden and Waterbury Railroad*, 1983.

Fennelly, Ann. "Plank Road Was Once Just That: A Plank Road!," *Cheshire Herald*, May 14, 1987.

Landmarks of Old Cheshire, Cheshire Bicentennial Committee, 1976.

Meriden, Waterbury and Conn. River Railroad, Conn. Valley Chapter of the National Railroad Historical Society, August 1953, and publication of the New Haven Railroad Historical Society, May, June, July, August 1982.

Miller, Charles Somers, *The Plank Road*, manuscript, 1941.

Mortison, Lou. "*Lester Green's Kowless Farm*", *Waterbury Republican*, Nov. 16, 1947.

"*Old Cheshire Toll House Landmark of Bygone Days*", *The New Haven Register*, Oct 29, 1922.

Story of the Waverly Inn, The, booklet, 1952.

Turner, Gregg and Melancthon Jacobs. *Connecticut Railroads: An Illustrated History*, Conn. Historical Society, 1986.

Wood, Frederic J. *The Turnpikes of New England*, 1919.

12

Baker, Mrs. Mark. *Prospect Pleasantries & Peculiarities*, 1977.

Connecticut State Register & Manual.

Connolly, Frank B. *Local Government in Connecticut*, 1992.

Cowdell, Nellie. *Prospect Primer of History*, 1977.

Prospect Pages.

Prospect Annual Town Reports.

Prospect Town Charter, Third Revision.

Records of the Prospect Historical Society.

Rockey, J.L. *History of New Haven County*, 1892.

U.S Census Records.

Waterbury Republican-American.

13

Anderson, Joseph, D.D. *History of Waterbury*, 1896.

Connecticut State Register & Manual.

Connolly, Frank B. *Local Government in Connecticut*, 1992.

Cowdell, Nellie. *Prospect Primer of History*, 1977.

New Haven Register. The.

Prospect Town Charter, Third Revision.

Prospect Reminder.

Prospect Annual Town Reports.

Prospect Pages.

Records of the Prospect Historical Society.

Waterbury Republican-American.

14

Anderson, Joseph, D.D. *History of Waterbury*, 1896.

Beach, Joseph Perkins. *History of Cheshire, Connecticut*, 1912.

Cowdell, Nellie. *Prospect Primer of History*, 1977.

Levermore, Charles H. *The Republic of New Haven*, 1886.

Prichard, Katherine A. *Ancient Burying Grounds of the Town of Waterbury CT*, 1917.

Prospect Reminder.

Prospect Pages.

U.S. Census Report, 1840.

Waterbury Republican-American.

15

Prospect Chamber of Commerce Phone Directory.

Paly, Melissa. *The Prospect Property, Prospect, Connecticut*, 1982.

Cowdell, Nellie. *Prospect Primer of History*, 1977.

Prospect Reminder.

Prospect Pages.

Roth, David M. *Connecticut - A Bicentennial History*, 1979.

Waterbury Republican-American.

16

Cowdell, Nellie. *Prospect Primer of History*, 1977.

Prospect Pages.

Prospect Reminder.

Prospect Times, The.

Prospect Grange #144 Celebrates 100th Anniversary, booklet, 1995.

Records of Intersport USA.

Records of the Prospect Town Hall.

Waterbury Republican-American.

17

Curtis, George D. *Souvenir of the Centennial Exhibition*, 1877.

Manuscripts from the Plumb Farms.

Prospect Pages.

Prospect Reminder.

Prospect Annual Town Reports.

Taylor, William Harrison. *The One hundred Anniversary of the First Meeting of the General Assembly*, 1919.

Waterbury Republican-American.

18

Clark, Clifford P. Manuscripts.

Cowdell, Nellie. *Prospect Soldiers 1775-1783*, Prospect Bicentennial Commission. 1976.

Hitchcock, Watson C. Manuscripts, at the Connecticut Historical Society.

Prospect Reminder.

Records of the Prospect Town Hall.

Strumpf, Babette. Military service records.

Waterbury Republican-American.

19

Blanchard, Mathilda. *Manuscripts*, provided by Jane Fowler.

Cowdell, Nellie. *Old Prospect Factories [paper]*, 1947.

Highways & Byways of Connecticut, G. Fox & Co.

Monagan, Charles. *Greater-Waterbury - A Region Reborn*, 1989.

New Haven Register, The.

Waterbury Republican-American.

20

Prospect Pages.

Prospect Reminder.

Records of Prospect businesses.

Waterbury Republican-American.

21

Anderson, Joseph, D.D. *History of Waterbury*, 1896.

Beach, Joseph Perkins. *History of Cheshire, Connecticut*, 1912.

Beers, J.H. Commemorative Biographical Record of New Haven County, 1902.

Clark, Clifford. Manuscripts.

Cowdell, Nellie. *Prospect Soldiers 1775-1783*, Prospect Bicentennial Commission. 1976.

Historical Records Survey. Works Progress Administration, 1937.

Prospect Times, The.

Prospect Pages.

Prospect Reminder.

Records of the Prospect Historical Society.

Rockey, J.L. *History of New Haven County*, 1892.

Waterbury Republican-American.

~

INDEX